THE ROLLER COASTER YEAR

Essays by and for Beginning Teachers

Editor
KEVIN RYAN
Boston University

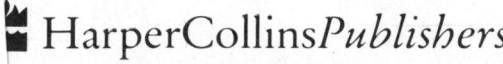
HarperCollins*Publishers*

To William Lauroesch
Mentor and Friend

Sponsoring Editor: Christopher Jennison
Project Editor: David Nickol
Art Director/Design Supervisor: Mary Archondes
Cover Design: Edward Smith Design, Inc.
Production Administrator: Beth Maglione
Compositor: BookMasters, Inc.
Printer and Binder: R. R. Donnelley & Sons Company
Cover Printer: New England Book Components, Inc.

THE ROLLER COASTER YEARS: Essays by and for Beginning Teachers

Library of Congress Cataloging-in-Publication Data
The Roller coaster year : essays by and for beginning teachers /
  editor, Kevin Ryan.
      p.   cm.
    ISBN 0-06-045687-6
    1. First year teachers—United States.   2. First year teachers—
United States—Attitudes.   I. Ryan, Kevin.
LB2844.1.N4R65   1992
371.1—dc20   91-14521
                                                         CIP

91 92 93 94   9 8 7 6 5 4 3 2 1

Contents

Preface

> Teaching is a great career. I can't imagine a better one. But what a beginning! I felt as if I were riding a slightly out-of-control roller coaster.

This statement by a veteran teacher reflects the experience of the overwhelming number of first-year teachers. The initial year is strong stuff. The excitement and the novelty of teaching are great, and the stakes are high.

Some teachers find the first year to be trouble-free and quite satisfying. They are in the minority, however. Most have difficulties of some kind that frustrate them and often diminish their commitment to continue teaching. When I showed up for the "New Teachers Meeting" in the last week of August 1959, the department chairman, a former Army sergeant, tersely told me, "Decide now to teach a second year." Characteristically, he didn't explain himself, but I figured out what he was getting at in the following months. The first year is not a good sample of what a teaching career is like; it is not a good basis upon which to make an important professional decision.

The events of the first year teach some negative lessons. Research shows that many young teachers change dramatically from September to June. In September the new teachers are often humanistic and pro-student, but by the end of the teaching year they have assumed a custodial attitude toward students, an attitude of having to manage them. Many teachers acquire negative stances toward students—students become their adversaries, a far cry from that which drew them into teaching.

Why does such change take place? First, it does not happen to all teachers. And second, the change is a matter of degree: from mild guardedness toward students to open hostility. There are many causes of this and other problems experienced by first-year teachers, ranging from lack of teaching skill to having too much to absorb all at once.

When difficulties hit, though, it is usually a surprise to new teachers. They are caught off guard on what they thought was safe and familiar ground. Had they not spent most of their waking hours from age 5 to 17 in and around schools? Why would they be bushwhacked on terrain so familiar, so similar to where they had spent so much time? It is understandable that people starting out with a new firm who are unfamiliar with the products, the procedures, and the sales territory would have problems of adjustment. Or that freshly minted engineers might have trouble applying what they had learned in courses on metal stress to the problem of putting up a skyscraper. But a teacher?

The fact is that while the terrain of schools is familiar to new teachers, they only know it from one perspective. They know school from the point of view of a student. They have spent thousands and thousands of hours in classrooms, but they have only seen the work of the teacher from an outsider's perspective. Except for a brief stint of student teaching, new teachers have had very limited—if any—experience with the phenomenon of being in charge. They are stymied by basic teacher moves and skills, such as the simple act of passing out a set of papers, actions that seemed effortlessly natural when they were students. Now, as teachers, performing these simple tasks seems like tap dancing in molasses.

I have been observing the problems of first-year teachers for over 30 years, starting with my own struggles to learn to teach. Once I had my own pedagogical sea legs, I watched and worked with newer and younger teaching colleagues. Later as a teacher educator, I watch my own students grapple with the problems of adjustment. There are a predictable set of problems faced by new teachers. Some are more severe than others, and some more common than others. Most of the problems had been addressed in the new teachers professional preparation programs. Most future teachers find, however, that the presentation of both the problems and the solutions has been too abstract. Instructors and textbooks are forced to be rather general, in the hope of being applicable to a wide variety of cases. And teacher-education students learn skills in a general way. They do not know how to apply them in their classroom of twenty-three fifth-graders who academically and socially are spread all over the lot and who are crowded into a hot room with a banging radiator and a classroom that is continually being disrupted by Paul poking Peter and Peter poking Popeye and by someone who thinks it is hysterically funny to leave the guinea pig's cage open, letting the obnoxious little creature make daily and unscheduled scampers for freedom.

The purpose of this book is to allow the future teacher to see the work of the classroom and the school through the eyes of first-year teachers. With the exception of the final chapter, the book is composed of accounts of beginning teachers, accounts written the year after the teachers' first year in the classroom.

Those planning to teach comprise the primary audience for this book. They will gain valuable insight into what teaching looks and feels like from the inside. They will read of things to do and things to avoid, and will be able to ask themselves whether or not they would have responded to various situations in similar ways. They will discover things they need to learn before their first year begins. Reading these accounts should make them more serious students of education.

Another audience is first-year teachers. While they will learn things to do and avoid, perhaps most important lesson is that they are not alone. Many beginning teachers are quite disappointed with themselves, feeling that they are failing their students, administrators, fellow teachers, students' parents, and, often most painful, themselves. To know that others who have gone before them—smart and good people—have problems similar to their own can be very reassuring.

Still another audience for the book is that of educators who work with beginning teachers—administrators, department chairs, supervisors, curriculum coordinators, and mentor teachers. A friend once told me that the greatest gift God has given us is our capacity to forget—to forget all the insults we have received, all those embarrassing moments, and all those big and small failures. Most people who work with first-year teachers have been first-year teachers themselves. Much of what happened to us is blessedly forgotten. These accounts should remind this audience of the special world of the beginning teacher, and enable them to be more empathetic in their supervision and support of new teachers.

Reading their accounts for the first time, I was struck by the highs and lows, by the sudden turns and dips, by the slow spots, and by times when things seemed simply out of control. I kept thinking of an experienced teacher's description of her first year of teaching as being on a roller coaster, roaring around a track that, although familiar and manageable to her veteran colleagues, was thrilling yet frightening to her as a first-time rider. The more I thought about the roller coaster, the more I realized how apt it is for describing this exhilarating time.

ACKNOWLEDGMENTS

Edmund Burke wrote that "to read without reflecting is like eating without digesting." He might have added, "to write without acknowledging is like stealing without conscience." This book belongs to many, many people. First and foremost it belongs to the dozen teacher-authors who have so faithfully stayed with this project and so candidly told the tales of their first year of teaching. Their willingness to let us see what they saw and feel what they felt and to share their gropings toward competency for some and adequacy for others proves that they are truly teachers.

Second, there were several who helped me with the many tasks of organizing this project and editing the manuscript. My wife, Marilyn Ryan, spent weeks at the dining room table sharpening and shaping this book. Skip Winestock and Cathleen Kinsella Stutz gave me useful insights and helped me with the discussion questions. Laureen Carroll and Peter Pendleton, my ever-faithful work-study helpers, did myriad tasks from typing drafts to handling the correspondence.

Third, there is a vast "support system" of colleagues and friends that will inevitably go unacknowledged. However, certain names and faces cry out to be recognized. Stephan Ellenwood, my close friend and department chairman, has been supportive of this project and many of my less-fruitful efforts from my arrival at Boston University almost ten years ago. Janet Stankiewicz, for whom Steve and I both work, has created an organized and warm work environment. Two deans, first Paul Warren and currently Peter Greer, have stimulated and encouraged me over the years of this project. Then there are the colleagues—faculty and doctoral students—who have helped out quite directly or in ways they are hardly aware of. Among the many are Sezai Kaya, Thomas Culliton, Joan Dee, the late Ann Breslin, John Cheffers, Myles Striar, Mary Williams, Alice Lanckton, David Greenhalgh, John Sullivan, Marty Kokol, Kerry Heffernan, Len Zaichkowsky, Burleigh Shibles, Jane O'Hern, Judith Schickedanz, Mary Shann, Miriam Marecek, and Gerald Abegg.

Kevin Ryan

Chapter
1

The Rookie

Margaret O'Bryan

INTRODUCTION

I wanted to be excellent, to excite, to invigorate, to sympathize with, and challenge the students, as well as be their friend, mentor, and a stimulating professor. I also wanted to survive. The following is an account of my first year as a teacher.

After graduating college, I had worked in the financial field for several years before deciding that the profession held no interest or thrill for me whatsoever. Instead I needed to be in a profession that challenged me, excited me, and made full use of my skills. I chose teaching. To be honest, I had a romantic notion that teaching would enable me to feel and be all I had hoped. And it was during the first year that reality hit the fan. I wanted so much to be perfect and fulfilled—it's why I chose the profession to begin with—but it just didn't happen that first year. There is too much to learn, and you are dealing with human beings all the time, be they students, teachers, administrators, or parents, not just numbers. I was also trying to explain my decision to many friends who thought I had a screw loose for spending a fortune on a master's degree and then taking a salary cut.

That first year was tough. And if you are lucky—and I truly consider myself one of the lucky ones—you come away from the experience feeling competent as a teacher with the knowledge of where and how to improve your teaching. I came away from my first year with those feelings. But I fear that as I describe the events of that first year to you, you will wonder why I consider myself lucky. I am happy with the choice I have made, but it is not because I was perfect or enthralling. It is probably because I discovered I like kids, I like learning, and I like having a job at which I can always improve. You should also know that I have been rehired—I also like just plain having a job.

Forever a slave to alliteration, teaching breaks down into "p" words for me: paperwork, people, programs, and politics. So, I shall break down my essay into these categories. First, I should explain briefly the environment in which I worked and why I was hired. I work in a suburban school district that is well funded, stable, and deals with students that are generally college-bound. Central School has an older, established staff and does not often deal with brand-new teachers; their "new" teachers have usually taught for several years in a rural or urban district that did not pay as well or offered considerably more headaches. Fate was smiling on me when I got this job. Several factors led to my employment. First, the district had offered an early-retirement program, which opened two social studies positions, thus giving them leeway as to the qualities desired in aspiring candidates. Second, there was an emphasis on recruiting young teachers. Third, one position they were trying to fill required working with low-ability/low-motivation students, something well-matched with my student-teaching experience in the inner city. I believe this last factor to be the main reason I was hired. The student-teaching supervisor's absolutely wonderful reference—bless her soul—must have impressed someone somewhere because they hired me. Oh, and there could have been some tokenism, since I am the only female in the department. But who cares? I got the job. And it is a good one, especially for a rookie.

PAPERWORK

Ugh! Paperwork was to become the bane of my existence. It never ends. If I was not planning lessons, I was correcting homework; if I was not correcting homework, I was taking notes and reading up on my subject; if I was not reading up, I was running off copies; if I was not running off copies, I was filling out forms requested by guidance, the department, the administration, or the students; if I was not filling out forms, I was reading memos that were left in my mailbox by the truckload; if I was not reading memos, I was working on bulletin boards. And if I was doing *none* of the above, I was feeling guilty. If there is one thing about teaching, it is a *lot* of work. And making sure I was organized and timely about performing the necessary tasks was vital to my teaching. For example, I never used to put page numbers in my lesson plans. I cannot tell you the number of crimes committed while I looked up the page numbers to tell the students in class. Joe would talk with Susie, Ben would let fly with a piece of paper, Tammy and Marie would catch up on their weekends, all in the five seconds it would take to look up the page number. Then, it would take me five minutes to get everyone back on task. (By the way, "on task" is a term educators just love. Add it to your vocabulary.) The attention span of ninth- and tenth-graders is not exceptional, and if I was not organized with my work and could not run that classroom whiff, bam, boom, I would wish I was on another planet. I remember the sense of dread that would overtake me if I misplaced a worksheet. I think kids live for the moment their teacher is unprepared. I remember how their faces lit up if I started searching for something or if the movie projector broke. The chatter and games would start immediately, and I'd then be disciplining and looking for a solution. A little voice would start to say, "It's all over, they're winning." Usually I found what I was looking for, and eventually I learned to have a small bag of tricks handy in case of such an emergency. But those moments when the control slipped due to technical difficulties were no less than frightening.

The hours it took for me to achieve a modicum of organization are as follows:

7:30 AM–4:00/6:00 PM: I was at school, teaching, making photocopies, disciplining, coaching, and so on.

8:00 PM–10:00 or 11:00 PM: I worked at home on paperwork.

Weekends—8–20 hours: I worked on lesson plans and paperwork.

I had basically no social life until spring, when I really lived it up by going out about once a week, on the weekend. I also began playing tennis once or twice a week with a friend of mine who was one of the basic skills teachers. I learned by then that friends are very important to one's sanity. My previous job as a marketing associate never entailed such consuming work. I mean I was physically exhausted. I coached in the fall and I felt like I was ready for a sanitarium by the fifth week. I would come home Fridays at 8:00 PM after a game so exhausted that even watching television required too much mental concentration. Often I would drink a couple of beers, watch the most inane show available, and go to bed by 9 o'clock. I would not move again until 11 or so Saturday morning, trying to catch up on a week's lack of sleep. Then, after the only breakfast of the week I could enjoy, I would start correcting papers or planning lessons until later in the evening, when I would watch another inane, escapist show and repeat the same procedure on Sunday. Sunday has come to represent the true meaning of bittersweet for me. There was so much to do for the next week and yet I could still drink my coffee slowly and actually ponder its taste. It would be the last day I could do so for another week.

Luckily, starting in October, I became part of a pilot mentor/intern program funded by New York State. I had been asked during the summer if I wished to participate and wholeheartedly answered yes, and to this day am thoroughly thankful I was one of the participants. I dropped one class and during that time would meet with my mentor. Jerry was a member of the social studies department. He saved my sanity. The mentor program, I believe, is responsible for the positive and realistic picture I have of my first year. This will become more evident as the story progresses. Anyway, our first goals were to put out the brushfires, which were mainly organization and getting the paperwork under control. He gave me his notes for the tenth-grade curriculum, a "bag of tricks" folder for rainy days, and reviewed my tests. I began to feel more in control. Later we would work on grading, different methods of getting the students to get more out of their readings, test results, and so on. I still worked as hard but by the end of November I began to feel as though I was getting somewhere. If there is ever a job in which you can second guess yourself, it is teaching. I would sweat over a problem that really wasn't a problem at all and at the same time be quite ignorant of a situation that required my attention. For example, I would be concentrating on Greek mythology and freaking out because I could not list the gods in their hierarchy, but I was totally ignorant of the fact that I was solely in charge of the low-level mid-year exams and should be considering their format and content. With Jerry's help, I learned to set up a realistic hierarchy of tasks to utilize my time and awareness of the more important shape of events.

Of all the paperwork, grading is the nitty-gritty of teaching for me. Students take their grade as the bottom line of your class. It is the end all and be all of the class. To me, a grade for a class is, or at least should be, a combination of ability, attitude, and effort. Put bluntly, how do you nail a kid who really tried with an F? Or, how do you reward a lazy, snotty punk with an A? My school requires that your grading system be in writing and given both to the students and posted in the classroom. I used the following combination in my grading policy:

> Low-level classes: 20 percent notebook, 20 percent homework, 20 percent class participation, and 40 percent tests

> Honors classes: 10 percent class participation, 20 percent homework, 70 percent tests

I felt that the inclusion of homework, notebook, and class participation would comply with both the need for a standardized system and the need for fairness. What I didn't realize was that I created a living hell for myself. When I had 40-some-odd notebooks in front of me I wanted to shoot myself. I had to go through each one, check the handouts, check the written notes, check dates, organization, neatness, and so on. Then, for the quarterly grade, just getting the calculator out to work up a homework grade and then tally the varying percentages for the overall grade made me rethink my values. I decided not to change the approach (I'm still young and have that vigor of youth). But, I now know why teachers lose values along the way. Values can mean a paperwork nightmare.

Grading became easier as I became more familiar with the process. I also became more familiar with what I thought was an A or F. You recognize it when you see it, or at least think you do, but as the year progressed I began to have specific point values. For example, I began to give certain point values to essays for introduction, and body, and conclusion. There had to be a minimum number of examples to give cause to an argument. This made it much easier to translate to the students just what I was looking for. By the way, if it seems I am a genius who by trial and error saw the light, I am misleading you. My mentor and department head both worked with me on grading. I also read the essays graded by the two other teachers in my subject area and asked them how they graded. This points out that while instinct is good, I certainly did not rely on it absolutely. I learned a lot from others. While they didn't change my whole grading system, they certainly helped me make it comprehensible to my students and less time-consuming for me. In the end, I felt my grades were fair. I also felt my planning and execution of lessons was satisfactory. It's a good thing I felt this way, because after the mid-year my teaching methods came under attack.

The social studies department gives its own mid-year and final examination to ninth and tenth grade classes. With the exception of the low-level classes, for which I was responsible for creating and administering the exam, the classes receive a department examination. This translates into my honors group. The results for this group were not outstanding. I had few 90s, mostly 80s and 70s, and one failure. I was thoroughly depressed. Our review had been cut short by a snow day and it was the first big test these kids had taken. The exam was a two-hour affair including 75 multiple choice questions and two essays. I had been working myself to the bone to cover all the material necessary. Jerry had warned me earlier to prepare them, and I had started using the other teachers' test questions on smaller tests to get them used to similar questions on the mid-year. I was hoping they would do really well and take that as evidence of my teaching abilities. Never put all your eggs in one basket. The results were quite reasonable but average. For the honors class I had been hoping to see more. I really got down on myself. I was not Mr. Chips. All that planning, organization, and paperwork did not seem good enough. There I was, in debt, no social life, working around the clock, and having a very hard time rationalizing my decision to become a teacher. I had yet to realize that the good times were just beginning.

PEOPLE

During that first year it was people who would cause me my greatest problem, and people who would help me to solve it. It depended, of course, on the personality and desires of those involved as to the side of the equation on which they fell. Some students were my worst enemies, some were my best friends. The same applies to their parents. The teachers and administration were almost all pillars of support. The problem I refer to now simply as the mid-year incident, had to do with my first-year goal—to be a good teacher. I really cared about fulfilling that goal and was working harder than ever to achieve it. It was like a kick to the groin when I found out some of my students decided I was "ineffective." Thus began the incident. Incident is one of those antiseptic terms that removes images of war, hatred, loss of innocence, despair, and so forth. I use the term purposely now because the scar has healed and I worked very hard not to take the whole issue personally.

Let me set the proper scenario for what was to become the major crisis of my first year of teaching. As previously explained, the mid-year results were mediocre for the honors group. Again, I stress that they were not out of line with the norm for the higher level. At about the same time as the mid-year, the local newspaper came out with a story concerning the mentor/intern program at Central School, a story, complete with my picture, detailing that I was a first-year teacher. So, word had gone out to the community that I was a rookie. In what I later considered to be no accident, a parent dissatisfied with his son's performance on the mid-year called the student's guidance counselor requesting that the student be switched from my class to a more experienced teacher's class. You see, my "teaching methods were ineffective" according to that student. No meeting was set up with me, the student, the parents, or the department head. The guidance counselor simply told the parent to write a letter to the department head requesting the switch. As fate would have it, I was at an "effective teaching" seminar when my department head received the letter. This too, I believe, was no accident—the student hand-delivered the letter when I was not in the school. I was pulled out of the seminar to take a phone call from Joe, the department head, who told me he had a two-page letter in his hand requesting that Jay be moved. He asked if I knew anything about it. After I told him I didn't, he replied that he would look into it. I then spent the rest of the afternoon listening to lectures on how and why teachers are ineffective. It really buoyed my spirits.

The next day I went into Joe's office after my first-period class to discuss the matter. That's when I discovered the chain of events that led to the letter. The irony of this situation is that for all my "ineffectiveness" the student had the same low grade on his English mid-year and a lower grade in social studies the previous year. Now it looked as though I might be grading too easily. So far, I could handle the situation. I had gotten little sleep the night before worrying about my "effectiveness." Also it was the day before winter vacation and I was exhausted from working like a dog on the weekends preparing for mid-years, then correcting them, and then getting out the grades. Still, I could handle the situation and its apparent outcome. The student had let off a little heat from home by blaming the grade on me.

Up to that point I could handle the situation. I then checked my box and found a note from a different guidance counselor about "a situation developing in my honors group." I went to see this guidance counselor right after speaking with Joe. He asked if there were any "problems" with my mid-year grades. He had a couple of students requesting to transfer out of my class because of my "ineffective teaching methods." Funny, but they were close friends with Jay. This guidance counselor was still speaking as the tears started to well up in my eyes. I was too tired and upset to rehash the situation. As he saw this, he tried to cheer me up by saying, "You know, Margaret, they really like you as a person, they just think you're not effective as a teacher." It was devastating. I didn't go into this business to win the Miss Congeniality award. I just wanted to be exactly what these students were claiming I wasn't: effective. I could no longer be rational at this point. I cried. And it was no Bette Davis single tear down the check; I turned bright red in teary blotches and nearly choked. I mumbled some kind of apology and quickly left his office. I then sprinted for the ladies room to let loose the torrent and—I hoped—to shape up in time for class.

In the bathroom I ran into another teacher. And guess which teacher? Cindy, the one whose son is in my honors group. She asked me why I was crying, I told her. She was very kind and considerate and full of encouragement. Considering that her son was not at the top of my class and that she of all people could best judge my "effectiveness," she went above and beyond the call of duty, telling me how tough teachers have it the first year and relating some problems she had her first year. I calmed down. I then left the security of the bathroom and looked for Jerry. I found him and heated right back up again retelling the story. He, too, was a soul of kindness. I calmed down again. I had to—my next class was about to begin.

I looked a mess. Makeup can cover up only so much crying, and I had gone way over the limit. It was pretty obvious to the class that I had been crying. This particular class was probably my most volatile low-level group at the time. I received strange looks from most of them as they filed in. Then Sue, the queen of the smoking lounge, came up to me, gave me a little hug and said, "We're glad you're back, Miss O'Bryan." She was referring to my absence during the seminar. The rest of the class went very smoothly. You could never tell it was the day before vacation. They knew I was upset and they were taking care of me. Let the other teachers bitch about the smokers and swearers and the nonconformists. They were taking care of me and I am never going to forget that. They're great people.

Meanwhile, the saga of the ineffective first-year teacher was continuing. Jerry spoke to Joe and told him something had to be done before the situation got out of control. Joe came into my honors class at the end of the day and spoke to them. It was a good speech. Joe, always in tune to social studies issues, framed his speech as a social question. It was based on rumors and how rumors and false information affect people. In this case it was the rumor that I was ineffective and that my mid-year results were inadequate. He spoke on as to how rumors can ruin a person's reputation. The conversation then went on to specifics. He told the students that according to his standards and the school's standards I was a fine teacher. He also told them he would not approve any transfers to another class unless it were to a lower level. The cavalry had come. The class was subdued. I left for vacation tired, bruised, and depressed. Still, for the misery the day held I was impressed by the support I received from the students, the teacher in the bathroom, my mentor, and my department head.

The staff support grew even stronger after vacation. Someone, I believe Joe and Jerry, spoke strongly to the guidance counselors. The one counselor who sent the letter was pretty embarrassed when I walked into his office to discuss the matter. I got a song and dance about the reason the situation went as far as it did, but I also received an apology. He seemed genuinely sorry about the whole issue. Also, teachers came up to me in the lounge and sympathized with me about the situation. I was to learn that parental dissatisfaction is one of the major headaches in this school system. In other words, this situation was by no means unusual for Central School. It was an initiation rite. In the end, the mid-year incident would boost my confidence. Like a cornered cat, I began to fight back. Instead of second-guessing myself, I worked even harder on my teaching strategies with Joe and Jerry. The support I received from so many people aided my efforts a great deal.

Not all of my contact with parents was as negative as the mid-year problem. I do not want to make parents out to be the bad guys. In fact, I usually

performed pretty well in case conferences and parent meetings. Take the following example. One very glib, young woman's mother came in to discuss a
drop in her grades. Before the meeting I reviewed the student's tests and
labeled which questions were missed and why. Whenever I make up a test,
some questions would come from notes, some from the text, and some would
ask that current information be related to general topics discussed throughout
the year. I made note of each of these and found that this young girl most
often missed those questions that required paying attention in class. Because
she often told jokes or gossiped in class, this was no big surprise. I had been
warned by another teacher that this mother could be a "problem," therefore I
was pretty nervous. I practiced on Jerry. He felt I was on solid ground, but
suggested I try to get a sense of her concern before whipping out too much
paperwork. Well, the meeting went really well. She was concerned that her
daughter was too social and just wanted to check why the grades had dipped.
I showed her the tests, explained her lack of attention at times to be a prob-
able cause, and offered that if the behavior improved before the end of the
third quarter, I would be willing to consider that in the class-participation
part of her grade. The mother seemed pleased. The next day the daughter
told me her mother thought I was very well organized and was impressed
with our meeting. Score one for the rookie.

The most important people to a teacher, of course, are the students. The
mid-year incident instilled in me a sense of betrayal, and it took effort to keep
those few complainers from coloring my whole perception of upper-level students. I found that while I had a great deal of patience with the lower groups,
the upper groups caused me a great deal of consternation. There were several
reasons for this. First of all, I have generally found the lower-level kids to be
more honest. Personally, I appreciate honesty more than brains. If they don't
like you, they call you a bitch. You then assign them to detention. They stop
calling you a bitch for a couple of days. And, generally they will like you if you
come across as liking them and treating them fairly. Since they are not really
interested in school for the most part, they are interested in you as a person.
And they treat you as such, whether they like you or not. On the other hand,
I found some of the honors types are your best friends until they get a 75. Jay
fits into this category. One even stated that if I was really smart, I'd be a
doctor or lawyer not a teacher. These are the troublemakers in the honors
group. I had to watch making assumptions about the whole group from that
minority. But a devious minority can spoil the best intentions.

Perhaps the best examples of lower versus upper student behavior stem
from my observations. When I was observed in a low-level class, I was shocked
by their behavior. It wasn't my class: They were taking notes, they were asking questions, and raising their hands before doing so. I started laughing at
one point. I just couldn't take the good behavior. But it really warmed the
cockles of my heart. Again, they were watching out for me. They knew why
Joe was in there and they wanted me to look good. Now, in the honors group
observation, a couple of students decided the time was ripe to put Ms.
O'Bryan through her paces. They started asking the most picayune questions

about India—looking for dates, names, and historical trivia. The observation went well, but it was a pretty obvious attempt at sabotage. Needless to say, they did not warm the cockles of my heart. Later, I found that there were a fair number of kids in that class that really liked my class and thought I was a great teacher. One girl's mother spoke to me this summer about how much her daughter enjoyed my class. I always work to remind myself of that fact when I remember the honors students. I found the intelligent troublemakers so obnoxious that they really overshadowed the greater number of their good-natured classmates. On some days, like the day of the observation, it took a lot of effort to keep from hating that class.

It is very different from my school days and my previous work to be known as Ms. O'Bryan. I had authority in previous jobs but none of it compares to the relationship between student and teacher. The main difference is, obviously, that students are not adults and school is not, in their eyes, a job. The authority associated with being a teacher is much greater and more difficult to achieve. I couldn't give raises or fire students. I also felt the pressures of being a role model. But students also show greater joy when they are having fun and you sense a greater impact on their lives than you do with adults. It was the contact with students in and out of the classrom that was my favorite aspect of teaching.

Perhaps one of my most memorable days was the day I wore a very fashionable, bright pink dress to school. It seems a stupid thing to remember, let alone write about, but I never realized the impact an outfit could have on students. I have never received so many compliments as that day. In homeroom, Sam commented on how pink was my color. Len told me I looked really sharp. Cindy said I should definitely wear it on my next date. Students in every class kept up with similar compliments. Even the staff joined in and one teacher to this day calls me Loretta Young because of the dress. The dress was like a magic charm and from that day forward I wore it if I felt like I needed a boost.

The pink dress touches on one facet of my life that fascinated the students: my social life. Their first question when I wrote my name on the board as Ms. O'Bryan was, "Is that Miss or Mrs.?" So much for women's lib. And the minute I told them it was "Miss," I was hounded for the year about my single status. And the more I avoided their questions, the more curious they became. During bus rides, the soccer team I coached would beg me to describe my boyfriend. Whenever there was a single male substitute in the building, the students would offer to introduce me to him. They would also debate as to which of the young, male teachers I was dating. I never dated any of them and I never spoke of my social life, but the facts did not seem to matter. I was incredulous at the speculation. The worst of this, however, was when I was seen at a movie with a date. Like most people, I hoped to impress the young gentleman. While we were standing in line, I heard pounding on the glass front of the theater. Six girls were waving madly, giggling and giving me the thumbs up sign. My date wondered if they were "friends of mine." The next Monday in school, students approached me all day and asked about my date.

After school is a great time to get to know the students. It is usually during these moments that the students and I could relax and get to know each other. Some students get too relaxed, such as the young man who wanted to know if I went to bars. It seems he went to bars often and dated older women like myself. Without having had practice warding off the advances of a tenth-grader, I'm afraid I came down on him a little too hard. "How old were these women?" I asked. "You know, college age, 20, 21," he replied. "I'm 28, Sam," I said. His face suddenly darkened and he exclaimed, "Wow, that's old!" I'm not sure who felt the worst, but that was the extent of the crushes on Ms. O'Bryan.

I also had a regular crowd of afterschool students that consisted of my ex-soccer players. They would usually be told to be quiet in the hallway by another teacher and then pop into my room to avoid trouble. We spent many an afternoon playing hangman or going over all the ninth-grade gossip. Of course I had a million other things to do, but I was honored to be accorded the right of listening to the gossip. I also enjoyed it. Soccer had worn me out in the fall, but the minute I received a shirt from the girls with "Coach" emblazoned on the back of it, I knew it was worth it. It also became evident that coaching was one of the best things I did when every afternoon the crew bounded into my room and asked, "Are you busy, Coach?" It was fun, plain and simple.

You also came to understandings after school. There was one young man, Bret, who almost every day tried to disrupt class. His usual tactics included sitting on the radiator, throwing spitballs, making his sneakers squeak when he walked across the floor, and a host of other equally dignified pursuits. So, Bret was a regular at afterschool detention. It was here I learned that Bret bore me no malice. He just hated school and often couldn't resist the temptation to bug a teacher. He hoped I did not take it personally. I never did. We had an almost businesslike relationship. We recognized each other's role and played the game accordingly, but outside those roles we liked each other as people. We appreciated each other's honesty and on days when one or the other seemed unusually sensitive, we left each other alone. Still, I can't say I was overly excited when Bret told me near the end of the year, "You know, you'll have my sister next year. She's as bad as I am." Bret and I looked at one another and he started to laugh. I joined him. This summer, I saw him at one of the schools with his sister. He introduced us and told his sister, "She's not bad, . . . for a teacher."

Jan was another discipline regular after school. Again, Jan and I got along fine out of class. She just had the unfortunate habit of always showing up late to class. Here again, detentions were business as usual. And after school we would often talk. The talk usually centered on the Grateful Dead, her favorite group. After I saw her in a Grateful Dead t-shirt, I told her I had once been to a Dead concert. Thereafter, she continued to pump me to see if I had once been "cool." I never let on one way or the other. Then, one afternoon, she announced to me that she decided I must have been "cool" if I had been to a Dead concert. Then she wanted to know what god-awful incident had happened to me that made me become a teacher.

Then again, not all students had rave reviews of me or my class. "This class is run like a prison!" Eric exclaimed loudly after I refused to let him go to the bathroom. Class policy allowed bathroom visits at the beginning or end of class but not in the middle. Eric wasn't going to let it go. For ten minutes he would let out the occasional side comment about me being Hitler in drag. Finally I'd had it. The rest of the class was working in small groups on an assignment. Eric was still busy with his Fifth Amendment right to go to the bathroom. And that led to detention. Even then there was no sign of Eric letting the issue rest. Now, the whole class was watching just to see how tough Ms. O'Bryan would get. Sometimes students force you into a no-win situation. You can lose control with too much understanding or too little. Or, you lose control with too much understanding or too little. Or, you lose control of the many when trying to reason with the few. Anyway, Eric was going to be publicly slaughtered for the many. He refused to be quiet and refused detention. I wrote up the discipline slip that meant an automatic trip to the assistant principal's office with a copy sent home to the folks. Eric looked a little shocked. He then took the slip, crumpled it, said "fuck this" and left the room. Eric and I never had a big confrontation again, but neither did we ever hit it off. The rest of the class never pushed the bathroom issue. But, I can't really say I'd won, even though the negative behavior stopped.

Another showstopper of a more serious nature left me speechless one day. As students were taking notes on Martin Luther, Maureen stood up, pointed at another student, and bellowed, "Tell this fucking bitch to stop staring at me!" The whole class was speechless. So was I. We were frozen for a few moments with our mouths hanging open. I then quietly gave Maureen a pass to the assistant principal. She took it and left the room; the rest of the class continued with their notes, still a little too stunned to comprehend the outburst. It took days of talks between Maureen, her friends, her other teachers, the assistant principal, and me to get her back in class, in a new seat.

There are many, many more stories about students. I'm full of them. I'm always trying to analyze their behavior—and mine—and how the situation could have been handled in another way. Those moments with students, negative and positive, are the most challenging part of the job for me. I like history and geography, but I still find the interaction with students more fascinating.

Teaching is a people business—with all the good and bad that that implies. I think the most important thing for a first-year teacher to remember, though, is that you too are a person. There were days when I was tired and cranky. I tried to be "super-teacher" and not let the lethargy show, but it didn't work. In fact, when I set for myself the goal of becoming Mr. Chips, I often ended up feeling worse. If I got up and felt really cranky, I found it better to admit that to myself and try to avoid confrontations. It was when I tried to perform super-teacher tricks on a not so super day that I snapped. I don't want to give the impression that if I felt down, I thoroughly gave in to that emotion, sat at my desk, and had a nervous breakdown, but I found that if I relaxed and perhaps had the students work in small groups as opposed to lecturing to them, that the class would run better. You'd be surprised at how long forty-five minutes can seem some days.

Occasionally, I even hit on a great idea. One day when I was tired a lecture was going very poorly. The class was acting up and I was short on patience. If I stayed on the track I was on, someone was going to end up spending time in detention. I thought something new was needed. I had Sam come up to the front of the room and be the "teacher." He was to have the class read a selection and go over their homework answers. To have some fun, I pretended to be a student. Well, the next thing I knew, the students are calling Sam "Mr. Jones," and he was calling me Margaret. If none of the students had an answer to a question, he would call on me. We laughed a good deal throughout the rest of the class and although we didn't get through all the answers, we answered most. Everyone enjoyed it. The kids were begging me to do it again as they left class. They then went into math class and begged Ms. Baird to let them go over their math homework that way. She did. Ms. Baird and I caught up with each other in the teachers' lounge and she told me what had happened. We both laughed over their enthusiasm for the "Teacher Game" and how serious some of them became in front of the room. It wasn't the first time I had ever had the kids go over things in front of their peers but the game quality of pretending to be a teacher really added something to it. It was a happy ending to a mediocre beginning. Usually, nice things happened when I let my hair down and became a person instead of super-teacher.

Being human has its limits though. Many times, as in the incident with Eric, I had to set limits and be a disciplinarian. Showing I was human was sometimes mistaken for weakness. For instance, I never pretended with the kids that the sun rose and set upon my knowledge of social studies. I would look up answers I did not know. At home I worked exceptionally hard brushing up on background knowledge, but the students could not see me at home. So, if I could not rattle off the specific date the Qing Dynasty ended, it would be taken as a sign of weakness. It did not matter if I could lead them to the significance of that era upon China's development. It was this honesty that led to the mid-year crisis. It didn't matter how many questions I got right, it was the ones I held off to look up that determined my intellectual capacity.

Benny, a very bright boy but one who did not do a lot of studying, used my "newness" as an excuse for his lower grades. In fact, he started all the mid-year rumors. The interesting twist is that Benny never wanted out of my class; it was the best excuse for his purposes. Of course, when he found out the others listened to him, he enjoyed the power over me and the grief he caused. On some days, Benny would start asking trivial questions just because it got on my nerves. Jane, the other mentor, knew Benny from her own class, in which he often applied similar tactics. She suggested I try her trick. When Benny started asking questions specifically designed to disturb the teacher, turn it around and tell Benny "that's interesting, why don't you look into it for tomorrow's class and bring us the results." While transparent, it was effective in quieting him during class. Outside of class he would continue with snide comments and he did do damage with his remarks. His tale of my incompetency went home through the mouths of other students in my class. I should have been braver in the beginning and stopped him the day the comments started. But there was always that fear of failure hovering in the back of my brain. I had to confront myself before I could deal with Benny. Jane and Jerry helped me see his ploy and fight back, but as I said, the damage had been done at that point. Still, I wouldn't have and still won't now change my approach toward honesty. Honesty can make you an easy target, but I'd rather be a target than unapproachable. I think as a teacher, if you aren't approachable and open to questions, you don't learn anything yourself. However, in the ninth and tenth grade they don't always buy the open approach. I'm not sure they want life that complicated.

There are more people involved in teaching than just students and their parents. There are teachers and administrators. And at first it's funny to see them from the perspective of co-worker rather than student. The staff at Central School was very supportive. I can't recall any incidents of hostility toward me. There are a couple of people I would not choose to talk to at great length, but on the whole I really like the staff, especially those in my department.

I remember being terrified at the first department meeting. The whole department is male, and with the exception of another teacher hired along with me, they are older. I don't know if social studies breeds particularly opinionated people, but this group was wild. Everyone in the department has an opinion on almost every subject, has no qualms about voicing those opinions, and usually does so with acerbic wit. During that first department meeting I was sure I was going to be eaten alive. And trust me, I am by no means a bashful person. It is rare that I am in awe of a group of people, but in awe I was. Needless to say, I did not open my mouth during the first meeting. And all I could think was "How am I ever going to live up to the standards they've set?" Well, I am still in awe of this group but as I said before, I really like my department.

Jerry is the key to many of my friendships in the department. Once I was comfortable with him, I got to know other members of the department. It was usually through jokes that I got to know them. One running joke centered around the fact that I was the only female. My first day at school, Ted (the other new social studies teacher) and I were talking in his classroom. A couple of female teachers came in to chat. They made a joke about my solitary status in the department and one of them said, "I hope you can hunker because that's what your department does in the morning. The boys all sit around a table and hunker." It was obvious by her tone that she did not find their hunkering too pleasant. Anyway, I told Jerry at one point my apprehension concerning the department and the "hunker story." He laughed, said it was true, and suggested I surprise the group by sitting down to hunker with them. I never did, but the story made good copy, and the group often teased me about it. As a private joke we nicknamed the department photo "Bambi and the Forest Creatures."

One of the teachers who teased me was Fred, who also taught the ninth-grade curriculum. Fred is a football coach who, on the surface, lives the term *macho*. But his teasing turned into useful talks about, and help with, teaching strategies and materials. It then turned into my raping and pillaging his files. It was the kind of support I needed, both the jokes and advice. I found many of the social contacts in the teachers' lounge to be real goldmines of information. It became a very important source of knowledge as well as a good time. I was very pleased the day I showed Fred one of my readings with worksheets and he asked for a copy. It will take five more years to even the score, but I'm glad I've started.

I also became friends with the other social studies teacher hired at the same time. Ted is my age and we met over the summer at a seminar on African Studies. He had taught several years in other districts before coming to Central School. Over the year he has been a good friend, a good listener, and very helpful. One lesson of his I borrowed was a big hit with my classes. It concerned the Triangular Trade and involved paper cutouts of guns, slaves, and rum. The students moved about the room from Europe to Africa to the Caribbean. They then translated the physical activity onto worksheet diagrams, which became the basis for a further study of the slave trade. The activity was also an excellent one for me to see how creative lessons benefit the students. Ted and Fred were always a good source of ideas and they sparked in me the desire to really polish my own plans. I was lucky to see and use these ideas my first year. Again, teaching is a people business. Interacting with all kinds of personalities, young and old, mature and immature, pleasant and unpleasant, is a big challenge. It takes a special combination of being tough and tender to be successful. I didn't always get it, but it is a good feeling when you do play a situation right or have an excellent lesson.

PROGRAMS

The mentor/intern program deserves special mention. It helped me in many areas of teaching my first year. I'd hear of this idea in education while studying for my MAT. My sister, also a teacher, talked to me several times about how she felt such a program was necessary for new teachers. She wished she had had a mentor. So, when the letter asking if I was interested in participating in such a program arrived, I replied "Yes." Luckily, I was chosen to participate along with another high school teacher and two elementary-school teachers. New York State is interested in making a mentor experience a requirement for new teachers. I cannot tell you whether that bill has passed the legislature or not, but it was expected to be mandated for 1993. In preparation, our school district was chosen for a pilot program. 1986/1987 was the first year. It was interesting coincidence—a rookie program for my rookie year.

Because of delays by the state, the progam was not put into effect until October. Therefore, I had one full month of teaching alone. And I felt alone. I felt like I was scrapping to stay alive. With coaching a soccer team and the beginning of the year, I was physically and emotionally drained. After that first month, I came to really appreciate the mentor program. First, I dropped one class. The class only consisted of seven students, but the extra time during the day was still a relief. Luckily, Jerry and I had a free period in common, so it was easy for us to meet on a daily basis. The other mentor and intern in the high school had to meet during hall duty, which made it more difficult for them. The other intern teacher was Elaine Baird and her mentor was Jane. They were math teachers. Jane became a mentor to me as well and Jerry the same to Elaine. As a group we got along very well. It was good to have Elaine there especially. Misery loves company. But seriously, it was very nice to have someone going through the same ups and downs. Everyone on staff referred to us as "The Rookies."

Luckily, the mentor/intern program was a pilot program so we had no guidelines or mandates to follow from the state. We were guinea pigs. We had to fill out forms for the state and for an evaluative group for the district. But, other than that we were on our own to do whatever we felt was needed. I call this lucky, because I feel the whole benefit of a mentor program is to have a person there that you can tell all your deep dark secrets about your teaching. If the state requires too many reports on your activities, it could hamper communication. For example, if Jerry had to write comments about observing me to others, I might feel I was being evaluated—in the same way the principal or department head does. Needless to say, I would feel a little less relaxed in that situation. As it turned out, I felt very relaxed with Jerry as a mentor and I feel the program will make me a better teacher in the long run, and it certainly saved my sanity in the short run.

Jerry and I worked at first at just getting the paperwork under control. In fact, I used the first couple of weeks spending that extra period photocopying. He helped me with notes, and he observed one of my classes before Joe was scheduled to come in. I was very nervous about being observed. Even if he wouldn't tell anyone, I didn't want to be a total loser. Who does? And I was nervous about observations because of my student teaching. My professor picked the absolute worst days of my life to observe me. So, I felt as though I never came across well in an observation. If I were nervous the same result would occur once again. I also made the decision not to really work up the lesson before Jerry came to observe. I wanted him to see exactly how I was teaching. I mean that's what the students were getting on a daily basis and I wanted to know if it worked.

Well, it went pretty well. Jerry didn't marvel at the sight of first year super-teacher, but I performed just fine. I was really pleased by what he said. He opened up the discussion of the lesson with a funny observation. One student had asked me a question about the power of the queen of England. In trying to convey the subtleties of the situation, I spent about five full minutes rambling on about the queen. The student was just looking at me blankly when I finished and I realized I'd overdone it. It was a little like using a sledgehammer to kill a mosquito. Anyway, Jerry opened up our discussion by teasing me and saying, "Boy, Margaret, you really know your queen!" We both laughed. He then complimented me on how I handled a student who was nervous abut answering a question. The student at first refused to answer, but I told him I knew he had the right answer (I had looked at their papers earlier). Jerry then had one main criticism, telling me to make the students work a little harder and have myself work a little less. I generally tended to give information and rely less on the students to get it. He suggested I ask more questions and wait longer for answers. He also described how we could work on teaching strategies to accomplish this. Otherwise, I should do just fine during observations. That boost really helped. As it turned out, I received good marks on all of my observations.

The other situation that got a lot of laughs behind the scenes was the case of the pornographic comic book. I caught one of my students with a book of "men's-magazine-type" cartoons hidden in his notebook. So, as a responsible teacher, I confiscated the notebook and then had absolutely no idea how to proceed. I never had brothers, so the hormones of young boys really escaped me. I never read a chapter on porn material in any of my books at school. Well, it became my query of the day to my mentor. Well, my dilemma prompted a number of yuks from everyone. Jerry suggested I tell the student he could get the material back if his mother called me with the name of the book and claimed it was all right for him to have the material. Otherwise, he felt I should just keep it under my hat because, as he put it, "he's a fourteen-year-old boy." Well, needless to say the mother never did call me and the student was not caught with sleazy materials in my class again.

Of course, my mentor and I had much more serious discussions. It was nice to have Jerry as a sounding board for my ideas. Luckily we shared similar philosophies of life and got on very well. I was not discouraged to try things and I also was not molded into a mini-Jerry. In fact, as the year went on, he coached me into asking questions and then giving my own answers to them. He would also mention situations that arose in his class and ask me how I would handle them. He left me with the feeling that teaching requires a lot of judgment calls and that no matter how good you are or how long you have been teaching, you will still have problems. Since it feels like all you have your first year are problems, it was reassuring to know it wasn't because I didn't have "the right stuff" to become a teacher. Then again, it is almost depressing to know that this is a job in which you will never be perfect, skilled perhaps, but never perfect. I guess that's the challenge.

Jerry and I talked at length about the problems I had by mid-year. A number of teachers came forward with "ineffective" stories. The parents of many of the students are professionals, many of whom feel they know better than the teacher. I'm not sure how I feel about the parental pressure. On the one hand, it is positive in that parents encourage their children to do well, are interested in the school, and are active in maintaining high standards. It is negative in the sense that often pedagogical standards are lost when Johnny's parents say "boo." I also see students who are being pushed and, I feel, have a negative self-image because they are being pushed. For instance, one of the mid-year students was really having a hard time in the honors group. You could see it in her homework. Although it was always meticulously done and contained a lot of writing, it never put forth anything beyond parroting the book. She was missing the connections and regardless of the energy she put into her work, she was not an A student. You could see she felt frustrated and would come in for help. This helped her grade. Later in the year, I found her parents felt I was ineffective. Their child was "ivy league material" and I was jeopardizing this future. Although I was a new teacher, I had been in school a number of years, and had friends who went to ivy league schools. I recognized many bright students in my class, but I really felt I was not ruining brilliance here. But I could also see the need for this child to tell her parents that I was the problem—it got her off the hook. I'm not claiming I was an excellent teacher, but I refused to take the responsibility that I was damaging ivy league material. It took me a while to get to that admission. There was a lot of insecurity as a first-year teacher. The mentor program, and more specifically my mentor, helped me gain confidence, and allowed me to take pride in my teaching efforts and move forward to try new ideas. I could have second-guessed myself into oblivion. I felt a much better chance of improving as a teacher once I quit beating myself up.

POLITICS

Politics in teaching is to me the art of balancing the people and the paperwork. It is setting up a hierarchy for all of the millions of decisions you face every day. Consider this example: My first-period class just ended, and I now have a free period. The following tasks await me. Erik acted up and I need to see his basic skills teacher and the assistant principal; Joanie, another student, has asked me to have a cup of coffee with her—a rare honor for a teacher; I have 50 tests that need to be stapled together before the next class; there is a guidance form for a student I am worried about that needs to be filled out by the end of the day; I need to review the notes from the ninth-grade classes and make up a quiz on their reading; it is near the middle of the quarter and I should be sending home scholarship reports; I need to read the available materials on the Holocaust and the role of the hacienda system in Latin America; I also have a stack of dittos and photocopies needed by the end of the week. Politics. What should I do first? And second? And what changes when I find out the principal is coming to my fourth-period class? That was my life as a teacher.

And this doesn't even represent a bad day or a full day. My mind would always be filled with an ever-present log of things to do, people to meet, and problems to solve—all within a specified period of time. Organization is the answer. But organization won't help you when Bret is performing birdcalls in the back of the room. Personality is the answer. Sure, but personality alone won't run the photocopy machine. Find out someone else's answer. Sure, that helps sometimes—but I'm not someone else. I can tell Rodney Dangerfield jokes, but that doesn't make me funny. What did I do?

I tried all of the options. And I tried them in different combinations and sometimes it worked beautifully and sometimes it didn't work at all. Over the year, I learned which instincts to trust more than others. For example, on the people issues, I relied mainly on instinct. Usually this worked to the best advantage in dealing with my students. They seemed to like me and I know I liked them. It was hard to make time, but I found talking with kids one of the greatest joys. I found a few of them trusted me with secrets, and I always tried to do right by them. Since a good portion of my kids got into trouble with the administration, I found myself a buffer. I talked with both sides and tried to do what was best. Sometimes this meant turning a kid in. One boy cut my class frequently. His grades had really deteriorated by the second quarter. I had to turn in the cuts or I could get in trouble. But, when he really started working third quarter I had him serve detention with me and we talked. Half the time he cut detention and I did not turn that in. I figured he was working in my course and not to press the issue. There were a lot of problems at home and he would use the time to see his girlfriend. As long as the cuts were infrequent and he completed his work, I decided not to be a shrew. When he did come to detention, he often brought along a friend and we talked about subjects other than school. I used this policy with a lot of the troublemakers. And I found that goodwill usually brought better results in reduced classroom problems and increased work. There were a couple of students this made no impact upon, but the majority appreciated the effort. I don't think I received any higher compliment than when this student told me, "You know, you really can teach."

However, there was another boy who failed my class and practically abused me during detentions. He was always trying to sneak out of detention with excuses and was consistently rude. I could play hardball, too. Sometimes it was the only thing that worked. I reported him consistently after it was painfully obvious that the "Ms. Nice Guy" approach did not work. I found honesty to work well with the administration as well. I got to know the assistant principal quite well through my various students. I once got one of my students to confess to throwing a smoke bomb during English class. I turned him over to the assistant principal, arguing for some clemency for his coming forward. The assistant principal got his man, the student's sentence was a bit lighter, and I felt pretty good. When disciplining, it is hard to know when to be soft and when to be hard. It is probably my best teaching quality, at least that first year. I had relatively few real problems.

I relied less on instinct when it came to dealing with parents. I usually talked with Jerry at length if a parent was involved. To be honest, the parents made me nervous and I knew my nervousness could wreak havoc with my judgment. I feel I had made real progress by the end of the year. However, parents voiced the same complaint about my "ineffectiveness" at finals time that they had at the mid-year. One of the parents came in to see me this time. Without talking to Jerry, I took this one head on. I felt I had to, after all I'd been through. I had the student's test out, had my gradebook out, and showed by example how some missed homework assignments were directly related to many of the missed test questions. The parent was not fully satisfied and claimed there had to be some merit to the student's complaint. In other words, I was not fully convincing. But, it was a draw. His face fell when he saw my examples. My facts and arguments were just as good, if not better than his own. In a professional manner, I stuck up for myself and my teaching and I had made a damn good case for both. It was no thrill to have an upset parent on the last day, but after it was over I felt really proud. I had made it. I gave my department head the results and told him I did not expect he would get any more flak about my finals. I was a little leaner and meaner . . . but I had made it.

It was a conscientious plan of organization that I had worked on during the year that allowed me to present such a strong case to that parent. For such things as lectures, readings, worksheets, plans, and ideas, I relied upon more than just instinct. Jerry and I worked to make the readings and worksheets and classes all fit together to reinforce the ideas and lesson plans. I took whatever materials I could get from the other teachers in my subject area. I asked them what they found worked best and why. I was a bit of a pest. "Beg, borrow, and steal" was my motto. I decided what were the most important ideas to stress and then attempted to design readings, worksheets, videos, and lectures to complement each other in bringing across those ideas. Seeing how time was such a precious commodity, the mentor program was instrumental in getting to that point. Jerry helped me shed my tendency to over-worry and helped me develop effective teaching strategies. Luckily I had this mentor, a supportive department head, and other teachers willing to share their time and ideas. It was because of a year-long effort to integrate my curriculum and student learning that I could say during that parental discussion, "Look, your son never turned in the homework assignments that stressed Africa's reliance upon foreign technology. Question #3 on the worksheet specifically deals with this problem and was discussed in class."

The blending of the paperwork and people is the job of a master politician. It takes a combination of common sense, practice, and luck. I feel I had talent to start, but I really appreciated the help I received during the year. It kept me from getting discouraged and showed me the positive energy that teaching can create. On that typical day I described earlier, I went for the coffee with Joanie, and the tests were stapled helter-skelter just before class. Another day I had to skip coffee—the photocopier was singing the song of the sirens. You do what you have to do.

CONCLUSION

I owe special thanks not only to my mentor, my department head, and the teachers and administrators who helped me, but also to my family. I moved back home for most of the year and my parents witnessed my ups and downs. It was not pretty. My father is an administrator for another district so I did education the favor of showing the man exactly how hard teachers work. He, too, helped me solve some pedagogical puzzles. My mother gave me emotional support as well as feeding me enough to stay healthy. And both of my sisters listened sympathetically to many long, boring phone calls detailing the throes of a first-year teacher. You only hurt the ones you love.

I haven't written nearly half of what I wanted to, nor did I get in all the fun and tears. The year was a roller-coaster ride. There were days I would come home, take a beer from the refrigerator, sink into the sofa, and ask myself what in hell I was doing. I would beg my dog to let me know I was okay. Then there were days when I would be singing "To Sir, with Love" at the top of my lungs and congratulating myself for being super-teacher. But, usually I would come home with a stack of papers, eat dinner, do my work, and get ready for another day. I would be listing in my head the 50 million tasks awaiting me the next day and tentatively plan my course of action. I would then go to bed and curse the alarm clock the next morning. All work and no play makes Margaret a dull girl.

I may have been a dull girl, but the story has a happy ending. My first year's conclusion was a good one. I received an excellent review from the principal and my department head. In my meeting with Sam, the principal, he stated the school was very happy to have me and that I made a welcome addition to the staff. He even told me I should "blow my own horn" about how well I was performing. It was pretty heady stuff for this rookie and I loved every minute of it. Again, I owe thanks to many people and to my own good karma for getting and keeping this job. It wasn't easy. I have a few battle scars. Still, I like kids, I like social studies, and I like the challenge of combining the two. And I bet you can tell this conclusion has been written only after reflection. Anyway, I look forward to my second year as a teacher. I have a lot of plans and I can't wait to see what the students will be like. I have my fingers crossed for another happy ending.

ADDENDUM: MARGARET O'BRYAN'S RULES FOR FIRST-YEAR TEACHERS

1. Eat, eat, eat. There is a tremendous germ pool in school—you need to keep up your strength.

2. Go out socially. It improves your mood and impresses the students if they see you out. Remember, though, it won't impress your date.

3. Get a pet. You need something around that accepts you totally and can't talk back.

4. Remember what brought you to teaching when you get your paycheck. Keep telling yourself you're fulfilled.

5. Most important of all, laugh—or you'll be crying.

EPILOGUE

Margaret O'Bryan's second year was a year of "mores"—more knowledge, more confidence, more organization, more respect, more results, and more fun. The students who questioned her abilities to teach moved on to the tenth grade, where several used the same modus operandi on a 20-year veteran. Margaret picked up two honors classes and her relationships with students were positive no matter what their level of ability. Her soccer team ended with a winning season. Her lessons were more varied and interesting and she asked fewer questions of her mentor and department head. She looks forward to more "mores" next year and the years after. The second year confirmed that she not only likes the idea of teaching but she now enjoys the teaching itself. Next year is her tenure year, which, interestingly, coincides with the expiration year of her stockbroker's license. Unless there is a debacle at school, she plans on receiving tenure and encouraging futures, not selling them.

QUESTIONS FOR DISCUSSION

1.1 It is because of a resentful student, his parents' unhappiness with his mid-year exam grade, and O'Bryan's vulnerable status as a "rookie" teacher, that she is labeled "ineffective" for a short span of time.
 (a) What does the series of events that occurs in this particular incident tell you about the potential power that parents and students in some districts have over the careers of tenured and untenured teachers?
 (b) Why do you think such attitudes exist in some communities?
 (c) What do such attitudes indicate about how some parents value teachers?
 (d) Why is it important for administrators to support and believe in teachers they know are doing a good job, despite complaints from students and their parents?

1.2 One of O'Bryan's honor students tells her, "If you were really smart you'd be a doctor or a lawyer and not a teacher."
 (a) Where do you think students learn such attitudes?
 (b) What are the social consequences of this perception and what can be done to change it?

1.3 O'Bryan's rapport with her students is such that they like to stop by her classroom after school to chat with her.
 (a) Why might it be useful and important for a teacher to get to know her students outside class?
 (b) How can speaking with students outside of class help a teacher to teach better in class? How can it hurt?

1.4 Many first-year teachers are not as fortunate as O'Bryan in having a mentor to consult with on a daily basis to help with teaching problems.
 (a) What are the primary areas that O'Bryan seems to have trouble with in her classroom with which her mentor proves to be of invaluable assistance?
 (b) In schools where a mentoring program does not exist, what can a first-year teacher do to obtain help without appearing weak or incompetent to administrators?

1.5 The issue of grades is a particularly sensitive one for many students and their parents. Teachers must be accountable to both students and parents for the grades they issue, because grades become a permanent part of a student's academic record.
 (a) When an irate parent comes in to complain about his son's grade, how is O'Bryan prepared to defend the grade she has given the student?
 (b) Why is it in the best interest of both teacher and student for a teacher to document diligently a student's academic performance throughout the year?

Chapter
2

Tightrope Walker

Mary Freeman

The summer preceding my first year of teaching was filled with apprehension. Sometimes I wanted the days to fly by so I could get started; other times I panicked because I didn't have enough time to plan everything and be fully prepared. These mood swings gained momentum all the way until the orientation day for new teachers.

The director of personnel made the opening remarks, saying several times that during the year, our first year in Brookline, we were going to be overwhelmed. This turned out to be the theme of the day: preparation for being overwhelmed. They seemed to have brought us there to tell us that something bad was going to happen and they wanted to let us know so we would be prepared. It took a while before I began to have a sense of just what was going to be so overwhelming. Apparently, we were going to overwhelm each other. Each one of us was going to be so intent on excelling that we were going to intimidate everyone else. It seemed a shame to start off the year feeling wary about other people's successes. I thought it should be a positive sign that everyone was so excited about their jobs, and yet I could feel my self-confidence wavering. What if I wasn't truly qualified?

How had I gotten this job anyway? The previous school year I student-taught in a sixth grade class while completing my master's certification program. My supervising teacher decided to take a leave of absence, opening her position for one year. I applied and was interviewed by a panel of seven, including teachers, parents, and the school's principal and vice-principal. After the interview, rumors floated back to me regarding concerns about my age (26 is too young), my gender (there was a preferred male applicant who had been teaching for several years), my experience (or lack thereof), and my lack of children. Lack of children! Several parents in the community felt that I would not be able to appreciate their role in the school if I didn't have first-hand experience raising kids. There was nothing I could do about any of these things. I breathed a sigh of relief that at least none of their concerns was really about my teaching skills. In fact, no one seemed to question my ability to be in a room with a group of children and create an environment in which they could learn. After weeks of debate, I was hired, although other teachers with many years of experience, and children of their own, had applied.

All this went through my mind as I thought about whether it was true that I was a good enough teacher. I finally calmed my racing brain and said to myself: Today is Tuesday, on Thursday you will meet your students and know whether or not you can teach.

By the end of orientation day, I had had my fill of being lauded for my choice of profession and honored for my placement in Brookline, a predominantly upper-class suburb of Boston that prides itself on its ethnic diversity. Various administrators had extolled the virtues of the student body and the teaching freedom in the system. I half-listened and half-concentrated on my new-found friends David and Carol, who would be teaching at a school near mine. We cemented our friendship by bemoaning the disarray in our classrooms and wondering whether we would be able to get everything organized in time.

The night before school began, I couldn't sleep at all. "What if they don't like me?" I kept asking myself, and each time I reprimanded myself because so many people had told me that the main pitfall of a first-year teacher was an overwhelming desire to be liked. "Try for respect, or consistency, but don't try to be liked," teachers and friends warned.

I lay in bed thinking about the next day. I would walk into a classroom, stand in front of a group of 25 children, and talk about supplies for the year. I couldn't imagine myself doing it. Then the first group would go to my teaching partner Alicia's room and a second group of 25 would walk in. I would tell them the same thing.

In our version of team-teaching, Alicia taught social studies and math and I taught language arts, science, and computers. We each had one group for half the day. Because we shared a group of students, we were able to discuss their progress extensively in daily meetings over coffee. We planned all field trips and many activities for the entire sixth grade. Of the 50 students that Alicia and I team-taught, 10 of them were new to the school and would be as tentative as I was. Of the new students, four spoke not a word of English.

On Thursday morning, without quite believing in myself, I put on my most teacherlike dress, picked up my plan book, which already had hundreds of tiny notes in the squares, looked again at the list of 17 supplies that the students would need, and went to school. I was shaking. I was scared to demand quiet. I was far too nice. But a miracle occurred. They listened to what I asked them to do, and they did it. We played a game that would enable all the kids to get to know things about each other's interests, and they seemed to be mingling.

In the midst of the game, the principal came in to observe. I was shocked to see her. Had I done something wrong already? She left a note on my desk saying that I should demand absolute attention before explaining directions. I was so angry over being criticized that my self-confidence improved immensely. The real test was to get through it.

At 2 o'clock, the students walked out of the room. Other than the principal's comment, that was the biggest shock of the day. They were gone. It was quiet. I had survived my first day of teaching!

On Friday, my second day, teaching took a turn for the worse. The newness of me had worn off for the kids, even though their newness was still glaring at me. In the middle of the morning, I realized that I had already completed all the activities I had planned for the first week. My sixth-graders were beginning to pipe up with saucy questions and I knew this was the beginning of the testing I had expected to start in the third or fourth week. During my break I confessed to Alicia that I had gravely miscalculated how much material I would use in two days. She said, "If you have an idea, really milk it—don't let the kids force you to whip through things. Draw them out. Take it at your pace." When I went back to class after break, I did just that. I asked more questions and thought hard about how to feed off their answers. Calm settled over the class once again.

It wasn't until the second day was over and the weekend arrived that the haze lifted and I began to make some observations about what kind of situation I had actually ended up in. Class size was the issue that took immediate precedence in planning. I thought 25 was a reasonable number, having myself been a student in elementary school classrooms of 32. My partner saw 25 as excessive, having had only 18 the year before. As it turned out, the legal limit in Brookline was 25. I had landed the largest homeroom in the town. Consequently, we were given an aide to help out with grading papers and doing some teaching. I was terrified to have to supervise an adult. I felt I had just stepped out of the student-teaching mode, in which I had felt very restricted and tentative. How would I be able to give effective guidance to another adult? I wanted to blunder along unnoticed by other people. I wanted to be alone with my students and try to work out a rhythm without being observed and judged. As the year progressed, the aide proved invaluable. Any teacher I know would consider it a godsend if he or she were offered another adult in the classroom part-time. But I didn't know how best to make use of the service, and I felt I often wasted it.

The next week, I nearly went into shock when my students actually brought their supplies in, especially the shoeboxes, which I had expected would be tricky for them to locate. It was quite a realization to me that I could ask them to do something and they would really do it. Each day I felt more confident in my ability to stand up in front of the group. But sometimes numbness would take over. When this happened, I would give directions very slowly, feeling my energy draining away even as I spoke. I fantasized about staying at my desk where no one would notice me, allowing me to read, study, and plan. The slightest hesitation on my part inevitably ended up in some upset, a fallen chair, a broken pencil, a pouting child, so I learned that I had to move quickly and confidently all the time, even if I wasn't actually being most effective that way. That was a depressing realization, because I knew that many times if I were able to think for a minute before I spoke, I would be able to speak more clearly. It seemed that classroom management was taking priority over careful and articulate thinking. Individual kids were beginning to assert their own special brands of teacher agitation. The class was becoming less a class and more of a conglomeration of individuals who lapped up every ounce of attention I was able to give them, both positive and negative.

True to the proclamations of orientation, my classroom was filled with students from all over the world, all with incredible stories to tell. Culturally, they represented 16 countries. Academically, their reading levels ranged from second to twelfth grade. Socioeconomically, the majority were from upper-class families, although a substantial minority were from working class homes. One-third came from homes in which one parent was absent. I had to remind myself continually of these statistics as difficulties began to grow out of them. As I found myself beginning to engage in personal power struggles with kids, I lost sight of a detached understanding of their backgrounds and became too emotionally involved. Three children in particular—John, Mariana, and Anne—stretched my patience to the limit.

I recognized John as standing out from the other students some time during the second week of school. It seemed that he could ask anybody for anything and be given it, even if that meant completed homework or an only pencil. I began to intervene in minor bullying incidents, and became the object of extremely provocative bullying myself. It seemed that John was going through adolescence before anyone else. His favorite phrase was, "That's not fair." If he didn't get to go to the gym on every single rainy day, he proclaimed, "That's not fair." He would bribe girls to give up their spot in the gym by paying attention to them. He had an unhealthy hold on the heartstrings of many of the girls in the class. There were no girls who would stand up to him, and few who said bad things about him, even behind his back. I felt alone in seeing him as an adversary. The classroom had to be smoothly managed to avoid his proclamations of unfairness and I sometimes felt I was planning classes around him. I knew that if that was the case, he would certainly be able to feel his power.

Mariana came to sixth grade with an outstanding record of academic excellence. I had heard several teachers sing her praises before the first day of school. When she first differentiated herself from the crowd, I couldn't believe she was the same child people had talked about. She was elegant in appearance, but decidedly abrasive in style. She was painfully aware of others' opinions: She seemed to have become an adolescent over the summer, and I was her first adult test case. She leapt at every opportunity to point out something I had overlooked or to give exceptions to any generalizations I made. If class ended at 10:20, she would raise her hand in the middle of something and point out that time was almost up.

Anne had the habit of staring into space or talking to her next-door neighbor throughout the ten minutes I was explaining a lesson. As soon as I was done, her hand would go up; and she would say, "I don't understand what to do." I was convinced that she was doing this to get attention, although as the year went on, I began to see that some of her chronic difficulties with following directions weren't entirely her fault. Her other endearing quality was that she arrived anywhere from 15 minutes to an hour late almost every day. When she walked in, she would sit down and immediately begin socializing, regardless of what was happening in the room.

I spoke with the mothers of these three children early in the fall in an effort to address the behavioral issues that were surfacing in the classroom. When I spoke to John's mother, she said that John was having problems getting along with his teachers. When I pressed her on the issue, she said, "Ms. Freeman, it's not a problem with his teachers in general, it's a problem with you." I was shocked. No stranger had ever criticized me directly to my face. How could I respond to that? My response was to apologize, and say that I hoped things would improve. I got off the phone and immediately called the principal, thinking that I ought to let her know: I suddenly felt that my job and my future were in jeopardy. The principal was very reassuring, saying that it was the mother's own difficulties controlling her child that made her readily blame teachers for the child's social problems.

Anne's mother stressed that Anne was being denied special needs services by the town of Brookline and should be given extra help after school and during class. She felt it was my responsibility to make up the time that Anne missed because she so often came in late. I tried to impress upon the mother that Anne would love for me to keep her after school for special help every day, but that I didn't have the time to give her that kind of attention on a regular basis, and that she really needed to be able to learn in an environment along with other kids. The idea that she should be given special attention was a theme that kept recurring throughout the year. When I mentioned the substance of this meeting to the principal, she became very agitated. It turned out that Anne was a tuition student. By law, tuition students were required to pay an extra fee for special services, and Anne's parents didn't or couldn't pay them. Anne was caught in a bind—she was getting an education in an environment with many advantages, but she was unable to get access to all the services she needed. The principal was concerned that I be asked to provide special services, which were not my responsibility. I chose to provide a level of support for Anne that wouldn't be too time-consuming, but would help her keep up with the rest of the class.

On the first day of school, my partner, Alicia, began to worry about Open House, which was three weeks off. I was so worried about the second day of school that I could barely anticipate an event so far in the future. But she talked about it every day, and decorated her room with the fervor of a mother preparing for her daughter's wedding. I began to follow suit, putting up bulletin boards and signs in the halls, and getting swept into her perfectionism. Alicia strongly recommended writing down everything I wanted to say about classroom management and curriculum. We bought flowers for the room and dressed up.

I had strange sensations when greeting parents that evening. I saw my own parents in everyone's eyes. I felt too young to be shaking hands with lawyers and consultants and discussing the future of their children with them. Yet they seemed too young to have children the age of my students. These parents were closer to my age than my students were! Suddenly I wondered whether they hadn't been right on the interview committee to question my ability to teach because I wasn't a parent. I couldn't imagine myself having an 11-year-old. My students were already people to me, not children that had been babies.

It suddenly struck me that with adults assembled and me at the podium, I would have to give a speech. Thank heavens for the notes I had jotted down. Parents asked many questions about how strict or lenient I was regarding homework and behavior. I hadn't previously thought about some of the issues they raised— for example, what I thought of the five-paragraph essay. There seemed to be two factions emerging—the "back to basics" crowd and the "open classroom" crowd. I found myself using some bureaucratic and ambiguous language to avoid confrontations. But confrontation was not to be avoided. At one point, a parent asked me about the computer curriculum. I told her they would be learning basic typing skills and LOGO. She said her son had learned LOGO at summer camp, so what was he going to do? I said that LOGO was the only curriculum, and that LOGO was a computer language similar to BASIC, with a wide variety of possible projects, and that was what I would have to teach. Then I tried to go on to the next question, but the mother would not let the issue drop. I reminded her that Open House was not the night for conversations about individual children. She became more and more distraught and demanded a solution to her son's dilemma. She said he was too smart for the current program. I finally deflected her questions, and the group moved to Alicia's room for the other half of the Open House introduction.

I later heard that next door, the same parent harassed Alicia about math, saying her son was too bright for the town math program, but the parent was even more invested in getting a solution. She kept speaking out until other parents were asking her to quiet down. Alicia finally asked her to leave the room. When she refused, Alicia's eyes filled with tears, and she had to leave the room momentarily. Many parents commented to me afterward about the inappropriateness of the persistent questioning. I felt that the stage for the blow-up had been set in my room and dreaded the awkwardness that might result between Alicia and me because the actual incident occurred in her room not mine. After all that preparation, we had been unable to stem the tide of parent anxiety and now the tension level was high.

The next day, a flood of notes came in from parents expressing their support of our exploratory approach to teaching computers and math and their unspoken apologies for the scene of the night before. Several people sent flowers. We were confused about how to proceed. Alicia was irate. How could someone have humiliated her in that way? What was the principal going to do about it? The principal's attitude was that it was unfortunate, but no big deal. She thought we ought to meet with the parent who had harassed us and talk over the problem in a methodical way, rather than let it get out of hand. We felt we couldn't face that mother. She was a hateful, despicable person to us. We didn't feel the principal should force us to undergo a second round of criticism.

This incident was my first exposure to what motivated our principal to act consistently on behalf of the parents at the expense of the teachers; she was terrified that criticism of anything going on in her school would filter up to the administrators in Town Hall. She was extremely susceptible to parents pushing for perks for their children. Her attitude about Open House—that we should justify ourselves to the parents again—upset me, but it angered Alicia. She thought we should receive more support. Many other teachers in the school expressed similar opinions. They also had been criticized by parents and had not been supported by the principal. I realized that this oppressed feeling was one that bound teachers together.

Now the fall semester was well under way. I was getting to know the kids pretty well and had gotten a taste of the negative aspects of the parent community. What about the people with whom I was working? Alicia and I were getting along very well, and I turned to her for advice in many areas, although the situation surrounding Open House had made me feel very vulnerable to being in the junior teacher role. I tried to determine what we could have done differently to avoid such a situation, but I couldn't think of anything. I felt so overwhelmed by all the details I had to work on in my own classroom, that I resented times when I caught myself getting bogged down in conversations about the unsupportive administration. I was also trying to figure out how to handle the myriad specialists who were making requests and suggestions about students. The Hebrew and Spanish bilingual education specialists asked that I inform them on a daily basis what I would be covering. This meant knowing at least two nights in advance exactly what I was going to teach.

This was a farce as far as I was concerned. I had developed the habit of thinking of three or four things that I might do the next day, and then choosing one of them at the last minute, depending on how calm or excited the kids were. This was obviously an unrealistic plan for any support staff to follow, and yet if I planned an assignment in advance and notified anyone, I invariably changed my mind the next day. Sometimes I forgot that I had given plans to specialists and then found that the bilingual kids were in a different place from everyone else. This continued to happen and I couldn't seem to break the cycle. Finally the situation resolved itself. The bilingual kids naturally divided into two groups, the group that ended up having a separate language arts program in the English as a Second Language room, and the group that could be mainstreamed. There were eight kids who had bilingual teachers, and I was constantly struggling to find time to give them the individual attention they deserved.

I was still self-conscious enough about my teaching abilities that when the principal sent the reading specialist to observe in my classroom twice a week, and help out if I needed it, I was convinced that the woman was acting as a spy for the principal, there to report back. It was a way for the principal to see how much control I had in the classroom without threatening me with her presence. I found the reading teacher almost as threatening because I was so afraid of disapproval. Every time I wasn't completely clear about where a worksheet was or whether something had been graded yet or not, I felt tremendous guilt. Did other teachers get all corrected work back the next day? Why did I sometimes have papers from a week ago that I hadn't finished reading yet? How could I keep having new things for them to do and still keep up on correcting work they had already done? I found myself revolted by piles of papers after I had collected them, because they represented the guilt I would feel when I couldn't finish all 50 of them for the next day. Feeling guilty seemed to have the effect of making me avoid looking at the papers altogether until two or three children had complained that they wanted their work back, which forced me to complete what seemed an unending task. I imagined an ideal situation in which I would grade all papers as soon as they came in and be able to have each of them back the next morning. But the meetings, the conferences, the planning, the cleaning, and endless notices from the office regarding details that required attention, never seemed to allow this system to work.

Talking to other teachers about this constant nagging feeling of ungraded papers didn't make me feel any better, because they were living under that shadow as well. I felt I could never escape from work. I thought about it from the minute I got up until the minute I went to sleep, although I wasn't able to motivate myself to respond to these guilty feelings more than half the time. When I found myself complaining to other teachers, I was dismayed by their echoing complaints. (I hated the idea that I sounded like this, complaining about too much work, beaten by the emotional drain taking place in my classroom, where the energy was decidedly flowing one way—toward the students.)

I didn't want to see myself in other teachers, because to me they seemed old and beaten. They talked about their families all the time. Many teachers had children my age. I felt that I had been wrong when I imagined that teaching was a noble profession. It actually seemed to be inhabited by people who wanted large families and used teaching as an extended parenting arena. I wanted to feel intellectually inspired, I wanted to feel that I was a professional in my work, rather than just another cog in the wheel. I didn't want to be beset with other people's marital woes, and feel that everyone's life was so torpid. What if it rubbed off on me? I was terrified of becoming complacent and of wasting my education. I wanted to feel that I was achieving something, and using the skills that I had acquired during four years of college: the skills of analyzing, of discussing issues, of researching. I felt that everything about the way the teaching job was structured made that impossible. I was depressed by the idea that I was going to fall into an abyss of boredom and paperwork in my first year as a salaried teacher.

To offset the fear that trying to keep up with rote responsibilities was going to damage my ability to be interested and critical, I gathered in responsibilities like a magnet gathering shavings. I joined the teacher's book group that met once a month to discuss important contemporary fiction. I joined the Sapperstein Support Group, which was supposed to promote professional rapport among teachers. I volunteered to be the union representative for the school because the position had been vacated, and no one else seemed willing to take the job. I consented to meet with the assistant superintendent to discuss some curriculum that I had adapted from a writing workshop I had attended during the summer. On top of all the weekly commitments that I seemed to be collecting, I signed up for every workshop that was offered in language arts, science, and computers. This was no small number in Brookline, where many teachers receive grants to present their work to other teachers. I found myself spending Saturdays learning how to teach typing, exploring the *Boston Globe* newspaper operation as a possible field trip opportunity, listening to presentations on the teaching of reading and writing, and looking at products that other teachers brought from their classrooms.

On display at the workshops were journals with extensive comments, beautiful artwork, and near-professional-level poetry. I wondered what sort of wonder children they had in their classrooms, or what sort of wonder teachers they were. How did they find time to make such extensive comments in journals and on papers? I was baffled by other people's achievements. I wanted to be able to provide consistent lessons, but I always found that kids were slipping through the cracks. I could implement things that would work for the majority of the kids, but I would lose track of some of the people who needed my help the most. I began to realize that I hadn't cemented my own teaching styles enough yet to appreciate other people's styles and to know what to incorporate from a workshop and what to leave as someone else's idea that wouldn't necessarily work for me.

Throughout the year, I had been following a model of teaching writing that I had learned about in an education course. I met with kids individually and asked them questions about their stories, gave verbal and written comments, and asked them to go back and do another draft. At first, I was unable to manage the class while doing these individual writing conferences. Every time I began to talk to one student, I would glance around and be convinced that other students were talking about topics unrelated to their writing. After a while I realized that it was better to be completely focused on whomever I was talking to and only get distracted when absolutely necessary. Whenever I was able to get myself into this mood, writing conferences were wonderful, and the rest of the class concentrated as well. I felt as if I had real contact with my students, as if they sensed my concern, and were clarifying their thoughts on the spot.

The first major unit we worked on was animal fiction. They had to research an animal and then write a fiction piece using at least 100 of the researched facts. The products of this unit were good and I realized that the long hours of conferences had been extremely beneficial.

After completing the unit, the assistant superintendent and the language-arts curriculum coordinator asked to meet with me to view the results of the project and to see whether I had developed anything that would be useful to other teachers in the system. I was quite flattered by their interest, and arranged a meeting for the following Friday at 2:30 PM. The next day, I agreed to attend a meeting on the special needs of one of my students at that exact same time. I wrote a note to myself—Friday, 2:30—promptly misplacing it and forgetting about it. Friday arrived and I was paged to attend the special services meeting and to answer the telephone right when I was expecting the assistant superintendent. I rushed downstairs to see if I could gracefully extricate myself from the special needs obligation. When I arrived back upstairs, it was after 2:30. Not only had the dignitaries arrived, but Anne's mother was waiting at the door, saying that she had made an appointment through the office that morning to see me at 2:30. As my head was swinging back and forth between the two parties, the mother launched into her speech about how Anne needed so much extra attention, and how she was very upset right now because she couldn't seem to get her homework done. I tried to explain that I had another meeting to attend right now, and that I would have to meet with her later, and eventually I was able to herd her out the door. The assistant superintendent looked at me empathetically, taking in the apparent futility of trying to cut off a parent who was concerned about her child. It's like trying to put out a forest fire with a glass of water.

By November, the power struggles that had ensued from John, Mariana, and Anne's testing of authority had been resolved, although it wasn't until the spring that I recognized I hadn't worried about these students in a while. The incidents of challenge are much more memorable than the resolutions. It was at this time that I began to notice two children who had had low profiles for the first two months. Michael had been quiet and reluctant to turn in any assignments. I began noticing his preoccupation with little trinkets and sometimes science fiction novels. When we took our first field trip, some teenagers on the bus teased him because his pants were too short and he wore thick glasses. When we got back to school he began ranting about the "commie drug dealers" who had tried to attack him, and accused Alicia and me of risking his life by taking him on public transportation. The more he thought about it, the more excited he became, yelling at the top of his lungs and walking around kicking chairs. We had to take him to the office and have his mother pick him up. She was angry with us, saying we had given him a stage to act on by paying attention to him, thus exacerbating the situation.

For the next month, I heard Michael muttering about this incident under his breath, practicing karate as he made daily solo rounds of the playground preparing for revenge upon the "commie drug dealers." He jumped into the limelight again one day after his homeroom had returned from art class. I was getting some paper towels from the closet. When I turned around, he was chasing after a classmate—Phil—with a large mallet. They happened to be running right toward me, so I stepped between them and held onto Michael, wresting the mallet from his hand. I hustled him out the door and into the hall, where he continued to struggle against me and even took off his belt, swinging it around and saying he was going to get that creep if it was the last thing he did. I grabbed the belt from him and laid it on the floor, talking calmly to him all the while. He was still shouting almost incomprehensibly, as

I guided him around the corner toward the office. We passed the principal on the way. She, apparently not noticing the crisis nature of the situation, mentioned something about a form that I needed to fill out and get to her. I told her I had to take Michael to the office, and asked if she could step into my classroom for a moment and make sure that everything was all right. When we got to the office, I told the vice-principal briefly what had happened, and that I had to get back to my classroom. When I got back upstairs, the principal had left and all the students were imitating Michael's attack and shouting things that he had shouted moments earlier.

In the subsequent meeting with Michael's mother, she insisted that his behavior was caused by his teachers' failure to recognize his inherent genius, and that he was frustrated in school. She would not entertain the notion suggested many times over the past five years, that Michael needed professional counseling. The meeting became an opportunity for her to discuss what she termed a prerequisite for Michael to continue in school—a specialized math program. Already this year, Michael had been given special permission to attend an eight-grade algebra class at another school and come to sixth grade one hour late each morning. We had just been told that Michael had failed the first term of this class. Then he was given the seventh grade entry exam to see whether he could be put in a seventh grade class. He got a D on this exam. The mother insisted that his grades were not reflective of his ability. The school countered that they had no other means than test scores at their disposal to find out what he could do. If he wasn't willing to display his ability publicly, we couldn't spend the next years of his education assuming that he understood the math.

Now he was left with sixth grade as his only option. To put him in the highest math group would have put him alone in a group with Phil, who had infuriated him enough to cause the attack with the mallet. His mother's suggestion was to create an individualized program for him. Alicia (she was his math teacher) insisted that Michael was not an independent worker, and that she would not be able to supervise him if he studied alone, because there were already three groups to teach. The mother said that she thought it was worth a try. Alicia said, "What am I supposed to do if he spends his math period working on 'Dungeons and Dragons' and staring out the window?" The mother said, "Then that's what he'll do." Alicia had the mother put that in writing, and that's how he spent the rest of the year in math, untaught and unguided because the mother thought him so special that he could not be taught with other kids. Why did the principal give in to this, the course least likely to advance Michael's math skills?

One day in mid-October, Aaron stood up during a silent writing period, and began to extol the virtues of John F. Kennedy loudly and fervently. I looked at him in surprise. The room had been studiously quiet. Even though other kids were beginning to chuckle nervously, Aaron continued to talk about some of the great decisions Kennedy had made, and bemoaned the fact that our current president wasn't as heroic. I walked over and quietly asked him to sit down. He did so, although he was still mumbling under his breath. I later mentioned this to the guidance counselor, who rolled her eyes, and said, "I hope this isn't the beginning of another round with him!"

When Halloween arrived many students dressed up for school, some wearing elaborate homemade replicas of Ancient Egyptian costumes to complement their work in social studies. Aaron showed up in an enormous fur coat that completely dwarfed him, and a colored paper plate taped over his face, in a shape vaguely reminiscent of a beak. I asked him what he was dressed up as. He told me he was the Devourer, a character in Egyptian mythology that ate people after they had died. He also expressed tremendous interest in Van Gogh's suicide, and I worried about his attraction to death. Several weeks later, Aaron was feeling under a great deal of stress because he had missed homework assignments for several days in a row. I kept him after school so he could complete his work, which distressed him tremendously. He couldn't stand the idea of being in school any longer than was absolutely necessary. I went over the assignment with him and showed him why the one line on his paper didn't fulfill the two-page assignment. I then turned to help someone else with his work. At some point I noticed that the student I was helping was staring at the other side of the room. I turned to look and saw that Aaron was tearing bites out of his assignment, slowing chewing and swallowing them. He wasn't being defiant, he was sincerely frustrated about his work. I made him spit out the rest of the paper, and talked to him for a few minutes before sending him home. He didn't seem to understand how unusual his behavior was.

When I mentioned this incident to the guidance counselor she was very reluctant to do anything about the situation. She had had years of experience with Aaron's mother, who didn't recognize her son as having emotional problems. He had not learned to talk until he was five, and she considered that he was just in the process of catching up, no harm done. "Why mention situations to the mother that are just going to get her upset?" asked the guidance counselor. I felt I couldn't ignore the fact that something was wrong, so I called the mother against everyone's better judgment. Her analysis was that I wasn't putting Aaron in the academic groups that would enhance his social abilities. I couldn't think of a single group to put him in where his alternating passivity and obstinacy wouldn't cause problems. Other students became impatient with his suggestions, which seemed purposefully counterproductive. His mother absolutely refused to consider having Aaron tested for special services assistance. The only problems she conceded that he had were troublemaking friends and trouble with physical coordination. I thought about how Aaron repelled his classmates with his monologues and nose-picking, but if she wouldn't consider counseling, there was nothing I could suggest.

Aaron's case made me realize that a teacher's effectiveness is very limited. Based on the guidance counselor's reaction, I could assume that there had been many interactions with this parent before to no avail. The mother didn't agree with my suggestions and I had to accept that.

I took Aaron's case to heart, feeling that I hadn't been able to make changes on behalf of this child. I began to feel that although I spent so much time with my students, I had as yet made very little impact on their lives. By Christmas I was looking back over my first four months of teaching and remembering all the things I had tried to do that had failed, all the things I had started and not finished. I had a foot-high pile of journals that I was supposed to have read two weeks before. I had just taught a science lesson in which the outcome of the experiment surprised me. I couldn't explain it and my students were frustrated. I felt reluctant to call parents about issues regarding their children because it always caused so much stress and so many meetings, and never seemed to resolve any issues. I was still piloting lessons I had made up myself with no idea whether they would work or not, and the insecurity was wearing on me. If for some reason the art or music teacher needed extra time with my class, I was relieved to let them go. The drive to teach had drifted completely into the background. The week before Christmas, I came down with a fever of 103. I had to call in for my first substitute. Making plans for the substitute was so time-consuming that I couldn't drag my hand across the page to do it for a second day, so I dragged my body in to school instead, even though my temperature was still high, and I looked gray. The principal took one look at me and told me to go home. I was out for three days, able only to get back to school for the last day before the holidays.

When I returned, I felt drained and I couldn't figure out what the substitute had or hadn't covered. I was relieved when Alicia planned a movie and a party for the whole grade so I could relax. When I first walked over to my desk, I was overwhelmed by a profusion of gifts awaiting me. More than half of my students had brought in carefully wrapped presents, many of them homemade. There were lopsided cookies, Mom's jam, a well-reviewed novel about Chinese-Americans from my most sophisticated reader, a vase, perfume, a basket from the Philippines, calendars, and more. I was taken aback. It seems I had completely lost the perspective that I might play a central role in these children's lives. I had become so focused on all the problems of teaching that I had forgotten about the exuberance of my students and their willingness to give. I began my vacation feeling warm inside about the rewards of teaching and how they came when you least expected them.

Over Christmas this warm feeling began to wear off. I reassessed my life now that I had become a teacher. My boyfriend was upset because I was complaining too much about work. He said that it didn't seem as though I enjoyed what I was doing. How was I going to be fulfilled in my life if I didn't enjoy my work? He was also perturbed that my self-confidence had sunk so low that I was unable to make the simplest decisions about what to do on a weekend evening. I found that I had to make so many decisions every day that I was completely unable to decide anything once I got home. I never read the newspaper or talked about the news anymore, which had been an important part of our relationship. I felt intellectually frustrated because it seemed as though I wasn't thinking about issues, only about managing my classroom. The overwhelming time commitment to my work meant that my friends were wondering what had happened to me, and whether I was ever going to be available again to do things with them. While catching up with people over the vacation, I found myself speaking negatively about teaching. I seriously wondered whether I had made a bad decision to commit myself to the job.

The only thing that saved me from getting completely depressed about my decision to teach was the poetry unit I started right after Christmas vacation. With the help of the poet-in-residence of the Brookline Public Schools, I began a six-week unit. She came twice a week and either presented an idea or talked to kids about what they had written that week. At the same time, I attended a workshop that the poet-in-residence ran for teachers in the system. I wrote poems and talked about them with colleagues. Suddenly I had the intellectual stimulation that had seemed absent in my life before Christmas. I was actually writing things that I liked, and going through the same stages that my students went through as they tried to write. I felt that I could be enthusiastic about their writing now instead of dreading that I would be bored with what they had written. The poetry workshop gave me ideas of how to see what was interesting in any piece of writing. In my classroom, we read each other's poems, as well as published works and generally thought about nothing else for an hour each day. Some students wrote poems to music, wrote rap songs, or memorized poems and recited them. Somewhere in the middle of all this, we decided to have a poetry reading and invite the parents to hear what we had written. Spontaneously, I had leapt over the barrier against parents that had been created early in the year, and was able unabashedly to call many parents and see whether they could bring refreshments to the reading. I felt good about what we were doing in school and I wanted to share it.

Monica began to stand out during this time as a central teaching inspiration. She was a round-faced Bolivian girl who had emigrated to Spain. Then Monica's mother passed away and she was adopted by an American missionary family. She was just beginning to learn English. Although I spoke to her primarily in English, we spoke Spanish as well, which created a special bond. I encouraged her to write poems in Spanish, and translated all of the poet-in-residence's lessons for her. After a week of work, she came to school one day with a three-page poem inspired by a Van Gogh painting of irises we had been studying. This is a part of that poem.

And the leaves (those wicked beasts)
Group together against the water without knowing
that the water could help them.
The leaves
mortally afraid
curl up in fright
while the withered flowers
regain their lost fragrance but . . .
it's too late
for the night has arrived
bringing the intense cold
and the poor flowers
fall frozen
and the night
thinks it has triumphed

and it's true
but someone triumphs.
The following day
flowers will bloom again.

Her poetry was breathtaking. I was heady with her success. I felt like I was a
good teacher. Because of the language barrier she faced, I knew she would
not have done this work if I hadn't been able to speak with her in Spanish
and encourage her. I was elated. This feeling stayed with me, even through
the difficulties of getting the proper space and custodial coverage for the
poetry reading.

We compiled all the poems in one booklet, taking great pains to have
each student's page carefully typed. It took two full weeks to collect everything, and take it to the printer. Even after all that effort, a student named
Alan had slipped through the cracks and avoided having his work published,
although it was quite funny. He was embarrassed by this poem:

The dreary month of February
is often dark and dirty
Because you have to do in 28 days
what you normally do in 30.

The poetry reading was a great success. Almost all the parents came. They
brought lots of goodies to eat, and everyone sat riveted through an hour-and-
a-half of reading. The only discomfort was that Michael's mother glared at me
with inexplicable anger throughout the reading. Later it turned out that she
had overheard some kids making fun of Michael's poem and blamed it on me.
I had learned that teachers are the first ones to get a finger pointed in their
direction. My skin had thickened a bit by this time.

Compounding my high spirits from the poetry unit was my principal's
evaluation. It was so flattering that it made me blush. She used words like
magnificent, outstanding, and productive:

I told Mary that she was born with "teaching genes" by which I mean that her
instincts are very much on target; she relates to students extremely effectively
and conveys expectations well. . . . In sum Mary is a superb teacher. I have never
supervised a teacher who in her first year has consistently developed curriculum
in as thoughtful, creative, well-organized and thorough a manner as Mary.

I was completely overwhelmed by this evaluation. It had nothing to do with
who I thought I was and what I thought I was doing. But my self-confidence
had a few more roller-coaster rides to complete before the year was out.

Just when I thought teaching was looking up, I was hit by a blow to my
ego from which I thought I would never recover. We had started to read
myths in conjunction with the social studies unit on Greek mythology. We
went directly from reading poems to reading much longer stories. I didn't
sense that the transition was going to be a hard one, and assigned 25 pages
over two nights, thinking they could handle it. I heard many students talking
in the hall that they were going to boycott the homework because it was too

much for one night. Instead of wondering why they were concerned, I got angry. I had worked so hard all year, and this was the reward for teaching them to work hard too. So I made up a quiz with four questions on the reading and gave it to them as a surprise the next day. They were very unhappy about it. More than half of them failed. I didn't comment about it at all, but collected the quizzes and told them how much it would count in their grade. I also said that the questions had all been from the first six pages of the story, and that anyone should have been able to get that far if he or she had tried. The rest of the day was a tense battle of wills. I knew that my quiz had caused much discussion. Alicia happened to be absent that day, so there was the added unstable energy of a substitute next door.

During last period, I was doing a creative writing lesson and most kids were working on their writing. I noticed that one boy had left the room without my permission. I went next door to find that all the students in the substitute's room were standing in a cluster in the center of the room. The sub was standing on the periphery looking lost. She appealed to me for help. I yelled loudly that students should take their seats immediately and work quietly on their assignments for the last half-hour of school. The students slunk guiltily to their chairs.

After school that day I found a letter in my mailbox in John's handwriting stating, "We think your being unfare, [sic] and mean!!" and was signed by almost all of the students in my homeroom and a handful of students from Alicia's homeroom. At the bottom, "Go Home" was scratched out and it said, "and a lot more and it's not forged." I was stunned. With tears in my eyes, I went immediately to the principal who took one look at the letter and instead of being supportive, asked me whether I *was* being unfair. I showed her the reading I had given them and tried to explain the outburst. What I needed was for someone to tell me that I wasn't a bad teacher. Instead I was given a lecture about what I could have done better. I was painfully aware that this wouldn't have happened if I had handled the situation differently. But at that moment, I couldn't think about lessons to learn, not just yet. While we sat and talked about it, movement from outside caught my eye. I looked and saw 10 or 12 sixth-graders racing by the window, trying to peek in and cover their faces with their jackets at the same time. It was a bizarre feeling to be the cause of so much anxiety. The principal dropped her jaw in amazement, saying she had never seen anything like it.

That evening I thought and thought about how I could respond to this situation. Before school the next morning I would have to face John and his mother and accept an apology. Then I would have to face my class. Meeting with John's mother was difficult because I knew she had questioned my ability to control the class since the beginning of the year. She was from South Africa and had very different ideas from the Brookline school system about how a classroom should be run. She wasn't alone in her ideas. The Chinese parents wanted more homework for their children, as did the Russians, the Irish, the Slavs. Many other parents complained of *too much* homework, perhaps because they put more emphasis on the child having free, unstructured time in their developmental process. The school was a place where child-rearing values of different cultures clashed.

At the meeting I was comforted that John's mother agreed that he had been in the wrong, whether or not the environment had encouraged his actions. Fortunately, the incident occurred in a substitute's room rather than in mine. Alicia would never have allowed that to happen while she was there.

I walked tentatively into my classroom. I stood before the class and said quietly that if they felt they needed to tell me something and they didn't feel they could do it in person, I would like them to please address me personally in their letters and sign their own names to what they wanted to say. Then I began teaching a lesson right away with no discussion. I decided not to entertain comments right then because I was scared of losing control. It was a relief to be teaching. They were so quiet that I thought we might do well to have crises more often. After I had given them something to work on, I went to my desk, and saw that it was covered with folded paper and envelopes. They had clearly been there before I entered the room but I hadn't noticed them. I glanced at some of the notes, and realized they were all apologies. These were just a few of them:

> Dear Ms. Freeman, We are very sorry for the rude note. We weren't trying to hurt your feelings. We hope you'll forgive us. Sincerely, The Class.

> I am very sorry that I signed my name on that nasty note. Sincerely, Aaron

> I think you are a very nice teacher. When I need help, you help me. Rhonda

> I am really sorry about that note yesterday. I didn't really know what it was. I thought it was a goodbye letter to José or something like that. Sincerely yours, Sally

> I am very sorry for what happened yesterday. All I can say is I signed the note because of peer pressure and that I'll try not to let it get to me again. Sincerely, Helen

> I hope you will forgive us for doing that. I hope you will continue to teach our class. Ruth

> I know that you do your very best to keep the class under control, and then I imagine how you feel when one kid messes it all up. I'm sorry. Love, John

> We're glad to have a teacher just like you. Those people tricked us, but they didn't get away with it. Love, Iris and Maria. P.S. We didn't sign that letter.

I realized how guilty and scared the whole situation must have made them feel, and I also realized again that these were kids, they were vulnerable to circumstances, and they didn't hate me. Still, I made a conscious effort to keep some emotional distance from my students for the next few weeks. I threw all my energy into making foolproof lesson plans and giving an exact and even amount of homework, I dressed in more businesslike clothing than usual. I felt the need to separate myself as an adult, whereas before I had put a lot of energy into keeping in touch with their personal lives. I thought if I got that emotionally involved in a dispute with my class, I had better back off. I think some students were hurt and confused by my distance for a while, but it was much better for everyone. Was I starting to feel too comfortable teaching? Was this a backlash from not working hard enough? I was convinced that it was, so I threw myself into my work with renewed vigor.

Experienced teachers had told me that most of the real work of the year got done in the fall, and that in the spring the combination of vacations and warming weather made serious study difficult. After Easter vacation, there were only eight weeks left until the end of school; everyone felt cooped up after being inside for several months. I began a unit on moral dilemmas, and around that same time, immoral things began to happen. I kept hearing about John's tempestuous behavior from the art, music, and gym teachers. He wasn't giving me a hard time, but I was still responsible because he was in my homeroom. We had to develop a behavior chart, which required a signature from each teacher and was sent to his parents. Somebody urinated in the heating duct in Alicia's room, so it was filled with asphyxiating fumes and the room had to be evacuated. Fifty sixth-graders were in my room for two days. The close quarters made everyone nervous and students couldn't stop speculating about who had done it. We couldn't figure it out either. It was eerie to think that one of our students might have been that irresponsible.

Around this time, Aaron's mother asked teachers and administrators to write letters of recommendation for his application to several of the most prestigious private schools in the Boston area. We were surprised that she made this request when Aaron was clearly below grade level in so many social skills. But she insisted, so we filled them out, feeling compelled to place him in the bottom of each social category listed. The principal, Alicia, the guidance counselor, and I wrote the recommendations together, and concurred on the major points. I felt frustrated writing the recommendations in a group, because I wanted to think of good wording to describe his situation, and everyone else wanted to do them quickly and get it over with. Under the column "relationships with adults" I wrote, "seeks adult attention to mitigate alienation from peers." (Aaron sought me out every afternoon to talk about sports and politics because he was so lonely.) The group decided the recommendations didn't deserve more time because it was an absurd idea that he would ever be accepted. Aaron was pulled out of school two to three times a week for the next month for interviews. He was falling miserably behind, and seemed to be coming late in the mornings more and more often. His eyes were glazed over when he came, and often he would forget to take out his work when the class began a new lesson. I felt sorry that his mother was dragging him through this.

The guidance counselor encouraged Aaron's mother to read the recommendations before we sent them to the schools, but she said that wasn't necessary. So off they went. Of course Aaron didn't get accepted, and his mother was irate. She called the guidance counselor saying that a friend on one of the admission committees had breached confidentiality practices and given her a copy of the recommendation. She was appalled by what we had written. She said we had sabotaged her son's future, and that she had written to one of our U.S. Senators and town's Superintendent of Schools in Brookline to say what irresponsible teachers Alicia and I were. She brought a lawyer to a meeting with us to demand that we rewrite the applications. I wished desperately that I had been more careful with my wording in the first place. Alicia and I didn't feel it was proper to rewrite the applications. How moral would we be if we bowed to this kind of pressure? As usual, the principal bowed under pressure from a parent, prevailing upon us to write a cover letter that modified some of the harsher statements about Aaron's inability to communicate.

We sent the letters, and shortly thereafter I was called by someone on the admissions committee. He said it was highly unusual to get letters like the one we had written, and asked if I could explain the discrepancy. I told him the truth, that the mother had threatened us with a legal action, that she had gotten access to the recommendations and wasn't happy with them, and that the principal had thought it would be wise in terms of the school's relationship with the mother to do something to assuage her anger. Clearly the school wasn't considering accepting Aaron, but the admissions officer thought the situation was curious.

At about this time, I became aware that two students who were good friends had been absent on the same days three times in the last two weeks. I called the parents to ask about them and we realized they were truant. I then called the principal to discuss a course of action. I correctly anticipated her response which was to ask, "What have you done to make them skip?" but I had mentally prepared myself for this and so was unfazed. Fortunately I had kept good attendance records and the recent work hadn't been terribly hard. I knew that these two boys required a lot of extra attention to get their work done, and I knew I hadn't been giving it to them lately. I often felt that I was unable to keep up the energy to stick to deadlines, so sometime in the spring I got exhausted from trying to keep everyone else from sliding under. With 50 students, it seemed almost impossible. And so even though it didn't surprise me that they had skipped, I still felt responsible. Their mothers had contrasting feelings about it. One mother was very clear that her son had done it because he just hadn't felt like doing the work, and the other mother, who had had trouble keeping her son organized all year was feeling a need for more structure in the classroom and very predictable assignments. All of those things require more teacher input. Realizing I couldn't say yes to everything the parent asked me to do, I would have to say no, I can't check your son's notebook every day.

We took the sixth grade to Cape Cod for a whale watch as the culmination of a science unit on whales that had been a big success. Alicia and I planned elaborately. We decided to be ambitious, buying and preparing all the food ourselves rather than paying extra to eat out. We wanted to have a healthy menu because we thought the students would be more responsive if they were well-fed. The meeting to brief the other chaperones was so detailed that they all got bored. We spent a day up north checking the cottages where we would sleep, reviewing arrangements with the owner, measuring distances between different points of interest, and making up a question sheet to be used at the Maritime Museum. We worked ourselves into a frenzy getting ready and the work paid off. Everything fell into place, and we had the added bonus that the two most excitable kids took medication for motion sickness and slept during most of the boat ride. One reward for the smoothness of the trip was that the staff members who accompanied us were enraptured with the sixth grade. They had never been on a trip that was so calm and fruitful. I breathed a sigh of relief at the end because I knew how many things could have gone wrong. Michael could have become obsessed with the ideas that someone on the trip was out to kill him. Aaron could have decided that the food was unacceptable and refused to eat. Phil and John could have torn apart the room we allowed them to share, and accused someone else of doing it. But none of those things happened. The whale watch was a success. We even saw some whales!

The year was sliding to a close. The weather was getting warmer and adolescent hormones were beginning to roar. Sometimes I felt as if my students barely noticed me, but were completely reliant on their peers for information. I began to wonder who was listening to me because everyone seemed to be getting directions from his or her neighbor.

Unfortunately, the year was not to end as successfully as the whale watch. I was unprepared for the tremendous transition anxiety that my students were going through at the end of the year. Just when I thought the end was smooth sailing, I got involved in a head-on clash with Phil, his mother, and the principal. It began somewhat benignly when Phil refused to sit down so other kids could see a movie. His defiance continued despite several requests. Typically, in such a situation I would send someone out in the hall and speak to them privately a few minutes later. When I asked Phil to leave he refused. Just a bold no. I asked him a second time and he said no. I said that I was not making a judgment or asking questions about what he had done, but I needed him to follow this simple direction now. He said no. So I sent him to the principal's office. As it turned out, he had already been sent to the office once by a substitute in Alicia's room. When the principal saw him, she spoke to him and they ended up in a shouting match. She finished it by saying he would have to go home for the rest of the day.

The next morning we were planning to go to the science museum on a field trip. Alicia was out with the flu, but I wanted to take the trip anyway. When Phil arrived at school, the first thing he did was to grab someone's paper to see their grade. I said something to him about it, and he blew up at me saying I always singled him out for reprimanding. I let it go. Later, when I announced the groups in which we would travel to the museum, Phil immediately began complaining that I had separated him from all his friends. I had made the groups arbitrarily because everything was a bit rushed with Alicia out and a substitute helping. I explained that to him, but no explanation was satisfactory. He was beginning to get stirred up and we needed to go. I decided to walk with him to the office and ask the vice-principal, who was also a counselor, to talk with him. I said I didn't think he would be able to handle himself on the trip. Going on a trip with a substitute was risky anyway, and I felt that if I was distracted from the rest of the group by Phil, a catastrophe might result. The vice-principal talked to him for a few minutes and deemed him able to handle himself.

I was not to be so lucky. Each minor difficulty that befell Phil that day became a stage upon which he could act out my incapacity to be fair. Sean took Phil's soda and drank it. When Phil told me about it, my response was to reprimand Sean and have him give Phil money for another soda. That wasn't sufficient punishment in Phil's eyes. He thought Sean should be sent home for committing this infraction. I think Phil would have liked to live in a "tar and feather" era. Throughout the trip Phil showered me with accusations of unfairness. I tried to be very patient, saying that he needed to calm down, be reasonable, and control himself if he was going to continue with us on the trip. The last straw came when one of the girls got carried away and flirtatiously splashed and soaked Phil with puddle water. He came to me demanding retribution. I was getting overwhelmed with being responsible for all those kids, and the substitute wasn't even able to keep kids walking safely along the street. I told Phil that I hadn't seen exactly what had occurred, and that he just needed to hold on until we got back to school. Well that wasn't nearly a strong enough response. Phil began yelling at me at the top of his voice. Nothing I said consoled him. Other kids began chanting "unfair, unfair, unfair." I couldn't see the faces of any other adults. I told Phil he wouldn't be able to go home on the bus if he didn't calm down. I would have to take him in a cab. He continued to scream and cry, as the bus pulled up and all the sixth-graders began piling on. Again I asked if he could calm down enough to get on the bus. His only response was to yell louder. So I stayed with him as the bus pulled off. No sooner had the bus left then Phil bolted. I chased after him for a half-block and then lost sight of him. I realized my predicament—I was responsible for all 50 kids, and now I was alone on the street with none of them. I turned back to the bus stop and sprinted after a bus that had just pulled away. I told the driver my situation, and she sped down McIntyre Avenue honking at the bus bearing my students. I hopped off one bus onto another to be met with accusatory glances and shouted questions concerning the whereabouts of Phil. I gave the student teacher who had accompanied us $10 for cab fare, and asked her to get off the bus and comb the area near the museum for Phil. I told her I expected he had headed for home, and to meet us back at school in an hour. My students did not understand why I had left him. They knew I was an athlete and felt I could have caught him if I tried. My judgment of the situation made them very uncomfortable. Hushed remarks about my "inability to control kids" began circulating among students. My only recourse was to talk to as many kids as possible and try to sound them out as to their perception of the situation.

When we got off the bus to make a transfer, I called the school office and explained the situation. The vice-principal said he would alert Phil's mother, and await our arrival at the school. By the time we got back to school, the class's anxiety had risen to a fever pitch. The girl who had splashed Phil was begging for trouble. I felt everyone was avoiding walking next to me. The other two chaperones didn't give me any feedback on the situation, and I thought they were accusing me of something too. I wished fervently that Alicia wasn't sick so close to the end of school. I felt sure this never would have happened if she had been there. That certainty made me call into question all of the joint successes of the year. Had sixth grade gone reasonably well only because of her?

Phil turned up at home about an hour after the other students had left for the day. The principal was firm in her resolve to handle the situation and did not ask me to attend the meeting scheduled for Monday regarding Phil's behavior. Phil was not to come to school until something had been arranged. On Monday morning, he arrived as though nothing had happened. Alicia was still at home in bed. The principal came and told me that Phil's mother had breached an agreement to keep him home, but that at this point it had been agreed that if he got into trouble again with a teacher he would be suspended for the last three days of school. The mother talked a bit about Phil's father, from whom she was separated, having stood him up at a ballgame right before the field trip. She attributed his behavior to his difficulties with this relationship. I felt wary of this (non)resolution, because I knew that suspending him would cause a near revolt among my students, who were championing his cause. However, I decided to avoid provocation at all cost and wait and see. During the disciplinary meeting, Phil yelled at the principal, but didn't get sent home. On Monday afternoon, he was kicked out of an assembly for disrupting the music class. He didn't get sent home. He seemed willing to avoid me during classes although he insisted on doing some irritating things—tapping his tennis racket against the desk, for example. I managed to overlook his provocations. Tuesday proceeded without incident. Then five minutes after the end of school, Phil walked into my room and from across the room, began telling me exactly what he thought of me. I looked him straight in the eye and told him to leave immediately. I had to ask him to leave four times. Another student who witnessed this outpouring of rage slunk away quietly.

I sat and thought about what had just happened. Did that qualify him for suspension? Had he gotten to that point because no one had followed through on their threats? If I told the principal, would I be doing it for personal reasons or because it was the best response to the situation? I went next door and talked to Alicia at great length. She bemoaned the fact that discipline problems in this school were never handled well at the outset, getting out of control and ending up having a heavy impact on our teaching. She encouraged me to act according to my intuition. I ended up walking to the office to talk the situation over with the vice-principal. I was visibly shaken by this new turn of events. I explained what had happened, and then tried to make him aware of how this mess had turned many students against me, and that I was reluctant to suspend him. At the same time, I thought that Phil had gained too much power in the situation, and that someone had to stop him. The vice-principal said he was willing to take responsibility for the suspension, and felt it was the right thing to do. He called Phil's mother. I left the office with a feeling of dread.

The next morning when I came to school, the principal met me at the door and told me that Phil's mother had not taken the suspension as a logical follow-up of the disciplinary meeting, but had decided that it was because I disliked her son. She had gotten on the phone with a number of my students to get their opinions on how I had treated Phil since the field trip. She called all the kids in his social circle, who supplied her with accounts about how overbearing and unfair I was with him. She wrote a five-page letter outlining all my incompetencies as a teacher and accusing me of engaging in a vendetta against Phil. This parent reaction prompted a conference on the last morning of school during which Phil's mother tried to get permission for him to return to school. She did not acknowledge that Phil's relationship with his father, or the fact that she was sending him to overnight camp for the summer at 3 o'clock that very day, had anything to do with his anger and pent-up emotions. The meeting lasted for two hours. Alicia attended and was clearly irked at having to be away from the class for so long on the last day. All our plans for wrap-up activities were becoming moot, and the mother talked on. I had to defend every one of my actions of the past four days. I talked about how there had been miscommunication among administrators, and how I felt the situation was left to smolder too long. I pointed out the agreement that had been made. But the mother insisted on raking me through the coals for as long as she could. The principal and vice-principal were very passive. This mother had a lot of power as an active parent in the PTO, and as someone who had donated money to the school. The administrators had decided to suspend Phil without regard for the political consequences, and now they were fearful. I thought how ludicrous it was that the whole incident had occurred because Phil felt he was being unfairly treated. Now it seemed that his behavior had been treated lightly for many years because confrontation with the mother was so unpleasant.

By the time Alicia and I were able to return to our classrooms, the kids were very agitated and excitable, making plans to outsmart the substitutes. They had no interest in settling down. The day wore on unproductively. Many students got into trouble in their art or music classes. Aaron bit a fourth-grader. Michael got in a fist fight with a student who beat him at chess. John kept standing on top of desks and shouting "party" as loudly as he could. Even popcorn didn't keep him quiet. When I tried to put my foot down to regain some semblance of order, one student said, "What are you going to do if we don't be quiet? Suspend us?" Phil was allowed to come back to school for the last half-hour to receive his report card, causing major disruption as everyone pushed and shoved to surround him and get his story. As soon as the day was over, I began packing everything up at random. All I could think was that I wanted to get out of the building. By 8 o'clock, my teaching valuables were out of the room and in my car. The year was over.

A week later, I found a short-term job doing some word processing for extra money. The ambience of the office was chilling, the staff was bored with their work, and the hierarchy was iron-fisted. I began reevaluating my year of teaching in light of what other options were available. I wanted a job that was socially useful, people-oriented, intellectually stimulating, and flexible. As the summer progressed and I thought back on the year, I realized that I was enamored of teaching despite its ups and downs, the emotional challenge, the long hours, and the frustrating encounters with kids and parents. Events of the year began to sound humorous when I related them to friends and family, and various people and places would bring back memories of jokes my students had told me or moments when a discussion had taken off on a lively tangent. The first year was behind me and I was confident that I could avoid many pitfalls and re-create high points in the coming year. I knew I would heal from the last-minute chaos and be able to begin fresh in September.

EPILOGUE

Mary Freeman completed her one-year position and was recommended for a sixth-grade opening within the system. She found her second year much less stressful and more rewarding than the first year had been. In part, the change had to do with intensive outreach to the parent community and increased management experience. Mary intends to continue teaching at the middle-grades level and wryly notes that fairness never disappears as an issue with this age group, although foreseeing complaints helps to avoid unnecessary confrontations. She encourages prospective teachers to take the plunge.

QUESTIONS FOR DISCUSSION

2.1 What specific areas in Freeman's experience as a first-year teacher seem to be most frustrating for her?
   (a) How does she deal with, adjust to, and surmount problems with students, parents, the school principal?

2.2 The trial-and-error approach to learning to teach has obvious limitations. Nevertheless, after having taught for only several weeks, Freeman says, "I wanted to blunder along unnoticed by other people. I wanted to be alone with my students and try to work out a rhythm without being observed and judged."
   (a) What merit do you see in Freeman's wish to "blunder along" on her own?
   (b) What inherent disadvantages are there in a trial-and-error approach to learning to teach?
   (c) Why might a trial-and-error approach to teaching be one of the best ways for a teacher to learn the craft?

2.3 When Freeman assigns her students reading homework in mythology that they feel is excessive, they write her a note expressing their feelings that she is being unfair and mean.

(a) Is there any validity to the complaints of the students?

(b) What indications are there that Freeman might have misjudged the amount of work she assigned?

(c) Why is the issue of a teacher being "fair" a sensitive one for young children?

(d) What other ways might have Freeman addressed this issue other than by becoming less emotionally attached to her students for a few days?

2.4 When Freeman attends a poetry workshop for teachers in her district, she makes a discovery that inspires her to return to her classroom with renewed vigor and enthusiasm.

(a) What is it that Freeman learns (discovers) at the workshop, that uplifts her lately drooping spirits so that she infuses her students with her own excitement about poetry?

(b) How is a teacher's personal growth related to her teaching?

2.5 Freeman spends much of her year struggling to find material to teach. This is a problem experienced by many beginning teachers.

(a) As a new teacher, is it better to have the curriculum decisions made for you? Or to have to make them yourself?

(b) From the point of view of parents and students which of these is a better policy?

2.6 Freeman finished her first year of teaching on less than an optimistic note due to an abusive student, his mother, and an unsupportive principal, who is afraid to confront parents even when they are wrong. Notwithstanding, the triumphs of the school year overshadow the disappointments and humiliations, and Freeman decides to return to teaching in the fall.

(a) What are some of the triumphs Freeman experiences that prompt her to remain in education?

Chapter
3

A Different Kind of School

Sean Glennie

WHAT AM I GOING TO DO FOR TOMORROW?

Once again, I find myself in this familiar position. Why is it that I always leave it to the last minute? No wonder everyone always talks about the Sunday night blues. If I could only find a cure for them, I'd be a millionaire. Then I could sit back and not worry about surviving on this meager salary. Thank God I'm married to Meri.

What will I do for tomorrow's lesson plan? Smack in the middle of team-teaching a three-week unit, one-half of my team is out sick. They said we teachers had to be quick on our feet. Oh, maybe I could wing it for a day. I already have a few "wing-it" lessons stored away after nine months of teaching. I imagine that a teacher with 10 to 15 years of experience has a much larger file of "wing-its." But, I always feel guilty using them. Who am I cheating more—the kids or myself? Throughout that first year, I was forever perplexed by this paradox. Occasionally, part of me would say, "Take a break tomorrow. Give yourself a breather. You're a teacher. Don't get burned out." The other half would always remind me, "Why slack off? You can teach. You're not burned out—not even close. You've only been on board nine months. Besides, remember the kids." But I'm getting ahead of myself. . . .

THE TEN COMMANDMENTS

I remember the class with Professor O'Keefe as clear as day. It was one of the last classes of the semester, and he was giving us his "do's" and "don'ts" for the first year of teaching. "If you can stick to these ten survival rules, I can pretty much guarantee that you will survive your first year of teaching. Not only survive," he assured us, "but you will probably go on to teach a second and third year." I sat with my pen poised, or rather, clenched, in my hand. I was ready for dictation. I was ready for the Ten Commandments. I didn't want to miss a single one for fear that if I had only nine, I would never survive the first year. These are the ten commandments we were given:

1. Promise yourself that you'll teach a second year before you enter the first year (because the first year is different from all the others).
2. If you aren't organized, *get organized.*
3. Love thy school secretary (and janitors—the "little people").
4. *Don't* isolate yourself from the faculty.
5. Get feedback on how you're doing. Open up to evaluation.
6. Come to terms with the fact that you are an authority figure. You're in charge.
7. Focus on the students' learning. Make sure that something important is going on. Focus on results.
8. Pay your body its dues, that is, visit, a health club, run, make time for workouts.
9. Find a *mentor,* so you can go to him or her to find out, what to do when . . . .
10. Don't get married two weeks before beginning your first year of teaching.

My jaw dropped at number 10. I think a friend of mine must have seen it, for she turned and looked at me, grinning from ear to ear. You see, she knew that my fiancée, Meri, and I were planning to be married on August 17, a mere 17 days before the first day of school. Uh oh, I thought to myself. I never thought of it in this light.

As I look back now over the few months before our wedding last summer, I can see that period of time a little more clearly. I think that I was so uptight about finding a job teaching that I had little time or energy to get nervous about the fact that I was about to be married.

HOW I GOT MY FIRST JOB, . . . BUT NOT MY LAST

Throughout the summer and the day of the wedding reception, everyone continued to ask about my future employment. I tried to keep a calm and controlled manner to my responses. "It's just a matter of time," I replied, trying to reassure myself at the same time. Somehow I think that my future father-in-law was a bit hesitant about giving away his only daughter to an unemployed teacher. However, he never made me feel uncomfortable and gave me only support and encouragement.

Being unemployed has got to be one of the most demeaning situations in which a person can find him or herself. You get the feeling that no one wants you. At times, I felt like telling potential employers that I would pay *them* to hire me just so that I could gain some experience. People who are unemployed and tell you that they are confident and at ease about finding a new job are lying through their teeth. Or maybe they are just deceiving themselves. It is by far one of the most scary and insecure feelings, one that does nothing but lower one's self-esteem.

"Teaching positions are tight in the Boston area," I was told, "but you'll be able to find something." I really believed that I would fall into something, that it was "just a matter of time." It just took me much longer than I had anticipated. And I certainly picked an unusual path to follow, though not by choice.

In the late spring I finalized the updated version of my résumé. I headed for the library to get my hands on Porter-Sargent's listing of local private schools and the Massachusetts's listing of public schools. If positions were scarce, I·wasn't going to let even one school slip through my fingers. I decided to blanket all of the local schools with résumés and application requests. I never took the time to fill out these applications if the school had no openings, although I probably should have.

Next, I began with all my previous professors, friends, and friends of friends. I was unemployed and desperate. I wanted to leave no stone unturned. I made sure that I always had a stack of résumés with me wherever I went. I gave everyone I knew or with whom I came in contact a résumé, smiled, and told them I appreciated their help. All of this time, I reminded myself that all I needed was just *one* job, not one hundred.

Each Sunday I camped on the living room floor with the want ads spread open. Various career counselors have told me that only 10 percent of new jobs originate from ads in the newspapers. Even though it was a long shot, I still had to try. I remember thinking that if the number of teaching positions that I found in the local papers was any indication of the market, I stood a good chance of being a carpenter for my first year of teaching. "Just a matter of time," I tried to reassure myself.

I continued to check the career resource center at school as well as local organizations that posted openings. For some unexplained reason, most of the open teaching positions were found in towns such as Casper, Wyoming, or Shawnee, Oklahoma. I have nothing against these towns, but it was a little unrealistic to think that I would be able to leave our rundown condominium on which we had risked all of our savings just a few months earlier. Nor was I about to uproot my wife from her place of employment (and our only source of income at that point). I was in Boston to stay.

I got nibbles through all of these sources but nothing definite. I had one offer to teach three-fifths full-time. I knew that we couldn't survive on that. I needed a full-time position. I continued to hold onto the hope of a permanent position in a local high school. We got married on August 17. The next morning, we left for Canada on our honeymoon. Despite being drugged with excitement from our wedding, deep in the back of my mind I still harbored thoughts of my future (un)employment.

Local schools opened on the Wednesday after we returned from our honeymoon. At 10:30 PM the next Thursday evening, the phone rang. I lumbered off of the couch wondering who would be calling at that hour. It was Barbara Tache, chairperson of the Social Studies Department of Oak Hills High School. I had done my student teaching at Oak Hills the previous spring and had become good friends with Barbara. "How would you like to teach social studies at Oak Hills this year?," she asked. Her question shocked me speechless. Things always work out somehow, I thought to myself. Or do they . . . ?

I went into Barbara's office the next day, day three of the fall term. The halls were full of students. My adrenaline began to flow and I felt excited, anticipating being in my own classroom. I was there to replace Jim Bobik.

Jim Bobik, a veteran teacher in the Social Studies department at Oak Hills High School, was applying for a nonteaching position within the city's school department, and had not made the usual preparations to begin teaching his assigned classes. He hadn't informed Barbara Tache of his plans either, but she had heard the story through the grapevine. She assumed that he wasn't returning to teach since he had yet to show up for school, and the term had begun. Nothing is ever sure in public schools. Some people say one thing while others are expressing the opposite opinion, and political maneuvers abound. Already I felt uneasy about the job, but my gut told me to accept the position.

I had had a recurring nightmare during training and throughout that summer that I would be assigned subjects to teach in which I had little or no background. Whatever the situation, I told myself, I'll surely have a few weeks in which to prepare. Barbara handed me the textbook for the European History course. I would have three freshman sections of that subject. That's not bad, I thought. Then she dropped the bomb. "And you'll also have two sections of advanced senior Economics." Uh oh, the only economics that I had ever taken was during my freshman year at college. I dropped it two weeks into the semester. I tried to tell Barbara that she was making a big mistake. But she assured me not to be alarmed. Just stay one chapter ahead of them, she told me. Yeah, an advanced class of seniors ready for schools such as Stanford, Dartmouth, and Cornell would never figure out that I was just one chapter ahead of them. They were going to eat me alive. Already, my heart was pounding.

I took the text home for the weekend and immediately began receiving tutoring in basic principles of economics from my wife. That Saturday night was a living nightmare. I was full of frustration and anger at myself. I never should have dropped that economics course in college. The more I tried to learn, the quicker I realized that it was hopeless. My biggest worry was the thought of letting the students down. I didn't want to give them short shrift.

Out of utter despair, I called Barbara at home late that night and explained my dilemma. "Come in early Monday morning, before classes," she said, "and we'll try to find a solution." As far as I was concerned, I felt like I had been asked to teach Russian without ever having had a lesson in that language.

I tried as hard as I could to remember what it was like to be a senior in high school. Will they really be interested in this stuff or are they just coasting through their final year? How sharp are these kids?

I walked into class on the first day. The nerves throughout my body twitched, but I tried not to let anyone notice. What a feeling to have 25 pairs of eyes checking you out from head to toe. Again, I tried not to think of what they may have been thinking of me at that moment. I realized later that a rookie teacher has to play amazing mindgames with him- or herself to maintain what appears to be a calm, collected manner. I imagine it's the same in just about every other profession.

Having decided earlier that I would first introduce myself and talk a bit about my background and life experiences, I soon realized that this wasn't a bad decision. Talking helped relax me, and it gave the student something to listen to and something on which to focus their attention. They seemed interested in what I was saying. Some of the students even asked questions about some of my experiences, especially regarding the Peace Corps. Positive feedback is nice to get on the first day, particularly during the first 20 minutes of class.

Now it was their turn. Each student stated his or her name. Since the student body of Oak Hills is multiethnic, there were several names that I butchered as I tried to repeat them. Without fail, this was always followed by an outbreak of laughter. Whether it was nervous laughter or genuine good humor, the laughter nonetheless made all of us in the room feel much more at ease.

I decided to get at least some idea of their writing skills, and, if nothing else, a brief personal profile on each of my new students. I encouraged the students to explain a little bit about themselves—personal background, sports, hobbies, likes/dislikes, anything that they wanted me to know—in writing. These, I assured them, were for my eyes only. The better we knew each other, the better we would understand each other. They did a great job. Many students noted their age and the number of siblings they had, as well as their favorite hobbies and sports interests. A few, much to my surprise, revealed some personal problems and fears about school. If this was only the first day, how close would I become to these kids over the next few months? This thought was somehow comforting. Being a new teacher, I think I needed to be needed. On the other hand, I suddenly realized the responsibilities involved: 25 students per class, for five classes. That meant 125 different individuals to try to get to know!

Over the next two weeks I was able to trade the two sections of Economics for two sections of U.S. History for lower-level students. As I soon discovered, this was just as challenging as teaching the advanced students. The problems I encountered trying to teach these kids ran the gamut from no class participation to the common use of profanity in the classroom to poor attitude and disrespect. They exactly fitted the images portrayed by the students in *To Sir with Love*. Only I wasn't Sidney Poitier.

When I'd turn my back, something would go flying across the room. I'd try to spin around quickly in an effort to catch the culprit. But, the closest I would get was to identify the general area from which the object was launched. And staring at me with smirks on their faces were usually the same six to eight kids. Another favorite trick was, "Can you identify this student?"

They loved to switch names on me when I was taking attendance. This would drive me nuts! A room full of 25 new faces and 25 strange new names seems like a giant jigsaw puzzle for the first few days. I learned quickly that I'd better become good at matching names to faces, or life would be miserable for the *whole* year. They could only get a couple of weeks out of this game before I had all the faces and names matched, but it was still enough time to cause some aggravation.

It was in one of these remedial history classes that I got my first taste of student disrespect, the "fuck you" backtalk. I had been warned of it in college and throughout my student teaching days, so I had been expecting it. But until it happens, you can't imagine your feelings and reactions. I felt a burning anger and my feelings were scorched. For a split second, I was speechless, and so too was the class—all awaiting my response, I imagine. That second of silence seemed to freeze into an eternity of silence and indecision on my part. My mind raced, searching for the "proper" response. My initial thought was that I had to set a precedent here to show that this behavior would not be tolerated in my classroom. I'd throw him out of class. But, I also wanted to deal with him one-to-one. So, as he walked out the door, I told him to bring a note back from the housemaster (disciplinarian) after class.

As I think of the scene in retrospect, it appears that I responded with the typical knee-jerk reaction: "Get out!" Certainly there must be other, more creative ways of dealing with this situation. Perhaps it's these types of situations that separate the average teachers from the extraordinary ones. One thing that I learned during the first year is that if I were angry, hurt, and upset that is no time to try to talk rationally to a misbehaving student. At that point, my listening skills are not going to be at their best. Maybe the student and I both need to cool off and try again in 15 minutes, an hour, or even at the end of the day.

So it turned out that this student came back after class to see me. He wasn't ready to talk or apologize, but I wasn't going to let him slip back out of the room angry and silent. My fear was that he could stay like this for the entire semester! Another one who would haunt me in my dreams at night—a terrifying thought!

We finally started talking about the incident. Tony hadn't known who I was. He also admitted that he was putting on a bit of a show for his buddies. I explained to him the type of respect I expected in my classroom. Trying not to put him too much on the defensive, I assured him that the students should respect each other, as well as expect an equal amount of respect from me. I explained to Tony that the normal disciplinary action would follow (detention after school), in addition to my request for extra written assignments and a written apology for the incident. It's amazing to me just how well a verbal and written apology have worked in similar situations since then. I think as long as your students realize that you, too, are human, they will respond in a similar fashion. I have made mistakes in the classroom and will undoubtedly make many more in the future. As someone once said, "To err is human." But it's important to me, and I think to them, that once I realize my mistake, I am forthcoming with an apology to the individual student or to the entire class. I respect them; they respect each other and me.

Tony turned out to be one of the most respectful kids in my class. Much to my delight, he also helped at times to keep some of his more rowdy friends in line in class. I had finally begun to understand this group of tough kids.

Throughout the first four weeks, the classes went fairly well considering the fact that I felt like I was scrambling here and there. I stayed ahead of my students, albeit not by much at times.

I could empathize with my students and their burdensome homework load from five classes. I, too, was carrying five full classes. Correcting 75 essay exams on the Middle Ages from three classes would take me days. Inevitably, written homework assignments from my other two classes requiring my immediate attention would come due during those same days. Ugh! I hoped my planning would get better as time went by. I thought that I would never make it. There was always more to do. Staying up late at night and getting up early in the morning was just allowing me to keep my head above water. It was so tempting to just scribble a letter or number grade on the top of those papers. But when I stopped and thought about my former teachers, there was nothing more frustrating than writing an hour exam and having it returned with not one comment written on its pages. I was determined not to follow their example. Some teachers just smirked and chuckled. "You'll learn," they assured me, "you won't have the patience or the energy to continue that for very long." Other veteran teachers, usually the ones I admired and respected the most, offered words of encouragement. The biggest reward was from the students themselves. They really seemed to appreciate the comments and effort that it took to grade their papers and exams. That made all the long hours and hard work worthwhile. I felt good that I was surviving, and the kids seemed to be getting something out of my classes and enjoying them.

What was bothering me was all the talk among the other teachers that Jim Bobik was returning and would be displacing me out of my job and back to the ranks of the unemployed. The story was that Jim Bobik did not get the nonteaching position within the school department that he was seeking. Facing a year of not teaching, and with his salary therefore in jeopardy, Jim was planning to return to his social studies teaching position. If this was true, I would soon be out of a job.

I was meeting daily with Barbara Tache, but I could never get a firm commitment regarding my status. I don't think she knew much more than I did at that point. The teachers were not the only ones to hear these rumblings; the students heard them as well. I began to get questions in class. "Are you staying?" "Why not?" "It isn't fair to us," they complained. All valid questions and comments, yet I tried to remain neutral in my replies. Ultimately, Jim Bobik did return, six weeks after I had taught my first "real" class. Because of his seniority and the fact that it is nearly impossible to fire a teacher from this school system, Jim Bobik returned to reclaim his place, and I was forced to leave. So goes the politics of a public high school. I had learned a lot in those six short weeks, both in and out of the classroom.

Saying good-bye to all my students was the toughest part. In such a short amount of time I had grown close to quite a few of them. Even though I knew them for only six weeks, and although it was over a year ago, I still have fond memories of them.

Two weeks after I had left Oak Hills High School, I returned to meet with a teacher with whom I had developed a close relationship. I wanted to pick his brain, on the chance that I might gain some clues on how to find another teaching position *quickly*.

I arrived right at the change of classes. The bustling halls brought back so many good memories. Even all the different smells had a nice familiarity about them. I reminded myself that I was no longer teaching there. I saw familiar faces go by here and there, students that I had taught for those six short weeks. I wondered if they had already forgotten me, and the thought was painful.

As I stood in the hall talking to my friend, two students approached us. They were two of the shyest girls I had instructed in one of my freshman history classes. They had hardly ever spoken, so little, in fact, that I was convinced that they were thoroughly bored with the subject and probably the teacher. They told me that they missed me in history class, and that it had suddenly become very boring and painfully uncomfortable to sit through with Mr. Bobik as their new teacher. Whether this compliment was genuine or not, it certainly did make me feel better. It was nice to hear, especially since I was now unemployed.

Leave No Stone Unturned   Once again I found myself pounding the pavement. By then it was the middle of October, and I figured that all teaching positions must have been filled. I really was going to be a carpenter for my first year of teaching. I'll accept it for now and try again in the spring, I thought. It was bleak having no prospects. My brother phoned one night to tell me about a local job fair that was being held for two days. He suggested that I check it out, giving me the old line of encouragement, "You never know what could turn up." Nah, I thought to myself, I don't want to work for some bank or enter a McDonald's training program. I was dead set against going, but for some unexplained reason, the minute I woke up the following morning, I knew that I was going to go to the fair. I still was not willing to leave any stones unturned.

My luck had turned. The only noncommerical, nonbusiness table at the fair was the one sponsored by the state's correctional department for juveniles. Little did I know that teachers were needed in these facilities. It makes sense once you think about it. A juvenile gets into trouble with the law. Depending on the case, the severity of the crime, and the record of past arrests, the kid may be sentenced to a locked, secure facility, shelter care, or even some other program, such as a group or residential home. While in the care of the state, a complete range of services, including education, is offered to the detained juvenile. I was amazed. I don't know if it was because I'm a country boy in the city or some other reason, but I had never thought of this line of teaching before.

I handed my résumé to the representatives of the Department of Youth Services at their booth at the fair. I was informed that a new shelter care unit, a residential, locked facility housing 24 juvenile males, had just opened in Boston. They were in the process of building the education department of the new Clipper Shelter Care and were looking for teachers. I felt revived! I just might teach this year after all. I wondered what it would be like teaching juvenile delinquents, streetwise and tough-talking city kids.

In my mind I had a grey picture of single cells, bars on the windows, and cold cement floors. Guards probably carried those huge keyrings, too, the ones that weigh about three pounds each. Much to my surprise (and relief), when I visited the shelter for the first time I found a warm atmosphere, with wall-to-wall carpeting and a fully equipped recreation room with weights, table games, and video machines. The four dorms, each a single large room with six beds, were clean and well organized. Contrary to my preconceptions, staff members did not wield guns, nightsticks, or shackles. The staff and the kids all seemed warm and friendly during my initial visit for my first interview. This isn't too bad, I thought.

I began to get an idea that working with this population might be somewhat stressful, perhaps causing one to feel what is so often referred to as "burnout," when I met Bill, the director of the facility with whom I had my first interview. He chain-smoked and guzzled coffee throughout our entire meeting. I have never forgotten my initial impressions from that first hour.

I was very excited about the opportunity, however. The person who would be my immediate boss, the education coordinator, seemed very friendly and supportive. I was informed that I might encounter an illiterate student in the same class as one with tenth-grade-level skills. The challenge I would face in the classroom seemed incredible: delinquent, tough kids, low skill levels, varied abilities, and behavioral problems. Since Clipper is a shelter care facility, there is a high turnover rate among its residents, I was informed. I might have a student for three months, or I might have a student who is in class today and gone tomorrow. I had wanted a challenge, and now I had certainly found one. The kicker was when they asked me how I would feel teaching behind locked doors. Would I feel claustrophobic and/or threatened? I swallowed hard and managed to reply, "Not if I felt that I was working in a relatively stable atmosphere." I needed to sit down and think about this. My knees began to feel weak. I have a good friend whose frequent advice is, "Go with your gut feeling." My mind had second thoughts, but my gut said take this opportunity. I accepted the position of social studies teacher.

Like the one I had encountered during my student teaching days at Oak Hills High School, the Clipper Shelter Care's student population was ethnically diverse. I liked the rich atmosphere this lends to the differing opinions and perspectives expressed in the classroom. That's not to say that tensions cannot reach their boiling point in such a mixed climate. They certainly did many times in this setting. But, I'll gladly accept the trade-off and risk a clash, rather than teach a homogeneous group of students.

MY TURN TO FAIL

Since Clipper is a shelter care facility, there is a high turnover rate. Some residents may be there for a day, while others may stay as long as four months. This, of course, all depends on their personal case background, charges resulting from the alleged crime(s) committed, and sentence(s). When I first began teaching at Clipper and was told of this trend, I thought that I would certainly forget many of the old names and faces as the days and months passed. But as most teachers would probably tell you, each name, when repeated, brings back certain special memories—some fond and others not so fond.

A fellow teacher and I keep a list in our heads of what we call our "Dream Team," a group of 10 to 15 special students whom we feel were simply a joy to have in class. While developing the Dream Team, we of course automatically began the checklist for our "Nightmare Team" as well.

Harry tops the Nightmare Team in my opinion. The first day in class, Harry's main goal was to find and test my limits. I guess most students do this in one respect or another during their first few days, but I had the feeling that inside Harry was a burning inferno of anger and disrespect for authority, especially teachers.

I introduced myself to him with a firm handshake. He didn't like the fact that he had to shake hands with me, but it had happened too quickly for him to avoid it. He did, however, avoid making eye contact with me. I felt as if I had the plague and must have appeared as an ugly green monster to his eyes. But class must go on, I assured myself.

I was waiting for his turn to read. Somehow I knew that he was going to refuse. Most new students do. However, most of the time with a little coaxing and assurance that you just want them to try, they usually relent and give it their best shot. Not this guy. Harry refused to read. "I'm locked up," he complained, "Why do I have to be in school?!" This loud exclamation was followed by a barrage of profanity. He was determined not to participate in class. I tried every method I could think of to encourage or coax him to read, write, or talk. None succeeded.

I began to view Harry as a personal challenge. I tried to talk with him alone outside of the classroom. No good. I inquired within the facility about his behavior outside the classroom. It was consistent—no participation, no fraternization with other residents, no improvements. This went on for days.

I started to get down on myself. Why can't I reach this kid? Harry's anger and silence soon expanded into provocative behavior. He intimidated other students in class and began to instigate verbal and physical fights.

Harry is one of those students that a teacher "brings home" at night. He was in my dreams. I found myself thinking of him constantly. How was he doing now? How would he be in class tomorrow? More profanity? Another fight? He was like a heavy weight I was carrying on my shoulders. And he was taking away more and more of my energy.

I never broke Harry's wall of silence and anger. He never opened up or participated in class. I tried every creative approach I could imagine. To this day, I feel a certain amount of guilt about Harry. Through his eyes, I probably seemed like another "typical" adult. Surely I could have tried *something* else, some other approach in an effort to reach him. In my own mind, I failed.

Harry taught me two valuable lessons. The first was that I was human. There will be more Harrys in my future teaching career—cold, angry, hurt, and impenetrable despite my best efforts. The second sad lesson was that I wasn't the first, nor will I be the last, "unsuccessful" teacher who tried in vain to reach Harry.

I JUST CAN'T TEACH TODAY

Every once in a while a day comes along, for one reason or another, when you just don't want to go to school and teach. It just doesn't seem like you can reach down deep enough inside yourself to pull out that extra enthusiasm that you'll need to teach effectively. One morning, on the day of our first wedding anniversary oddly enough, this very feeling came over me. On the previous evening my wife and I had had an emotional discussion (I wouldn't exactly call it a fight) about stress factors in our life.

Professor O'Keefe's tenth commandment had come back to haunt me, on the very anniversary of the day that we had been married. I wonder if he would be willing to add an eleventh commandment to his list: "Don't buy a house and try to renovate it during your first year of teaching (which we already know should not coincide with your first year of marriage)." Not only was I a newlywed during my first year of teaching, but I was also undertaking major renovations of the top floor of a three-family house. It was the only place near Boston we had been able to afford. We had purchased it during my days as a student working toward my Masters in Teaching. It was the proverbial "handyman special." This, as well as other factors in our lives, was causing more stress and headaches than this first-year teacher cared to confront on top of trying to teach that day.

Somehow calling in sick doesn't seem to be a solution. At the shelter, we don't have access to substitute teachers. The other teachers carry the weight of your absence. This, in my opinion, is one of the best deterrents to the abuse of sick days.

I arrived earlier than usual that morning to photocopy my lesson handouts and to organize my last-minute thoughts on the day's lesson plans. Would I have the energy today? They say that every kid can have a bad day every once in a while. What about teachers? Was this going to be mine? Ten minutes into the first class, it dawned on me. These kids were just the medicine I needed. I soon found myself enveloped in the material, my mind working at full speed again, all in an effort to handle what seemed to be an endless barrage of questions from the students. More important than anything else, I found myself joining in the classroom laughter. I love my classes to be lively, to buzz with excitement, and to be filled with laughter. I firmly believe in the philosophy quoted by Gilbert Highet in *The Art of Teaching:*

A very wise old teacher once said, "I consider a day's teaching is wasted if we do not all have one hearty laugh." He meant that when people laugh together, they cease to be young and old, master and pupils, workers and driver, jailer and prisoners, they become a single group of human beings enjoying its existence.

By the time my last class was over that day, I felt better. The kids were exactly what I needed. I hadn't known that four hours earlier, but I certainly realized it by the afternoon. However many times you come home exhausted and emotionally drained, the love, vibrancy, and spirit that these kids have to offer make it all more than worthwhile.

ACRONYMS AND MERVIN

There are so many new labels, acronyms, diagnostic tests, and agencies that we first-year teachers must confront and try to remember that it becomes absolutely mind-boggling at times. When it seems as if I am losing the battle, I am reminded of a teacher who wisely commented one time that labels meant nothing to her. In fact, she made it a point not to read the labels and diagnoses that could be found in a student's file. Why prejudice herself, she figured. Why not treat each student who comes along as an equal, full of limitless potential?

Because of the type of kids that we see in the system, our students arrive weighed down by a full set of labels. I try not to listen to all the "expert" advice that everyone is always so willing to offer on how to deal with kids with specific histories. The first questions out of so many mouths are often, "What's the charge? Why is he in here?" I don't want to know. In my opinion, it's human nature that I will alter my approach according to this information. I don't want to know.

That's not to say I never learn of some of their backgrounds, some of which are rather shocking to me. For instance, I would consider Louis to have been one of my most enjoyable kids in the classroom. He was always full of life and participated in class constantly. Louis never showed any disrespect toward me or his peers. He was clearly a candidate for my "Dream Team." Only after Louis left our unit to go on to another program did I learn why he was locked up. The head clinical worker at Clipper informed me that he had been arrested for raping his younger sister. Louis was 15. I was stunned to say the least. How does something like this happen? Why!? I am grateful that I hadn't known his background two months earlier. I'm sure I would have been angry with Louis. No matter how professional I would try to be, I have no doubt that subconsciously, or perhaps even consciously, I might have treated Louis very differently.

On the subject of categorizing or labeling the kids, I'm reminded of a 13-year old who was recently a resident at Clipper. While Mervin was short in stature, he was long on character. He was a real chatterbox, never at a loss for words. Mervin liked to be the center of attention in and out of the classroom. Once I figured out how to make the class revolve around Mervin, the 45-minute class period flew by, and it actually became a joy to see his smiling face every morning.

One day I noticed that Mervin had begun to talk out of the side of his mouth. Straight out of a gangster movie, Mervin added the furrowed brow and gesturing arms and hands to make his statements more forceful. He might have been intimidating with this new approach had he only been a foot-and-a-half taller.

Naturally, others took notice of Mervin's new communication style. From what I had come to know about Mervin's behavior, I figured it was just another attention-getting mechanism he had adopted. And he was certainly attracting attention from the other teachers, the staff, and his fellow students. He was the king, and more and more kids started to emulate his gestures. All at once, he had moved from being low man on the totem pole to one of the leaders of the shelter.

As you can probably imagine, Clipper's administrators wanted to have a psychologist come in and see Mervin. Surely something must be wrong, they argued, and so a psychologist was summoned. As is customary in most interviews and clinical evaluations, the psychologist began an amicable discussion, saving her big question for the right moment.

Mervin continued to speak out of the side of his mouth throughout the interview, carrying on with his gangster impersonation. I wonder if this began to irritate the psychologist as she tried to understand his behavior. Finally, she stopped and asked directly, "Mervin, why do you talk like that?" His response was quick and offensive. It certainly would have caught me off guard. "I don't know," he replied in a Bogart tone through the side of his mouth. "Why do you brush your hair to the side?" I'm told the psychologist was speechless. She quickly dropped the subject and continued her interview on another track. I'm not sure if it was ever clinically assessed as to exactly why Mervin was behaving in this particular manner. However, one thing was certain: Little Mervin had gotten the best of all of us this time.

BODY ACHES AND PAINS

Don't get the impression that this first year has been all rosy. It has had its share of unanticipated drawbacks and pitfalls. I remember Professor O'Keefe's advice that you must maintain a regular exercise schedule. It will help reduce the stress, he advised us. On occasions when I have found the time to run for more than two consecutive days, I must say it certainly did help to reduce my level of anxiety. My problem is that all too often I derail myself from that routine: I end up telling myself that "I'm too busy" or that "my schedule is too irregular." Of course I know that these are just excuses, but they somehow convince me at the time to ignore Professor O'Keefe's advice.

I don't know why, whether as a result of this lack of exercise or because of my job, but I have endured frequent headaches during the work week. I imagine that it's a bit of both. In fact, at one point a friend convinced me that I should go to the doctor and have a complete physical exam. Luckily, nothing turned up. The doctor's advice to me was identical to what Professor O'Keefe had told us a year earlier, "Get more exercise to relieve your stress."

The body reacts in amazing ways to the stress and activity of teaching. I sometimes wonder if all teachers feel butterflies each morning when they wake up. I have from day one. It's as if my adrenal glands are working overtime. Each morning before I leave to go to school, my stomach is full of butterflies and the adrenaline is flowing. Do these feelings subside as a teacher becomes more seasoned? Or are some teachers just more prone to these physical reactions? Once I enter the school I'm fine. There's no problem standing up in front of the class. By this time, the adrenal glands are back asleep waiting for tomorrow morning.

They warned us in school. They warn us on television, in commercials, and on posters in the doctor's office: "You must leave your work at the office." I always thought this was a bit odd, especially for teachers. You've got to bring your work home, both physically and emotionally, to prepare for the next day's lessons. I understand what they're trying to say, though. Your work directly affects your life at home. A bad day with one student or a lesson that has collapsed on its face can ruin a relaxing evening. This has happened to me this past year more times than I care to recount. You can't always plan on tonight's dinner being filled with candlelight and romance. On top of that, my wife's job is particularly stressful and she, too, has her ups and downs. It's been a big adjustment for both of us trying to balance life at work with life at home and not letting work take priority over our personal lives. It is particularly difficult in the first year of teaching, when you are out to prove to yourself and to others that you have what it takes to be an effective teacher.

On the other hand, I'm not so sure I want to separate my role at school from my personal life completely. My work is so much a part of my life. My students oftentimes feel like "my" kids. Their successes and failures seem to be mine also. It's natural for me to talk about them at home, to share the day's events with my wife and friends. I'm proud of them, no matter how well or poorly they do academically. There is so much more to a classroom than that day's multiplication problems or reading assignments.

At times I can't stop thinking about these kids, even when I'm in the shower or washing the dishes. And I dream about them constantly. Not all of these dreams are pleasant; some have even been nightmares. Before I started teaching, I guess I didn't anticipate what an impact these kids would have on me and my life. But, I wouldn't change it for any other job.

HOW DO YOU CHANGE MORALS?

Two of the most frustrating things I've confronted this year have been derelict attitudes and morals. Although I think this is an iffy area for teachers to be delving into, all teachers have a personal decision to make, a line to draw between remaining silent and speaking out personally on particular issues. I feel that it is my obligation as a teacher, if not simply because I am another human being, to speak out on such issues as crime, theft, violence, murder, and substance abuse. Maybe it's the environment in which I teach and the population with which I work that makes these issues so "hot" day in and day out for me. But I imagine almost all teachers, regardless of their subject area, encounter these issues and moral choices routinely. When I started the year teaching in a local public high school, these issues were certainly not absent from the classrooms nor the minds of the students. It's just that when most of your students are incarcerated for these very same crimes, the subject of morality is always close at hand.

Let me give you an example. Many of the shelter's residents have been convicted for auto theft. If not convicted, many still are very knowledgeable about the "trade." It seems to be the prime starter crime, the steppingstone from which many kids move on to "bigger and better" crimes. At least, that's how it is here in the Greater Boston area.

The statistics are alarming. Somewhere in the vicinity of 60 percent of all stolen cars are taken by juveniles. Usually they work for someone else. They may be filling a wish list of parts for some mechanic or simply selling the whole car to a chop shop for some quick cash. Why so many juveniles? According to all the kids that I've spoken with, it's quick, easy to learn, fun, exciting, and if caught, they'll tell you, they'll often get off scot-free. After the third or fourth time arrested, maybe a kid would be detained for a couple of months. It's a gamble, but the benefits clearly outweigh the costs for these kids. Try telling one of them that crime doesn't pay. He'll brag about his money, new sneakers and clothes, jewelry, and most important, his image.

This is a subject that we talk about often, in class and informally around the facility. It seems that most of these kids see nothing wrong with stealing cars. They're not molesting little children, nor snatching pocketbooks from old, helpless women, they'll tell you. They're stealing cars. "Yes, but that belongs to someone else," I'll suggest. "They've got insurance, don't they?!" is the typical immediate response. "In fact," they add, "we've done insurance jobs for people. So, we know that the insurance companies pay." At this point, there is usually someone in the class who volunteers their own story of such a "job." I try to explain that the victim's insurance rates will inevitably rise, as well as those for the general population. As the occurences of theft in a certain area rise, so do the rates for everyone in that area. But this falls on deaf ears. Little more is heard when I suggest that the victim probably won't get the full value for the car from the insurance company. The car decreases in value from the first day of ownership. Have you ever looked up the value of your four-year-old car? It's depressing. I continue by trying to describe the agony and annoyance of having to go out and replace the stolen car. And, we haven't even begun to talk about the most important point—the feeling of having something stolen from you. What a helpless and infuriating feeling. My coffee cup was stolen from my room one day. Such a small thing and of little value, but the feeling that someone had stolen it was enough to make me go on a tirade. I stress these feelings with the kids, but I get little empathy in return. "What do you guys feel? Any remorse? Pure satisfaction? What? What?," I yell to myself.

It all came to a head when my brother-in-law was up from Virginia for his college break, working in Boston for the summer. He had just recently purchased a second-hand 1978 Toyota Corolla. Like my first car, it was a bomber, but an invaluable bomber. We got a telephone call from him one morning at 12:30 AM. His car had been stolen from in front of his apartment. As we stood in the police station that night, he was visibly angry and hurt at the same time. For some reason, I felt the same way.

I went into school the next day to plead his case with my students. I don't know what I was looking for, maybe an explanation, or comfort, or perhaps individuals at which to vent my frustration. The only thing I did know was that I was speaking to a group of individuals who were very knowledgeable about the subject.

I told the story, and of course got snickers and outright laughter in return. It was as if the criminals had beaten the system again. I tried to remain calm and explained that this particular theft struck particularly close to home. Still I heard comments such as, "I bet my boy took it," and "I bet you'll find it in a few days, but it will be all stripped." Great, I thought. Which is more painful, the initial theft or later finding your property totally destroyed? What's going on in their minds? Do they have no compassion for anyone?

At once, I decided to put the shoe on the other foot. "Have any of you ever had anything stolen from you that was yours, that you owned?," I asked. A few students responded. I pursued one individual in particular. At last, I thought, he will make it clear to the others how it feels to be robbed. After all, don't they say that we learn better from our peers, or at least listen more closely to them?

"What did you own?" I inquired.

"A dirt bike, a bike, and a moped."

I wondered to myself about that amount of material wealth for a kid from a low-income family. Nonetheless, I continued. "So, what happened to them?"

"All the stuff was on my back porch, and one night a couple of kids stole it all when we were asleep."

"So how did that make you feel?" I asked. I was getting close. Soon all the others would see the light.

"I was pissed! I felt robbed! You know, like they had no business taking that stuff."

"See! Do you guys see? John had some of his things stolen. Look how he felt. Now can you understand a little better the pain and grief that others feel when they are robbed? Have you ever stopped to think how you would feel if some kid stole your car that you had saved for and bought with your own money?"

"By the way," I asked the student, "how did you buy the bicycle, motorbike, and moped? Did you save your money from your job?"

"Oh, . . . Oh, no, I stole them from someone else . . . ," he responded, wearing the smile of a Cheshire cat.

My heart fell. I don't think they *can* understand, I yelled inside myself. Is it useless to try to communicate to them this feeling of being violated? Can you teach feelings? How could I get them to understand? I felt like banging my head against the wall. Too many of these kids have grown up in poor neighborhoods. They have never owned, or should I say earned and bought, things of value. For some, it was enough to worry about their next meal. If you grow up as a have-not, you tend to crave the things possessed by the haves. Isn't it only natural for the haves to have to surrender some of their worldly goods to the have-nots?

But is it natural? Is it normal or right to steal from others? Is it ethical? In my opinion, no. But how do you teach this, if you decide to at all, to those students who have never known differently? How do you impress upon a student that drugs can kill? Or if they don't kill you, that they can cause some serious problems in your life? If the kid doesn't know any differently, if his parents have been substance abusers and criminals all of his life, he may perceive this behavior to be normal and acceptable, perhaps even morally right. As teachers, we all face these issues. Our job is difficult because we each have to make a personal decision regarding whether to broach a controversial subject and then we must decide what we are going to say to our students about it. I didn't have a problem entering the classroom discussion of morals on drug abuse and theft. My difficulty and frustration arose when I felt that I should teach certain feelings and morals. How does one induce a student to see the wrongness in stealing someone else's car? I'm still struggling with these issues.

LEAVING A LASTING IMPRINT

One of the things about teaching that can be both frustrating and rewarding is not knowing the impact that you have on the students you teach. Knowledge or the sharpening of one's analytical skills can be very difficult to measure. Oh, there are mechanisms such as tests that can be administered or class discussions that may reveal to the teacher a pretty good idea of the students' growth. But it is not always clear-cut.

Some areas in which we influence our students are much less obvious to us. I wonder if it is to the students as well. One time during my training, a professor asked all of us in class to think back over all the years of our schooling. He asked us to identify the good teachers and to explain the qualities that separated them from all the other teachers we had had. The qualities that sprang to my mind were fairness, a good sense of humor, willingness to talk with us as equals rather than down to us as inferiors, and willingness to sit and listen to our fears and comments about life. Good teachers offered much more than academic guidance. It was a simple yet effective exercise. At once I saw clearly that my former teachers had given me so much more than biology facts and an exposure to Shakespeare. They had given me invaluable tips on life, listened when I needed to talk, laughed with me, and mourned with us when a classmate was killed. They had been teachers and friends. In training, I guess they would call these special teachers "excellent role models."

I quickly realized that there was so much more to being a good teacher than just mastering the subject area. The frustration with all of this is that we never really know how much we have touched our students' lives. As more-seasoned teachers will tell you, often you never find out until months or even years later, that is, if you find out at all. I often wonder how many of my students will remember me as a good teacher.

My wife and I and a good friend of ours were on our way out of a theater one night, headed back to our car. We were in the heart of downtown Boston and had to walk about eight blocks to the parking garage. There is a small, seedy area of downtown Boston, called the "Combat Zone," through which we had to walk from the theatre district to get to our car. Since it was after 11 PM, I thought we would certainly get an eyeful of nighttime characters in the Zone, not to mention catcalls directed at my wife and our friend. I suggested to them that we just ignore all comments directed at us and continue to the car as quickly as possible.

We were about halfway through the Zone when we passed a car with its lights out parked in a narrow, dark parking area. All at once the horn sounded, causing us all to jump. I think it's safe to say we all were a bit on edge after that. A guy started hollering out of the car window at us. It was tough to tell if he was speaking with a broken accent or if he had had a little too much to drink. My guess at the time was both. As my wife and our friend nervously glanced over their shoulders, I told them to ignore him and to continue toward the parking garage.

The man continued to yell at us, telling us to stop. That was the last thing I was going to do! At this point we were about one block from the car. We picked up our pace a bit, but he continued to yell at us. My wife informed me, as she continued to look over her shoulder, that he was getting out of the car and coming toward us. By now, my heart was pounding! I told the women to walk very rapidly to the parking garage, and that I would try to talk my way out of the situation. I'm no heavyweight, nor do I hold a blackbelt in the martial arts, so I had no idea what I was going to say or do.

As I turned toward the man, who was now 30 feet away, something about him struck me as being familiar. I thought I recognized his face and his walk. Sure enough, it was Julio, a former student from the Clipper Shelter. All this time, he had simply wanted to say hello and had been calling out to us. Did I ever feel stupid! I was actually glad to see him. He laughed because he knew what all of us had been thinking just moments before. He's only 15 years old, but he knew he had just gotten the better of us.

We talked for a few minutes and caught up on each others' lives. Of course I asked him what he was doing in the Combat Zone at that hour of the night. He said that he was waiting for his brother who had just gone into an adult book store. Several months later, I found out that Julio had been sitting in a stolen car that night. He really had gotten the better of us.

I may not have been able to convince Julio to stop his criminal ways, but I felt I had had some impact on him. The fact that he had wanted to stop me to say hello made me feel good. Who knows . . . perhaps he learned more in class from me as an individual than I realized while teaching those classes. I hope so.

IT'S MORE THAN JUST THE CLASSROOM

One of the benefits that I have enjoyed about teaching is the extracurricular activities—sports, trips, vocational programs—in which I have participated with my students. It allowed me to see them in a different light and vice versa. It helps erase the "us" and "them" attitudes that both students and teachers develop. The "us" and "them" are suddenly fused into "we." That's a nice feeling. "We" win and lose together. "We" laugh and cry. "We" learn together.

I'm reminded of all the basketball games over this past winter. If you want to become a humbled teacher, join in a scrimmage with the students on the school team. Every Wednesday night and Saturday morning we had games against other schools. In one game, we were getting blown out by 17 points at the half. We were lucky to be that close. We walked to the locker room with our heads hanging low. It was embarrassing for all of us. After much moaning and groaning, one of the kids said, "Hey, we're only nine buckets down! We've just got to take them one at a time." It was just what the doctor ordered. No coach's pep talk could have put it in better perspective than this one player had just done. All at once, energy and excitement started to surge in all of us. Suddenly, we all felt as if we really could beat this undefeated, first-place team. We ran out for the second half warm-ups all pumped up. The others players and their fans were laughing at us. Their cheerleaders were the most offensive, slinging blatant insults at our team. But our players ignored them. They were on a mission. We battled back to within two points with only a minute left to play. The other team tried to stall the ball and run out the clock. The ball was stolen by our team and a basket was made. Our bench went crazy!

It was bedlam all around us. On the return trip down the court, the other team missed their shot and a chance to take the lead. With little time left on the clock, we grabbed the rebound, ran it down the court and sank the winning basket. You can imagine the mad hysteria on our bench, and the utter silence from the rest of the gym. We had won the game, stolen it from the champs. There were no more insults or ribbings from the other players or their cheerleaders. We were the champions, for at least those few isolated moments.

Throughout that game I felt extremely close to all those kids. For that short amount of time, they were no longer my students—they were my sons or perhaps my younger brothers. There was a bond out on the court that was so special, one very different from the close student-teacher relationship that develops in the classroom.

I find a similar reaction in both myself and the students when we travel to a nearby vocational high school. It is here at Constitution Technical High School that our students participate in a three-hour afternoon program teaching different trades. The goal of the program is to turn the kids on to a specific vocation and eventually lead the students back to school, an environment and institution they have long since discarded as useless and a waste of time. The technical school, we hope, provides the facilities that will spark the students' interest in learning a trade. If a student still refuses to go back to high school once he is discharged from the shelter, perhaps he will leave with enough skills to be accepted into a neighborhood apprentice program offering local employment. In essence, we hope that he will choose this new career path, either by continuing on with it in school or by entering the job force, instead of following the same old pattern of crime.

I was given the responsibility at Clipper Shelter to act as the shelter's Constitution High School coordinator. My job was to see that the program ran smoothly for our residents. I have a particular interest in vocational trades. I love to tinker in auto mechanics and the building trades. Besides, my wife and I were in the midst of renovating our condominium, and I could stand to learn as much as possible.

I rolled up my sleeves and went to the classes with the kids. I was just as turned on to this new world as they were. I didn't always pick up the trade secrets as well as they did. It's nice being taught by our own students for a change. They taught me such things as how to put a small engine back together. Often, they would lean over patiently to reexplain a new technique to me. I was constantly amazed at their work. While some could wire a two-door home chime system together with their eyes closed, others were cutting and laying tiles as if they were master masons.

As we learned together, we grew together. Not only were our student-teacher relationships back in the classroom enriched, but the feeling of that special bond was in the air. I think part of it is explained by the fact that both the student and the teacher see each other from yet another perspective. The more angles from which you view an object, the more detailed the picture becomes. While I might see a troublemaker in the classroom, I may find myself looking at a very talented and knowledgeable electrician in this new setting. I had students who couldn't read the first line of a simple story, but put them in one of these trade shops and they could fix or construct masterpieces with their hands. I guess we all have something to offer this world. The key for me as a teacher is to remember that that gift may not always be visible from the front of a classroom. Experiences such as helping to coach the basketball team and learning with my students at Constitution Vocational High School, experiences outside of the classroom that allow us to relate to one another, have definitely sharpened my ability to approach these kids, and other people I encounter, with an open mind.

FINAL THOUGHTS

I look back over my first year of teaching with mixed emotions. It seems to have flown by, but at times the days and weeks couldn't have dragged more slowly. I've seen a lot of students, had my share of ups and downs, and I have certainly learned a lot. The more I grow, the clearer I see that I need to learn all that much more.

One area on which I continue to focus is my unit and lesson planning. I have learned that I cannot survive on a day-to-day or even week-to-week basis. It's just too much of an emotional and physical drain. Being prepared, as the Scouts would say, enables you to be in a better position to confront and conquer any unforeseen problems that arise.

Although it was Professor O'Keefe's tenth commandment that had made my jaw drop, it was my new wife who was always there with encouragement and support. Typical of many employees in their new job, I often wondered if I was accomplishing anything. It certainly helped to have someone there to keep things in the proper perspective.

While writing these words I've realized just how valuable those ten commandments, more than anything else, have been during my first year of teaching. The ones that I have been able to incorporate into my daily life have been a dependable source of guidance. The others that I haven't yet mastered indicate areas in which I need to improve.

The first commandment kept me going through those certain times when I wanted to toss in the towel and become a carpenter. Yet, that is the one that I no longer worry about. I'm sold on being a teacher. I can think of no other profession that could possibly bring me so much joy and satisfaction.

EPILOGUE

Sean Glennie, a former member of the Peace Corps in West Africa, continues to teach social studies at Clipper Shelter Care. His college background includes Colby College and Boston University's M.A.T. Program. What keeps Glennie's interest most is that each day is a challenge and never like any other. The students at Clipper Shelter also continue to teach Sean, in the classroom as well as on the basketball court and in vocational classes. They are a large part of what makes his job so enjoyable. Sean plans to continue his work with this diverse and special group of students at Clipper Shelter Care.

QUESTIONS FOR DISCUSSION

3.1 Glennie believes that it is essential for a teacher and his students to respect one another.
  (a) What does Glennie do to get this idea across to his students? Do they respond positively? Why?

3.2 Glennie quotes Gilbert Highet, who, in *The Art of Teaching,* wrote, "A very wise old teacher once said, 'I consider a day's teaching wasted if we do not all have one hearty laugh!' "
  (a) How and when can a teacher use humor as an effective tool to promote learning in the classroom?

3.3 Glennie firmly refuses to read his students' files, which contain information about their background and past behavior.
  (a) Why is such a decision helpful to both Glennie and his students?
  (b) How can becoming familiar with a student's past be useful to a teacher?

3.4 Glennie observes, "I quickly realized that there was much more to being a good teacher than just mastering my subject area."

   (a) What are the qualities that make a teacher "good" and memorable to his students other than teaching content or one's academic specialty?

3.5 What kinds of experiences does Glennie have outside of the classroom with his students that directly affect his feelings and attitudes toward them?

   (a) How are these experiences part of his own education as a teacher? What does he learn?

3.6 Glennie asks himself the question, "How does one induce a student to see the wrongness of stealing?

   (a) What suggestions do you have?

   (b) Should the teaching of morals or ethical behavior be part of the school curriculum, or should a teacher avoid such issues, which may be better dealt with in the home or through religious training?

Chapter 4

Riding the Roller Coaster

Amy Shea

Big yellow buses were bursting with clammering children. Cars lined the street. Teachers waved and smiled. The pavement was very hot, and I was bothered by the whole ordeal. Saying good-bye is never easy for me. I avoid it whenever possible, preferring to slip out the back door. This time it was inevitable and painful. For the past 10 months I had planned for them, conversed with them, argued with them, played with them, worried about them. They filled my dreams at night and challenged me daily. Now I was saying good-bye and I didn't like it at all. These children, my students, twelve 10-year-old boys and twelve 10-year-old girls had been my companions all year. I wanted the best for every one of them. I was able to help them all in some small way. I couldn't reach all the goals I had set—it was impossible to reach some. Nevertheless, I was very fond of my students, and I was nervous about letting go.

The same anxiety had pervaded my first day at Cider Mill. I woke very early that morning and took a great deal of time getting ready. I wanted to make the right impression and wear the right clothes. I ate a good breakfast, hopped in the car, and was off to the first-day-of-school meeting at the Applewood High School auditorium. The last time I had felt this same nervous apprehension and excitement was back when I, myself, was a public school student. "Who would I sit next to?" "Would my friends remember me?" "Would I get good grades on my report card?" Those questions filled my mind throughout grade school and high school, and, now, in the same respect on my one-hour drive to Applewood, questions carried on within me: "Would I make friends with my fellow teachers?" "What kind of children would I have?" "Would I like teaching?"

Notebook in hand, I entered the high school auditorium to find that I was the first of over 200 teachers to arrive. I sat nervously at my too-early arrival and resorted to writing my thoughts in my journal notebook. Soon clusters of teachers began to arrive. I sat in the back and watched them. Cliques laughing and exchanging huddled whispers about summer escapades reminded me of cliques of high school students arriving on the first day of school. I overheard a few teachers discussing my school and introduced myself to them. Now I had a group to sit with, and I could begin to learn about this new place.

The superintendent talked for a long time. He recounted last year's highs and lows and urged teachers to meet goals for the coming year. His speech was incomprehensible to me as I didn't know any of the history. I didn't recognize any names. At the end of the meeting, my mind was on overload and I was suffering from a headache. I was anxious to see Cider Mill again. I had only visited the school twice: Once for my interview in early July and then again in August to preview the school schedule and take a look at my classroom.

A modern one-story brick building, Cider Mill sits proudly on one acre of grassy, tree-dotted land. Surrounded by well-manicured, single-family homes and gardens, the school is the focal point of the neighborhood. Cider Mill's interior is warm and inviting, brightly colored carpets, displays of students' work, framed prints of famous paintings and illustrations, photographs of school events, and sunlight welcome students, teachers, parents, and visitors.

Plagued by the prominence of the "open-school" philosophy of the sixties, Cider Mill has virtually no walls between classrooms. The walls were knocked down to create an openness and greater flexibility within the building. It was thought, then, that schools without walls would allow students greater freedom of choice and, therefore, greater motivation to learn. The open-school philosophy passed but the walls were never rebuilt. Hence, within the warmth and abundance of Cider Mill, bookcases, file cabinets and chalkboards create barriers between classes. The noise level can be excessive, and concentration is difficult. However, Cider Mill still provides a dramatic contrast to the urban school in which I taught last year.

As a student teacher, I was assigned to The Belmont School. The Belmont School was located in Dawson, a major eastern city located near Applewood. The school was built in the early 1900s. It was a four-story, brick schoolhouse with decorative wood work inside and out. My class was an exciting mix of immigrant students representing 12 countries, including Vietnam, Cambodia, Laos, Greece, Haiti, and Ecuador. The diversity was rich, as was the range in academic ability and experience. The Belmont School and Cider Mill were both public elementary schools, yet the quality and content of education differed immensely. Cider Mill offered students a vast array of materials and experiences. Children at Cider Mill were not only exposed to a rich menu of activities in school, but for the most part, their families provided them with exotic trips, family vacations, video games, and computers.

The Belmont School was a school for moderate- to low-income children. Home life for many was a small apartment in the city, crowded and noisy. Afterschool life for these Belmont School 11- and 12-year-olds usually meant babysitting a younger sister or brother or working at dad's gas station or around the house. School life at the Belmont School did not include abundant materials. My lessons were compromised by the fact that I could not use the photocopy machine, and there weren't enough chapter books to pass around the class. The library was small, and many of the books were outdated. Special music events were part of the schedule, and we crowded into the basement, which served also as a makeshift gym, auditorium, and lunchroom. Gym, art, and music classes were offered on a part-time basis by special teachers, but most often they were the responsibility of the classroom teacher as was computer education. The playground resembled a parking lot with a few basketball hoops. I always cringed at Cider Mill when they would complain of their grassy playground spotted with trees, flowers, swings, slides, jungle gyms, climbing poles, and paved areas for basketball, four-square, jump rope, and hopscotch.

Teacher schedules at Belmont School left no room for planning, and the available resources did not stimulate creativity. Their contract called for a 3:30 dismissal (a half-hour after the children's dismissal time). Once the children had been dismissed from their classrooms, many teachers were quick to run from the building, and drive off before the students had boarded their buses. The Dawson Public Schools teachers' contract early dismissal time was a response to frequent threats of crime within the urban school system. Meanwhile, teachers at Cider Mill had the freedom to stay as late as they wished after school. Many Cider Mill teachers could be found in the building at 4, 5, and even 6 o'clock preparing lessons, meeting with parents, attending workshops, and providing remedial help to students.

The Belmont School provided me with a rich experience and foundation for my first year of teaching. However, as a first-year teacher, I chose to teach in a system such as Applewood's. I felt that Applewood could provide an environment in which there were few limits to educational resources and expertise. Cider Mill was rich in educational supplies and experience. Many of the teachers were veterans of 15 or more years of experience. In each area of the curriculum, Cider Mill assigned a teacher as team leader. The curriculum team leader ordered new materials, provided overall planning within the subject area, and planned in-service workshops and one-to-one demonstrations. Workbooks, paperback novels, mimeo books, paper of all sizes and colors, pencils, pens, colored pencils, scissors, and rulers were all abundantly supplied at Cider Mill. A lesson rarely had to be modified due to a shortage or quota on supplies. A rich assortment of specialties was also provided by Cider Mill. Each week the children had gym, art, music, and library period. During the year music, mime, drama, and science events enhanced the schedule. A poet-in-residence and an artist-in-residence provided children with first-hand poetry and weaving experiences. A Poetry Night and a specially designed Cider Mill Weave celebrated the significance of these events. Cider Mill proved to live up to its statewide reputation as an excellent elementary school. My choice to begin in a strong and affluent system such as Applewood's proved rewarding. Although, even in such a vital and enriched environment, the fact remained that I was a first-year teacher with a lot to learn.

All summer I had plotted and contrived plans for the school year, and to my dismay, could never get beyond the first three days. Preparing the first three days of learning for my students took me no less than 100 hours. I labored over those initial plans, making sure that I had adapted theory properly, included a place for children of all abilities to succeed, encouraged critical thinking and creativity, fostered appropriate social skills, nurtured self-esteem, utilized challenging content, and met the available time limits. Hence, I spent 100 hours creating a perfect mathematical formula using educational theory and practice to craft lessons.

Greeted by fresh coffee and warm blueberry muffins, the Cider Mill staff meandered about the library. Paul McCormick, the principal, arrived soon after and called the Cider Mill staff meeting to order. Weary still from the long faculty meeting at the high school, I found a comfortable spot in the library "pit," a colorfully carpeted area reminiscent of a theater's orchestra pit. Paul McCormick, a middle-aged man with a welcoming smile and manner, greeted us and introduced me and the other two new teachers. I was honored by his laudatory introduction and comforted by the staff's applause, waves, and smiles at our arrival.

The principal had interviewed me in July. His questions were sincere as were his concerns about hiring a first-year teacher. He had been an elementary school teacher himself for a number of years and recounted many tales from his own teaching days. He explained that it had been a difficult choice to leave the classroom for his administrative role. Respected by his staff, at times Mr. McCormick seemingly felt alone and without comrades in his position as leader. His vision for the school was enormous. Standing in front of the Cider Mill staff, Mr. McCormick shared his vision with the teachers and his feeling that a school staff should be much like a family, supporting and caring for one another. Cider Mill's community and sense of pride was evident.

Encouraged and enthusiastic, I left the library and headed for my classroom. I put up bulletin boards, photocopied the work I had prepared for the children, aligned the desks and rehearsed my plans. Wearily I drove home in anticipation of the first day of school.

They arrived. As if on fire, the children ran into the classroom.

"Is that her?"

"Are you Ms. Shea?"

"She's a new teacher. She won't know any of the rules."

"We can get away with anything!"

"We're even!"

"What do you mean?"

"There are 12 girls and 12 boys."

"One girl for every boy."

Like any group of people who share a common experience and have been away from one another for a long time, the children chatted away without any conception of time and place. I watched intrigued and, I might add, a bit frightened.

The best laid plans never work out. At least mine didn't. I considered all the factors graduate school had taught me to consider—self-esteem, hands-on methods, group process, question types—but I had not considered the human element. I had not considered the fact that I had really never worked with 10-year-olds before. I student-taught at the sixth-grade level (12-year-olds) and the fifth-grade level (11-year-olds) but at the young ages of 1–12 each year makes a significant difference. Fourth-graders were a new challenge for me. I had tediously planned the lessons without the knowledge that I really needed about children. I needed to know about their skills, their interests, and personalities. Hence, when I assigned the first few lessons, the children were dumbfounded at my complicated instructions and my quick execution of directions. Neatly typed ten-step direction sheets are baffling to fourth-grade students as was my planned "Dr. Seuss Play" lesson.

I had copied a Dr. Seuss play from my language arts text—a two-page play with simple words. I could read the entire play in approximately ten minutes. Then I carefully planned the lesson as follows:

1. I would read the play to the class. All the students would follow along.
2. Children would choose groups of four with whom to practice the play.
3. Children would rehearse the play, and then perform the play for the entire class.

Simple enough, you say. Well, I had 45 minutes to teach the lesson. I spent the first 15 reading the play to the children, and they spent the next 30 minutes arguing over who should be in each play group. We eventually finished the lesson—one week later.

To my surprise the lesson was far too complicated and intense for fourth-graders, particularly on the first day of school. My perceptions of teaching and students would obviously undergo some dramatic changes in the days and weeks to come. Not only did this modification of my first lesson occur, but each lesson proved to be a learning experience for me.

One lesson really succeeded. The plan had been suggested to me by a fellow student at a summer course. It was the "signature" game. I had drawn up a chart listing a variety of children's activities. Each child received a copy of the chart and the following directions: "Find students who do the activities listed, such as piano-playing, ballet, hockey, and sewing, and have those students put their signature on the correct block. You must not make a sound during this game. It is a silent game." The final direction was added at the last minute. I was beginning to match my plans with the open-school environment. The game was fun. Children hurried about using all kinds of nonverbal signals, such as pointing, acting out a scene, and writing words down to ask questions and communicate with fellow students. The game lasted about 30 minutes and we had 15 minutes at the end to recapture the best parts of the whole process. I was beginning to learn.

The first few weeks were a time of adjustment. Adjusting lesson plans, classroom seating arrangements, and most challenging, adjusting discipline technique. I knew I would have to discipline the children. I knew I wasn't supposed to be "too nice" at the beginning. I had had practice as a student teacher calling for the attention of the class and putting all things in order. But as a student teacher there had always been a master teacher sitting and glaring at the misbehaving children from the back of the room. I was second in line then; these children were my responsibility. My main focus at the start of the year was creative and innovative lesson-planning. I had left much of the discipline technique up to the fact that if the lessons were intriguing, the children would not have a need to misbehave or act out. That was true about 1 percent of the time. There was that rare occasion when *all* children were invested in the lesson at a single moment, but the normal situation was that there would always be someone within the classroom with a different agenda in mind.

For example, during an initial math lesson we reviewed addition and subtraction facts—a simple lesson including math storytelling. I often told stories involving math concepts. I would choose a student in the class to be the main character in the story. That student always enjoyed the attention and the excitement of being the successful and glamorous main character. Some children resented these stories, particularly when they were not the main character. On one occasion, a child's resentment affected the entire math lesson. As I spoke, she busily passed notes about the classroom.

"Frances, please stop the note passing," I instructed. For a moment the notes stopped, and I returned to my story only to find the notes were being passed again.

"Frances, do I have to change your seat? Please stop passing the notes."

"Okay, Ms. Shea," she replied, glaring at me. As soon as I turned my back, I could hear the quick rustle of notes passing around the room again. Exasperated, I thought to myself: I planned this lesson carefully. I'm only trying to help the children out. I'm not teaching addition and subtraction facts for my own benefit!

"Frances!" I screamed, "Please leave the classroom and see me at the end of the period."

"I'll do that, Ms. Shea," Francis replied with a satisfied grin. She had rattled my cage and was pleased.

Feeling guilty about yelling, and frustrated with the now anxious mood of the class, I stopped to collect my wits. I overheard the teacher next door calling out number facts and quizzing the children. The children were responding with confidence. I took her cue (open schools are advantageous at times) and began the same rote quizzing in my classroom.

"Thomas, 2 + 4?" I called out.

"Six," replied Thomas.

"Mary, 2 + 3 + 2 = ?"

"Seven," responded Mary.

"Very, very good!" I exclaimed.

"Steven, 5 + 4 + 1 = ?" I asked. I received no reply and asked the question again: "Steven, 5 + 4 + 1 = ?" Most of the children looked at Steven who suddenly realized I'd just called on him.

"What?," asked Steven. In a loud voice, I called out, "Steven do you know the answer to 5 + 4 + 1?"

"Ms. Shea, isn't it time for lunch?" Steven inquired.

"Steven, I asked you a question. I am not concerned about lunch at this time."

The children were packing up their books and counting their lunch change. It was time for lunch, and I was too weary to persist with Steven.

"The answer is 10, Steven!"

Jean, a quiet and sensitive girl in the front of the room sensed my mood and asked, "Ms. Shea, can we go now?"

"Yes, you are all dismissed."

Frustrated, I collapsed into my chair only to find Frances staring at me.

"You wanted to see me Ms. Shea. Remember?"

Too weary and confused to think of a way to deal with Frances, I simply replied, "Frances, let's not pass notes tomorrow and please work on your listening skills."

"Have a good lunch, Ms. Shea," Frances replied knowing she had won the battle.

The quick exchange of math class for lunch occurred, and I ran out to the playground for my 15-minute lunchtime duty. Discouraged and frustrated, I gained the ear of the teacher next door. A master teacher and math team leader, Marlene Fray had been teaching at Cider Mill for over 30 years. She treats the children with respect, and has been a tremendous right hand for a new teacher. Frustrated and anxious, I recounted the story to her. She provided a bit of advice. We stood at a five-foot distance from each other, as teachers are not allowed to converse on the playground. A difficult rule as that often means the only time we have for adult communication throughout the day is a 20-minute lunch period. I had to talk and get this off my chest in order to get on with the day and the afternoon lessons. Marlene recounted a couple of incidents that occurred during her own first year of teaching and suggested that I set a proper tone at the start of each lesson to encourage listening skills and interest. The next day I put her suggestions to work during math class. It worked! A quick drill of math facts at the start of the lesson put the children into the right frame of mind for math. From that day on, I was to begin math lessons in this way.

Frances and Steven proved to hinder as many math lessons as they could throughout the year. Steven was a chubby 10-year-old who had moved from Massachusetts to Colorado and back approximately 10 times in the past 10 years. He had begun school many falls at Cider Mill only to transfer to a school in Colorado in late fall or early winter. His records were sketchy. This time, Steven was with his mom and his little brother in Applewood. They had left their dad back in Colorado. During the day, Steven was lost in his own thoughts most of the time. He rarely heard me when I called on him. He would not follow classroom directions until they were extended to him personally. He wandered about the schoolyard during recess and lunch all by himself, hands in his pocket, staring at the ground. Sometimes he would ask me if he could stay in for recess so that he would not have to go out. This was rarely possible as I often had recess duty and children could not be left in the class-room alone. On those days I didn't have duty, I needed a break too, particularly from students like Steven, who would wear at you all day.

Steven would not play games, work with other children, or answer questions. He would do everything possible to distract me from teaching, such as asking questions about lunchtime, end of school, and my personal life. He always asked these "crucial" questions during the climax of a lesson I had planned. He rarely did his homework or completed classwork. During the December holiday season I had the children make calendars for "someone they love." Steven's calendar was never completed. The pages he did complete were filled with pictures of weapons and soldiers. His stories were sad, and he complained to me that he did not get along with his mom. He then complained to his mom that he did not get along with me. Steven required attention every five minutes and with 23 other students, many similarly needy for attention, that was not possible.

I consulted the school psychologist, principal, and other teachers with respect to Steven. We determined that he worked well in small groups and needed extra attention. His mom agreed with that, too, and we developed a "special needs" program for him. With the cumbersome paperwork, testing, and number of children requesting special needs help, we were not able to get Steven the extra help until late winter. His tests confirmed our expectations. Steven was a bright child with substantial emotional needs due to his family situation and persistent travel from one state to another. He continued to plague me each and every day of the school year as I tried to control my temper and see him as the needy child he was. This is very difficult because at times I wanted to blame him for his terrible behavior and lash out at his inability to pay attention and his willingness to distract other children from their work. At other times, I tried to keep him after school for extra help. Steven would agree to the extra help and even request it at times; but when the end of the day came, he rarely stayed and my first-year difficulties organizing 24 ten-year-olds made it very difficult for me to remember or catch Steven before the end of the day.

Steven's mom was agreeable and helpful at first. She agreed to work with Steven at home. I agreed to keep Steven after school, and we suggested the special needs plan. She was really trying. As the year progressed and Steven's progress did not, she began to blame me and the rest of the school staff for his problems. She lashed out at me for not letting her know right away when he did not behave and demanded to know why I didn't keep him after school as often as I had promised. She was very angry and felt we were not helping her little child. I explained during the meeting that we did care about Steven, and yes, I did not keep him after as much as I had promised. I learned not to make promises, as situations can change so quickly in an elementary school. What is promised one day may be impossible the next. Finally, I explained that Steven was a very difficult student who persistently interrupted lessons, did not complete schoolwork, and was distracted most of the day.

Steven was the most challenging student of my first year of teaching. The next time I work with a "Steven," I will be better prepared. I will get help quicker. I will notify school officials and parents immediately and put the child on a consistent behavior plan. I did not know what could be done in a case like Steven's, and neither did the rest of the school personnel—he was new to us and his records did not indicate this emotional problem. The end of the story is sad: Just when we were beginning to understand this child, and just when his schoolyard behavior began to exhibit friendship and companionship, Steven left for Colorado again, this time to live with his father. According to Steven and his mom, "The schools are much better in Colorado." I wish they had waited. A year is not a long time for a child to begin to understand his feelings and cope with the separation of his parents. Next year he would have been returning to a school that understood him and a special needs package prepared to help him.

The school year introduced me to Steven and many others with similar emotional weights. Divorce, separation, and economic problems hinder many children. Kennedy told me once that his house was a "dump." A freckled faced 11-year-old, Kennedy was one of eight children who lived in a small shack at the edge of town. Kennedy's mom and dad had separate living quarters, and his dad spent a lot of time getting drunk.

Kennedy liked to sleep on the floor because his mattress wasn't very comfortable, and they all stayed away from the kitchen at night because there was no heat there. Kennedy and I did not get along at all during the first weeks of school. He would shout out when he did not agree with me. He constantly accused me of picking on him and staring at him during lessons. He was a tough kid who did not want any teacher pushing him around. A big blow-up came in early October. Kennedy kept talking out and using foul language while I was trying to conduct a lesson. I reprimanded him and eventually asked him to go to the library (fourth-graders hate to leave the classroom). When he returned he said, "You're always picking on me, Ms. Shea."

"You are always talking out," I replied, defensively.

"No, I'm not. What about Frances and Heather? They were talking out too!"

Fairness in the fourth grade is the foremost ingredient to teaching.

"I heard you!," I exclaimed.

Together we argued for about ten minutes, until Kennedy ran from the room, filled with tears and angry words.

I collapsed at my desk crying all too loud. "How could I hurt that child?" I wondered, "How do I deal with him?"

I put my head on my desk.

Marlene Fray and her team-teacher Claire overheard our argument. They came to comfort me and ask if they could help. They were always there to help when I needed them, but I still didn't know quite how to take their help. Could they be trusted? Marlene and Claire made many suggestions, and most of all they encouraged me to relax and go home.

Preparing for my trip home, I heard the hushed footsteps of Kennedy. I did not want to talk with him now, I needed time to think. Hence, I pretended that I did not hear him at all. He picked up his books and ran quietly out the door.

That was our last big battle. I took the advice of Marlene and Claire and talked to Kennedy the next day. I told Kennedy that he would have to control his temper, and I would, too. I told him that if he called out too much, I would have to ask him to leave. I also praised him for his good work and consistent homework completion. Against all odds, Kennedy was one of those children from a tumultuous home who had an inner energy to achieve and do well. He wanted to please others, particularly the teacher. He wanted people to see and treat him as a "good kid," not a troublemaker. I learned a lot about Kennedy in the first few months of school, and by early January I began to look forward to seeing him each day. I could always count on a hug in the schoolyard, a homemade cookie, and, most important to a teacher, excellent attention and hard work. Kennedy was making great progress, and so was I.

I discovered that I had a temper during my first three months of teaching. I hadn't really experienced a problem with anger since I was 16 and undergoing all the trauma of high school. I found myself anxious and itchy. I wanted the children to behave a certain way, and when they didn't, I began to yell. I was yelling too much and getting so frustrated that I would shake and sweat. I was afraid of myself during these temper tantrums, and I could tell I was making the children very nervous. "Why didn't they listen?" I would continually ask myself, "Don't they understand?"

Finally, I lost it. It was a Friday at 1:15. The children had arrived from gym excited, hot, and thirsty. They lined up at the water fountain for drinks and the badgering that goes along with post-gym excitement and last period Friday anxiousness.

"Carl's drinking all the water, Ms. Shea!"

"Lisa cut ahead in line."

"What are we going to do this afternoon?"

"Let's play a game."

Anxiously I watched the clock tick away. I had planned this period for science. We were way behind in the science curriculum. The lessons took a lot of mental as well as physical preparation. I had to find the equipment, put it together, and copy the charts. I knew every minute counted, and I didn't quite know how to get the whole thing off the ground. The lesson was a worm experiment. The children had to work in small groups, which I assigned. After their moaning and groaning about whom they would work with, I asked Kennedy to pass out the worms. He and Bob had collected the worms after school the day before. I had to bribe them to collect worms as I didn't know I was suppose to care for the ordered worms, and they had all died that Monday. Kennedy began giving preferential treatment to friends by supplying them with the largest and fattest worms. Hand-picking worms became a source of argument, and the children began to complain. The clock was still ticking away and we hadn't even passed out all the worms. We only had 15 minutes to complete the lesson.

"Kennedy, just pass out the worms."

"They are my worms, Ms. Shea, and I can pass them out in any way I want to."

"Kennedy, let me pass them out?"

"No, if I can't pass them out, I'm not going to let anyone have them. I collected them!"

"Kennedy, please leave the room." Angrily, Kennedy left the room, with the worms!

"Go get those worms from Kennedy, Bob." At that point a group of children got up to leave.

"Where are you going?," I asked.

"We've got band practice." I had forgotten that every Friday afternoon half my class would leave at various times throughout the day for musical instrument practice. During the week two students leave for speech, eight children leave for resource room help (special needs), not to mention a half-dozen weekly dismissals all at different times of the day. The elementary school classroom resembles a three-ring circus most of the time. The instrumental group left, and I attended to Bob, who waited patiently and quietly with the worms in his hands. I took the worms from him and passed them out to the students prior to giving directions. Once all the children had the worms I quickly gave the directions, both to save time and in response to the children's inability to listen. They were too busy playing with the worms.

The lesson had begun. Noisily, the children attempted the experiment. Their noise made me nervous. I knew the class next door was having a quiet circle lesson. I flicked the lights on and off and requested that the children keep the noise down. They responded with a moment of silence and then resumed their noisy speculation and playfulness with the worms. The experiment proved difficult and the directions forgotten. It seemed that all at once the children were all crying for my personal attention. I began helping one group when Sandy from across the room let out a screech of horror. It seemed that Jeremy had become bored with the lesson and began burning the worms on a light bulb.

"Jeremy, what do you think you are doing?" I cried.

At that moment, Becky and Elizabeth had spilled all their soil on the rug, and Danny was demonstrating to the class how to make mud pies from the soil and water. At this point I screamed, "Danny go outside and dump that mud! Elizabeth and Becky clean up the floor! Everyone else you've got one minute to clean up your experiment and return to your seats!"

I had completely lost my temper and control. The children knew I meant business, as did every other teacher and student in the five-classroom open area, library, and computer room. Quickly, they returned to their seats. Still angry, I exclaimed, "Line up!"

I began to sweep up the muddy mess and clean the classroom as the children stared at me in dismay. The instrumental group had returned to a chaotic environment and were busy questioning, "What happened?"

"I do not want to hear another word!" I shouted.

I continued sweeping with a vengeance and muttered, "This f- - - - - - lesson." The bell rang, and the children filed out. I cleaned, packed my books, and was off. I could not take another minute of this classroom life. During the ride home I relived the situation a hundred times. I had gone too far this time. I mustn't raise my voice anymore. My expectations for these 10-year-olds were too high. I had to control this temper. Guilty and saddened by the disastrous ending to the week, I relaxed and related the story to friends.

As early as 8 the next morning, the principal tracked me down to a friend's home in another state. "Oh no," I thought.

He confronted me with the situation at hand and asked for an account. He had received a note from a parent telling of my disastrous Friday afternoon. It seems she had been the Boy Scout carpool driver, and my profanity had been the topic of the drive.

Glorified and exaggerated, my total disaster had become a catastrophe in the eyes of parents and students. My hushed remark had become a boisterous comment directed toward innocent children. At once, I was devastated. All the time, effort, money, and heart I had invested in teaching may have been wasted. I had failed and lost the respect of parents, students, and the principal.

Cautiously, Mr. McCormick warned me several times at the beginning of the year that Cider Mill's parents were *very interested* in their children's education and that I should promote a positive attitude at all times. He guarded my behavior and reputation and placed me next door to Marlene and Claire. He took a risk hiring a first-year teacher, something many systems will not even consider. However, throughout the year, persistent questions, warnings, and advice convinced me that he was still nervous about this decision.

I tried to recount the story to him. The whole scene was a blur to my mind. My anger had been so great that the details were fuzzy. I wondered if I had screamed out the "f" word in front of the class. I did my best to convey the situation, and we ended the conversation with a scheduled appointment for the first thing Monday morning. I hung up the phone tearfully, asking myself what I had done.

From the phone call early Saturday morning until Monday morning I recounted the event continuously. On Monday morning, I felt like I had a clear vision of the entire situation. I arrived at school at 7 AM and began typing up the story for both my records and the principal's information. Mr. McCormick arrived a few minutes later. We spoke, and Paul was encouraging. Obviously he had run the scene through his mind a few times too. We decided that he would interrogate the children involved during the morning and that I would apologize to the class first thing.

I had consulted my father over the weekend as to how to deal with this situation. My father had come to my rescue in sticky situations many times during my life. He suggested that I use the event as reason for a lesson about losing your temper and telling the truth. In this way, the children would see the error as a human mistake from which one can learn.

Upon arrival, I could tell that last Friday's catastrophe was still fresh in the students' minds. There was lots of hushed commentary and quizzical stares coming my way. I tried to overhear as much as possible and found that the children knew a mother had called the school and that the principal was involved. As soon as the first bell rang, I called the children to the front corner of the room (the corner farthest away from any other classroom). I asked them to sit close to me as I had a very important message to share. Once I had the children's attention, I began my rehearsed speech:

"As you know I lost my temper last Friday," I quietly admitted.

"We know!," responded the children enthusiastically.

"Since becoming a teacher I've learned that I have quite a temper and that I'm going to have to learn to control it. Last Friday, in anger, I said something I shouldn't have said."

"What did she say?," a child asked loudly.

"Shhhhh," remarked another child, protecting my integrity.

Soon, however, a whispered message was sent through the group mimicking what I had said. The message was accompanied by surprised and astonished expression.

"I want to apologize to all of you as I said something that was inappropriate, and I will never say it again. I think we can all learn from my mistake that we should be very careful when we get angry about the things we do and say. Does anyone else in the group ever lose their temper and get angry?" I asked. Most of the children were satisfied. I had apologized, and they had accepted with smiling nods and gestures. Only Eric, the boy whose mom had related the story to the principal, and a couple of his friends were still preoccupied with the incident. The other children began relating stories of angry experiences and lost tempers. The Friday disaster became a point of communion for the class.

The incident itself was not easily forgotten, as I still had to contend with Paul McCormick, parents, fellow teachers, and my own feelings. I spent the next two weeks walking through the school with my head down, avoiding the stares of fellow teachers who knew something was wrong, but had not been told of the exact incident. I ate my lunch in the classroom rather than the teacher's lounge. I had several meetings with Paul McCormick, who continued to support me cautiously and boost my spirit and confidence.

Not more than two weeks following the worm experiment, my $56 book-order money was missing from my desk. I had been warned to lock my desk from day one at Cider Mill, yet I had never located a key, and, hence, never locked it up. I was afraid to tell Mr. McCormick about the incident, but I knew that honesty pays in most situations and that he would eventually find out anyway. There had been a great deal of stealing in my classroom. Almost every day snacks, lunches, milk money, erasers, and favorite pens were missing from children's desks. Therefore, after numerous searches through my desk, I assumed the money had been stolen. I consulted with Marlene, who instructed me never to accuse a child of stealing unless there is concrete proof. Hence, I did not accuse anyone, but Mr. McCormick and I spoke to the class as a group about stealing in general, and, in this particular case, the missing $56. We encouraged "the stealer" to own up to it and guaranteed that there would be no punishment—only help. We reminded the students that the money still could have been lost and that there might not be a thief in the classroom.

Mr. McCormick stood by me in this incident with some reluctance. I could tell he was beginning to question his hiring me.

I pushed forward with the encouragement of family, friends, and colleagues and the inner notion that my investment in this endeavor was very great. I was not going to quit because of a few mistakes and unfortunate incidents. Hence, I obtained a key from Mr. McCormick for both my desk and file cabinet to lock up any money and other valuables left in my desk. The $56 was replaced with money from a school "slush" fund used for miscellaneous situations. Harried, I left the school that afternoon only to lose the desk key! Now my desk was locked, with the new $56 check in it, and I had no way to get it. I knew if I told Mr. McCormick now that I had lost the key, all would be lost for me.

This time I would ask Charlie, the school custodian, to help me out. I humbly related the tale of the stolen money to Charlie and asked him to open the desk drawer. He warned me that I should tell Mr. McCormick, and that he would have to break the desk drawer open. I kindly begged Charlie to open the desk, and he begrudgingly consented. I asked Charlie to keep the lost key a secret, and he reluctantly agreed again. Thank goodness for Charlie.

The disastrous worm experiment, stolen money, and lost key events affected me for a long time. One month following the incidents, Eric began to use the incident over and again to relate his anger and frustration to me. Numerous parent conferences with Eric's mother, and teacher consultations with the school psychologist, and special education teachers led me to conclude that my teaching patterns had been too strenuous and distant for this child who needed one-on-one attention, simple written and oral directions, praise, and encouragement. I applied this conclusion to the entire class and modified my expectations. I made more room in my schedule for the day-to-day "sensitivity" issues, such as listening to the many stories children want to tell, watching their moods and attitudes more closely, and taking the time to enjoy their youth rather than be frustrated by it.

The Christmas holiday was approaching. Holiday concerts, gift-giving, parent conferences, and report cards filled the calendar. The spirit of the season quelled my anxiety as did the positive attitude of my students' parents during conferences. The parents expressed pleasure overall with my classroom manner. Their compliments and stories encouraged me. Mr. McCormick completed my first ten-page written performance review. His tone was very positive and his minor criticisms helpful.

Cold and snowy January came, and marked a new beginning for me. I returned after a well-needed two-week holiday break. I had slept a lot and thought a lot about the months of teaching to come. I knew my students now and had a good sense of the fourth-grade mentality. Energized, we began the new year with a spirit of growth.

Cider Mill's fourth-grade social studies curriculum excited me. Essentially it provided children with a world view. Throughout the year, children compared and contrasted lifestyles of children the world over. To get a feel for these comparisons, we planned an international luncheon. The class was divided into committees including planning, shopping, cooking, serving, and cleaning. We had "brown-bag" lunch meetings to discuss the foods we would prepare; we shopped at a local grocery store after school; and, the day before, the luncheon children cooked in school and in their own homes. Parents had volunteered time and money to make this luncheon a success. Their contribution was a sign of support and confidence in me as well. Our classroom was transformed to a festive restaurant with bright balloons, tablecloths, paper plates, and plastic utensils. We invited Mr. McCormick, the special needs teachers, and the parents who had contributed. Together, on a Tuesday afternoon late in January, we delighted in foods from Mexico, Thailand, India, Ireland, China, different African nations, and the United States.

The international luncheon was the first of many exciting and innovative group projects. Others included a robot unit for which we visited local museums, wrote letters to robot manufacturers and inventors, read books, watched video tapes, created illustrations, and eventually wrote our own *Robot Report*. We learned about economics by creating a small marketplace in the school cafeteria. With play money we bought and sold homemade cookies, cakes, computer game time, raffle tickets, and ice cream cones. I read the children *21 Balloons*, and we invented our own balloons with colored pencils and paper and hung them from the ceiling. We performed in plays, created ad*verb*tisements to learn about verbs, wrote stories daily, and played math games. Having learned about the "human factor" and teaching, I was able to mold my lessons to my class's abilities and aspirations. My lesson-planning was beginning to succeed and the fruits of this planning were evident.

I wanted to share every success and failure with my fellow teachers. However, my fellow teachers who had been at Cider Mill for approximately 15 years each, were not invested in the day-to-day successes and failures of a first-year teacher. This was difficult for me to remember, and many times I felt very alone at school.

Teachers were often complaining about salary, and more often complaining about the latest administrative decree. One incident in particular stands out in my mind. Pamela Rosen, the librarian, and Paul McCormick disagreed about Pamela's request for emergency personal time. Pamela did not receive permission to visit her mother who was in the hospital. The specifics of the situation are unclear to me, however, the reaction was not.

Pamela's "disobedience" cost her her job. Upon returning to Cider Mill, she found out that she had been fired! The teachers were up in arms and were calculating the outrageous amount of sick time they had accrued. Marlene, math team leader, computer teacher, next door neighbor, master teacher, *and* building teacher's association representative suggested that I not get involved, because I was a nontenured teacher. I gladly took her advice—I had had enough of my own conflict in this first year of teaching. The teachers met with the union representative to discuss the situation. They drafted a letter in support of Pamela and waited for a response. In the meantime, Pamela and her lawyer worked together to combat the dismissal and eventually won Pamela's job back, with a three-day unpaid penalty.

Pamela's conflict and dismissal provoked strong negativism and distrust in the building. Teachers were angry at the administration's authoritarian role. Paul McCormick was frustrated; the teachers conflicted.

As a first-year teacher, I could sense an administration-versus-teacher conflict. It seemed at teacher meetings, in administrative conferences, and during my own difficult periods as if teachers were students who needed to be reprimanded and praised. Unlike other professionals, many of the decisions regarding teachers are left to the administration rather than the teachers themselves.

On a lighter note, teaching provided an endless source of humor and rich memories. Love blossomed in my classroom. Kennedy and Heather fell in love. One afternoon just before dismissal, I was sitting at my desk writing a note to a parent. Out of the corner of my eye I thought I had seen them kissing. I said to myself that I was mistaken, and let it go.

The next day I saw it again. Heather and Kennedy were kissing in the corner of the classroom. It wasn't any peck on the cheek. It was a real lip-to-lip kiss. I ignored it. Jokingly, I entered the teachers' room the next day and relayed the story to my colleagues. Their mouths fell open, and the looks on their faces were serious and concerned.

"That is too young for that kind of behavior," said one teacher seriously.

"If you're not careful," cried another teacher, "you're going to have your whole class kissing."

My mood changed, and I could see that I had misjudged the situation. I spoke to Kennedy and Heather after school and told them that kissing was not allowed in the school or playground. Although angry, they both agreed to show their affection for each other in shared snacks and games during recess.

Another day, engrossed in the subject of nouns, I stood in front of the class introducing the lesson.

"What is a noun?" I inquired.

"A person, place, or thing," Janet quickly responded.

"Name one word that is a noun?" I asked.

"A monkey," chuckled Gary who began scratching his underarms with his fingers.

Suddenly the children's eyes were staring at my feet. Sandy began shaking her hand wildly in the air. Still enraptured with the lesson, I was somewhat unaware of their diverted attention.

"Sandy, do you have something to add to the lesson?" I asked innocently.

"Ms. Shea, why are you wearing two different shoes?" she asked, giggling. The whole class began to laugh as I looked down at my feet and found that I had a black shoe on my right foot and a blue shoe on my left.

Embarrassed, I thanked Sandy for informing me of my "color blindness" and began to laugh myself. As a teacher I was always the subject of my students' careful study.

My first year of teaching was busy and tiring. Only now, during summer break, do I realize the number of hours during the schoolday, nights, and weekends that I spent wondering and worrying about the planning for those mischievous and playful fourth-graders. The end of the year was like the end of any childhood fairy tale or fantasy.

By June I had successfully completed visible projects such as *The Robot Report*, a class poetry book, and a fun-filled trip to the science museum's new planetarium. Parents were very supportive and complimentary. My second and third performance reviews were excellent. Mr. McCormick took it for granted that my contract would be renewed in late March. He notified me of the news at my third performance review meeting.

The children were beginning to reveal true progress and develop social skills. Steven had many friends now and was never alone on the playground; Eric's mom wrote me a wonderfully supportive note at the end of the year, thanking me for the time and effort I had given to Eric; and Mary, a troubled but capable student, had produced a fantastic project, overcoming a lack of confidence and discipline.

To my surprise, the $56 thought to be stolen from my desk had never been stolen at all. The money had dropped between the drawers in my desk. I discovered the manila envelope when searching for a misplaced lesson plan. I was feeling very positive about my experience as a teacher and had recently received approval for a summer study grant to create a hands-on natural science unit for fourth-graders.

The tumultuous start had become a sensational finish. Early in the year, Mr. McCormick and Dr. Snider, the superintendent of schools, had nominated me for a first-year teacher award. In the final month of school I received notice that I had been chosen as an "outstanding first-year teacher." What a boost! All the hard work as a special needs volunteer, working as a secretary to earn my way to graduate school, graduate school itself, and numerous part-time jobs as waitress, bookkeeper, and preschool teacher to pay for my degree had paid off. I was overjoyed and humbled by the award. I felt I had deserved it, as it is hard for an educated person today to choose teaching as a career. The money and prestige are not equal to that of a doctor, lawyer, architect, or businessperson. I also realized that this was only the first step of many to becoming an excellent teacher. I was only at the beginning.

I wanted the beginning of the school year to welcome the children with open arms. In the same way, I wanted the children to leave on the last day of school with a positive feeling of achievement and pride. I laboriously planned the final day so that there would be a mix of activity and a special time to exchange feelings about the past year. The day began with a schoolwide assembly regarding safety. We then returned to class and read a special fairy tale. Reading to the children had been my favorite activity of the year. The students were entranced by the beautiful stories and would beg me to read to them daily. This was no problem; I enjoyed the stories as much as they did and enjoyed losing myself in *King Arthur and the Knights of the Round*

Table, The Secret Garden, and *Aesop's Fables.* Next, I introduced the children to a bubble-making lesson. With strings and straws we blew giant bubbles about the schoolyard and watched them radiate rainbow colors as they floated through the air. After the bubbles it was time for our pizza and ice cream picnic. At this time I announced to the children that I would be getting married soon and quelled their year-long probing of my love life. They applauded my announcement and buried me with questions about my loved one, our wedding plans, our future plans for children, and so on. The day was closing quickly, and I was beginning to lose eye contact with those I would miss the most. Kennedy avoided me the entire afternoon, as did Carl and Diane. Heather and Penny hugged me all the way around the schoolyard, and Shelly photographed the entire class in a multitude of crazy last-day-of-school poses.

With a half-hour to go, we gathered in a circle in the classroom. I told them that I had tried to do my best for them this year and that I thought they were a fabulous class. I admitted that I had made some mistakes and that this was normal for any human being. We then exchanged our memories of the best moments in fourth grade:

"The planetarium," exclaimed Robert jubilantly.

"I liked the planetarium too!" Kelly shyly replied.

"You . . . you . . . uh . . . let us get away with a lot," laughed Kennedy.

"I like Kennedy," Heather said confidently.

Other responses included the international lunch, new friends, reading stories, and making bubbles. I liked Ned's response the best. He said, "Ms. Shea your teaching was like a design. Like today we had a story and then made bubbles. It wasn't always paper and pencil."

I felt satisfied—that was just the teaching plan I'd intended for the year.

"My favorite part of the year was your final reading projects," I added. "Those projects were the most creative and thoughtful work you produced all year. From viewing your plays, poems, puppets, and drawings I could tell how much you have learned this year. You are certainly ready for fifth grade."

I gave each student an individualized book cover to remember me by and a package including their report card, miscellaneous photos I had taken of them during the year, a reading list, and next year's school schedule. The children excitedly compared report cards and book covers. The room was a mass of emotion, and I stood there in the midst of it and watched. My role for this year had ended as far as the children were concerned. Tomorrow I would return to Cider Mill without the students and pull the loose ends, including student records and next year's supply list, together. The bell roared, and the children ran from the room stopping for quick hugs and handshakes.

"Have a great summer, Ms. Shea." one exclaimed.

"I'll write," said another.

"See you next year!" A bit confused by all the commotion and emotion, I wandered to the front of the building to join the other teachers. The year had come to a close.

EPILOGUE

Amy Shea continues to teach fourth grade at Cider Mill Elementary School. She looks forward to a life-long career as an educator and continues to seek better and more meaningful ways to educate elementary school children.

QUESTIONS TO DISCUSS

4.1 Teaching in an open classroom like Shea's has advantages and disadvantages for both teachers and students.

(a) What are some of the strengths of an open classroom setting?

(b) What drawbacks do you see?

(c) What types of suggestive or "symbolic" messages are being given to students by having them learn in an unstructured open space?

(d) Does the open structure of the Cider Mill help or hinder Shea's experience as a beginning teacher?

4.2 Shea's expectations of what it will be like to teach, and the reality of actual classroom teaching, turn out to be quite different from each other.

(a) In what specific ways does "real" class life differ from some of her expectations on teaching?

(b) What discoveries does she make about herself? Her students?

(c) How might Shea's student-teaching experience have been designed to prepare her better for her first teaching position?

4.3 Shea quickly learns that domestic problems, such as divorce, separation, and family financial pressures, can spill out of her students' homes into the classroom as children misbehave.

(a) Is it possible for a teacher to empathize with emotional problems a student may have, and, at the same time, make it clear to the class that behavior that prevents students from learning will not be tolerated?

(b) How does a teacher perform this balancing act of caring for students and being understanding, yet setting firm guidelines of appropriate classroom behavior?

4.4 After the school librarian is fired by the principal for disobedience, Shea notes, "Unlike other professions, many of the decisions regarding teachers are left to the administration rather than to the teachers themselves."

(a) Why wouldn't an administration wish to consult with teachers themselves and use their experience and expertise in helping to identify and address school problems?

(b) What advantages are there in having teachers in a particular school help make important decisions regarding school policy?

(c) How important is a principal's role in the life of a school? Why?

Chapter
5

Different Worlds

Anne Edelen

1

I heard about the "taxi lady" from a teacher who had been at the school a few years. Hired to teach art, she had gone through orientation week with the anxious confusion of all new teachers. But over the weekend she brooded too long about the prospect of being alone with a roomful of teenagers, and when the first day of classes came she never appeared. Instead she sent a taxi, carrying a cardboard box containing her teacher's editions, grade book, and school calendar. The cabbie carried the box into the school office, and handed the secretary a note the lady had also given him. "I'm sorry," it read, "but I just can't do it."

I know how she felt. The first day of teaching brings the sweaty panic of inexperience, the pounding insistence of the question: "What am I doing here?" You watch helplessly as students—laughing, shouting, whispering, staring—come through your door. They sit, and you are left facing them.

My first class is U.S. History. The students, remedial-level tenth-graders, know that history is a book of random facts, too heavy and boring to be worth carrying home. I want to chip away at their definition, so I start by asking them each to write what they think a historian looks like. They giggle nervously, look at me to see if I'm really serious, and look down at their papers. I wait, and they begin to write. "A historian is somebody really old, looks like their [sic] about to die." "A historian is real upper-class. He smokes a pipe, and has white hair." "A historian is like a mummy that they have in the museum." I read these out loud, and the students seem to enjoy hearing them. Next I tell them, "I'm an historian, and you all will be too by the end of the year." They look confused.

I ask them to write down what they would like to learn in U.S. History. One girl wants to know about "human kind." Another lists "slavery, nuclear power, cultures, and well-known court cases (ex: Charles Mansion [sic])." One girl has written in letters of increasing size "our relationship with Russia, the making of computers, the making of refrigerators."

I never thought I would teach in a Catholic school. I became a teacher because of my concern about our public schools, and had intended to teach in one of them. But after a bad experience student teaching, I worried that I'd never survive a full year. I heard that the urban Catholic schools were succeeding where the public schools were not, and so decided to apply to some of them. In a few days I heard from Sister Louise, dean of students at Pope Pius High School.

Sister Louise conducted my interview, with Sister Barbara, Sister Francis, and a large picture of Jesus overseeing the proceedings. I was relieved that the nuns wore street clothes, and that I didn't have to use the answer I had prepared on my feelings about the Catholic Church. I liked the questions they asked me, particularly the one about my thoughts on how a school administration can best support its teachers. After the interview, Louise gave me a tour of the building, which had none of the graffiti and/or signs of vandalism that scarred other city schools I had visited. Pius has 400 students, Louise told me, most of them from single-parent homes, and many from the local housing projects. Scholarships and jobs at fast food restaurants make it possible for even the poorest students to pay the $1000 tuition. By the time I left for home, I'd become hopeful that at Pope Pius I could teach the students who most concerned me and not be destroyed in the process.

My second day doesn't go as well as the first. Drug Education, after a fairly lively start, is flat already. Every day for the past week I've phoned Sarah, the teacher who designed this course and whose job I filled, but I still can't figure out the file drawer of manila folders that form the curriculum. I don't know anything about drugs, don't understand the desire to take them, and can't keep the difference between smack and crack and bennies and dexies straight. I give the students a multiple-choice drug quiz that Sarah guaranteed as a surefire way to start the course. "They love doing this questionnaire," she tells me. "I usually end up spending two or three days on it." My students finish in 20 minutes, and start checking their watches to see how much time they have left in the period.

All the students at the school are girls, which appeals to me. I, too, had attended an all-girls' school, but had spent the nine years since my high school graduation in male universities and male professions. In the boardroom of the *Yale Daily News* you can find among the framed photographs of tuxedoed men the picture of the 1981 Editorial Board with me, sitting stiffly in my black skirt and white blouse, in the center. By the time my photo had appeared in *Newsweek* and *People*, I had tired of the question, "How do you feel about being the first woman editor of the *Yale News*?" In the photographs of the 1982 Rhodes Scholars I sit in front with the 14 other women, our ankles together and hands held primly in our laps as instructed by the photographer.

We are dwarfed by the four rows of men behind us, smiling in front of the stone walls of Rhodes House. I liked the idea of returning to an all girls' school, and the break it would give me from being the representative of my gender.

After Drug Ed comes study hall, which I proctor each day in addition to the five classes I teach. The study hall has 26 girls, none of whom I have in class. I don't know any of their names, so I'm forced into a general shout of "Girls! It's much too loud in here. Please stop talking." My pulse rate rises and falls with the noise level, as each confrontation makes me more tense and more frustrated. I try another strategy—walking over to whichever group is the loudest. This silences the girls I've approached, but two new clusters erupt for every one that I quiet down. I feel totally destroyed at the end of fifth period, and still have two more classes to teach.

One of these is U.S. History, and my tenth-graders, after their initial willingness to guess at the looks of historians, are testing. Right before class begins, I notice that a student has turned her chair so that it faces the back of the room. I look on my seating plan to find out her name, walk back to where she's sitting, and say nicely, "Monique, could you please turn your seat around to face the front of the classroom?" She looks up, turns her chair to face the side of the room, and sits back down. I decide not to push it, and return to the front to start class. It is already five minutes into the period, and I'm worried we may not be able to finish the lesson that I'd spent an entire afternoon preparing. Another student, noticing a friend walk by one of the windows, runs over to shout a greeting. I already know this girl. Yesterday, in answer to my "What would you like to learn?," she wrote "I don't want to learn nothing in history. I hate this class. I'm no good at it I flunked it last year and I'm going to flunk it this year." I'd learned her name then: Debbie. Barely scraping five feet tall, she has the freckles and fair skin common among our Irish-American students. She wears her blonde hair cropped close, which makes her large red earrings even more prominent. I walk quickly to the back of the room and close the window. "Debbie! Get in your seat!" I'm surprised at my ferocity. She looks at me as if I'm being wildly unreasonable, then smiles and returns to her desk.

Later in the day I mention the incident to a teacher who has Debbie in her homeroom. "Debbie? Wonderful kid, wonderful kid. Did you know she's the sophomore class president?" Five minutes before class was over Debbie had gone right back to the window and started shouting again.

I live about five miles from the school. The stench of urine is so strong at the subway stop where I get off for work that I've learned to breathe through my mouth until I get outside. From there it's a 15 minute walk to Pope Pius. The route goes past stores covered with plywood, and doorways in which empty bottles of cheap liquor have been left by whoever slept there the night before. I next walk under the overpass for the highway that cuts off East End, the neighborhood where I teach, from the rest of the city. Next to the sidewalk the door of a rusted blue Porta-Potty swings crazily in the wind. I usually have to wait here for a break in the traffic. Once under the highway I cross a bridge that lifts me above a web of railroad tracks and an abandoned tip of the harbor, where remnants of rotted piers rise out of the filthy water. I have crossed into East End. Pius sits on the edge of the neighborhood, wedged in between two bars.

The school building is a pleasant place to work, a relief from the ugliness that surrounds us. Drawings and paintings from the art classes brighten the student lounge and front office, and posters for bake sales and basketball games decorate the hallways. I look forward each morning to entering my classroom, with its five-foot-high windows that let in the southern sun, and always notice the care with which the janitor has swept clean the paper scraps and dust of the day before. I've hung a Picasso print above my blackboard, and I'm beginning to feel at home.

My comfort is disturbed by the symbols of Catholicism that adorn the school: a crucifix above my bookshelf, a statue of Jesus in the parking lot, and a glowing white portrait of the Pope after whom the school was named. The painting is not in my room, but hangs in the hall outside in such a way that when my door is open, the Pope stares in. It seems strange that in a school for girls, run by women, the only portraits are of two men: the Pope and Jesus. I'm sure these symbols give strength to the people who erected them, but for me they're reminders that I work in a school run by a church whose assumptions disturb me.

While I shy away from the paintings and crucifixes, I'm drawn to another side of this parochial school: the care that is given to each student. One teacher spends her lunch period phoning recent graduates in search of an old uniform for a student who can't afford one. Sister Barbara, the principal, makes call after call trying to find a home for a girl whose mentally unstable mother refuses to let the child in the house. I'm amazed by the contrast with the public school where I student taught. There, I was the first to notice that the reason two students were flunking history was that they didn't understand English. That was in March; the two had been at the school since they arrived from the Philippines the previous September.

I've been trying to give my ninth-grade World History classes an understanding of how people wrote the history they'll be studying. I bring in some "artifacts," and have each group write a short history based on one of them. They have fun doing this, since all of the objects tell them something about me—a bulb from my garden, a photo of me and some friends. They identify the latter as "a group of historians." For homework I ask them to bring in an artifact of their own, and a paragraph explaining what the object tells about its owner. I want them to see how historians can learn about people by studying their possessions.

The artifact exercise turns out to be closer to Show and Tell than I would like, but through it I learn about my students. They are younger than I had thought: "This is my Teddy Bear Pukka. It is my favorite stuffed animal. I am going to save it and give it to my own daughter." Another student brings in a coin and writes. "This is a 1976 silver whole dollar coin, from the United States of America. This centamental [sic] gift is important to me because my mother gave it to me two years ago, for Christmas. What it says about me is that I am capable of saving money. My sister and brother also received one from my mother but one lost it and the other spent it."

The following night I read the personal histories that the students in my Drug Ed class have written. The anonymous histories focus on the role of drugs in the students' lives. I wanted to know the extent of drug use among the girls, and to get them to examine this aspect of their lives. I'm more shocked by the papers than I thought I'd be. One student writes:

> I like getting high. But one time me and my friend smoked a joint with dust in it, but we didn't know until afterward. I though I was gonna actually flippout [sic]! If I'd known dust was in the joint I wouldn't of [sic] smoked it. I did valiums too. They're alright. I have to be in a certain kind of mood to take them though. They relax ya. But one time I took like 4 (I never took more than 5) and I was so bitchy. (excuse my language.) I forgot everything I said. Once me and 3 of my friends took "T." It was alright but it didn't last long enough. Two of my friends were punching themselves because they felt numb. My favorite drug is mesc. I took acid. That's okay, but it's more of a spacy trip. Mesc just makes you laugh and laugh and laugh! I *love* it! I'll probably trip this weekend. I started taking mesc when I was 14 ½ and I started taking acid at 15 because mesc was scarce. But now mesc is back around.

Some are not as flippant:

> My experience with drugs is hard to talk about for me because I took valiums one day, drank a bottle of champagne and had about 9 screwdrivers. I was celebrating St. Patrick's Day. But the only thing is I don't remember how I got to the park, who I seen there. I went with one of my friends but I lost her. Then after the picnic was over I just remember being on Elm Street standing in front of a motorcycle accident.

The first week of school closes with a pep rally to begin the Spirit Drive. Spirit, I find out, means raffle tickets, and each of us has to sell five books of them. The whole school gathers in the gym, and is led through a series of chants and shouts by two teachers my age. I, like the first-year students, am rather appalled at all the screaming and yelling, and stand to the side of the gym with my arms crossed. My reluctance to join in the mania makes me feel old and schoolmarmish. I am relieved when the bell rings and the rally ends.

2

After three weeks I'm starting to feel less overwhelmed, but I still can't get used to the pace. I arrive at school at 7 AM and spend the next hour meeting with students, photocopying, taking care of paperwork, reviewing my day to make sure I have everything I need. Then the onslaught: homeroom, U.S. History, World History, Drug Education, study hall.

Lunch gives me the first break in my day. I can eat in one of two teachers' rooms—smoking or nonsmoking. The smoking room seems designed to encourage you to leave it. Three elements dominate the space: a row of defunct toilet stalls, a giant photocopy machine that is continually thumping through copies of tests and worksheets, and a table with foil ashtrays full of cigarette butts. The teachers gathered around the ashtrays seem to have interesting discussions about politics and education. But the smoke and noise give me a headache, and there's a clubbiness to the group that makes me feel I need an invitation to sit down. I eat my lunch in the nonsmokers' room.

Here there is a sofa and two beat-up armchairs, several small round tables for eating lunch, and, on a shelf behind the refrigerator, a one-foot high statue of Mary next to a case of empty beer bottles. Three other teachers share my lunch period: Helen and Sue, who are also new, and Arlene, who has returned after a three-year absence. The marriage that freed her from the need to work has now ended. Thirty pounds too heavy, Arlene wears her weight as a shield against the students. She fears them, and often reminds us of the wisdom in living in another town. "Sure it's a longer commute, but at least I don't have to worry about any of *them* showing up at my doorstep." Helen, who came to Pius after teaching in a neighborhood of large brick houses on landscaped lots, does not fear the students, but instead views them with contempt. Sue is the only one of the three with whom I can talk, but her friendship with Helen and Arlene makes me uncomfortable. Usually I eat my lunch silently and listen to the conversations.

"I hate this class," Sue says. "If they don't do well on this test I'm going to strangle each one of them." Like me, Sue has never been a high school teacher before this job at Pius. She is grading a pile of vocabulary quizzes as she talks, marking each answer with her red pen in a smooth rhythm: red x, red x, red check, red x. "Forty-nine—great grade, huh?" Red check, red x, red x. "I hate teaching. I suck at it." Helen responds, "Well, you've ended up in one of the worst possible places to teach. The kids here don't want to learn. It was a totally different story at the school where I taught last year." Sue disagrees. "No, it's not the kids," she says. "I like the kids. It's just that I work too hard for what I get paid." Helen won't give up. "I tell you, you'd like teaching a lot better if you weren't at this place."

We are studying Ancient Egypt in World History, and I have been experimenting with ways to make the subject less distant to my ninth-graders. I focus on the lives of the rich and poor, a theme with which they easily connect, and ask them to write two stories, "A Day in the Life of a Servant in Ancient Egypt" and "A Day in the Life of a Pharaoh." Most of the essays come in as I had hoped: The students have built interesting stories from the information we've studied. But my favorite essay is Mona's. Involved in her story, Mona has completely forgotten about Ancient Egypt:

> I started the day by making breakfast for King Tut and his wife. The King said that he wanted to talk with me in private in the study which is down the hall from the master bedroom on the third floor. I went in there and he told me to sit down and he would be with me in a moment since he was finishing proofreading a bill. When he finished he said in a very serious way "You are the best servant I have ever had. That is why I have to tell you something." He stopped for a little bit.

"You have been very good to me these long five years. I've gotten to know you over these five years." He stopped again. He started again. He told me that he was getting a divorce. He said he didn't love his wife anymore. But he asked me something that could very well change my life forever. He said in a soft yet serious voice, "Will you marry me"? He said for me to take my time and tell him tomorrow. He told me he had to fly to Mexico and sign the divorce papers.

I had become engrossed in the story by this point, wondering about little Mona, who never volunteers an answer in class and responds to questions in a whisper. I doubt she's learned a thing about history, but see some success in this first step out of her silence. The story ends with the wife being packed off to her parents' house. "I was sad to see her go but I was also very eager to get her out of our lives forever so that the King can marry me and we'd live Happily Ever After. THE END. BY MONA."

I'm very lonely here. The teachers make an effort to be friendly, and we chat about the weather and World Series while waiting in line at the photocopier or passing in the hall. Even Arlene, with her fear of adolescents, will make nice comments about a dress I'm wearing or a new haircut. But after a month the chat seems hollow. I want to talk about new approaches I'm trying in my classroom and hear about what others are doing. I want to discuss the latest wave of books on American high schools. I want to feel that I'm working *with* the other teachers rather than beside them.

Part of the solitude seems to be the nature of teaching. I can go through an entire day with no more than a few words to anyone older than 17. Before school I'm too busy with students to talk with adults. After school, I have no time, but go home to grade papers and prepare lessons frantically, with the hope of grabbing a free hour or two before I go to bed. I'd thought our faculty socials might provide a chance for some conversation about education, but there such talk seems inappropriate. Most teachers here see different teaching strategies as nothing more than reflections of different styles. You do your thing, I'll do mine; and we don't need to talk about it.

Part of my loneliness comes from being different. Of our faculty of 36, about one-third are nuns. Of the 25 who aren't, only a few besides myself have not grown up and gone to college in this area. Three of the teachers even attended Pope Pius as girls. Out of place here, I don't fit in with the people I know from Yale and Oxford either. Before school started my husband Rick and I attended a mini-reunion of Rhodes Scholars at a Chinese restaurant in Harvard Square. I looked around the table filled with bowls of rice and tea, and ticked off all the current occupations of these people who came to Oxford when I did: Harvard Law, Yale Law, Harvard Architecture, Yale Law, Harvard Med. Pope Pius didn't quite fit on that list. People asked what I was doing but then uncomfortable with my answer, quickly skimmed the conversation past teaching and onto familiar ground. By becoming a high school teacher, I had left this Ivy League world. To the people at this table, my walk over the bridge to East End made me disappear.

We are studying the Boston Massacre and I ask my students to write a newspaper article about the incident from either the British or the American point of view. I want them to see how an historical event can be shaped to serve the needs of the person describing it. I'm excited about the results. Most of the students have picked their omissions carefully, and produced convincing examples of propaganda. Some have even displayed their articles with inch-high headlines and photographs photocopied from their textbook. But I don't know what to do with one of the articles I receive.

The author does not live in East End, but comes from a neighborhood several miles from the school. Maria's dark hair and eyes are those of a romance novel heroine. I'd noticed people, including myself, stare at her, as if trying to understand or memorize the looks of someone so beautiful. Her beauty gives her a self-confidence rare in an adolescent, a presence so strong that I am always surprised when I see her papers: misshapen letters crawling unevenly over the page. She has written a brief account:

> BOSTON: Today Americans are angry about the events of the Boston Massacer [sic]. British soldiers and Americans were standing around when snowballs began to be thrown. Crispus Attux [sic] and some other blacks started throwing rocks at the Americans and soon everybody was fighting. Luckily the British killed Crispus and most of the blacks. What Crispus did makes me mad but mostly blacks back then were OK. Now they're rude and not thankful for what they get.

I ask Maria to come by after school. She arrives, impatient about the time she's losing, and I explain why the Massacre was not the race riot she described. But I'm not able to touch the racism that led to her version of the event. "Blacks just don't know their place," she says. "Things were better when they were slaves." I end the meeting by telling her I will not allow racist comments in my classroom. If she is going to make them I will ask her to leave. Unable to teach her, I've had to resort to discipline. She asks if she can go and I, feeling totally defeated, say yes.

I have been able to break through the wall of polite conversation with two teachers: Carolyn, the head of our three-member department, and Sister Beth, the head of discipline. In her twelfth year at Pius, Carolyn answers my questions about the school routines: "Does anyone care if I don't take communion at mass?" "What's an NEASC meeting?" "How many raffle books am I expected to sell?" I'm thankful that I can go to her with problems—a class that's too rowdy, a student I can't reach—but wish I could hash out new ideas with her. Carolyn is protective of me, perhaps rightly, and so meets my suggestions about field trips and curriculum changes with warnings about potential problems. I appreciate her concern, but wish she could be more enthusiastic.

Beth's room is called the Planning Center. The name is right out of Orwell, but the small room feels friendly and students really do make plans here, plans for how to improve their behavior. On the wall Beth has hung a poster of Harriet Tubman. The poster comes from a play that links Tubman's work on the Underground Railroad with the current Sanctuary movement to protect Central American refugees. Beth sits at a desk underneath the poster and spends her days talking with girls who have been sent to her for being disruptive, violating uniform regulations, or failing to come to class prepared. She gives me the support I need to feel I'm not confronting discipline problems alone.

Study hall can still ruin my day. The solution, of course, would be for me to say, "Who cares?," and let my charges do what they want. But I can't stand the chaos, or the injustice of allowing the chitchatters to prevent the other students from studying. Today Joyce, who lost her sign-out privileges last week when she cut study hall, comes in five minutes late. Still angry, she walks up to my desk and puts her hand on the paper I'm reading. "I want to sign out to go to my locker." I look up. "Joyce, you lost that privilege last week." I assume she's just testing, and will go sit down at her seat. I'm wrong. "What do you mean I can't go to my locker! You can't do that to me!" She has the entire study hall's attention. "I'm going to see Sister Beth! You can't get away with this!" Joyce stomps across the room to the door, turns, pauses, and shouts: "Bitch!" She slams the door behind her. The study hall waits for the show to continue. I try to appear calm, and go back to grading papers. After study hall, I stop by to talk to Beth. Joyce has written down her version of what happened. "I needed to get a book from my locker but Mrs. Edelen wouldn't let me so I said I wanted to go to the planning center. I called her a witch because she wouldn't let me get my book." I recount my version, and Joyce is kicked out of school for the rest of the day—automatic suspension for cursing at a teacher. I feel somewhat vindicated, but still cry on the phone when I tell Rick about what happened.

With half of first term over, it's time to send Warning Slips to girls who are failing. I decide to use the opportunity to let all my students know how they are doing. I have been amazed at comments they make about grades. Those with As ask if they are flunking; others who rarely hand in assignments ask if I think they'll get a B. They make no connection between their own efforts and the grade they receive, but see their mark as determined solely by the teacher. Of course, there is some truth in their view of the arbitrariness of grading. But I don't like the powerlessness it implies. "I don't give you your grade," I tell them, "You do." I give each student a printout that shows their mark and exactly how they earned it: the mark for every homework, quiz, and test. I ask them to write a paragraph about how they feel about the grade.

The comments of the students who aren't doing well interest me the most. A girl with a D− writes: "I never got a good grade in History. It's hard for me to understand. I always study the wrong thing. I really want to pass. My father things [sic] I'm just stupid but I want to prove him wrong. I'm gonna start coming for extra help." Debbie, the "wonderful, wonderful kid," has a D+. In the past month, she has emerged from the sullenness of her first week. To conclude the study of the Boston Massacre I had staged a trial of Matthew Kilroy, one of the British soldiers involved in the shooting. Debbie, with a swirl of the graduation robe I'd lent her for her role as judge, presided over the event. The energy of the class made me glad I was a teacher, and Debbie's excitement was the greatest of all. I'm starting to understand why she's class president. When she's interested in a discussion, her involvement rouses the whole class to participate. "I think I good [sic] do better if I do my homework," she writes about her D+. "But I am happy with this it is the highest I got since I have come here."

3

With the start of November first term ends. I find in my mail drawer a card from "The Pius Spirit" that says "Thanks for a great First Term!" With the card comes a gift, a mug painted in green with the motto "A Woman's Place Is Everywhere." I like the mug, and wonder whether the "Spirit" knows that I still struggle with my decision to work in a traditionally female profession. Usually I feel good about my choice, and think it's a better one than simply plugging into the values and structures of traditionally male professions. But sometimes I feel as if I've taken a big step back to a place from which most women are still trying to fight their way free.

To end the term I give my students printouts showing how they earned their final grade, and ask them for written responses. Wonderful, wonderful Debbie, whose grade is the same D+ she received at midterm, writes, "I ain't doing good in nothing. I don't know how I'm going to improve and I don't care." The switch from her pleasure at last month's D+ to her anger at this month's confuses me. The next day Debbie, to my amazement, gets a 98 on a quiz. I know she'll be excited, so at the volleyball game that afternoon I seek her out in the crowd to let her know how she did. I find her amid a loud group of friends, to whom she announces her result. I go back to my seat, and as I sit down, I realize that she had cheated, and exactly how. I feel betrayed and foolish.

I come home with what I call "spaghetti head"—so spent that I'm sure my brain resembles the overcooked spaghetti that's sold in the cafeteria. When I get like this, I can't stop replaying all the little failures that brought on the condition: The question I didn't answer as well as I could have, the homeroom incident I should have handled differently, Debbie's decision to cheat. When I tell Rick about my day he asks, "Didn't anything good happen?" The answer, of course, is yes. I found a tutor for Annie. Martha's article, the one I helped with last week, appeared in the neighborhood newspaper and she's been showing it to anyone who'll stop and look. But somehow I always focus on what went wrong. In our mail drawers this morning we received a bright yellow paper entitled "Ten Commandments for Dealing with Stress." "When you experience a setback or defeat, reestablish your self-confidence by remembering past accomplishments." I'm not sure why I can't forget the failures. I thought it was because I wanted to do better next time. But maybe I'm just too tired to relax, too tired to fight the temptation to overanalyze my day. "Don't strive to be a perfectionist," the sheet admonishes.

Sue, the tolerable one of the trio who share my lunch period, has become increasingly frazzled. Arriving at school just before the bell, she'll run up to her classroom without even taking time to hang up her coat. Sometimes she'll shout from the stairs to whoever is closest: "Now what is it they're supposed to know about adverbial phrases?" or "Where do you put the period after a quotation?" Her inactive social life, which she blames on teaching at Pius, depresses her. With only three men on the faculty and no time to meet people outside of work, she has little chance of finding a beau. At lunch today Sue is more agitated than usual. Stopping halfway through a candy bar, her lunch, she asks, "You know what I say when I get up every morning? I say, 'I wish I was going to work in an office where I sat at a desk all day.' I see business-women with leather briefcases and Brooks Brothers suits and I say 'I want to look like that. *That's* how I want to look.' "

Helen responds, for once setting aside her usual disdain for students and teachers. "But it's not as nice as you think it is. It's not all peace and quiet. You've got your boss bitching at you all day."

"But here you've got 100 teenagers bitching at you all day," Sue replies.

"Well, if you don't like it, maybe you should think of something else. Work is an important part of your life."

Sue pounces on Helen's answer. "Work is my *whole* life! I'm not married. I don't have kids. I don't even have a boyfriend. Work is my whole life and I can't stand it!" She stuffs the unfinished candy bar in the trashcan, and rushes out of the room.

This month's faculty meeting focuses on student pregnancy. Of the 400 girls at Pius, 7 are due before the end of the year. I still do a double-take whenever I see one of the pregnant girls, her school books held high against her chest to make room for the rounded belly. Some of the other Catholic schools, against Archdiocese policy, encourage pregnant students to leave. Pius encourages them to stay. This policy has given the school its nicknames: Home for Unwed Mothers and Big Belly High. My students swing between anger and laughter when they tell me these names. When I ask if they think pregnant girls should be made to leave, they say no, of course not.

The faculty meets in one of the larger classrooms, where the student desks have been moved into a circle so that all 36 teachers can see one an-other. The talk centers on self-esteem. I had read of the link between teen pregnancy and poor self-image, but had never thought about the specific self-esteem problems of teenage girls. "Our girls get the message very early on that they are second-class citizens," says a guidance counselor. "Most of the attention of the family is focused on the males." Another teacher continues. "Our girls are not the initiators of sexual activity, or of any activity in which a man is involved. They don't even see it as an option that they *would* have, *could* have control over their sexual activity. Their boyfriends make those de-cisions for them."

During the meeting I feel the same sense of camaraderie I experienced during the faculty liturgy held in September. I remember how good it felt then to sing "Amazing Grace" with the other teachers and to say together the Faculty Covenant, a statement of ideals about teaching, which begins, "We stand together."

Around the middle of the term, Louise, the dean of students, visits my class to make a formal observation of my teaching. Some of the other teachers grumble that these observations erode our status as professionals. Don't they trust us? But I've been looking forward to this. I can't get used to the vacuum in which we work. Sometimes I feel as if I could teach that Hitler followed Roosevelt as president, and no one would say anything about it. Last week Sister Barbara, the principal, stopped by to tell me about a conversation she'd had with one of my students. The girl sat next to Sister Barbara at a basketball game, and told her about my class. I made history interesting, the girl said, and I made the students work hard. The praise made me happy, but still I thought it odd that the only evaluations I'd received of my teaching came from teenagers.

We are studying the Constitution during the class Louise attends. My students don't understand what a constitution is, so I have them write their own. I am surprised with how seriously they take the project. Loud debates pop out over whether the drinking age should be 14 or 15, and the different factions pull me into their arguments. "Ms. Edelen, don't you think that kids should be able to work no matter how young they are?" "Ms. Edelen, Kelly says death penalty for rapists and I say no death penalty allowed. What should we write?" I look forward to reading their documents once I get home, and am interested to see that all of them include a version of this group's statement: "Everyone should be treated equal and have equal rights." I am most affected by a rule written by four students who don't do well in school: "We are free people, even the children."

The next day I find Louise's evaluation in my mail drawer and open it right away. I want to read her thoughts on the way I handled class discussion, which I'd asked her to watch in particular. But the report, while complementary, was written for my personnel file instead of for me. "Ms. Edelen used a variety of teaching techniques which included input of subject matter, hand-out materials, a discussion and good practical questioning methods." The evaluation continues like this for a page. I recognize that Louise is trying to be supportive, but can't believe that after only three months I've become a model teacher, as this report implies. I want to improve my teaching, and this evaluation doesn't help me.

The day after Parents' Night, Marianne, one of my ninth-graders, comes into class with a black eye. Last night her mother found out that Marianne had gotten an F in History. I ask Marianne to stay after class, and almost start crying when I'm talking to her. "My mother said all the teachers would ask me about my eye," she says. "They didn't hit me. I slipped and hit my head on the bedpost." During my lunch period, I tell the guidance counselor that I suspect Marianne's been abused. I respect this counselor; she's worked with these kids a lot longer than I have and is committed to helping them. She's concerned, and says she'll talk to Marianne. I also talk to Sister Barbara, whose advice I trust as well. She shakes her head slowly before answering: "Marianne is the third . . . [in her family] . . . who's come through this school, and we had an incident of abuse with her oldest sister. I thought the parents had stopped, but maybe I was wrong."

I have a hard time concentrating the rest of the day. Marianne is a fragile girl, very quiet and pretty, with curly red hair. She spends most of her time daydreaming about her boyfriend, and decorates all her papers with drawings of hearts and hot air balloons on which she has inscribed "Marianne luvs Mark" or "Marianne-n-Mark, now and 4-eva" She signs all her papers with her boyfriend's last name as well as hers. I can't stop thinking about her.

The guidance counselor is waiting for me at the end of the day. She has talked to Marianne, and believes the explanation about the bedpost. To me that seems too easy. We talk about their conversation, and the counselor gives me the reasons for her conclusion. I want to believe Marianne and the guidance counselor, but I struggle with my image of a good teacher. A good teacher does not walk away from possible cases of abuse. "What do we do now?" I ask. "Watch her extremely closely. If there's any sign of abuse, act." I still feel uneasy, but decide to defer to the judgment of the guidance counselor, who I know has helped students who've been abused. I'm not sure what else to do.

Over the next few days, I ask advice of my department head, Carolyn, who teaches a course on child abuse. I talk again to Sister Barbara, who feels we've taken the wisest course. I talk to Rick, my mother, my sister, my friends. But no one can make me certain that we've done the right thing. By the end of the week Marianne's black eye is gone, but I still think about her.

The day before Thanksgiving is Christian Awareness Day, when regular classes are suspended and students and teachers attend workshops about such issues as AIDS and alcoholism. I listen to the keynote speaker, who tells the teachers to remember that our students are still children. I think about her request on the way home. I find it so easy to forget that these girls, who've survived experiences I will never have, are not yet grown.

In December I'm asked to serve on the Rhodes Scholar selection committee for my state. I'm excited about this. It brings me back to my old world for a short visit, and gives me the recognition I don't get as a teacher. The first set of interviews takes place in a high-ceilinged room, equipped with bartenders and maids in black-and-white uniforms. I've been spending so much time with inner city teenagers that I'd forgotten how comfortable I can be at these cocktail parties of the elite. I enjoy the witty conversations with bright people, and the broiled scallops that are passed around on little silver trays. I'm having fun.

The next morning the selection committee interviews candidates one at a time. I am the youngest on the panel, down from Oxford only two years earlier, and once again the only woman. My vacation from this role seems to have done me good. In the past I had always felt pressured to act in ways that would show that women could fit in where they had once been barred. But my perspective has changed, and now being the only woman makes me feel free to be different. Instead of feeling defensive as the sole teacher in this group of professors, real estate brokers, and lawyers, I'm more certain of the importance of teaching than I've been since I began at Pius. I'm surprised and somewhat annoyed that my self-esteem can receive such a boost from being chosen for this panel. But it does, and so I have the confidence to stand by a choice different from those of the other Rhodes Scholars.

The Rhodes candidates enter awkwardly, trying to establish eye contact with each of us as they've been coached, and giving instead the impression that they're lost. We interview several future politicians and then hit a student who wants to be a high school teacher. The head of the committee, a corporate lawyer, jumps all over him. "With all due respect to Ms. Edelen, aren't you shooting too low? As a teacher the number of people you will reach is really very limited." I smile at the comment on the way home, as I think of the 120 students I work with each day. I smile too at the thought that of the two candidates selected by the committee, one was the teacher. Most of the committee members had cast their vote with the idea that he would grow out of this desire to teach. But I hoped he wouldn't.

In U.S. History we have been learning about different Americans who tried to end slavery: Harriet Tubman, Harriet Beecher Stowe, Nat Turner, John Brown. I'd gathered readings from books at home and in the library, since my students' history book dealt with all four people in seven sentences. I rarely assigned readings in this book. Its superficiality reduced history to nonsensical trivia, so I couldn't teach from it with a good conscience. Instead, I developed all my own readings and exercises. I knew this approach helped my students learn better, although I wearied from the constant loss of weekends it required.

To bring the struggles of the abolitionists into the present I ask the girls to explain what they see as the most effective way to change what is wrong. Debbie's mood has improved since the low of her first term D+, and I've had no more cheating incidents. But her answer is much more hopeless than I had expected. "There's nothing you can do about it. There two [sic] many people who are rapists or who abuse there [sic] wives. The only thing you can do is watch out for yourself." I'm surprised at this response, since Debbie does try to change what's wrong. Last year two juniors put mescaline in a ninth-grader's soda. Debbie, also in ninth grade, saw what happened and, rather than maintain the safe silence adopted by the other witnesses, went to Sister Barbara. Without Debbie, the girls would never have been caught.

After class, I ask Debbie if she would like to write an article for the neighborhood newspaper on an upcoming school play. She still can't get above a D in history, and I have been looking for some success to give her. She shrugs and says, "I won't understand what's going on. I won't know what to write." I tell her I'll come to the play the same night she does so that we can try to understand it together.

Rick and I go on Saturday night, and the performance, a medley of dance and song choreographed by Pius's drama teacher, impresses us. I love to see students whom I know only in the classroom perform in another context. I even get a little teary seeing one of the girls from my homeroom stand alone at the mike and sing a perfect "We Shall Overcome." I look around for Debbie, but don't see her and worry that she's decided she's not smart enough to write the review.

On Monday Debbie shows up before school to show me her article.

"How'd you write the story if you didn't come to the play?," I ask.

She smiles: "I was there. I seen you come in with your husband, but then you sat down next to Sister Beth and I wasn't comin' near you then."

"What, did you think she'd send you to the Planning Center?"

Debbie laughs, and I read the article while she waits nervously. She wants to make her mother proud, but can never bring home the A's and B's she needs to do so. Being president of her class and a varsity basketball and softball player isn't good enough. She wants to be smart for her mother. Her review is barely coherent, but luckily short enough to salvage. "An article by me in the *Tribune*—my mother will never believe it," she says.

My relationships with my students discourage me at times. I'll think I've established a good rapport with a girl, but then commit some unintentional offense and find her grumbling about how much she hates me. My students want to categorize me as either friend or foe, and can't let me rest in the gray area in between. Some of the seniors tell me I'm a hard teacher for kids to figure out. "We can't tell whether you're mean or nice." And so I swing from ally to enemy, never sure on Monday if I'll be starting at the same place I left off on Friday.

As Christmas approaches, my students' moodiness seems to mellow. On Christmas Decoration Day my homeroom students cover our door with a large foil Christmas tree that we decorate with flashing lights, tiny candy canes, and small packages, one for each girl in the homeroom. As "Jingle Bells" plays over the PA system, we stand back and admire our door, feeling pleased that people stop in the hall to admire it with us. "This is the *baddest* homeroom in the whole school, Ms. Edelen," says one of my students. I've received a number of Christmas cards as well. I laugh at one from a junior I don't even teach: "I'm glad you came to Pope Pies. [sic] I love your study hall because it's always so quiet. Have a Merry Christmas and a Happy New Year at our school." I save the card from a girl who writes, "You're the best teacher. Be happy forever."

After the students leave, the faculty gathers for a Christmas party. I'm impressed the school works so hard to bring the teachers together, but dread these events and find excuses to stay in my classroom so that I can arrive late. I still feel like a stranger on the edge of a crowd of friends. With no free time except lunch, I haven't gotten to know anyone except Beth in the Planning Center across the hall, Sue from my lunch period, and Carolyn, my department head. Carolyn continues to watch out for me, and Rick and I spent a contented Saturday with her at her beach home. But Carolyn, looking for a new job, can't help me feel more a part of Pope Pius.

At the Christmas party I go over and talk with Sue, who has overcome her earlier frenzy and begun to enjoy her work. Last week she announced at lunch, "You know I was teaching *Death of a Salesman* last week and I noticed that I was really loving it. I surprised myself. I thought 'You know, I really love this.' " As we sip our punch I tell her, "With the exception of you, Carolyn, and Beth, I don't know anyone here any better than I did in September." Sue doesn't seem surprised. "Everyone's afraid to talk to you, Anne. They're afraid you'll think they're stupid." Her comment upsets me. I rarely mention anything about my education, so as not to put off teachers who might be intimidated by it. But maybe I just can't erase that difference.

Midterm exams follow Christmas break. Carolyn has warned me not to take the tests too seriously, since my students won't. Instead I start the week of review with a little talk. I'm pleased with the pitch I've decided on: If you study hard you'll feel good about yourself and if you blow off the exams you'll feel bad about yourself. My students are into it on Tuesday and Wednesday, and some even come during lunch period to get questions answered or to make sure their notes are in order. But by Thursday most of the girls have lost interest. It takes almost ten minutes to get the class started, and a few students indicate total ignorance about what's transpired over the past months. Debbie, depressed by the prospect of bringing another series of low grades home to her mother, has retreated into an attitude of resigned defeat. "I'm going to flunk this test," she announces. "Have some confidence!" I reply. She looks down at her desk and says, "How can you have confidence when you know you're stupid?"

World History is the worst. Christine asks if I'm sure we've studied Ancient Egypt before. On a review map I get Saudi Arabia labeled as the Mediterranean Sea, the Mediterranean labeled as Europe, and Rome floating atop the Atlantic. Their knowledge is totally fragmentary, lacking any pattern that would make it worth having. They remember that Spartan youths went to military camp at age 7, but have no grasp of the issue of the relation between the military and society, which gives this bit of trivia some meaning. I'm not even sure if they all realize that these child soldiers are no longer walking around in Greece. Mona, who may still think pharaohs got divorces by flying to Mexico, raises her hand and says, "The Spartans were just loony weren't they?" I find myself agreeing.

By the end of review week I've begun to doubt the value of what I'm teaching my ninth-graders. Of course there's the old line about the need to understand the roots of our civilization. But that connection between Ancient Rome and the United States, a fairly cerebral one, won't happen if the students have no understanding of American civilization. "Why do we have to study about the Romans?" one student asks. "What do they have to do with us?"

"You can't change the world and make it better unless you understand what's come before you," I reply.

"You can't change the world anyway," she says. "You can't change anybody. People do what they want to do and no one can stop them."

"I don't believe that," I answer. How can you believe that and have any hope?

I make the mistake of giving back the midterm exams at the start of class. Among these is Debbie's D−. Upon seeing the grade, she crumples up her exam and arcs it into the trashcan. When we start the day's lesson she just plays with her earring, daring me to confront her. I walk back to her desk and tell her she has the choice of participating or going to the Planning Center. "I don't want to be here," she says, and leaves. I wonder whether I should have just ignored her and let her stew.

After school Debbie comes by to talk about what happened. I sit on my desk, and she walks up, turns her back to me, and crosses her arms. She's wearing her basketball uniform, blue and gold #17, and I'm surprised at the chubby little legs sticking out from the shorts. They are the legs of a child, not a woman.

"Can you look at me while we talk, Debbie? I'd be much more comfortable that way."

"I don't want to look at you." I don't say anything, and she shifts a little in my direction.

"Mrs. Meyer wouldn't have noticed I wasn't taking notes. You noticed. That was good." I'm surprised at the compliment.

"Thanks for saying that. I'm glad you know I care. But I'm still upset about what happened. I thought you and I didn't have to play those games, Debbie."

She surprises me again by apologizing. "I'm sorry, but this is a bad time for me. Around exams I just go inside myself and don't come out for two weeks." I feel sick that she did so poorly when she wants so badly to do well. My response is weak.

"I'm sorry you didn't get the grade you wanted. I think you may have to accept that this is a difficult course for you. You should be proud that you're doing the best you possibly can."

"You think I should be proud of a D? You think a D is a good grade? I'll never be satisfied with a D. Why'd you give me a D−? You might as well have flunked me."

"You make it sound like I just think up your grade on the ride in to school. You know I calculate those marks based on the work you've done, you know I spend a lot of time on them. I didn't give you an F because you didn't earn one." She pauses before talking.

"You're right. I earned that D, not you. I shouldn't blame you for it. It doesn't matter anyway. I'm not going to be at this school next year. I hate myself. I hate this school. And I'm not going to be here after this year."

Now I pause.

"That would be awful, Debbie. You contribute more to this school and your class than anyone I know."

After Debbie leaves, I start to cry. I'm not sure why, exactly. I assume it's her anger at herself, and the truth of her statements. While I'm crying, Beth comes over from the Planning Center to see how the conversation went. We had talked earlier about Debbie's reaction to her D−. I tell her what Debbie said, and then she tells me about Debbie. "I love that kid more than any other in the school," Beth says. "Her father's in prison for murder, life sentence. She visits him about once a month. She's his only child and the mother's remarried and won't go, so Debbie goes by herself. I'm not sure how she manages to get herself out there. It's at least an hour by car and Debbie doesn't even have a license. But she goes. She never talks about the visits, but sometimes she'll stop by my office in between classes and say, 'I saw my father last night.' "

On Wednesday I wake up feeling like I've been punched in the jaw. By Thursday the pain is so bad I can barely open my mouth. At the doctor's office, I learn I have Temporomandibular Joint Disorder. I've screwed up my jaw by grinding my teeth at night. "Have you been under stress?," the nurse asks. "No, not really," I say. I don't want to admit I'm having a tough time being a teacher. The jaw is not the first sign of stress, only the most upsetting. In September I lost ten pounds because I couldn't eat. In November my hands broke out in a rash, and I laughed at the idea that I might be allergic to chalk. But it was eczema, another stress symptom. The nurse hands me a pamphlet on stress reduction seminars along with the prescription for my jaw.

The first thing they teach you in stress-reduction class is to recognize when you're experiencing "symptoms" so that you can break the cycle before it gets worse. I start watching myself, and see before me a madwoman. I've tried to remain sane while teaching. I jog every day, eat right, sleep seven to eight hours a night, keep up interests outside of school, see friends. But all this comes on top of writing curriculum for three different courses, conscientiously responding to the work of 90 students, and running two extracurricular activities. I thought I'd become incredibly efficient, but really I'd become a maniac. If the drive home takes five minutes longer than allotted, I panic. My schedule has no room for such delays. I'll have to run my three miles five minutes faster. I grade papers while I eat lunch, read mail while I'm photocopying, empty the dishwasher when I'm on the phone. I know I'm in trouble one Friday, when I leave for work in a rush without having time to wash my hair. The same thing had happened on Tuesday.

5

The new semester offers another beginning. The students feel it too. "I'm gonna do really good this term, Ms. Edelen." "Hey Ms. Edelen, see my new notebook?" I've made some adjustments to my approach with U.S. History and Drug Ed, but with World History I'm starting over. For the second semester, the course changes to World Culture and Geography. I'm appalled at my students' lack of knowledge of the world today, and have become convinced that this ignorance limits them far more than their ignorance of Ancient History. I want to do something about it.

For most of my students, the world stops at the edge of East End. They don't know where Iran is or what NATO means or why the South African mineworkers are striking. They can't read the newspaper and understand the events as more than a disconnected series of violence and meetings. With no context other than East End, they're immigrants in their own country. Given this situation, sticking to the curriculum and serving up what's next, the Middle Ages, seems pointless.

My students' parochialism has amazed me since I first came here. They ask what part of the city I live in and when I answer they respond, "East End's better." They write all over their notebooks, in letters as large as those used to declare their romantic affiliations, "East End #1" and "East End Rules." This defensive pride in East End imprisons them inside it. Why go downtown to the main branch of the library? East End has its own library. Why be friends with anyone from outside East End? East End's better. I'm determined to expand the boundary of my students' world. We'll start with India.

I'd forgotten how bad study hall can be. By the end of last term, it had settled down to the point where I was glad I'd been assigned study hall instead of lunch duty. (I'd heard about the day when the power went out, leaving the basement lunchroom totally dark. Two students had decided to scream "Rat!" to see what would happen.) But with a new semester comes a new study hall, filled once more with faces I can't attach to names.

One girl is so practiced in disruption that she makes last semester's students look like amateurs. Patty arrives 20 minutes late for the first study hall of the semester. Rather than come up to my desk to explain her tardiness, she speaks from the back of the room, loudly enough so that I, and everyone else, can hear her. She begins the monologue before I realize what has happened:

> Now Ms. Edelen I understand that you may be a little upset with my tardiness and I think you're absolutely correct, absolutely correct to run these studies as strictly as you do. In fact I've often defended you in the lunchroom to ignorant students who complain that you're too strict, but my tardiness today results from such outstanding motives that I know you won't give me a cut and force me to stay for detention—you see on my way to study I remembered my friend Chrissy who's home today with the flu and so I decided to call her to cheer her up you know how depressing it can be to be home sick don't you Ms. Edelen and what with all the teen suicides today I thought it important to do my part to stop this terrible epidemic and save my generation from destroying itself. So I did stop to make that call Ms. Edelen since I thought what a small sacrifice is being asked of me ten minutes of my study time to help a friend who's feeling low and prevent yet another needless death and I knew Ms. Edelen that with your reputation for compassion and fairness you would support me in this gesture of Christian love and ignore this slight infraction of the rules.

Today I find Patty's strategy less amusing than her opening monologue. Whenever I'm not looking up she lets out a short, loud whistle, a sort of soprano fog horn. I ignore her, and practice my stress breathing. Slow breath in. Slow breath out. Focus on a pleasant image. She keeps up the whistles and I see the students who aren't giggling start to get annoyed, and look at me as if to say, "How come you're not doing anything?" I ask Patty to stop, three times, and when she doesn't I tell her to go to the Planning Center. Outraged, she slams her books together and marches to the door, muttering about injustice. By depriving her of her audience, I'd broken the rules of her game. As she steps into the hall, she turns and shouts her farewell. "Crap! You're full of it!" I take in a deep breath, and by the time I let it out she's gone.

After starting the unit on India with geography, a foreign language to my students, I decide to challenge their ideas by looking at some of the cultural differences between India and East End. I give my students translations of some of the marriage ads from the classified section of a Delhi newspaper and we compare how Indians and Americans find their spouses. I ask each student to write an ad for her ideal husband, and read aloud the results. After going through several descriptions of the stereotypical teen heart throb, I hit an ad that cracks up the whole class. "Attractive 16 year old girl seeks very rich 90 year old man with no living relatives. Men with termonal [sic] illness preferred."

During the class it comes up that I'm married. "You're married?," my students ask. "We didn't know you were married! How come you say your name is Ms. Edelen if you're married?" For them, Ms. means liberal single woman. Everyone uses Mrs. once they have the privilege of doing so. After explaining the history of the term Ms., I tell them that my name now is the same name I had before I got married. "You mean you and your husband had the same last name?," one asks. No, we had different names, and had both decided to keep our names when we got married. "You mean your husband *let* you?" They don't understand that I don't need his permission to keep my name. Arlene continues to fill the lunchtime conversation with her complaints about her students. "Margo has no business being in this school," she says, looking at her apple with such loathing that I assume she's picturing Margo's face on its surface. "Either she's bouncing off the wall on an upper or asleep at the desk on a downer." I hate how Arlene throws around these accusations of drug use. I think she fears the possibility of an attack from a drug-crazed youth, and so assumes that every aspirin is an amphetamine, every running nose the sign of a cocaine addict. "That girl looks terrible," she continues. "She's going to be dead within the year if she doesn't stop popping those pills."

Looking for relief from Arlene and Helen I get up from the lunch table and wander over to the teachers' bulletin board. One flyer advertises a workshop in April, "Classroom Strategies for Confronting Prejudice." A note on the flyer says to ask questions of Beth, so I go up to the Planning Center to find her. We had talked once before about prejudice, when I told her of my incident with Maria and the Boston Massacre. Beth and I had begun to share our ideas about education, and we decide to go to the conference together.

That afternoon I stay after school to preview a movie on cocaine, and Debbie drops by to talk. This pleases me. I wasn't sure whether our conversation about the D− on her midterm exam would drive her away or bring her closer. She's upset about her reading teacher, who told her she'd progressed from a sixth-grade reading level to seventh-grade. "She's telling me I'm at a seventh-grade level like I'm supposed to be proud of it. I'm in the *tenth* grade." I know Debbie is picturing all the little 12-year-olds who are her equals, so I tell her about Olivia, the 30-year-old woman I tutor one evening a week. Olivia reads on the second-grade level. Separating grade level from age seems to make Debbie feel better, and she goes off to basketball practice.

Other students have also begun dropping by. They come in the morning, or after school, or sometimes during my preparation period, their lunch. Often they do nothing more than check in to show me a grade on an English paper or tell me about the result of last night's game. But sometimes the chat serves as prelude to discussing a problem. Denise, one of the handful of black students at the school, comes in early one day to get some advice. I love my talks with Denise. Her stories about her trials with her sisters get both of us laughing so loud that I have to shut the door to keep from disturbing others. But today she's worried about Robin, another black student. "Robin won't talk to any of the white girls, and she does things to make them angry, like flash around her Liz Claiborne bag—you know the ones that cost about $50?—and talk about how much money she has and how she's going to spend it." As she talks, Denise folds and refolds a gum wrapper, smoothing the creases with her fingernail and then unfolding the small square to start over again. "Now I know Robin," she says, "and I know where she lives. It don't cost much money to live in the projects, and Liz Claiborne bags don't cost $50 when you shoplift them. But even if Robin wasn't lying, she shouldn't be bragging in front of other people." Denise thinks Robin is making the other black students look bad, and that they'll be ostracized by the white girls because of it. She wants to talk to Sister Barbara, and after checking that she's talked to Robin about the problem, I encourage her to do so.

India has been going over well. An English teacher tells me that when she introduced a story about Mohandas Gandhi, one of my students shyly raised her hand. "Gandhi is also known as The Mahatma," the girl said. "Well thank you. That's right," said the teacher, and another of my students raised her hand. "Ask us anything about India. Ms. Edelen taught us all about it." To end the unit, I arrange a trip to an Indian restaurant. Sue has agreed to skip lunch with Arlene and Helen to help me manage this troupe of 15-year-olds, so we set off for the subway with her in front and me in back. During the ride, I try pointlessly to count my students, as if by doing so I'll keep from losing one. But just as I've gotten to 12 or 13 the train stops and a new load of people pours in, interrupting my count and forcing me to start over. To my surprise the same number of students get off the subway as got on. The owner of the restaurant, whom I'd warned about the event, greets us nervously. But the girls make me proud and he does not have to leap from his post at the kitchen door to halt a food fight. I'm pleased with the curiosity with which most of the students approach the strange food, but surprised by their awkwardness around me and the other adults. In addition to Sue, I've invited Rick and our friend Keith, who's travelled to India, to the restaurant. I wanted to give my students a chance to talk with some adults other than teachers, but they don't seem to know how. They giggle or look down at their plates whenever Rick or Keith asks them a question. Later, I describe their shyness to another teacher, who doesn't seem surprised. "Our girls don't know how to talk with adults because they never sit down and have dinner with their families," she says. "And I'm sure that all but one or two had never been to a restaurant other than McDonald's before. I'm surprised they talked as much as they did."

A friend from Yale has decided to marry, and he invites us down to New York for the engagement party. I had been to his parents' Central Park penthouse once before. The sculpture garden on the roof deck felt like the one at the Baltimore Museum of Art, and downstairs I counted two Rothkos and a Jackson Pollack. I had noticed over the couch a tapestry that reminded me of Picasso's paintings, and commented on it. "Oh yes, that's one of three tapestries Picasso designed." When we arrive the apartment has already filled with guests in silk dresses and Italian suits. Paul greets me with a hug and, realizing that I don't know many people at the party, tries to make me feel comfortable by introducing me to some of the guests. Before each introduction he whispers something about the person I'm about to meet. This person is a Rockefeller. That person just put in a bid to buy Harcourt Brace Jovanovich. Did I read about it in the papers? Then he makes a notch in the circle for me to enter. "This is Anne Edelen. She was the first woman editor of the *Yale Daily News*." After this happens a few times, I turn to him and say "Paul, that was five years ago. I'm a teacher. Introduce me as a teacher." After a while, Paul's father takes over the introductions. "This is Anne Edelen. She's the next secretary of education."

6

On Friday Nicole, president of the senior class, gave birth to a baby she named Clarissa. Yesterday, Clarissa died. The seniors, many of them crying, talk together in small groups, attempting to make sense of what happened. The death shakes the faculty as well, and even Arlene seems touched. "She'll have other kids, but she'll never get over this one." The entire twelfth grade attends the funeral. I had assumed they would take the rest of the day off, but after lunch I notice that many of the seniors have returned to school. I walk across to the Planning Center to see if Beth has an explanation. "Yeah," she says, "you know almost all of them have come back here. They need to deal with this in a place where they feel safe and loved. And for most of them that place is here. That place is right here."

My relationship with Debbie, which I'd really begun to enjoy, has fallen apart. It happened when Debbie's friend Lisa was expelled. Lisa's outbursts at teachers had brought her to the point where one more serious incident meant expulsion. Meetings with Lisa's mother made clear where the tendency came from. Sister Barbara once had to threaten to call the police to get the woman, screaming abuse in the school hallway, to leave. But the school's expectations of students are firm: We understand the situations many of you come from. We care about you and want to help. But those situations do not excuse you from making your best effort on school work, or from treating students and teachers with respect. I believe in this approach. It seems the only way to break the cycle. Lisa directs her final outburst at me. When Debbie learns her friend had been expelled, she knows whose fault it is: mine.

By the time I figure out what's going on, it's too late. Debbie stops handing in assignments and her grade, brought back to a D+ through several months of steady effort, falls to a D−. Furious that her report card, her offering to her mother, might contain such a mark, Debbie strikes back by refusing to participate in class. The grade sinks to an F. My attempts to talk with Debbie fail since she's convinced I have betrayed her and thus will no longer trust me. I try one last time to salvage the relationship by asking her to write another article for the newspaper. After agreeing to do so, she misses three meetings with me and never writes the story. I'm worried she's going to flunk for the year.

On the morning of our March faculty meeting we receive in our mail drawers a copy of an article from *Time:* "The Baby Bust." The article comes on top of rumors about troubles recruiting a freshwoman class, and teachers whisper about the possibilities. The Archdiocese wants us to increase our tuition, but that would prevent the girls who need us most from attending. The more obvious choice is layoffs, so I try to work out who would be most likely to go. As the new person in a department that teaches mostly ninth- and tenth-graders, I'm high on the list. I wait for the afternoon meeting to see what will happen.

Sister Barbara begins by stating that Pius will not have to raise tuition next year. But she says our ninth-grade class will be lucky to reach 60, 40 fewer than the present senior class. Layoffs it is. Sister Barbara, usually refreshing in her directness, hides behind verbiage. "I think there will definitely have to be a reduction in faculty size. Our faculty-student ratio will just be too high."

The possibility of being laid off takes away my energy. It's hard to give so much when you may be gone in a few months. For the first time, I want the weeks to pass quickly. I count and recount the weeks until April vacation, and always find the total too large. I'm bothered that I feel this way. I want to like teaching, and usually I do. But right now I'm too worn out to care.

Bonnie, the president of a student group I advise, has broken her leg in a biking accident. Bonnie has cheered me on some of my low days this year. On a Friday when I'd decided that study hall duty would end my teaching career, I found a note from her in my bag when I got home: "To Ms. Edelen—Have an Awesome weekend!" My work with Bonnie and Students Against Drunk Driving has been some of my most successful this year. I know we're filling a real need with the Alateen group we started last month, and the performance by a local acting troupe, for which we'd raised the $500, had students thinking for weeks.

The day after her accident, Bonnie hobbles into my classroom and sits down on the edge of a desk. Grimacing, she lifts her leg, enlarged by its white sheathing to twice the size of the other, onto a chair and then slowly rubs her armpits to rid them of the soreness from the crutches. One of the few athletes among our students, Bonnie is crushed by her loss of mobility. I've borrowed Rick's car for the day, and offer her a ride home. "Thanks," she says, brightening at the proposal. "That bus ride was murder this morning."

I have never been farther into East End than Pope Pius, and Bonnie lives in an East End housing project about a mile from the school. She directs me through the blocks of brick buildings and rusted chain link fences and finally tells me to stop at a building as drab as the rest. "That's home!," she says, and laughs. I'm not sure whether the laugh means anger, embarrassment, or acceptance, but feel privileged that Bonnie has shown me where she lives.

In U.S. History we have fought World War I and are about to give women the right to vote. I start our work on the suffrage movement by giving my students the following puzzle:

> A boy falls from a tree and breaks his leg. His father calls the ambulance and they are whisked to the hospital. The boy's leg needs surgery. Upon seeing the patient, the surgeon exclaims, "My boy!" Another, unrelated, doctor must be found to perform the operation. The boy is the surgeon's son, but the surgeon is not the boy's father. Explain.

Only one of my students can see that the surgeon is the boy's mother. For homework, I ask them to write a definition of the word "feminist" without using the dictionary. My students don't understand what this word means. For me its power comes from its history. By saying I am a feminist, I link myself with Susan B. Anthony and her imprisonment for voting, with Margaret Sanger and her work to give poor women access to birth control, with Alice Paul and her three week hunger strike to protest her arrest for picketing outside the White House. But my students don't know that history. They bring in their definitions the following morning and raise their hands hesitantly. "My mother says feminists don't want to have kids or wear a bra." "Feminists are lesbians." "Feminists are liberals." I ask what a liberal is. "You know. They wear backpacks." A girl raises her hand a second time. "But isn't it right that feminists are lesbos?"

The workshop on prejudice that I'm attending with Beth falls on Saturday, April 11, the first day of spring. March 21 had passed like any other winter day, but April 11 is glorious, warm enough to dig last year's sandals out of the bottom of the closet. Rick and I start planning a bike trip, but then I remember. I'm going to be in a classroom from 9 to 4, learning about prejudice.

By the time I drag myself to the workshop, Beth and 15 other teachers are already there. We begin the session by breaking into groups of four and going through an exercise called roadmapping, in which you draw a map of major points in your life. The exercise gives kids a way to share themselves and creates the atmosphere of trust needed to succeed in teaching about prejudice. Beth and I join the same group, and she uses her key ring as her map. She talks about the key to the convent, and her key to Pius, and how she's more and more convinced of the power of good education to change lives. She talks about the key to her moped. I never knew Sister Beth had a moped.

When we break for lunch Beth and I sit on a hill in the sun and eat our sandwiches and apples. I had never talked with a nun before I came to Pope Pius, and had always thought the decision to become one was bizarre. I feel comfortable enough with Beth to ask her about her choice. She talks about it, and I'm surprised to find she didn't become a nun until she was older than I am now. I ask her how she reconciles her political beliefs with those of the church. "I have friends who call me a Cafeteria Catholic, because I pick what I like and ignore the rest," she says. "But I tell them that the Catholic Church has always grown from dissent. *I'm* in the mainstream, not those wimps who don't want to think for themselves!" We laugh, and head back into the workshop.

The final duty before the start of April vacation is Parents' Night. I sit in my classroom beside report cards and printouts as the line of parents, always mothers, comes through the door. I recognize the mother of a student who has come for extra help every Thursday this year, and smile. I value my morning sessions with Wendy, for they give me a chance to know one of those invisible students who never speaks in class. Wendy's grades have improved as well, which has given her some confidence.

The last parent of the evening is Debbie's mother. She has brought Debbie, as well as a younger brother, who bounces around the room shouting, "This is where I have Sunday school, Ma! This is where I have Sunday school!" In her jeans and long blonde hair, the woman doesn't look much older than Debbie. As she introduces herself and her son, I remember the comment I wrote to go along with Debbie's F. Since friendliness hadn't softened Debbie's anger over her friend's expulsion I had decided to try being blunt: "I enjoyed teaching Debbie during the first two terms; she tried hard and always participated in class. During the past term, however, Debbie has stopped trying and stopped doing her assignments. In class, she's been rude and uncooperative, and has had to be sent out of the room on several occasions."

Mrs. Callahan speaks first. "Ms. Edelen, I'm very concerned about this comment. I was up in Debbie's homeroom with Mrs. Nash, who was telling me that Debbie is the nicest student she has ever worked with in all her time at Pius. And then I read *this*. I came right down to see you." Mrs. Nash thinks Debbie is wonderful. Why don't I? I look over at Debbie, to see if I've been wrong. She glares at me, and then returns to playing with her earrings. "I'm sorry I can't be more positive about Debbie's performance this term, because as I said she can be a real pleasure. But in the past few months her attitude has been unacceptable." "Well Debbie has never liked history," Mrs. Callahan replies, "but I know she can pass if she tries. With this kind of attitude she's only hurting herself." I am disarmed by this show of support. I had assumed Mrs. Callahan would come to Debbie's defense. She continues talking for several minutes, a script a teacher would write for a parent: the importance of history, the importance of respecting the teacher, the importance of doing well in school. The longer her mother speaks, the more upset Debbie becomes. I try to end Debbie's misery, and say, "Mrs. Callahan I really appreciate your support. I think the best thing for us to do is just put Term Three behind us." She turns to Debbie: "Is there anything you would like to say?" Debbie is crying now. "Is there a problem between you and Ms. Edelen?" Debbie shakes her head no. She can't talk and keep the tears from turning to sobs. I feel lousy, and say, "It was nice meeting you, Mrs. Callahan." Debbie stands and mutters, "You didn't have to write that I was rude." She walks quickly over to her little brother, picks him up, and leaves. I head for home and a week of vacation, unsure whether I've lost Debbie for good. We still haven't heard about layoffs, and I wonder whether I'll return to find out I have no job here next year.

7

We come back from April break to learn that two of the new teachers have lost their jobs. Sue and I will be rehired, but Helen has been laid off. Despite her contempt for our students, Helen wanted to stay here and is upset about the prospect of applying for jobs elsewhere. The school has worked hard to keep me. Of the five courses I'll teach, two have been snitched from other departments. I owe Beth for one of them. Her Holocaust class drew an extra section for next year and she requested that I be the one to teach it.

Sue asks me to sit and talk with her during her lunch duty, my preparation period. Surprised at the ease with which I walk away from my Things To Be Done List, I go. "I'm gonna turn down the job offer from Pius," she says. "I just can't handle anymore not being able to afford moving out of my parents' house." I'm not surprised by her decision, but upset that she would have to make it. She's worried that she's going to hate her new field, banking. "I had this interview yesterday with First Fidelity Bank. Here's the job: Somebody wants to buy 30 shares of IBM. They call me up and say 'I want to buy 30 shares of IBM.' I type up the form: 30 shares of IBM. The next guy calls: 50 shares of Coca Cola. I type it up: 50 shares of Coca Cola." "It sounds really boring," I say. And what a waste of your talent, I think. "It sounds really boring," she says. A girl comes up and hands Sue a candy bar. It's become a game among the students to see who can buy her lunch. "What do I owe ya?" she asks the girl. "Just take it as a bribe," the girl answers. "Subtle, real subtle," says Sue.

In U.S. History we are studying the effect of World War II on life in America. I've gotten a range of material from the National Archives—recruitment posters, tapes of anti-Hitler propaganda, memos about rationing—and each girl is studying a specific document. I want them to understand the different ways in which the war affected people. They struggle with the project, but seem intrigued. "Where did you get these Ms. Edelen?" "We've never seen stuff like this before." Debbie, working on a poster urging people to buy bonds, says "You know, if my mother came in here and saw us working on these posters, she'd never believe this was a history class." "But this *is* history," another student responds. "I know, I know," says Debbie. "But my mom would never believe it."

The lunchroom scene has deteriorated. Sue got that job at First Fidelity and will start next week, one month before school ends. I can't believe she would leave before she's finished the year. I feel betrayed, as if she never meant what she said about caring about her students. Arlene is afraid of facing next year without her new buddies, and explains her own choice to stay. "I'd leave here in a minute," she says, "but I can't with a 2-year-old at home. With a 9-to-5 job, I wouldn't get home 'til 6, and I'd hardly see him." Helen directs her bitterness over being fired at her students. "I hope none of them ask me to sign their memory book," she says, "because I know what I'm going to write—'I hope I never see you again. My days are going to be wonderful now that I don't have to see you in class.'" Sue and Arlene laugh. "No, I know what I'll do," Helen continues. "I'll just write LOSER in big letters across the page. Loser. Loser. Loser. They're all losers."

Nancy, the student who's helped run my homeroom all year, looks upset when she arrives at school. She usually comes about five minutes early, but today she's here 15 minutes before the bell. "Ms. Edelen, did you hear what the seniors did to Mrs. Blesser yesterday?" Yesterday was the last day for seniors, who finish classes five weeks before the rest of the school. I wonder whether Helen, Mrs. Blesser, wrote "Loser" on their memory books. I usually won't talk with students about other teachers, but today I can't resist. I ask Nancy what happened. "As soon as she shut the door to start class they all pulled out water pistols and started firing them at her!" I know I should act shocked, but it's hard to keep from laughing. "Some of them had those battery-operated kind so they could get her *really* wet." "What did Mrs. Blesser do?" I ask. "She just walked out of the room and didn't come back." The incident upsets Nancy, so we talk about it for a while. Then Nancy moves to another subject. "Did you know Miss Foster was leaving?" Sue must have told her students about her banking job. "Yes, I did. Does that make you sad?" "Yeah," she answers. "Are the teachers going to give her a party?" For what? Bailing out before the year is over? "No, I don't think so," I reply. Nancy goes on. "Miss Foster doesn't want to leave, but she got laid off so she has to find a new job." Laid off? I can't believe Sue has told them that. But then I didn't believe she'd leave before the end of the year.

A few weeks after Sue leaves a teacher whom I've been trying to get to know comes down to the lunchroom to share her budget woes. Now that the seniors have left, she's free this period. "Well, I'm 750 bucks short, but I don't want to work this summer since I'm taking classes for my master's," she says. "It's just too much to work on top of going to school full-time." Helen has a suggestion. "How about fast food?" I think of what it would be like to work side by side with our students all summer. "Yeah," adds Arlene, "Papa Gino's is up to six bucks an hour. Hard to beat that." I try to imagine a doctor or lawyer working at McDonald's to pick up the cash needed to pay the bills. This thought makes me angrier and angrier as the day goes on. Usually I'm content telling myself, "America's values are screwed up, but that doesn't mean those values have to be mine." But today, worn down by the months of long hours, I'm angry. For the first time it's really clicked that with the exception of the nuns and a few of the other teachers, no one I work with views teaching the same way I do. For most it's a job like any other. Judged by the measures of money and power, it *is* the equivalent of fast food.

I'm still upset when Rick gets home from work. We go for a run and I'm shouting: "To teach in America is a totally irrational decision!" I count off the reasons on my fingers: "Long hours. Stress. Loneliness. No prestige. No money. I just read that the median income of this country is $27,000, and I make $10,000 less than that. I make less than I made my first job out of college, and I've gotten two master's degrees since then. It's not noble to teach. It's foolish. It's totally irrational." People are staring at us, but I want them to hear. Rick tries to calm me down. "Your problem is that all along you've assumed that people agree with you, that everyone thinks talented people should go into education instead of corporate law or investment banking. Do you really think that all of a sudden people are going to drop those huge salaries and say 'This is selfish. Sign us up to save the world.'?" I don't answer, so Rick goes on: "I think you're right about the other teachers. They don't understand your decision, and would probably give a lot to have what you've passed up." Rick laughs, trying to get me to see some humor in my situation. "Basically, people *do* think you're crazy."

The Saturday of graduation is so hot that by the time I reach the cathedral my blouse is sticking to my back. Parents and boyfriends sit in the pews fanning themselves with their programs, and teachers gather in the back of the church to help calm the nervous seniors. The girls, draped in their blue and gold robes, rub the sweat from their temples and adjust and readjust their caps. The music begins, and the seniors march slowly up the aisle in pairs. I can see them count silently as they walk, making sure not to move faster than the girl in front of them. Bonnie, off her crutches just in time for the big day, sees me watching by the side, and gives me a hug before starting her march up the aisle.

After graduation, the teachers meet for drinks at a restaurant on the waterfront. Glad to be out of the heat finally, we relax in the cool of the air conditioning and watch as boats move by the window. Waitresses bring drinks decorated with pineapple spears and paper umbrellas while we joke about events of the past year. I'm disappointed that Carolyn's not here— she left for the beach right after graduation—but feel happy sitting in this room with these people. I listen as teachers laugh and retell old stories, and feel the tremendous release from pressure offered by the freedom of the summer.

Proud of completing my first year, I think a bit about my second. I look forward to working with Beth on the Holocaust course, and with another teacher I admire on a program for our first year students. I wonder how Debbie will greet me in September. Refusing to let go of her anger, she stopped doing any work in U.S. History and flunked for the year. When I told her she'd have to go to summer school she replied, "I'm terrible in history. I knew I'd fail." I'm not sure she heard me when I said she could have passed the course. Maybe next year I'll think of a way to help her gain some pride in herself.

The second round of drinks has almost been finished and, suddenly very tired, I begin to gather my belongings to leave. I start saying my goodbyes, and as I stand to go, Beth leans over her piña colada to tell me one last story. "Hey," she says. "Did I ever tell you the one about the Taxi Lady?"

EPILOGUE

During Anne Edelen's second year at Pope Pius, teaching continued to be a challenge. There were, however, many more days that ended with the elation of getting it right, and far fewer that closed with the despair of getting it wrong. She will be teaching at Pope Pius again next year.

QUESTIONS FOR DISCUSSION

5.1 Frequently new teachers find themselves working in a school setting very different from their own background. While some things are familiar, others are new and strange.

  (a) What are some of the differences that Edelen observes between teaching in a public school and teaching in an independent Catholic school?

  (b) Is it appropriate for Edelen to teach in a school having a different world view from her own needs? What are some of the advantages and disadvantages of teaching in a private school?

5.2 As a first-year teacher, Edelen reflects, "I feel very lonely here."

  (a) In what way is "loneliness" or teacher isolation actually built into the profession of teaching?

  (b) Can you think of different ways a school could be set up, or activities structured, so that teachers might experience a stronger sense of community and camaraderie?

5.3 When Edelen attends a mini-reunion with friends (who—like her—are all former Rhodes Scholars, she feels uncomfortable about telling other Ivy Leaguers that she is now teaching at a girls' Catholic school.

  (a) What does this reveal about her attitudes and goals?

  (b) Why is the profession of teaching in the United States not held in as high esteem as law or medicine or architecture?

  (c) In what ways is the value that most Americans place on education at odds with the public view of teaching as a profession?

  (d) What kinds of things do you think that schools and educators must do so that the teaching profession is viewed with greater respect by the American public?

5.4 What additional steps might Edelen have taken with her student Maria to try to alter her racist attitudes toward black people?

  (a) Do you think it is a teacher's responsibility to try to change the attitudes of students who are prejudiced? Why? How?

5.5 Debbie, one of Edelen's students, tells her: "I'm going to flunk this test," and "How can you have confidence when you know you're stupid?"

  (a) How do you think a teacher should respond to a student who has low self-esteem, low personal expectations of academic achievement, and a poor image of herself?

  (b) Should a child's self-esteem be an area of concern for a teacher, or is this issue better left in the hands of parents, guidance counselors, or school psychologists? Why?

5.6 One of Edelen's students tells her, "You can't change the world. You can't change anybody. People do what they want to do and no one can stop them." And another student remarks, "There's nothing you can do about it. There are too many people who are rapists or who abuse their wives. The only thing you can do is watch out for yourself."

(a) How do you think a teacher should respond to students who hold these beliefs about people?

(b) Should one of the functions of schools be to teach students that they can and should change society to make life better for the common good? Or should schools stay away from potentially controversial issues of societal values and concentrate on teaching the "basics" of reading, writing, and arithmetic?

(c) Should a teacher be concerned with moral and ethical issues, issues dealing with the difference between right and wrong behavior? Why?

5.7 Edelen talks of becoming discouraged in her relationships with students. She thinks she has established rapport with a student and then the same student says she hates her.

(a) Is she too sensitive? Is she naïve in thinking she will have real relationships with people she doesn't share background education or neighborhood with?

(b) What are some realistic expectations for new teachers to have about their relationships with their students?

5.8 Near the end of the school year, Edelen, in a burst of anger, writes, "It's not noble to teach. It's foolish. It's totally irrational." Yet, even though she feels resentful and unappreciated, she decides to return to her school the following year.

(a) Why do you think she makes this decision? What is it about teaching that Edelen, obviously, finds personally rewarding and fulfilling, despite the frustrations and disappointments?

Chapter
6

New Kid on the Block

Margaret Lewis

AUGUST: PRESCHOOL MUSINGS

Well. In two weeks I start teaching at my own school with my own classes. I've been surprisingly cavalier about preparing for the coming year. I've read the texts and other teachers' old lesson plans, but how do I prepare for *my* classes, which will of course be unlike any others in the history of education? I must admit that I don't know. I have ideas, but will they work? What will the kids be able to do in 45 minutes? What will they like? What will they scoff at? I feel like a teenager learning to drive in the snow: Until I've done it, no one knows whether I should be trusted with the car. Still, I have to be trusted with the car in order to find out whether I can do it. My sense is that I'll just have to feel my way until I am in control. Then again, maybe I'm just lazy and shirking my duty.

Actually, I think the problem is that I don't believe that in two weeks I'll actually be standing in front of a class and that they'll be listening to me. Won't they know that it's just *me*, and not a *real* teacher? I have the odd feeling that I'll be found out, that they'll know I'm an impostor. The administration will decide after the first day that they've made a terrible mistake and will send me home with two weeks' severance pay. Real teachers are the teachers I had in high school. You don't *become* a teacher, you just *are* one. I'm too young, too silly, too inexperienced, too irreverent to be a real teacher.

But I shouldn't be quite so diffident. Student teaching was a success overall, and I do feel more confident about my ability to run a classroom and explain material than I did before. And for better or worse, it didn't completely cure me of entertaining grand ideas of being the Pied Piper of public high school. With me in the classroom, the students will learn anything with ease and joy. Ha! Some days it does feel a little like that, and it's glorious. Other days, I could be Barnum and Bailey (perhaps I should say Madonna) and I'd still go over like a lead balloon.

Will my students like me? That should not be my primary concern, for I'd be a poor teacher if it were. It's more important that they like my class or my subject. But it's a tangled web; can they like my class without liking me, at least me as teacher? I don't think so; I have never been that kind of student. For me, classes are much more enjoyable if I like and respect the instructor.

In my certification courses, one professor warned about taking students' performance personally, about seeing the teacher-student relationship as one in which they are achieving for the teacher, not for themselves. This admonition struck a chord, because I always have enjoyed pleasing the teacher, and if the truth be told, I look forward to students trying to please me. Although I'd like to pretend that I'm above wanting my students to like me and my class, I'm not. I do see the danger of taking everything in the classroom too personally, for I have already fallen prey to it during student teaching. It's painful and unproductive. I don't want to be one of those teachers who tries to be every student's best friend, nor do I want to be a power wielder, dispensing and withholding favor on the basis of performance. Nor do I think, as I said, that their liking me is nearly as important as their learning and understanding. But it does hurt when they don't do well on a quiz or when they don't do their work, or when they're rude. And why shouldn't I show it, appropriately? Their performance and behavior ought to matter, and to an extent it *is* directly related to me, for teaching is so highly interactive. If it matters, then I know that I care. What's more, they'll know too. Perhaps in five years this will all sound incredibly naïve, but I hope not. It's usually easier not to care, and so people don't, especially in a field like teaching. It's human, but it's wrong.

I love both of my subjects and want my students to, at the least, find points of interest within them. But I don't love academe to the exclusion of all else, and I want them to know that, too. Somewhere along the line I acquired the silly idea that to be a true student, and certainly to be a teacher, one had to love one's subject before all else. Despite my academic success, I don't, and it's made me feel guilty at times, like an impostor. I will expect discipline and application from my students . . . but not utter devotion to Russian or English. Some teachers make students feel as if they're only interested in the kids who like or who are good at the subjects they teach. This is understandable—again, the do-they-like-me self-gratification syndrome. Still, there are more important things in life than studying English and Russian. I know that, and it hits me sometimes even when I'm teaching. I want my students to know that I am as interested in their being good people as good students. I want them to know that "normal" people, not just nerds or brains, can be strong and motivated achievers. I want even the average-ability student to get a kick out of school. Big dreams, eh?

Despite elaborate essays on job applications, I have no philosophy of education. I did like an article I read in my general methods course that discussed the teacher as having many roles: as good example, educator, counselor, police officer, parent, judge, moral yardstick, and so on. A teacher may not want to accept the responsibility of all these roles, but the fact remains that he or she will be expected to fill them for different kids and even parents and colleagues at different times. I'm not looking forward to patrolling the halls asking for passes. Yecch. But it is part of the territory. On the other hand, teachers should also prove to students that it is all right to be human; that one person cannot be all things to all people, and that the students themselves should prepare to accept and play their own wanted and unwanted roles in life.

I am particularly pleased about having landed this particular teaching job. I liked the administrators I met on my first visit. Polite yet informal, they seemed sharp and perceptive. Eleanor Nickle, the foreign language and English department supervisor, is an elegantly fragile older woman with impeccable style, manners, diction, and a formal air. She's rather intimidating at first, yet she eventually put me at ease by slangily and conspiratorially telling me, "Don't worry. There aren't too many really jerky kids here." I think that she likes me, and I'm glad. I am particularly glad to be working for someone that I will find easy to respect.

Bill O'Connell, the principal, has a casual yet tough manner. He's friendly even as he obviously takes your measure. He seems to be a bit of a showman, but he struck me as honest and straightforward. I think I'll like him too.

Everyone I spoke to had mainly positive things to say about Woodfield and the schools. Woodfield is a suburban blue- and white-collar town of about 20,000, with a high school of about 950 students. The parents are very interested in the education system, although it does not have any particular reputation for academic excellence (or weakness). About 60 percent of the students attend college or some other school after graduation; a good number of those are children of parents who have not attended college. The consensus of the teachers and administrators I spoke to seems to be that although there are not that many very bright students at the school, most are pliant and cooperative, and there are few to no major discipline problems. At least this won't be one of those teaching jobs where half my time is spent yelling and kicking kids out. That's a relief. The teacher-as-police-officer role appeals to me very little.

SEPTEMBER: TEACHERS' MEETINGS

The two days before school started consisted of teachers' meetings—discussions of goals for the year, changes in policy, introducing new staff, and so on. For me they were two days of smiling, handshaking, and getting nervouser and nervouser, as Alice might say. Not wanting to be too early since I didn't have anyone to talk to, I managed to be late to the superintendent's first meeting for new teachers, held at the (to me) ungodly hour of 8 AM. I had actually driven on time up the long driveway to the school, a typical 1960s jumble of brick boxes and rectangles. I was so jittery about going in, though, that I sat for a while in the car in the parking lot, watching the other teachers walk in, wondering who they were and whether I was dressed appropriately and whether I really planned to go through with this. When my watch said 7:57, I went in and was greeted warmly at the door by Bill O'Connell, the principal. As jittery as I was, I was painfully grateful that he remembered my name.

Unfortunately, when my watch read 7:59, the school clock read 8:04. As I finally walked in to the spacious, high-ceilinged school library full of books and unfamiliar faces, I thought I sensed surprise that a teacher, especially a new one, would be late. Not disapproval necessarily, but surprise at not adhering to rules. One man in particular seemed to be glaring at me. Uh-oh, I thought, I'm a rebel already and not even for the right reasons. I smiled brightly to cover my embarrassment, and my teaching sojourn at Woodfield High School began.

Those two days were a shock, beginning when I learned that I did not have my own classroom, nor even two classes in the same room. I therefore had to find, count, and lug all my books down the long, brick-lined, polished (not for long!) hallways to classrooms all over the building. Established teachers had done this last June and most paid little attention to me, but one of the more sympathetic found me an elevator key. Seventy-five books here, 30 there. . . . The building is not that large, but it seemed, as all schools must to all new teachers, an endless labyrinth.

That done, I realized I had no supplies. I was directed to a little janitor's closet where they were stored. But what did I need? White or yellow paper? Should I really use red pencils? Too classic. Besides, only real teachers use those, I'm just a new kid. And where would I put them? Would people share with the vagrant teacher or (horrors) would I have to bring my own chalk and paper to each classroom? This had not been discussed in General Ed 101.

And after those momentous decisions, a little something for myself: an unused desk scavenged from a friendly colleague. Unlockable, flimsy, and squeaky, but at last something that could be mine! Unfortunately, I had absolutely nowhere to put it; the hallway seemed somehow inappropriate. Never would I have thought that I would so covet a rectangular room sporting student desks, blackboards, pastel-tinted bathroom tile walls, broken venetian blinds, and gray industrial linoleum. After some consultation with a helpful vice-principal and another friendly teacher, we settled on the corner of a science laboratory, wedged kitty-corner between the last row of lab benches and the walls into a space of about 6 by 3½ feet. Though every time someone, including me, tried to walk past the front of my desk all the books got knocked down (since the clearance between it and the lab benches was about a foot), still the location gave me some rare and valuable privacy, as the science lab was generally unoccupied. At the least, it was impetus to remain thin so I could manage to squeeze in and sit at it. It was a far cry from the spacious office I had had in a previous job, complete with file cabinets, rug, window, shelves, and telephone. My new desk introduced me to the (in)dignity of teaching. More was to come.

The most striking first moments of all, however, came when I met the faculty. They were nearly all warm and welcoming, including me in their post-summer greetings to one another, introducing me to people I should know. I had student taught at a very traditional school with a frigid social atmosphere, and in contrast this warmth seemed like paradise. And, as I was feeling faintly hysterical, people's friendliness calmed me down. Eleanor in particular was very kind, leaving me welcoming notes, giving me a notepad and Russian stickers for students' papers, and answering my myriad questions.

But I also picked up faint social danger signals almost right away. For one thing, almost no one looked under 30 (and almost no one was), and I was 26. For another, there was little talk of courses, of students, of school. But that was all right, I supposed. Time enough to talk of that later. My panic set in, however, on a lunch trip off-campus.

By lunchtime, I was feeling slightly defeated, wondering whether I hadn't been crazy—like everyone said—to leave a good job (and desk!) for teaching. I was pleased to be invited to lunch by some teachers I had met that morning, and I hoped that the meal would bolster body and spirit; maybe they'd tell me about the school, the kids, about teaching in Woodfield. By the time we reached the restaurant, however, my wistful new-teacher hopes had withered to dismay. The women I was with were talking animatedly— but about dinette sets, lazy husbands, aluminum siding, children's clothing, divorce, and pregnancy and labor. I felt as if I'd stepped into a commercial for laundry detergent.

I am more a listener than a talker, especially around new people, but this time I had little to say because I seemed to have so little in common with my companions. There was nothing about their conversation that would identify them as educated people interested, not to mention working, in education. One woman, noticing my quietness, asked me where I lived. My apartment is in a university town about ten miles from Woodfield, very culturally oriented and nurturing of the avant garde. When she heard this, she made a face and exclaimed with genuine distaste, "Oh-oh, you're not one of those artsy types, are you?" I wasn't sure whether to be more taken aback by her closed-mindedness or her tactlessness, so I just smiled, albeit less brightly than I had that morning.

The meal depressed me terribly. Others asked me about myself, but my answers were met largely with polite blankness and, I imagined, an air of "She's not like us, is she?" I had nothing interesting to add about dinette sets and therefore didn't belong. Still, I didn't *want* to have anything to say about dinette sets. I didn't even want a dinette set. I did want to fit in but didn't see how I could when we seemed so different. These were teachers, but I hadn't heard an off-duty word all day that pertained to ideas, or emotions, or school! I went home glumly, and comforted myself with the thought that these were only a few of the many people I would meet this year. I was secretly convinced, though, that I would go through the year branded as the unmarried intellectual child who actually was (how odd) interested in her students.

SEPTEMBER: THE FIRST DAY OF SCHOOL

The first day: upset stomach, masses of teenaged faces and names I'll never learn to match or distinguish, friendly encouragement from colleagues. Easy for them to say. Bells, bells, bells, or more accurately, electronic beeps, beeps, beeps: horrible Pavlovian sounds to mark the end of class. Look at the clothes those girls are wearing! They didn't wear clothes like that when I was in high school. (Did I really say that? I must be old.) Feeling self-conscious and disorganized, rushing from classroom to classroom just like one of the students. I wish I had a room. These halls are zoolike. What do I *say*?! Should I give homework? Do I write my name on the board as in grade school? Should I start right in or just hand out books and learn names?

I'm not sure exactly what happened. I didn't give homework; it seemed unnecessary. I wrote my name on the board; I felt stupid but it seemed the reasonable thing to do. When will this feel natural? Will I have to fight the impostor syndrome all year? I gave them books and a personal questionnaire that I had created, made seating charts amidst groans, and mispronounced names. I told them that I was new to the school, carefully avoiding spelling out that I was a brand-new teacher. I told them that the thing I cared about most was respect, for me and for each other—no rudeness, no unkind teasing, no disobedience. I then wondered if they had the faintest idea what I was talking about, as disrespect is part and parcel of adolescence. I wondered if other teachers ever said anything like that or if my concerns and hopes and questionnaire marked me painfully clearly as a greenhorn. Regardless, everything went smoothly. No one threw spitballs at me. In fact, I was treated with respect.

The worst part of the day was fifth period lunch duty. May no first-year teacher encounter such a thing on the first day! How do other teachers maintain that air of placidity amidst the noise and haste of a high school cafeteria? I felt like an absolute fool on parade strolling up and down and around the long rows of tables in the big sunny room surrounded by a welter of stiff, feathered hair, hamburgers, metallic shoes and purses, ice cream, sweatpants, and teenage noise. This was definitely another one of those "teacher roles" mentioned in grad school that I was not too comfortable with, and that nothing could have prepared me for. Why was I *here*? Why was *I* here? I recognized nobody and imagined that everybody was staring at me. I was not just imagining it: many of them were. I looked different: uncomfortable, young, unfamiliar. Kids aren't shy: "Who are you?" some of them called out. "What's it to you?," I wanted to say, but instead lamely replied, "I'm a new teacher," for lack of a better response. How I watched the minutes crawl by.

One of the things I remember most about the beginning of school is the rudeness and noisiness of the students. In large part, it's not intentional; they just don't seem to realize that not holding a door or screaming in your ear in the hallway or interrupting you in the middle of a sentence is unacceptable. Still, that's no reason to let it pass. I don't know what to do about this; I'm not ready to play schoolmarm and loudly call attention to each infraction. My style of raising an eyebrow and shaming them into good behavior only works on the ones who already have some sense of manners. Well, human nature adapts easily; in six months I probably won't notice half of what drives me crazy now. And perhaps when I know them better I'll feel more comfortable with reprimanding them. But boy are they obnoxious.

The day ended and I went home with sore feet and sore ears and a sore brain. I had lived through it and was ready for a well-deserved vacation. Unfortunately, there was one more day in the week and I felt sure that my supervisor would prefer me there, so I went home to think all over again about what I would say.

SEPTEMBER/OCTOBER: LEARNING WHAT TO SAY

Having recently moved to a new apartment, I had to reregister to vote. When the woman asked me my occupation, I replied "teacher," and then started to laugh. Me? A teacher? The impostor syndrome still lurks.

But I must be a teacher, for I have five very real classes. Not only that, but I stand in front of them, talk, wave my arms, and write on the board and they actually listen and take notes. It's exhilarating! Two of the classes are sophomore-level English at the C, or average, level and three are Russian, the subject I trained for in graduate school. One of my college majors was English, but the English I'm teaching here bears little resemblance. Very little.

There are four course levels in the school: A (honors), B (general college prep), C (average), and D (special help). My English students are in the C level, which means that they range in ability from those who belong in the D level but don't want to be there, to those who actually are average (whatever that means), to those who are capable of the B level but who don't want to be there or don't achieve consistently enough to justify moving them up. Most of the students in C level plan to work after high school; a very few will attend four-year colleges, a few more training schools or two-year colleges. As a result of this heterogeneity of abilities, motivations, and behaviors, the consensus among teachers is that C level is the hardest to teach. This may be "average" in American high schools, but it's not what I've been used to recently. Life in the rarefied atmosphere of college, the professional world, and graduate school has spoiled me. I strain to think back to my own quite average high school, and remember ruefully friends and acquaintances of mine who were just like these C level students—nice people, but the sort whose idea of a fine film is one that stars Sylvester Stallone. I sigh and adjust my sights, for that is what teaching requires; but I am determined not to adjust them too low.

My two sophomore classes are very different in some ways; Period 1 is large, mildly rebellious, and mostly male. There are some good kids in the class, male and female, but the overall atmosphere is dominated by a few cliques of boys not fully willing to be nice to the teacher. Fortunately, none of them is fully willing to jeopardize his future and be an absolute stinker, either—at least that's my hope. Period 4 on the other hand is a small, friendly, constructively talkative group, with a more even male/female mix. From a teacher's point of view, the difference can be summed up this way: There are several students in Period 1 who would want to tell me if I had chalk on my face, but they probably wouldn't because they'd get snickered at and so would

I. The kids in Period 4 do tell me, however, and they don't laugh at each other or me when they do. A minor point, but it effectively contrasts the relaxed camaraderie of one class as opposed to the adolescent warfare undertone of the other. I get chalk on my arms, hands, and even face all the time but I have solemnly sworn never, ever to lean against the chalk tray and get one of those awful stripes across my backside. It will happen eventually, though. It's a teaching rite of passage.

But regardless of temperamental affinities or hostilities, we will have difficulty with each other, this C level class and me. I seem to be expecting too much of them in terms of sheer comprehension; they seem completely unused to exerting themselves mentally and especially to listening carefully. Or are they testing me to see how much they can get away with, how dumb they can play? I don't feel as if they are, but I can't rule it out.

Most maddening to me is their difficulty with simple mechanical requirements. They forget pens. They forget books. I have to repeat page numbers four times. Small details, but they build up to become absolutely infuriating and disruptive both to my train of thought and to class. I do not know how to deal with this; I don't like the idea of them going through class without a pen or a book, especially if it seems to have been an honest error. So, I let them go to their lockers or I lend them one. But that seems so wimpy! It doesn't teach them any responsibility at all! Yet to allow them to sit through class without the essentials would probably please some of them no end, so that's not a solution. Interestingly, this happens much more frequently in Period 1 than Period 4, and I don't think it's just because it's the first class of the day, either. I suppose the thing to do is to lean hard on the repeat offenders and excuse the rare lapser; but then that's a breach of consistency, something I try to avoid. Aargh! I never would have thought that piddling details like this would be so important. It would seem, though, that piddling details are exactly what drive teachers crazy. I can see why.

But not all the problems are peripheral; some actually involve subject material. After assigning a reading in the text the night before, I spent ten minutes explaining and showing examples of the writing concept "don't use the word 'however' at the beginning or end of a sentence." As I talked, I thought to myself that I didn't fully agree with this rule. I didn't want to be ambiguous, for fear I would confuse them. You could explain your disagreement to a more capable class, but not at this level. Yes, I agreed with my mythical advisor . . . No! I didn't. Why should I feed them hard-and-fast rules that don't necessarily apply? That's exactly the problem with schools! And so I added the disclaimer that occasionally, "however" does sound better at the beginning or end of the sentence. Instantly I saw annoyance and confusion: Huh? The teacher just contradicted herself! Still, in the few faces of those more comfortable with language, there was relief and agreement. Aha, I thought; some do understand. But were there enough of them to justify having confused some others?

The acid test: some examples on their own. Most dutifully stuck "however" somewhere in the middle of each sentence, though in a few cases with little regard for sense (well, you didn't say you wanted it to make sense); some tacked it on the beginning or end (uh, I didn't hear you say you wanted it in the middle); a few listened and put it in the right place.

How can I possibly give them an ear for language when they're already half-grown? Should I get mad at them for not knowing the obvious? How can I be angry when a student tells me earnestly that she honestly didn't realize that I wanted it to make sense? Exasperation melts into laughter when I realize the warped logic (schoolwork doesn't necessarily make sense) she applies to school; perhaps I should cry. Should I explain that writing rules are meant to be contradicted, but not by them yet? They do hate ambiguity, it's true; some will probably conclude that I just don't know the answer and that's why I teach it both ways, and so they'll tune out. But life is full of ambiguity. Is it fair to deny knowledge to those who can grasp it? Yet is it fair for me to present material that most of them won't understand?

At this point, I feel the real question is: Is it fair to expect me to do the impossible? For that's how this feels. I seem to recall saying that I "only" wanted my students to be hardworking and good people at the same time. Have I changed so much so fast that now all I want is that they bring their books to class and listen quietly? Yes. No. I don't know. This is very trying. I'm tired.

Happily, my Russian classes are a contrast to my English classes. I am more comfortable with and excited by the subject matter, and on the whole, these were more motivated students (mostly A and B levels and a few C level). Well, motivated not necessarily to learn, but at least to get good grades. While the two are not interchangeable, they are sometimes indistinguishable, and it will take me a while to realize who is who. In the meantime, I will enjoy the contrast; in Russian, everyone does the homework and no one forgets a book, even if they can't distinguish between direct and indirect objects.

I have one Russian II class of nearly all seniors, who are marvelous. I inherited them from last year's teacher, and they were very helpful early on about what they had covered last year. In fact, they were startlingly revealing about exactly how this teacher had taught them: Fridays off, lots of discussion about his personal life, hopelessly simple quizzes, hardly any homework. Here we had the proverbial "gut" course: take it, show up, smile at the teacher, and get an A. Don't smile? A C. At first I was amused; it explained why they were regarding me with a little wariness, and it was fascinating in a horrible way to hear about this teaching travesty.

After the entertainment value faded away, however, several bleak realizations sank in. One was that most of these charming and talkative Russian II students didn't know anything significant about Russian. A few did; the very bright ones had been able to learn despite the teacher. This only complicated matters, however, for now I had one class with at least two wildly disparate knowledge levels within it, and all the students expected easy grades regardless of effort and ability. Some of them obviously needed much of Russian I again; others were ready to pick up right where they'd left off last June. How to teach it? Review, yes; but for how long?

The other revelation was that of all my Russian I students, many must have signed up on the advice of previous students that an A was easy and the class was a joke. My Russian II students even confessed to such proselytizing. I thought I had sensed some surprised dismay at the workload I had assigned the Russian I students; now I knew at least partly why. Great. Not only did I have to make my own reputation, but I had to live someone else's down. Well, too bad. I was there to make them not only enjoy it but also work, and work they would.

But not all of them were getting more than they had bargained for. A schism similar to that in the Russian II class soon appeared in one of my Russian I classes. Several students came to my desk after the first week or so and said, a little self-importantly, "Ms. Lewis, although the pace you've been going at is fine for most of the class, and maybe even too fast for some, it's too slow for us and we wanted you to know."

My first reaction was impolite and unprintable; my second, brilliantly, was "Oh." My third was, "Thank you for telling me; I'll see what I can do." My fourth, kept to myself, was, "What in the world am I going to do now?"

So, I was aiming too high with most of my English students and both too low and too high with small percentages of the Russian classes. Suddenly my English classes appeared downright homogenous in comparison to Russian, for I needed only adjust in one direction—down—to serve most of their needs. But how was I to teach three different levels in one Russian class? It was just as well that I didn't make lesson plans in August; I hadn't anticipated this at all.

There was no satisfactory solution. Other language classes have the luxury of greater enrollments than Russian and hence classes grouped homogeneously by A, B, or C level. The Russian classes, while good-sized, were still too small for a public school to justify separating the 9 A students from the 24 B and C. My first action was to recognize only two levels for credit and workload purposes: A and B. C students could get by at the B standard; I was not about to teach three different levels in one introductory foreign-language class during my first year.

The students accepted this without question. I then assigned honors students extra work on projects or in translation. It was not ideal, but it worked smoothly enough. I had wanted to work with them separately, especially as I remembered being bored myself in high school, but I couldn't figure how to take the time away from the class as a unit, especially since I was still feeling my way. There was just never enough time. And as with English, it would not be fair to teach the course to the best students and lose the bulk of the class. Once again, how to teach? I was learning that the answer was compromise plans, juggle and squeeze time and effort, and hope.

Though I am a vehement advocate of public education, to me this is one of its major failings and unfair sources of pressure on hard-working, conscientious teachers. Regardless of demand, only cost-effective classes exist. But in most academic subjects, it just doesn't work to lump high-ability students with low-ability students, for both are disserved. Being cost-effective is by no means the same as being educationally effective. People who decry academic tracking as elitist and wrong cannot possibly be teachers, and they must not remember being students.

NOVEMBER/DECEMBER: LEARNING HOW TO SAY IT

I've been "observed" by Eleanor and Bill recently; that is, they've sat in on my classes. Although the pressure made it seem as if I've been watched all day every day, it has been only five classes so far, with more observations due in the late winter. Although I was terrified beforehand, I got accustomed to having them there and eventually even appreciated having an adult in the classroom for my more obscure jokes and asides.

Observation was revealing in many ways. First, I learned that the students were basically on my side, as they were very well-behaved. A little misguidedly well-behaved, for they were so quiet that I felt I was teaching mannequins! They must think that a teacher's idea of an ideal classroom is a morgue. I also realized how I'd relaxed about preparation since those first days in September. Though I never want to be boring, I quickly learned that at five classes per day, each and every class I teach can't be a gem of perfection, interest, and organization. When I was observed, however, I felt tremendous renewed pressure to be scintillating and creative in every class, every minute. I studied for class. Silly? Possibly. Do Eleanor and Bill understand that it's impossible to be continually riveting? Of course; they've both taught too. Nonetheless, in the evaluation game, there's an unspoken assumption on both sides that perfection is attainable despite the fact that it's not.

Both evaluations were helpful. Some of the suggestions were basic, but I hadn't thought of them. Bill said to close the door when class has begun. Eleanor advised not to call on someone right away after asking a question: Make them all think before choosing someone. They also picked up my nervous habits. I pace about the front of the room, sometimes aimlessly, which can be distracting. Eleanor recommended that when I move, I move into the class between the rows, putting the motion to some purpose—intimidating a talker or bringing people into the class more. Much to my horror, Bill said that I use "okay" as a sort of verbal punctuation. Okay, I must change that.

They also recognized some larger weaknesses that I was hoping they'd overlook. At the same time I am glad they didn't, since it means I'm gauging myself relatively accurately. I do not use my voice very effectively yet; I'm rather soft-spoken. Nor am I always a commanding figure in front of the classroom—again, partly a function of using body and voice to fullest advantage. While I agree, I feel a little unfairly judged. They can't expect me to be Dale Carnegie at this point. It is hard to think about much else when I'm learning to explain the material clearly and read faces for questions and the like. I do think that physical presence will come to me more easily once I'm more comfortable in the classroom in general; but I suppose they're right to mention it to me now so that I'll be aware of it.

Interestingly, Bill thinks that I seem apologetic when I give students an assignment or homework. I do feel that way sometimes. The more I learn about my students' lives and remember my own, with jobs, activities, crazy home situations, boyfriends, girlfriends, and the like, sometimes it does seem unreasonable to give homework on top of that. Then again, I must remember my role as taskmaster; that's partly why I'm here. He also was sensitive to my use of difficult vocabulary with the lower-level students. I'm glad he said that; I used to hate teachers using big words in order to impress students (or so I thought). That's certainly not my intention. What I've decided is not to completely change my way of speaking, but to listen to myself more carefully, stop when I've used a "big word" and find out whether the students understand it. If not, they'll learn it right then and there. After all, how else will they increase their vocabularies unless these words are heard and explained?

Eleanor made the remark that was the toughest for me to take. She said that I needed to work on heightening students' motivation, on making them want to work. Good grief. Doesn't she suppose I think about that constantly, especially since I am still struggling with having A, B, and C level kids in the same class? Don't teachers across America worry about that daily? I'm not saying I do an amazing job, but I do try! This was especially frustrating because she didn't seem to have any specific suggestions on how to increase motivation. Well, I will continue to muddle along, keeping it in mind but again feeling a little resentful, since only experience and guidance will help.

Despite her criticism, our relationship has been good so far. To some other teachers, department supervisors and administrators are the "them," not unlike what teachers are to students. I don't take this approach, though, and have talked comfortably to Eleanor whenever I have had a question. I seem to be a favorite of hers (according to other teachers), and I have enjoyed her rather maternal attitude toward me. Others say that she either takes to you or she doesn't, and have pointed out with what sounds in some cases increasingly like jealousy, that she's taken to me. I suppose anyone who consorts with "them" is suspect, so it's a tricky relationship at this point. I want to be a favorite but not necessarily openly favored; I cannot be pleased about my good rapport with my supervisor but instead must feel on guard against appearing to be her protégé or, well, teacher's pet.

In any case, they then showed me their written evaluations after we had discussed the classroom visits. Both of them gave me quite positive comments, and checkmarks, which pleased me very much and surprised me somewhat, since they had just spent so much time telling me what I was doing wrong or what I could fine tune or what they would have done differently. It almost made me angry to see their positive comments after they'd just spent so much time picking me apart! Teachers are supposed to write encouraging as well as critical comments for students; even good superiors, like mine, should remember to do the same when discussing teachers' performances with them.

And what about my colleagues and their dinette sets? Well, since those initial fateful days, I've found some friends. I've become more accustomed to the group I first met and they to me. I've met many others, too, whom I hope to know better. Perhaps not surprisingly, the people I'm most interested in seem to be either young, or single, or in my disciplines.

I never fully realized before how much one's lifestyle determines one's friendships. I have found myself gravitating not only toward people around my age, but also to single people, regardless of age. I'm not on the lookout for a mate, for I am involved in a good, long-standing relationship; it's just that we seem to have more in common. Many of the married teachers are very involved with their families and houses and all that goes with that, and talk of little else. While I don't share that with them, I admire them for being able to handle an entire outside life as well as teach. I seem to spend every waking minute thinking about and planning for school or correcting papers. If I had a family now they'd disown me for neglect! In fact, my boyfriend, while supportive, feels closed out of my life and I don't blame him. I don't feel as if I have time for anything anymore, including myself. Either I'm overworking or everyone else is underworking . . . or maybe it's just first-year syndrome. I hope it's the latter. I'd like to sleep late or see a movie again some day.

But despite all the time spent on and in school, in a way I feel as if I still hardly know anyone. There is so little time to sit down and talk to another teacher. The day is hectic; our 20-minute lunch is short and impersonal, the half-hour after school is for students or paperwork, and at 3:05 most teachers are out the door. I spend all day with and talking to people, yet at the end of the day I sometimes can't remember actually conversing with anybody!

Being the new kid on the block, I was assigned to a number of duties and extracurricular activities that no one else wanted. Luckily, one of them was the Teachers' Senate, a body of faculty representatives from each department designated to collect concerns, complaints, and desires about the school and school life from the entire faculty and report them to the administration. It is nonbinding, but seems effective. I suppose no one covets it because it requires staying after hours, but I have been enjoying it. Why? Not because I am political or especially interested in reforming the school. No, I realized one day as we were heatedly discussing whether girls' teams were short-changed in the athletic budget and whether teachers should be informed by the administration that a student has serious home problems, that here I was with other teachers *talking about school*! We were not in the lunchroom, where someone always sneers at discussing business; we were not in the classroom, where the teacher is the only adult; we were not at faculty or department meetings, where necessary but often tangential or boring business is discussed and then everyone hurries out; instead we were spending our own time talking to each other about issues that concerned us and our students. It was all the more special for its rarity.

In addition to Teachers' Senate, I have found two friends in particular with whom I buck the isolation phenomenon. One is the man I thought was glaring at me when I was late to the superintendent's meeting in September; he claims he was merely pleased to see someone who looked like a kindred spirit. John is a Spanish teacher, also new to the school, single and close to my age. The other, Andrea, is a music teacher who's been here for years; also single, she has a dry sense of humor and lives in the city. We have fun puzzling out inane school rules, arguing over points of grammar, discussing our students, comparing teaching methods, and groaning through lunch duty together. It's good to have peers.

Speaking of lunch, something is strange about the teachers' lunchroom. It's sex-segregated, like a junior-high school dance, with the boys on one side, girls on the other. The line is not uncrossable; a few men eat with women and vice versa, but it's the exception. The stereotyping is almost funny: the men talk about sports; the women talk about housewifely stuff; everybody talks about each other.

Some of the stereotyping, however, is not so funny. I had to fend off dozens of remarks from men about pretty smiles getting me places or repaying favors after school, in tones ranging from innocent teasing to paternal to sneering. That I can deal with. I was hurt and angry, though, at hearing secondhand some much more distasteful comments about me. Apparently I play a role in the fantasy life of some of the male faculty, and apparently they amuse themselves by discussing it. My informant seemed surprised I wasn't flattered; more sexism. Were the same people I thought I was making friends with leering at me as soon as I turned my back? It's almost a corny cliché, but I felt violated. I wanted to wear baggy dresses to school; I wanted to avoid all male teachers; when I went into the lunchroom I wanted to scream that they were all middle-aged and overweight and boring. I recovered; let them talk. I still feel resentful, though, and on my guard. I wish it weren't so.

Along the same lines, John and I eat together when we can, and since such male-female fraternization is slightly unusual, and we're both young, everyone has decided that we're an item. It's a bit like having gone back in time 20 years. Well, it's not that exciting a school; let them talk about that too. Socially, grownups aren't all that much different from teenagers; too few realize the scant difference.

On the other hand, many of the teachers I've met have been willing to share advice and even materials and plans, which is a godsend. There is much more talk of teaching than I had originally encountered, and there are many dedicated caring teachers here. Still, the burnout that pervades the profession does exist too. One day John and I were sitting at a lunch table animatedly complaining about how much we were annoyed by the buzzers used to signal the end of class, and we decided to go and ask whether there were any alternative. Suddenly, a teacher whom I had heard say little all year raised her head from her sandwich, looked at us glumly, and intoned, "You'll learn, yes, you'll learn soon enough not to question, not to question." We looked at one another, initially taken aback but then overcome by the ridiculousness of it. Not to question? It would be time to leave teaching when we learned not to question and not to teach our students to question. And it was certainly time to leave that table, so we did, smothering our giggles.

Teaching a class is much easier now. I'm learning not to overprepare, not to give graduate-level lectures, not to feel nervous, not to leave the door open. I do wish that there was more time, though. I would like to digress more in class. I want to sit down with each of my students and talk to them about themselves. I did this as a student-teacher and was amazed at the good effect on their attitude and behavior. If there's one thing that works, it's showing an interest. Now, though, with my one free period a day usually taken up with photocopying or busywork, there is little opportunity for chatting outside class with students, just as with the faculty. It's the same paradox: surrounded by students, interacting with them constantly, yet still isolated from them!

I had a shock the other day. In the middle of class, it struck me that I was being boring. Truly boring. I couldn't even bear to listen to myself. I had prepared for class, but the material was so dull, and so was I. It was the strangest feeling, standing in front of the room knowing how enervating the lesson was for all of us, and not knowing how to escape. I was tempted to call a halt to it all, but somehow and for some reason I plugged on. Whew. It's one thing to know that even if my students aren't always hanging on my every word, most classes go well; it's another thing entirely to hear myself talk and wish that that blatherer would shut up!

I am worried about keeping my Russian II class together. I originally thought these kids would be my favorites, but we're getting on each other's nerves, for I'm expecting more than they're accustomed to giving, and their academic weaknesses are painfully apparent now. We have been doing what should have been review for three months now; some of the class is learning Russian for the first time; the others are going bananas at all the rehash, though they are too polite to say so. I feel terribly frustrated. Well, as one student who hasn't passed a quiz yet says, "I like you just fine, and you're a good teacher, but I hate Russian." I think it's a compliment but I'm not certain.

I am also frustrated by one boy in there who is brilliant. His knowledge appears all-encompassing; his memory is superb; he is creative and witty. Sam is two years younger than the others, but years beyond them intellectually. I'll bet some teachers are terrified of him; I just make notes of all his startlingly sharp or obscure questions that I can't answer and bring him the answer on a note card the next day. Just teaching Sam alone would be as big a challenge as anything else I've met this year! As happens often, however, Sam's mental agility is not fully equaled by his social graces. He gets along tolerably well with the other kids, but he demands too much of my time in class asking fascinating but tangential questions; lost in his own intellectual cloud, he argues with me about very fine points, annoying the other students and me; he eagerly gives answers, cutting off others in the process. I should talk to him privately, but I'm not sure he'd handle it very well. He's a tiger in the classroom, but awkward one on one and suspicious of personal questions. I know, I've tried to find out how he feels about being a student here. We'll see.

Cheryl is a different type of problem in what I consider to be my "worst" class, Period 1 English. She is just plain rude, talking during class and making brash remarks and asides, then self-righteously and disruptively denying any wrongdoing when confronted. I have learned to take a very low-key approach to bad behavior, for if I react to it as strongly as I did at the beginning of the year, I will have an ulcer by Christmas. And I was right in thinking that much of the behavior that appalled me in September I now hardly notice, for better or worse. Cheryl, however, is the sort of person who makes me steam on contact, despite my best efforts. I have the funny feeling that she honestly thinks I am unfair; nonetheless, she does not accept my very clear signals to behave, and let's face it, I am the teacher.

We have had many minor confrontations; finally we had a major one. Angrily accusing me of picking on her, she went to the vice-principal from class with my consent to complain about me. I spent the rest of the day and night furious and then afraid; how would I live with this kid for the rest of the year? Though I was sure I hadn't, what if I had been handling things unfairly? What if her parents complained about me to the school board?

The next day the three of us sat down in Fred's tiny cluttered office and had a chat. Fred, the vice-principal, is brash, irascible, and often loud beyond the point of rudeness himself. I originally had been aghast at his being a school administrator. Further contact proves, however, that he is reliable, consistent, and knowledgeable, and can display surprising sensitivity and tact when dealing with teachers and students. This was one of those times. He told Cheryl that I was by no means the only teacher who found her a problem, and that since as the teacher I had to adapt to many more personalities in class than she did, that she better try harder to adapt to mine since it was easier for her. I promised to try not to "pick on" Cheryl if she would try to stop being the center of all class disruption; she promised to pay attention to my danger signals and clam up when I told her to, for her own good. We shall see.

I have another boy in the same class, named Michael, who concerns me. He does nothing. Opens his book, if he's brought it, and sits there. Homework? Forget it. In-class writing assignment? He leans forward, looks at his paper, and when I come around, tells me he doesn't know what he's supposed to do. I explain it to him, leave, and he lapses back into oblivion. Though he passed with a D+ first quarter, he'll fail this one. I have spoken to his parents, and his mother and I started a weekly phone call to each other which had some effect at first, but now nothing. On parents' night I looked up from my desk to see a stricken-looking man and woman walking toward me— Michael's parents. Apparently Michael is doing the same thing in every class and several teachers recommended psychiatric help for him and counseling for the whole family. I'd recommend a good swift kick in the pants for our young friend.

I teach a deaf girl in my other English class. This is Anna's first year in a mainstream high school, and it is a struggle. She can speak, but she is very difficult to understand. To comprehend others, she lip reads, which means that at best she gets 60 percent of what is said. This puts great constraints on her teachers; whenever we speak we should stand in front of her facing her. This means no writing on the board and talking, no giving general instructions from someone's desk as I walk around the room, none of the aimless wandering of which I'm so fond. I try, but it's nearly impossible. Another minus is that she hates English. Her effort is so-so; she gets a great deal of help from home. I was warned about her fifth grade vocabulary—if you can't use a word, why bother to learn it, I suppose—but the papers she works on at home are comparable to others in the class. Is Mom doing them? I think so. Perhaps I can give a double grade, one for Anna and one for her mother.

JANUARY/MID-YEAR: HALFWAY THERE

I gave all of my students course evaluations to fill out. After all, everyone else is telling me how I'm doing, why not those who know best? In all fairness, though, other teachers here have been very generous in sharing compliments they have overheard from parents and students, which is gratifying. I'm glad I'm working with people who are considerate and supportive enough to pass along good reviews.

And good reviews are largely what I received from my students. They seemed taken aback by a teacher's asking for their opinion, but they then took the forms seriously. Two unusual comments stick in my mind; one stinging, the other pleasing. The stinger: "She acts like she thinks she's one of us." The pleaser: "I like her. She's normal, which is more than you can say for most teachers." Are they merely different views of the same behavior?

FEBRUARY/MARCH: THIRD-QUARTER BLUES

My English students' intellectual naïveté is both charming and distressing. They don't understand how to read or how to think about reading. After finishing an O. Henry story with a surprise ending, for kicks I asked them to make up a few paragraphs about what they thought happened after the story ended. Some of their accounts were very clever and we read them aloud. As I handed them back, one girl raised her hand and asked: "What really did happen after the story ended?" At first I thought she was teasing; then I realized that she truly expected me, the teacher, to know. Sometimes I do fancy myself omniscient, but. . . . Not all requests are so endearing, however. When they're especially frustrated or bored with whatever novel we're reading, they ask, "Why can't we just watch the movie?" I try not to scream.

English is a bit of a muddle; the course has now switched from an emphasis on writing to literature. I think I move too slowly; there's so much to show them and explain and talk about. We'll never make it through the material I'm supposed to cover. Is that so bad? No, if they learn how to read a book carefully; but yes if it means I'm incompetent. Beware of just getting through the curriculum for the sake of getting through it, they said in graduate school. Yes, but . . . the pressure is there, and don't I owe it to my students?

My frustration must show. The principal called me in one day and gave me an unsolicited pep talk. How many other principals would do that? I was gratified. Bill feared that the English classes were getting me down and he didn't want me to lose my enthusiasm for teaching and for Russian . . . I didn't have the heart or the nerve to say that everything seems to be getting me down.

I'm losing my Russian II seniors. Grades have been sent to colleges, the newness of the new teacher has worn off, and most of all this class is certainly not the breeze they had bargained for. They respect the fact that I'm actually trying to teach, which their other teacher didn't, but I can see in their faces that they wish I'd come a year later so that I wouldn't be teaching *them*. Other teachers commiserate, saying all seniors are terrible this time of year; I have heard that chairperson Eleanor primly tells all complainers that *she* never had trouble with her seniors' motivation. Well, la di da. I do.

I feel guilty about it, but I dread going to that class. This also makes me realize what a good schedule I have in general, for the idea of regularly dreading a class is novel since I've been at this school. It's getting to the point where Sam, a few other good souls, and I are the only ones truly involved in class. When I get visibly frustrated, they still say they "like me but hate Russian," but I'm not placated by that anymore. In fact, I've found myself semiconsciously retaliating at them for their apathy, giving them long, complex, dull assignments. This is probably stupid of me: They'll hate not only Russian but me too.

I'll try to marshal the energy to liven up the rest of the year, but what if they don't do their part? Is it my fault or theirs? When I wasn't yet a teacher, I would have placed the blame on the teacher; now I am sorely tempted to place it on the students. Yes, partly out of wanting to escape responsibility, but let's face it—how much can I give if they don't want it? Is class 100 percent my responsibility? No. Or maybe I'm just fooling myself.

Not having a classroom is the pits. I'm always leaving something behind, always carrying 20 pounds of books around with me. I'm often late to class since I'm not about to run off on a student who wants to ask me a question at the end of the previous one. I end up writing the same thing several times a day since the blackboards I use aren't my own. I have no home base. Grumble.

There is a bright spot. Russian I is going smoothly, even with different levels in the one class. I don't like it that way, but it's under control. I am most able to relax and enjoy myself in Russian I, for they are the most mine— my subject and my students not inherited from anyone else. Mine mine mine. Probably another unhealthy attitude. Oh well.

I'm adapting to all of my roles better, too. In the fall, I never asked students in the hall to be quiet or to "get to where you're supposed to be"; now I only think twice instead of five times about saying it. Lunch duty, while still a chore, is not nearly so much an exercise in self-consciousness. Students who forget to say "thank you" get reminded about it. I don't know, though, about getting accustomed to bathroom duty.

The women teachers have to sit outside the girls' bathroom to make sure the girls don't smoke in there. Basically, we listen to them use the toilet and watch the stalls for rising "smoke signals." It's ridiculous, and what makes it more ridiculous is that just seeing smoke is not enough to nab a student; we have to see them with a cigarette. What kid is going to be that stupid? I like one teacher's approach: If she sees smoke, she throws a cup of water over the top of the stall. When the girl yells, she sweetly says, "I'm sorry, I saw smoke and thought there was a fire in there." Entertaining solutions aside, it's a silly situation, and teachers and students are embarrassed by it. Some things are just beneath one's dignity, and teachers command little enough respect as it is without being toilet attendants.

As I feel more comfortable with teaching and (most) other duties, the people around me have become a bigger part of my life, for better and worse. I think about school constantly; I dream about my students, and most of the dreams are no longer about disciplinary nightmares. Cheryl has changed her tune, lapsing only occasionally. I should take pleasure in small victories, for Michael is now frightening in his apathy. I want to ignore him because he's so disconcerting. My efforts have proved inadequate and I want to conserve my resources for those who want them. Maybe he does need professional help; everyone is mystified by him.

Another one of my students, David, is convinced that I'm the witch who did something horrible (he won't say what) to an older sister of his years ago; when I explained that this was impossible, he became downright malevolent and accused me of lying. The class and I looked at him in shock both at his behavior and his disregard for reality. He growled further unpleasant remarks at me during the ensuing days. I stopped saying hello to him in the hall and spoke to his guidance counselor; since then he has mellowed. Did he find out that he was wrong? Is he awaiting revenge? Strange.

What I find particularly enigmatic is that in the two courses (Russian I and English) that I teach two classes of, one class of each performs significantly less well than the other. One of the two low-ballers is my Period 1 "bad" English class, full of underachievers and lazybones; the other is my sixth-period Russian I class, which I love. Why those classes, I wonder? Is it my fault? Period 1 I'm still stiff, not warmed up to teaching yet; I'm also less fond of that class than of its fourth-period clean-cut counterpart. Third-period Russian is much larger and has a less-defined personality than sixth period, in which disparate types click and enjoy great camaraderie. I always look forward to sixth period: The class is small, friendly, and fun. Perhaps too much fun, if they're not doing well. I wonder how much of the difference in performance is caused by differences in my demeanor and approach.

But everyone's grades are going down, in all classes. Third-quarter slump, I suppose, but I find it alarming. Most of the students don't seem to, though, and as I grow more jaded, I ask, why should I worry if they don't? But I don't really mean that; it's my own slump showing. I do worry, and I still believe that if I don't worry, then I don't care. I must find the happy medium, as the Greeks and Romans would counsel.

In a way, my grades have gone down, too. I have rebelled. I am tired of spending practically 90 percent of my own time on school. In need of escape into another world, I have started reading books again, voraciously. I've become a little blasé about preparing for class. I still prepare, but not the detailed plans I once clung to with terror. I wing it a lot more, and it goes fine. Partly I'm coasting, partly I feel more confident. Still, I'm not like the teachers who casually remark at lunch that they have no idea what they'll do next period. Are they lying, or showing off their skill, or are they idiots? I can't imagine ever getting to that point. Then again, I couldn't imagine getting this far through this year either, and I have.

But I feel old. Long-time teachers say that teaching keeps them young, but I feel as if I've aged more than my due this year. Being young, I have to act old to fit the expectations others have of me. But all those roles I'm supposed to play get to me; the pressure to keep up with paperwork and preparation is unrelenting; it's annoying to have to act and think like an adult all day long. It feels more and more natural, but even that bothers me. Do I really want to feel comfortable with being an authority figure to people I don't even know? Do I want to accept the responsibility of opening people's minds every single day? Not particularly. It sounds noble in the abstract but it's darned tough in reality. Some days I wake up and I just don't feel like talking to anyone. I don't want to try to be interesting or enlightening. I just want to sit around and read the newspaper. But I can't, because I'm a teacher, lighting the lamp of knowledge for today's youth. I can't even play hooky because I'm not organized enough to leave comprehensible lesson plans behind. I hate school. Bah, humbug.

But I must admit that it is wonderful when Christine comes up to me with tired eyes and a big grin and dares me to guess what she did last night. I bite: What? "This book is so good that I read five chapters ahead of what you said!" Or when Jared, one of my bright underachievers in C English, gives me a stunningly good short story as his in-class free writing assignment and offhandedly yet proudly tells me he has a few notebooks full of more like it at home. Or when my Russian students dress up in babushkas with me for the Foreign Language week dinner (one was in an Arab headdress, but no matter) and make a bowl of borscht with USSR written on it in parsley. Or when I receive marriage proposals from sophomores. Or when Tom, whom I've teased and prodded into working harder, starts asking me shyly to correct his quizzes as soon as he's taken them, for now he's studying and getting As and Bs. Or even when I stay at school until 4:45 on a Friday afternoon waiting for Sandy to rewrite a paper because she has told me with shining eyes that she suddenly thought of the perfect argument for her thesis and she desperately wants to work it in to the paper but still hand it in on time. This is fun. I don't hate school.

APRIL/MAY/JUNE: THE END

Courses for next year have been selected and Russian enrollments are up by about 35 percent! I am relieved, for part of my unofficial job description was to raise enrollment in Russian. I'm mostly happy, though. It means I must be doing something right. I'm especially glad in light of the fact that I had to turn the course's reputation around. I had hoped that the increase would mean four Russian classes for me next year instead of three, but despite the school's wanting me to increase enrollment, they're not willing to separate next year's Russian II into one class of level A and one class of level B. Not again. . . . Though I understand the situation, I did some mild complaining about this to Eleanor and Bill for the record, wondering whether if I continue to increase enrollment all I'll get are the same number of Russian classes, only larger, and not a schedule with more Russian classes. I got a disappointingly and uncharacteristically unintelligible answer from the principal having to do with scheduling problems and seniors.

Joan's answer was clearer: It was a slap in the face. Coolly, she suggested that I should have recruited even more students and that if I had, I would "deserve" the extra Russian class. Unfair! If the increased enrollment is still too small to justify another class, fine; but proportionately, the increases were quite good (from 13 to 18 students in Russian II, from 33 to 46 in Russian I), and she gave me no credit for that at all! Besides, Russian isn't offered at the junior high with the other foreign languages, so I'm at a disadvantage to start with since I need to "steal" my students from other languages. I guess I'm not the golden girl any more. Well, now I can join the rest of the department in the doghouse and be one of the gang. We'll see what happens next year. If I deliver the goods but get the same runaround, I'll make more noise.

Actually, I heard the news of the enrollment increase without knowing for certain whether I even had a place here next year. Eleanor has assured me that I have nothing to worry about, and Bill has discussed next year with me as if I'll be here, but there's no proof. The superintendent held a meeting recently for all untenured teachers explaining that some of us would not be rehired. In fact, before anyone could be rehired, we would all be officially fired in writing. A strange system if I ever heard one; the point seems to be to forestall lawsuits from teachers not rehired. Fred, the vice-principal, squeamishly hand-delivered the demoralizing "firing" letters, but there wasn't one for me—a good sign, but still not a definitive one. Suddenly in the faculty room one hears whispering: "Are you coming back next year?" "Did you get tenure?" "Did you hear about Joyce?" It's a little tense.

I'd like to come back; I want to try again. One piece of valuable graduate school advice was to commit myself mentally to teaching for at least two years, for the first year is unlike any other, and the second year is much easier. Give it another chance before you even start. Everyone asks me if I like teaching, if I will stay in the field. I don't know; I tell them to ask me next year at this time. It's been a good year on the whole, no catastrophes, but I wouldn't want to live through it again. It had better be unlike any other. If it stays like this, I don't see how anyone could stand to stay in teaching.

When I was in school I loved it. Summer was welcome, but June was a little sad, and I anticipated September and the cycle of the new year. Times have changed. I can't wait for school to end! As of mid-May, there has been a pervasive sense that it's all over and that we're just playing out a charade. It started with the students, but I caught the bug quickly, much to my dismay. I think I had more discipline as a student than as a teacher! Sunshine and blue skies are calling; college students are coming back to hang around; baseball season is in full swing. It's been a hard year and it's time for it to be over. I've made mistakes, and I have a good idea what they are. Now I want to think and regroup and work out new ideas. And I want to go to the beach. . . .

To counteract this feeling, I've forced myself to finish the year tough. As a result, I've learned some things I needed to know but would have been happier not knowing. I hadn't checked desks for signs of cheating since the fall; I was amazed at what I found. So much for the laissez-faire approach. I'm being taken advantage of. Consequently, I've been looking more closely and walking around more during quizzes, and have nabbed several cheaters. Most of those accused have shouldered the blame; the worst is when they've been caught redhanded yet argue about it. I wonder if they realize that I too feel terrible when they're caught. What a way to end the year, thinking of my students as petty cheaters. It's not that I don't understand the urge to cheat; I know that it can be very tempting, and I tell them so. It's just that I would rather have them tell me if they don't understand. Still, it's likely that some of them are just cheaters and my loose honor system won't stop it. My fault; what a shame. Next year, I'll have to be careful about trusting them so much. Put it on the list of things to ponder over the summer.

Before the end of school, a contract appeared in my mailbox. I signed and returned it almost without stopping to think. Once I had sent it away, I got nervous. Did I really want to come back next year? Was I trapping myself by merely taking the easy way out? Yes and no. I hate the job search and don't want to go through it again, but that's not my reason for staying. I like it here. I never thought I'd say so, but I enjoy the mix of personalities and backgrounds on the faculty, even if it's not exactly diverse. I like my students, from the brightest to the dullest, from the slackers to the pluggers, from the quiet to the boisterous. And though I'm tired and want a break, I like teaching. Next time my kids can't teasingly call me "the rookie," and I won't feel so much like an impostor; next time maybe I'll feel more like the real thing. Besides, Gabrielle, a C-level English student and an avowed hater of the subject, stopped by on the last day of school and said, "I was talking to my mother last night and I told her that you were my favorite teacher. You know, I really liked English this year. I learned a lot."

How can I not come back for more?

EPILOGUE

After a summer as a student herself, Margaret Lewis returned to Woodfield elated, full of confidence, ideas, and insight, not to mention anticipation of her own room, a familiar system, and old friends' greetings. She felt like the real thing! In her excitement about classroom, curriculum, and cronies, however, Margaret had forgotten about the shock of reacclimating to the students. By October she was desperately and tearily paging through the help wanted ads. But by Thanksgiving she had stabilized, and she chugged through to June contentedly if not beatifically. Though basically happy and much more satisfied with her second-year performance, she continues to reserve judgment about a lifetime career in teaching.

QUESTIONS FOR DISCUSSION

6.1 One of Lewis's concerns about becoming a teacher is whether or not her students will like her.
   (a) How important is it for a teacher to be "liked" by his or her students? Do you think students "learn" more or less from a teacher they "like"? Why?

6.2 Resiliency and flexibility are two useful and essential qualities for a teacher to demonstrate in the classroom.
   (a) Why do you think this is so?
   (b) In what ways, and in what situations, is Lewis both flexible and resilient?
   (c) What other personal qualities do you feel are important for a teacher—especially an inexperienced first-year one—to possess?

6.3 Lewis writes, "in most academic subjects, it just doesn't work to lump high-ability students with low-ability students, for both are disserviced."
   (a) Do you agree or disagree with this statement?
   (b) What might some of the advantages be of homogeneous grouping of students according to academic abilities?
   (c) What disadvantages do you see?

6.4 A large part of a teacher's time in school is devoted to teaching; however, Lewis also experiences certain "indignities" in the profession that have little to do with teaching or student learning.
   (a) What are some of these indignities, and if they are, indeed, indignities, why do they still remain as part of a teacher's responsibilities?
   (b) In what ways might these indignities undermine the professional and contribute to the decision of some talented young men and women to leave teaching?

6.5 For the most part, Lewis's maiden voyage as a teacher is a relatively agreeable experience. In what specific ways does each of the following influences contribute to the positive nature of her first year in the classroom?
   (a) Evaluations and suggestions by her supervisors?
   (b) Help from experienced colleagues?
   (c) Lewis's ability to be open-minded and self-critical of herself and her teaching?

6.6 As a young, unmarried woman who is just entering the education profession, Lewis has very mixed feelings about the education and social values of many of her colleagues.
   (a) In what ways do her values differ from those of her fellow teachers?
   (b) Do you think, with time and experience, Lewis will "see things differently" and begin to accept some of the attributes of children and education that her colleagues seem to have adopted? Why?

Chapter
7

The Discipline Game

Michael Knoll

When the mailman rang my doorbell in early August and handed over a certified letter my first response was fear. I imagined a variety of disasters, relatives who might have been hospitalized. The letter's return address though, the Meadowfield School Department, argued against the disaster theory. I had no relations among the Meadowfield School Department. Simultaneous with that realization was the question: "Is *this* the letter?" Several months earlier I'd been interviewed by Meadowfield—and several dozen other schools—but I'd mentally written it off as yet another in a growing string of rejections. "I like your writing degree," the department head had mentioned, "but I'm reluctant to hire a teacher with no solid experience . . ." It had seemed to be the classic Catch-22: I couldn't be hired without experience, and I couldn't acquire the experience without first acquiring a job.

The letter in hand, signed in ink by the superintendent of schools, required a second reading before the message hit home. It indicated that I'd been appointed to a one-year position and made a reference to salary and a contract. The contract was to go into effect on the first of September, less than three weeks away.

The full impact washed over me slowly: The emotionally draining process of interviews and what seemed like inevitable rejections had finally paid off. With the contract in hand, I could now call myself a teacher, complete with graduate degree, state certification—and a job. I proclaimed it out loud: "I'm a teacher!"

Between the day I received "the letter" and Opening Day only a brief period intervened. The bulk of what I had to accomplish involved interpreting the "Meadowfield Curriculum Guide," which seemed wide-ranging and overly general, and translating the document into individual lessons. In doing so I felt handicapped by having only a vague sense of the academic capabilities of my students. During a brief telephone conversation with my department chairman, Dr. Morrison, I learned that four out of my five classes were classified as grade 9 "general" (non-collegebound) students. The remaining class was tenth grade general level. Though I understood that general-level students were those who'd not been tracked as college prep or honors, I was less certain just what abilities or problems they might arrive with. (It wasn't until weeks after Opening Day, in fact, that it became clear that the general category encompassed almost any student who couldn't make it in the higher-level classes—either for academic, behavioral, emotional, or "other" reasons.) Nevertheless, I did my best to draw up some lessons intended to be flexible enough to accommodate these uncertainties, but specific enough to provide necessary direction and purpose.

Proceeding with my early, preschool planning I felt my initial mix of euphoria and professional pride waver beneath the swelling emotions churning inside. Because I'd had no personal contact with the young people who would soon become my students, I was in essence dealing with a fear of the unknown. While still completing graduate school I'd been compelled to read and discuss articles with titles such as "How to Survive Your First Year in the Classroom" Those anxiety-generating titles were reinforced by the "war stories" that circulated among my fellow teachers-to-be, stories that read like articles from one of the supermarket tabloids: "First-year teacher molested, beaten, raped. . . ."

The memory of those stories was mitigated somewhat by the physical appearance of Meadowfield. I'd made a return visit in order to speak personally to my department head and learn what I could about the school and my students. Dr. Morrison described the students as "predominantly" middle or upper-middle class, with a strong penchant for designer clothing and Gucci accessories. During my partial tour of the school's interior I was struck by the spotlessness of the corridors. The halls conjured up images of students who respected cleanliness, order, manners. Those images persisted until I realized that the students hadn't set foot in those halls during the previous two months, during which time the custodians had been busy cleaning every square inch of that immaculate interior.

The exterior of the building resembled other schools that had been erected in the past several decades. It looked like a fortress: all grey stone walls, lined with small windows set wide apart. The building was situated on an elevated expanse of land bordered by a thin belt of trees. The trees and foliage were sufficient enough to lend a sense of suburban respectability, dignity, and serenity.

Those impressions contrasted vividly with most of my experience in the city's public school system, in those schools where I'd taught first as a substitute and as a student teacher. Those schools had been typical urban institutions, afflicted with a multitude of racial and other problems associated with big city educational systems. Though I'd felt as if I'd learned more in those schools than I'd learned in some of the graduate courses I'd taken, I was still relieved to have been hired by one of the suburban schools.

The downside of this was the immense distance, academically and culturally, between the schools where I'd been trained and the system in which I was going to teach. In addition, there was an even larger distance between Meadowfield, the schools in which I'd worked previously, and the school where I'd been educated myself. My own career as a high school student had occurred in a rigidly authoritarian, parochial school (Chaminade Catholic) that compelled its all-male population to wear sport coats and ties, attend Mass daily, and maintain the length of one's hair well above the eyebrows and ears. Rather than instilling blind obedience and submission in me, the dictatorial nature of the school fostered an enduring sense of defiance and a reluctance to conform. My personal rebellion had resulted in numerous suspensions and had fueled speculation among both students and staff as to whether or not I'd graduate. The only class I could tolerate, actually, had been English, where we were occasionally permitted to do purely creative writing. For me, such writing represented a form of sheer bliss, while providing the imaginative freedom from the school and its restraints. While I did manage to graduate eventually, I had no intentions of becoming a teacher myself. If I'd mentioned that I was considering teaching as a career, no one would have taken me seriously. Not in a million years.

My Catholic School experience, during which I'd been compelled to learn through fear of punishment and eternal damnation, had an eventual effect on my own philosophy of education—even before I acknowledged it as a "philosophy of education." When I'd made the decision to enter teaching (some ten years after graduating high school), I'd already worked as a writer and part-time journalist. I'd chosen teaching because it afforded a means for combining my passion for language with my own need for a career that might be meaningful, gratifying, and creative. In considering the type of teacher I might want to be like, I thought first of the teachers I remembered—the Jesuit disciplinarians whose philosophy had traumatized me. Rather than appealing solely to authority, as my teachers had, I wanted to inspire students through my love of language and by conveying a sense of the beauty and power of words. I believed that if I could make a connection between what went on in English class and my students' lives outside the classroom, and maintain their attention at the same time—to keep them awake—then I wouldn't have to deal with the issue of discipline and authority. I thus spent the night before Opening Day reviewing those strategies and exercises I thought might best succeed in inspiring my students-to-be, though I admitted to myself that I didn't have a clue as to what they'd look like, think like, act like. Jokingly, I told my wife I *did* know that my students had a preference for Gucci accessories and certain designer fashions. . . .

Opening Day, the subject of my extended and imaginative speculation, daydreaming and insomnia, was a definite anticlimax. As anticipated, my students arrived dressed to kill. This year's styles favored acid-washed denim (jeans, jackets, purses, shirts). The fabric was everywhere, though there was no Gucci in evidence. As I watched the students watch each other, evaluating clothing and hair styles, I realized what sort of preparation had gone into planning and purchasing what they were going to wear on this occasion. Obviously many of these kids had spent substantial portions of their summer earnings or allowances on fashions to be displayed here on Opening Day. In contrast to their colorful, up-to-the-minute wardrobes, however, their attitudes (as they filed reluctantly to their seats) appeared indifferent or solemn: They might have been arriving at a wake. The exception, in each of my five classes, was a small clique of students who seemed to know one another from junior high and joked and teased conspicuously against the general silence that pervaded. The attitude they projected when I attempted conversation before the bell was similarly indifferent, suggesting that education might not be too high up on their agendas. After the bell signaled the beginning of class—and before I could introduce myself or explain the basic objectives of the class—a few voices demanded to know what books we'd be reading. For a quick moment or two, the question boosted my expectations by suggesting that these students possessed a deep love of reading and a certain experience with literature that I hadn't anticipated. The book titles I responded with, though, elicited a chorus of groans and comments limited primarily to "boring" (from at least a half-dozen mouths) to entire phrases, such as "What a drag!" I replied that I appreciated their comments, even the negative remarks. I also promised to do what I could to make the reading list more interesting and contemporary. Though my response was sincere, and I said it enthusiastically, it didn't seem to have a major impact. In the back of my mind I wondered if *any* reading list could possibly inspire this group. And, if so, what titles such a list might include. . . .

Though I'd planned an introductory exercise intended to help "break the ice," I was compelled instead to assist students in filling out various forms and paperwork that had been given to me just hours earlier as I'd entered the building. The surprise paperwork included yellow "Who to Contact in an Emergency" cards, blue "Family Background" sheets, and a half-dozen or so others. The forms and papers had been given to me along with a bulging manila envelope crammed with information of every imaginable sort: Some of it was to be distributed to students, some was intended for me. My own unfamiliarity with the processes involved, and the fact that I'd not done any of this before, contributed to the overall sense of confusion that was escalating within the room. Compounding my difficulty in explaining the directions, which I barely understood myself, was the name problem: the fact that for me, the individuals in the room lacked a means of identification. Though I didn't know *their* names, they knew that I was the individual listed on their schedules as English "Teacher X" (a fact resulting from my having been hired in August after the computers were programmed). Thus, the more perceptive students began immediately to refer to me as "Teacher X," or, simply, "Mr. X." I didn't mind this situation as much as the fact that I had no names by which to refer to them. As a result I called the attendance sheet as slowly and carefully as I could. This list contained a large percentage of Italian names, a few of which caused me to stumble in my pronunciation. (The student population reflected the ethnic diversity of the city of Meadowfield, where Italian and Irish working-class families predominated. There were a small number of black families, but there were no significant racial conflicts.) Each time I mispronounced one of their names, I inevitably evoked laughter, while contributing to the overall noise level. I attempted to blame the problem on computer error, explaining that the computer was responsible for the errors in the list. Their faces implied that they questioned the validity of that particular explanation.

Blaming the computer did nothing to ease the noise level or improve the sense of order, which the room lacked. To try to move things forward I appealed to what I assumed might be a mutual desire to complete the paperwork and to begin the introductory exercises. I promised that these would be fun and I assured them that we'd walk out feeling more comfortable with each other. I'd scarcely begun to explain the exercise when the bell rang and the students, as if propelled by springs, shot out of their desks and lunged, *en masse* toward the door. I learned afterward that the clock in the room was slow by at least ten minutes and that it could seldom be counted on to provide an accurate sense of time. This information was provided courtesy of a student who was repeating the ninth grade and had been through it all before. Before the student left she mentioned that she was only one of several repeaters who'd been placed in Teacher X's class. I didn't have time then to question why so many repeating students had found their way into my classes. I suspected that this hadn't occurred by chance or any great respect for my ability to resurrect the failing academic careers of the repeaters.

After the surprise bell, which had cut short the previous class, I attempted to compress the paperwork so that we would at least begin the introductory Making Contact exercises I'd decided were essential. The students though didn't exhibit the same strong desire to make contact—or at least not in the manner that I'd intended.

Instead, they devised various distractions and diversions that prevented the class from making any forward progress. (When I refer to they or them during this first tedious week I refer not to the majority, but to only a handful of disruptive students, the Cool Few with their own specialized agendas.) If one of these students, however, demanded to use the restroom, a half-dozen copycats, envious of the first student's sudden freedom, made similar bids for freedom via the corridor pass system. The destinations requested for these passes became increasingly vague and obscure. "Building C," one student asked, while another requested a pass to "the cages." I wondered silently where each of those places might be, whether those locations actually existed within the walls of Meadowfield High School. I knew that if I asked where they were though, or worse, *what* they were, I'd further weaken my precarious position as a new teacher—Teacher X. I struggled instead to recall that portion of the handbook that dealt with the physical layout of the school, as well as the approved procedures for giving out corridor passes. According to what I could recall, a teacher was compelled to grant a pass to any destination designated as being necessary to the student's well-being. Beyond that, I had no clear-cut sense of as to what destinations might be essential to their well-being or how far their rights extended in this area. At the same time I wondered about the well-being of the instructor and how far my own rights extended. The school administration had chosen not to offer an orientation to new faculty members. I learned later that this decision had less to do with the administrations's policy regarding new teachers than it did the extremely small staff turnover. (The year I was hired I was one of only six new teachers, all of whom were required to orient themselves.)

Wanting to avoid the suggestion of a confrontation, a policy dispute in which a student might emerge as victor over Teacher X, I remained liberal in the granting of passes. Each time I bent to sign a pass, though, I vowed, with rising consternation, to reread and commit to memory those portions of the Meadowfield Student Handbook that dealt in any way with corridor passes— or classroom behavior generally. When the bell rang to signal the end of class that had been advancing toward anarchy, I gave a vague shudder of relief. I was sweating, disheveled, nervous, and disorganized. The remaining classes, with the exception of a tenth grade class (a small, miraculously well-behaved group), followed the pattern of chaos established by the earlier classes. When the day's final bell rang, and the last bunch filed out, resplendent in their acid-washed glory, the floor behind them littered with a carpet of gum and candy wrappers, I whispered a small "Thank God." It had been one of the longest days of my life.

I left school that day in a kind of stupor, my eyes fixed straight ahead and not registering much: the general blur and confusion of screaming, over-dressed teenagers, many shouting as if they'd just been injected with adrenaline. As if they hadn't a care in the world. I considered stopping and speaking to an English teacher who taught in a room adjoining mine. A few teachers had poked their heads in my room earlier, offering a hello and perhaps wondering who this new teacher might be. I decided not to stop and seek advice today, however. This, after all, was only the first day: We weren't expected to have taught anything yet. When I passed my department chairman on the way out, and he inquired as to how it had gone, I told him with a straight face that it had gone smoothly, with just a "few wrinkles—nothing I didn't expect." He looked at me curiously, as if I might have something more to add. I did ask if I might drop in and speak to him in a few days, though not about anything serious. In response, he invited me to visit any time, and to let him know how I was doing. Before he turned away, I considered, for just a second, asking him how the corridor pass system worked. I didn't let myself though. I didn't want it known that I hadn't memorized in full the Meàdowfield School Handbook.

It was the student handbook, however, that I read from cover to cover after returning home that afternoon. In my reading it was revealed—under a section titled "Use and Abuse of Corridor Passes"—that teachers indeed must issue passes to "students requiring immediate use of restroom facilities" and

"for purposes relating to matters of health." Had I stuck to those two categories, most of the students who today had been given passes would have remained within the confines of Room C313. The book, which was meticulous in
matters of routine discipline, added that students "must remain in the classroom for the entire forty minutes as required by state law. . . . Time spent
outside the classroom must be made up after classes have ended." The "afterschool" sessions required that the teacher write a disciplinary card to the
headmaster to insure compliance. The heavily punitive aspect of the policy
and sense of punishment recalled my own Catholic high school experience
and authoritarian techniques of various Jesuit brothers. It consequently called
into question my own scarcely evolved educational philosophy. Using that approach I'd hoped to maintain my authority without resorting to routine punishment and discipline. Having spent only one day in class, though, I decided
to defer judgment of those two potentially controversial matters until I'd acquired more experience. I spent the rest of the evening reviewing and revis-
ing my lesson plans for the week. The activity for the next day, assuming
we'd finally complete the introductory exercises, involved each student's writing a personal English profile.

The following morning, despite my uneven sleep of the previous night, I
arrived in Room C313 projecting what I hoped might be a fairly positive attitude. I'd concluded that the challenges of opening day had resulted from the
accumulated tensions that had been building inside the students during the
previous summer. I assured myself that those tensions would disappear if I
didn't call attention to them.

On this second day I opted for solutions that seemed the least threatening, while bearing in mind the need to maintain order and structure. I began
in class with a joke I'd borrowed from a Jay Leno routine and no direct reference to the corridor pass issue, which I hoped had been a kind of first-day
novelty. When I attempted to shift from the joke into the English profile I
immediately ran into problems. The students had enjoyed the joke, and now
many of them were trying out jokes of their own, many of theirs vulgar
enough for an Eddie Murphy routine—something that would certainly rate an
X. This continued as I labored to explain the nuances of the English Profile:

> I'd like you to simply list on the paper I've passed out the titles of all of the
> literary works you've read during the previous year. No big deal. Just the names
> of the books along with a statement outlining whether you liked or didn't like
> them—and why.

The most vocal students—the Cool Few—pronounced the English Profile
excessively simple and possibly lacking in purpose. Others asked me, in perfectly serious voices, whether I'd mind explaining the meaning of the term
"literary work"—and then looked at me strangely when I answered that it was
only a *book*, whatever they'd read during their previous English class. Those
who seemed to understand what was being asked for replied with comments
like: "I've never had to do anything like *this* for an English class. . . . I didn't
really *read* anything last year—not in English class anyway." And finally,

"Reading is so boring—are you serious? You're asking us to remember something that we were supposed to have read a *year* ago?"

I wondered only a second or two about the seriousness of their questions. As the questions—and the general attitude of the class—became more apparent I realized for the first time what the difference might be between a general-level class and an honors or college prep class: distinctions that before had seemed somewhat ambiguous to me. The students who'd been placed in my general-level class obviously arrived with attitude as well as academic problems. Despite the defiant undertones I attempted to respond as sincerely as possible to their questions and comments. I was caught in mid-response by a hand that shot up in what appeared to be an urgent gesture. If I had known the student better, I might have ignored her and proceeded to the next question. Instead, I called on her, still hopeful for some favorable response to the exercise.

"I gotta go," the girl declared flatly, offering no further explanation.

"Where would you like to go?" I asked, though I knew, or at least I suspected.

"Ladies' room," she replied, as if there were no other possible destination in life.

"Could it possibly wait until later?" I inquired, attempting a firm-but-fair tone of voice. "The bell rings in less than ten minutes. What we're trying to do here is important."

She stared back as if I hadn't said anything. "Hey, look, I gotta go *now*."

The attention in the room, which I'd had to fight for just a moment ago, now belonged entirely to the girl and myself. The girl, whose name I'd called from the roster at the beginning of class and now could not remember, had seemingly raised her hand in search of attention. Now, like a celebrity at a photo opportunity, she basked in sudden recognition. Meanwhile, the other students, hungry for anything resembling a confrontation, a story controversial enough to be retold over lunch, kept their eyes and ears riveted on Teacher X.

I weighed my options and decided that there weren't very many. I waited just a moment or two, staring at her, before I bent over to write the pass. I handed the pass over to her and I reminded the class that in the future they should find a more appropriate time to use the restroom. A few of the remaining students obviously moved by the force of my suggestion, promptly duplicated the first girl's request, citing their own need to utilize the facilities. I asked whether *they'd* read the handbook recently. I then mentioned that any time spent outside the room would be made up after school and that only one student at a time would be permitted out.

After responding to several protests I attempted to steer the class back to the English Profile, where we'd been when the pass request was made. Though no one else requested a pass during that period, the damage had already been done, the tone of the class shattered. The room was noisier, less structured, with students occasionally leaving their seats to wander briefly or chat with a friend in another aisle.

In my mind I imagined one of the students—a member of the Cool Few—who was keeping a running evaluation of my performance, grading the wisdom of my decisions and awarding points according to some arbitrary criteria. Clearly, by granting the pass to the pouting girl without first questioning her motives and possible intentions, I'd lost something in the eyes of my imagined evaluator. I wanted to believe otherwise, that in responding as I had to her request, giving her what she wanted, that I'd rise in the opinion polls. The noise that had begun to swell around me and nearly kept us from completing the profile before the bell rang, argued that I'd handled it inappropriately.

If that were true, that I'd mishandled the incident while at the same time adhering to the school regulations—and my own general philosophy—it left me in what seemed to be a difficult situation. I could have treated the request more casually, and perhaps sunk lower in the "polls" or I could have taken an extreme hard line, flatly denying the request or even ignoring it. The latter would probably have been even less popular than the first option, while violating my own still liberal philosophy regarding matters of classroom discipline: the legacy of my rigid Catholic school experience, a stance that argued against the excessive use of conventional disciplinary techniques. Obviously I'd have to rethink and reconsider my philosophy of discipline. That couldn't be accomplished at the moment though and, as the next class straggled in, I hoped that somehow the problem would fade away with the passage of time.

The second class was pretty much a repeat of the first. Two students requested passes (one to the restroom, one to the nurse), while the general tone alternated between mild chaos and uneasy silence. We made it through the English profile with no major challenges, though a few students poised questions that vaguely resembled the "I can't really remember having read anything" remarks that had been popular with the earlier group. The questions generated a certain amount of attention for the questioners, and succeeded in briefly bogging down the class. These challenges made me realize how important it was for many students simply to obtain the attention of their peers, regardless of how that attention was achieved.

The third class, the tenth graders, breezed through the profile with such ease that I was briefly astonished. I'd assumed that the exercise, and inevitable distractions and disruptions, would consume the entire period. This more mature group completed the profile in about 25 minutes. Afterward we talked briefly about which literary works they'd enjoyed and which they hadn't. Some of these students confessed that they found some of the reading done in school to be "boring," and one said that she "couldn't imagine reading outside of school." Their comments though didn't have the underlying sense of antagonism and defiance that the ninth graders had projected. The comments made by the sophomores led into a discussion about why reading turned off so many students, whether this attitude was to be condemned—or what might be done to change it. "My parents don't read either," stated the girl who'd commented earlier. "They usually only read the newspaper and my father runs his own business. . . ."

The ensuing dialogue, which involved most of the students in the class, was more or less what I'd intended to achieve with *all* of my classes. I didn't expect them to come in the door loving writing and literature. If they could talk about their attitudes though, and remain open to change, then it seemed like I could teach them. When the bell rang I considered briefly the emotional distance that separated freshman and sophomore high school students. At this point I had no theories about that "distance" or how to instill those qualities I found in my tenth-graders in the minds of the younger students. I was aware that the freshmen were under great pressure to adapt to the still threatening high school environment. As a result, their energies, especially those of the general-level students, were less likely to be directed toward academic objectives. For the moment, lacking answers to my questions, I was merely grateful that I had been given the class of sophomores.

The day's two remaining classes largely resembled the earlier ones: a few outbursts of noise, some half-hearted critiques of the English profile; three high-volume gum-chewers who had to be asked, repeatedly, to reduce their chewing activity, not because it bothered me personally, I assured them, but it did distract other students. Immediately after making this assertion I was informed by several members of the class, all chronic gum-chewers, that the gum-chewing and snapping didn't bother them, or anyone else, in the slightest. I then asked again that they turn down the volume on the gum. I asked, and was pretty much ignored. As a disciplinary issue, gum-chewing was largely a discretionary matter, one that the teacher could either tolerate or ban. At the present time I opted for compromise, informing them that they could continue to chew the gum unless the noise got out of hand. When a student asked me to define, exactly, what I meant by "out of hand," I explained that it was a matter of common sense and common courtesy. I was beginning to sense that issues such as the gum question were issues I could easily get stuck in. I wanted to teach them—not to spend whole class periods mapping out rules and policies that pertained to the volume of a student's gum-chewing, whether or not to allow students to escape the room and then devising means to have them come back after school. I hoped, as with other discipline-related matters, that they'd diminish as we became involved with the real subject matter of the course.

At the conclusion of the second day, however, I had definite doubts that some of the problems confronting me would simply fade with the passing of time. Instead of leaving school at the end of the final period I limped into the teachers' room, hopeful that someone from the English department would happen in. I eventually cornered a teacher willing to talk, one who seemed sympathetic to the issues I raised: the corridor pass problem, high-volume gum-chewing, questions designed to distract and garner attention for the questioner.

The woman, who turned out to be a history teacher, encouraged me not to take it personally, assuming correctly, that I *had* been taking it all personally. She explained, as I'd begun to suspect, that the ninth-grade general-level classes contained students with the greatest percentage of disciplinary and other problems—and the lowest test scores. "That isn't always the case though," she added, "some of the kids thrown in those classes are intelligent. Some could handle college prep or honors classes if they were motivated. . . . They get dumped into the general or SPED classes because they're not willing to make an effort, or because they have some additional problem that gets in their way."

When I questioned her about the additional problems she mentioned alcohol and substance abuse, suicide attempts, parental conflicts: "It was nothing like it was when I was going to school. All these problems. It's all different now. . . ."

Though I didn't press her as to the year that she might have attended high school, it was obviously a good 20 years ago. Possibly longer. She was similar in age, though, to many of the other staff members at Meadowfield, where the average age of the teaching staff seemed to be the early 50s. In the entire high school (with an enrollment in the neighborhood of 2000 students) there were less than a dozen teachers in their 20s.

As teachers drifted in and out of the teachers' room that afternoon, I introduced myself to several. Some seemed friendly and outgoing, a few merely quiet or reserved. What struck me most was the near absence of teachers my own age (most of the younger teachers turned out to be "subs") and the fact that the majority of the faculty lived in or close by the town of Meadowfield. This implied that the residents saw themselves as insiders and the nonresidents as outsiders. I wondered briefly if this generalization might indeed be valid, or merely the result of my sense of myself—as the newest English teacher on the floor—as an outsider.

In any event, I felt less outside the flow of things after my series of mini-conversations. The last teacher I'd spoken to, an English teacher named Elizabeth, confirmed that the general-level classes were often used as "dumping grounds" for students who couldn't be conveniently tracked in the higher-level classes. She spoke of a year in which she'd been assigned five freshman, general-level classes and the ongoing problems she'd experienced that year. She'd threatened to resign the following year if she were given a schedule like that again. The following year she was given all upper-level classes. Before she stood to leave she mentioned that the general-level classes now usually were given to the new teachers. "They don't have tenure yet, so they can't complain too loudly about it," she added.

Though I found her comments supportive and empathetic, we didn't get into specific problem-solving techniques or strategies that might improve some of my classes. The conversations and verbal exchange felt good though and were, I assured myself, a beginning: the possible start of my journey from "outsider" to "insider" in a system that I didn't yet understand. . . .

Earlier in the year, before I was even certain that I'd have a job, I promised myself that I'd do everything possible to convey to my students the range of possibilities and power inherent in language: its beauty as well as its practical applications. In conveying these ideas, which to a large degree had evolved from my own passion for language, I'd intended to implement teaching strategies that might make learning and teaching English both interesting and academically effective.

My teaching strategies were based, to a large extent, on the concept that students (and people generally) possessed a basic need to express and share experiences, feelings, and ideas with others. If I could create a classroom context in which students felt encouraged to explore the imaginative possibilities of words, then English class could become a stimulating and dynamic experience, for students as well as Teacher X. Built into this concept was a belief that language arts activities, properly designed and supervised, could work to transcend the English-is-boring syndrome, as well as overcome various behavioral and disciplinary challenges. In addition, I believed that the more traditional aspects of English (grammar, mechanics) might be handled by teaching them within the context of various writing activities and exercises.

While planning these exercises (before I'd authored my first corridor pass) I'd envisioned classes where students alternated between stimulating and meaningful discussions and silent writing/thinking exercises.

In reality, however, this wasn't the way it worked out.

Instead of the intense, content-focused classroom I'd imagined and planned for, what actually resulted were near daily battles for control. From the moment that the bell rang, when many of my students were still shuffling in—some minus books, notebooks, writing materials—I wrestled to assert control. Though it was never the majority of the students who engaged in these battles, the disruptive students depicted themselves as somehow heroic or worthy of the moral support, or at least the attention, of the others. More often than not they got what they wanted.

My initial response to the problem of classroom discipline was an attempt to channel disruptive energies into more positive directions. I announced that positive class participation would be rewarded when grades were issued: 10 percent of their quarterly grade would be based on in-class behavior (the verbal expression or reflection of whatever we were studying). I then explained that this component of their grade could be lowered or forfeited entirely if their class participation was consistently negative or distracting to me or the other students. This announcement resulted in few major changes, as the consistently disruptive crowd was relatively immune to the threat of poor grades. It thus became clear that a portion of my general-level students did not attend school with the intention of doing well academically. Some of them were clearly waiting until they became old enough to drop out legally. As a result, their objectives were not limited by anything as meaningless as a mere grade.

Despite their immunity to the threat of a failing grade, these students normally did maintain a social agenda of some kind and class participation for them represented an opportunity to cultivate relationships with the opposite sex. These students could thus be affected by shifting their seating arrangement. I did so with the intention of separating the talkative, "don't-threaten-me-with-a-failing-grade" type student from others who shared their desire to communicate and disrupt. Though I did achieve some success with the musical chairs strategy, there were definite problems with it. The first was that there simply weren't enough nontalkers available in most of my classes. The second problem was that, once a student was transferred to a more remote corner of the room, they sometimes felt a compulsion to overcome that new isolation by simply *yelling*—talking louder than before—in order to maintain communications with friends.

These noise-related problems and challenges were the most obvious and annoying of the issues that confronted me during my first few months at Meadowfield. Despite the negative effect these problems had on the class, as well as my own morale, I nevertheless managed temporarily to avoid taking a harsh stand on matters of classroom discipline. I had had several "heart-to-heart" discussions with my classes designed to focus attention on the problem of noise and with the hope of making it unnecessary to adopt harsh disciplinary measures. In these talks I described, from a personal point of view, how frustrating it was to be confronted daily with such a noisy classroom. I explained that this problem was keeping the majority of students from learning things that they needed to know. I wanted them to grasp that a few self-centered students, some of whom were admired by the others, were helping to cheat them out of an education. When given a chance to respond, some stated that they realized that they were talking too loud or too frequently, but did so only because the subject matter itself was so boring. The B word again. Others explained that they talked only because the person in front or behind them was also talking. We spent the rest of the period discussing their comments and attitudes. At the end I promised that I'd do everything possible to make the subject more interesting, including the use of films and videos. I stated that this would be possible only if they succeeded in improving the atmosphere in the room and keeping the noise to a minimum. I concluded by emphasizing the need as well as the benefits of greater cooperation.

For a week or so after the talk, the quality of life in Room C313 improved noticeably. The situation was eventually shattered, however, by a core group of students, small but influential, for whom the desire to talk—and attract attention—was more important than the needs of everyone else. It was this group that eventually managed to restore the near chaos that at times had reigned prior to our heart-to-heart discussion.

This dismal state of affairs continued until I began to receive warnings and comments from outside Room C313. The first came from a teacher whose room adjoined mine. She mentioned, as discreetly as possible, that on certain days my room was "excessively loud" or "boisterous." In addition, I heard more or less the same comments from a few of my own students, members of a cooperative faction that was exactly the opposite of the Cool Few. The other teacher and my own students offered variations on the same advice. Clamp down.

Their comments and advice affirmed what I'd been sensing internally: that I'd permitted a handful of students—most of whom wouldn't pass and didn't care whether anyone else passed—to prevent me from achieving and maintaining the necessary level of order. As a result, I'd been unable to implement many of the activities, including field trips, visits to the computer lab, small group activities inside the classroom, that I'd originally planned and believed were necessary in order to accomplish my academic goals. What we were doing instead was largely the type of activity I'd intended earlier to avoid: "busy work" and more conventional workbook exercises chosen to keep students occupied and quiet. Though these activities succeeded in keeping students active, they weren't inspirational or stimulating in any way. I'd thus been compelled to compromise the more imaginative and effective activities, including exercises I believed would stimulate a genuine interest in language arts, for activities intended to control behavior and maintain a quiet classroom. The result was a situation that alternated between periods of fragile calm and disruptive outbursts that had been the subject of the recent complaints.

Underlying this day-to-day struggle—and this is what hurt the most, the thing that kept me awake at night—was my own sense that I was failing in what I'd set out to do: that I wasn't fulfilling my own expectations or those of some of my students.

To add irony to the situation were the evaluations I'd received from my department head during the difficult first two quarters. Those evaluations, for the most part, were exceptionally good, almost enthusiastically so. I wasn't certain if my department head was doing this merely to build up my confidence, or whether he actually was impressed with what I was doing. On the days he'd come to evaluate I'd been blessed that some of my worst students, the coolest of the Cool Few, had chosen to cut class. I'd also planned lessons for those days that were imaginative and engaging. One lesson dealt with the nature of contemporary advertising and the ways in which ads utilized language. Department Chairman Morrison had himself taught such a unit on advertising when he was still teaching, so he thought the lesson was excellent. The evaluation looked amazingly good typed out on paper, so much so that I thought first it might have been intended for someone else. Even so, I felt lousy about the way things were going in the classroom.

When I finally got serious about making changes in my teaching strategy, abandoning the easy-going, liberal philosophy that had evolved as a reaction to the experiences I'd undergone in a strict Catholic high school, I was influenced by a combination of factors. These ranged from critical comments from the administrators on my floor to the theft of a quantity of blank corridor passes from my desk. After the theft, passes began turning up everywhere: some with my name forged on them, some with the names of other teachers. Each of the forged passes, about three dozen of them, eventually came back to me. Some were presented by angry teachers, some by angry submasters, and one, by the headmaster himself, as angry as I'd ever seen him. Although it was the students who'd stolen the passes, it was the teacher, he stated, who'd "created an environment where such ignoble behavior might take place."

I vowed then that this was indeed it. That life in Room C313 was going to change. . . .

One of the first changes made was my adoption of a disciplinary strategy that had been suggested earlier in the year by a teacher whose room adjoined mine. She urged me to totally isolate disruptive students by "sentencing" them to a quiet row, separate from the other desks. Offending students were permitted no conversation at all. The next day I wrote Quiet Row on the board in block letters and explained the implications. I informed them that any student who continued to be disruptive would be "sentenced" to silent time to be spent in the newly created row of seats.

Although the announcement triggered a chorus of laughter and questions intended to mock the idea, three students had received quiet row sentences by the end of the period. The next day these students found themselves sitting in chairs set well apart from their peers. They were given tedious writing assignments intended to keep them busy the entire period. Each time they complained, I reminded them that their "sentences" would be extended if they continued to talk during class. The arrangement, within two days, dramatically lowered the level of noise within the room. Furthermore, the "quiet" students now waited until *after* class before requesting to return to their previous seats. Despite those requests, I required each student to serve his or her entire sentence (ranging in length from two to four days, depending on the severity of their misdemeanor). The changed atmosphere in the room began to make teaching, as well as learning, a good deal easier. On the third day the "quiet row" concept had been in effect, I had at least two students thank me for silencing their disruptive comrades. Their gratitude signaled the beginning of a change in the way that the majority of the students perceived the class: the idea that it was their behavior, as much as the teacher's, that potentially determined what sort of experience they'd have in English class.

The quiet row was not the only change that month. I obtained from the office the phone numbers of the parents of my most problematic students. Most of the parents who could be reached seemed grateful to be contacted by a teacher. Not all of them were happy when I informed them that their darling offspring were creating problems, though they all promised some sort of action would be taken at home: a loss of telephone, access to the family car, or other privileges. Although a few of these parents were concerned enough to visit school and discuss the situation with me, some of the parents I wanted most to reach were unavailable. This affirmed my own sense that the students who did the best in school generally came from families in which the parents were concerned about the progress of their children in school—or at least were home when someone phoned to talk about their children.

The most positive, and unexpected, result of the get tough policies was that I ended up spending more time after school with my most difficult students. Many were kids whom I'd spoken to only in a negative manner. Thus I found myself in a closed room with students who for months had assumed the role of adversary—though I knew almost nothing about them.

During the first such sessions, with only a little hall noise trickling in under the door, we found ourselves in staring sessions in which nearly all of the conversation was monosyllabic:

"Glad you could make it," I'd begin.

"Whad'ya expect? Did I have a choice?"

"Well, you made a decision to come. . . . I'm pleased by that."

"How long are you going to make me stay?"

"That depends . . . on your attitude. Maybe 15–20 minutes."

Generally, the rest of the session was broken only by questions from the student regarding the remaining amount of time. Resisting efforts on my part to lighten the tone of the event, the student's expression usually ranged from sullen to angry, brightening only when I announced the end of the session.

That was the format that most of the initial sessions followed. The students who were compelled to return for additional sessions, however, sometimes opened up and began to talk—either out of boredom or personal need. During some of these conversations I was surprised by the kind of information that was expressed. Students who only a few months ago behaved like prisoners of war, revealing only their name and class rank, began to tell me personal information about their home lives, problems, families, friends, and jobs. Consequently I discovered that most of my afterschool crowd, the disrupters and distracters, possessed some form of emotional-adjustment problem. Their problems ranged from minor conflicts with their peers and parents, to more serious problems pertaining to alcohol or drug abuse, child abuse, and thoughts of suicide.

When a girl named Anna, who'd previously been one of my most difficult students, revealed that her father had recently claimed not to love her, I was momentarily stunned. I told her that she may have misunderstood him, and we spent the next 30 minutes discussing her troubled relationship with her parents, a situation that had recently influenced her to run away from home briefly. After we'd finished talking I escorted her down the hall and into the guidance counselor's office. After explaining the situation to the counselor, who agreed to continue the conversation regarding her problems at home, I left with an entirely different conception of my student and how I might best deal with her. I felt honored that she'd selected me to share her problems with, and I couldn't help but be bothered by the seriousness of those problems.

The students who sometimes were the most disruptive were often the most popular and influential. When some of these, including Anna, returned to class and began to make positive comments about Teacher X—now known as Mr. Knoll—it had a ripple effect. Anna, for example, had formerly and publicly loathed English class. When she returned after our "deep" conversation she projected a positive, almost born again attitude toward all things literary, including her instructor. These new attitudes gradually filtered through the room and the tone and behavior of the class began to improve. The word I received later, during another after-hours session, was that many of my former detractors were now describing me as "humane," "capable of relating," and able to discuss matters and issues unrelated to English class. When I heard these remarks I felt, for the first time, that I might not be failing after all, that on some basic level I was beginning to get through to them.

After the positive experience with Anna I continued to converse regularly with my afterschool students, often in the presence of a counselor when the situation warranted. More positive ripple effects began to circulate and I began to feel as if the stereotype they'd assigned to me had been broken.

In the absence of a clear-cut means of classification, they began to wonder what I might be like in real life. Thus, mixed in with questions about the nature of literature and the appropriate place to utilize semicolons there were other questions: "Are you married, Mr. Knoll?" "Have any kids of your own?" "What kind of music do you listen to?"

Though the questions were, to a degree, distracting, they weren't hostile or threatening, and I responded as openly as was appropriate. At the same time I attempted to guide the flow of conversation back to the subject matter. Steadily, the tone of the class became more subdued, tolerant, and cooperative. Though they were still far from perfect, their behavior—and the general ambiance of the room—was such that I could now implement the activities I'd planned months previously. We did exercises on the purpose of language. Writing exercises of all kinds. Interviews. Role-playing. Activities done in pairs or small groups. A three-day film unit prompted students as well as teachers from other classes to stop by and make inquiries.

Eventually I began to seek out new ideas and activities to supplement my own supply, which was beginning to run dry. It was the content now that was holding their attention, though there remained a general awareness that disciplinary measures would be taken if circumstances required. In my quest for new ideas and teaching strategies I was fortunate to be able to attend the annual spring conference of the National Council of Teachers of English (NCTE). The conference drew teachers, researchers, and language arts experts from across the country. For the three days of the conference I was exposed to presentations on every aspect of English. I left with three legal pads full of ideas and strategies, much of which I was anxious to try out. The only disappointing aspect of my participation at the conference was that none of the other English staff at Meadowfield shared the enthusiasm; some didn't seem to know what the N.C.T.E. was or that it even existed. These were the same teachers who discouraged the few new teachers from "talking shop" during lunch breaks and kept the conversation on matters far removed from teaching. (I'd twice initiated conversations in the lunchroom that had something to do with teaching or teaching strategies and had been told, both times, that such topics weren't discussed over lunch.) In one sense I understood why some veteran teachers felt like this. At the same time I vowed that I'd never let myself become that burnt out or indifferent toward my profession.

The combination of new ideas I'd acquired at the English conference and the improved atmosphere in my room carried me through the end of the third quarter with a minimum of problems. Despite the absence of major challenges I was nevertheless anxious for spring vacation. When it finally arrived my wife and I managed to escape for a brief few days in the Bahamas, something we couldn't afford, but felt compelled to do anyway. What was disillusioning there on the island, a good 1500 miles from Boston, were the hordes of drunken, shouting high school students who'd chosen to stay in the same hotel. It required some talking in order to persuade the hotel manager to move us to a guest house, which was slightly more expensive but isolated from the mobs of drunken young Americans. Our credit cards could handle the additional expense, but just barely.

My return to Massachusetts, and reality, was accompanied by an unexpected "pink slip" from the Meadowfield School Committee stating that they'd voted not to rehire any of the untenured English faculty. The decision was ostensibly based on declining student enrollment and a cutback in the city budget. Although the layoff was in no way a consequence of my performance, which ironically was improving, it was a difficult blow psychologically. In the wake of the notice I spent the next several days teaching as if I were on automatic pilot. I had almost no feeling at all for what I was doing. I felt victimized, exploited, and hurt, professionally and personally. When I'd taken the job I'd done so with the understanding (from my department head) that the following year I'd be able to do something more directly connected with writing instruction, which was my area of specialization. Dr. Morrison had hoped to develop a Writing Lab and a new course that would offer students specialized assistance with writing.

During the remaining portion of the fourth quarter, part of me wanted nothing to do with teaching. I wanted, at some level, to simply get through the required material, do it as quickly and superficially as possible, and proceed to the next job, the next school, the next set of challenges. Up until this point I'd channeled nearly all of my energies into improving the quality of my teaching and facilitating change in the attitudes of my students. Now at this point in the year, when many of my students *had* changed, they were the first to notice and display concern when my own attitude began to sag. It was obvious that they now had certain expectations about what was supposed to go on in Room C313. Many of them had gotten into the habit of dropping by after school—without a disciplinary slip. These students were a very different group than those I'd worked with way back in September. Their attitude helped keep my own spirits up after I'd received the pink slip.

I thus felt no choice but to proceed with the new ideas I'd seen demonstrated at the N.C.T.E. conference. I decided to utilize one of these activities, a collaborative book project, as the year's culminating writing event. In explaining this project to my students I said they'd be authoring a book together, with each student writing one or two chapters. The book's title and table of contents would be written together, in class, with the individual chapters to be authored later.

We'd selected a title—My First Year: High Lights and Low Lights—and were developing the table of contents when I noticed a disruption in the back of the room. Brian, a student who repeated grade 9, had a comic book open on his desk, while another student leaned backward to examine the book with him. Both of these students had been major problems throughout the year, requiring a variety of disciplinary tactics before they'd begun to improve. When I paused in my explanation to look at Brian and his friend, the other students immediately noticed, staring first at me, then back toward Brian. They watched me zero in on the situation and then they waited, expectantly, for something to happen. A confrontation? A disciplinary slip? A yelling match?

Before any of these things could happen though, one of the other students, herself a former member of the after-hours clique, nudged Brian and whispered something I couldn't hear. Brian put the comic book under his desk, opened his notebook, and stared attentively forward as if nothing had happened. As it turned out—nothing did happen. The tension in the room seemed to relax, a few students commenting quietly on what had taken place, or almost had, before we resumed work on the book project.

My First Year: High Lights and Low Lights turned out far better than I had anticipated. As the students became involved they added art work and graphics of various kinds. They assisted each other in editing their chapters and then rewriting them on word processors. We added covers made from colored paper and a color photograph taken with the school's 35-mm camera. When the book was finished it didn't look like something that had been done in school. And no one, not even the teacher, had imagined in September that such a project might be accomplished in June—not by a bunch of general-level students.

The book became a kind of academic and emotional catharsis. When it had been completed, photocopied, bound, and distributed everyone was surprised—and proud. For me, the book became a symbol of what my most difficult students could accomplish when challenged. For both teacher *and* students, the book became a physical, tangible reminder of what was possible when English class students, regardless of what level they were, learned to work together.

As the students filed out on the final day of school, exchanging handshakes and goodbyes, they carried their books with them—the books they'd made themselves.

EPILOGUE

Michael Knoll resides in Boston and continues to teach English, with a good deal more ease and significantly less frustration and insomnia than he experienced during his sometimes perilous first year in the classroom. He's abandoned his fantasy of escaping to Morocco and selling rugs and baskets to the tourists. He's hopeful about the future and states that: "After the first year things can only get better. . . ."

QUESTIONS FOR DISCUSSION

7.1 Knoll's past experience as a student shapes his philosophy and teaching.
   (a) In what ways is this influence useful?
   (b) In what ways is it counterproductive?

7.2 Knoll uses different techniques to control his students' behavior during the first half of the school year.
   (a) Why don't his students take him seriously?

(b) In what ways is he responsible for his students' poor attitudes?

(c) What specific steps does Knoll take to turn things around in his classroom so that students are able to learn?

(d) Discuss why and how each of the four methods that Knoll uses alters his students' behavior.

7.3 Imagine that your students complain to you that the books you assign to them "were boring." Would you try to make any changes in the course content? If so, what would they be? If not, explain why you would leave things intact.

7.4 The administration gives Knoll, a first-year teacher, all general-level classes.

(a) What hidden message are they giving Knoll and his students?

(b) Within the context is Knoll's humane and caring attitude toward students effective in changing negative attitudes and behavior?

Chapter
8

Something Today Made Me Cry

Jane Larsen

The first year of teaching is one of weightlessness and uncertainty. You move through it like a dancer who cannot hear the music. Potholes open up before you. People wearing masks dart out to greet you. Time loses meaning. If you sleep, you revive to find yourself thinking, not about your husband or your children, but about teaching. The fantasy arises that you are stuck in the moment, whatever you are in the midst of, whatever problem has stopped you dead, cannot be solved; your life will not go on beyond that moment. Though ordinarily creative, in the sleeplessness of the first year you may find yourself incapable of imaginative flight. Then, pray for a mentor or a colleague who will take over that function. Hope for a soul who has been teaching a long time to see your trouble and drag you breathless out of the holes into which you will fall. Search for a spirit who sees humor in the predicament. Hang onto those moments she shows you, for you will need them in your longest, most ungainly teaching year.

The indignities of the first year lend it a gracelessness and humor. The adept second-year teacher, for example, never falls into the trap of discussing a student's grade the minute he shoves the paper under her nose. But the first-year teacher says, "You don't like the grade? Your mother says it's a pretty good paper? You don't see how you could have gotten a C when you read Eli's paper and I gave him a B and yours is much better?" By now, she is hot under the collar, furious with the kid, and annoyed with her teachers, who "never taught her how to grade."

Borrowing from what the late Supreme Court Justice Potter Stewart said of pornography—I cannot define an A paper, but "I know one when I see it." How do you grade a paper? I have come to realize that I grade a paper according to percentage of accomplishment. I decide what would constitute a perfect paper and work down from there. Once in a while I look across the class to make sure of relative accomplishment, but for the most part I grade according to the ability of each student. A brilliant student not working will get a C on a paper for which a struggling student would receive a B. I will raise a grade to encourage a student who by luck or design finds himself on the right track. But, I still need to talk to someone about this. Am I right to think of grades as a coercion to move kids from one level to another? I need to talk. The wise second-year teacher buys some time. "Make an appointment, Matthew," he says. "Let's see. How's Friday at 2? Oh, and leave your paper." That allows Matthew to collect himself and allows the teacher to give some "serious" thought to the matter so that the discussion on Friday will give him an opportunity to teach Matthew something that he has been wanting the student to learn.

I left the first year with relief and the sense that I had left shambles behind me. I felt shame at closing the lid on the fist year, leaving all those "bodies" behind. The first year you trust maxims that satisfy the intellect but ignore the gut. I comforted myself with the maxim, "The second year will be better." As August approached my gut said, "Why will the second year be better? Aren't you the one who taught *Zen and the Art of Motorcycle Maintenance* and *MacBeth* as if they were the same work? Aren't you the one who gave the same paper assignment on *Typhoon* and on *Les Misérables*?" The fear was justified. It took me until March of the second year to feel that I understood what is meant to teach. A long gestation; or is it? We hope for giant steps; maybe we should be content with baby steps. I am embarrassed now by the obvious rightness of this conclusion.

Let us go back to the beginning of that long sleepless year, September of the first year of teaching. I would be part-time that first year. The plan was for me to teach two sections of a writing course in the fall and two sections of a remedial reading course in the spring. As things developed, I would also pick up a Humanities course in the spring.

A major player in my first year would be the department chairman, Trevor Donald, someone I had known a long time. I first knew of Trevor Donald when my middle child came home one day in his junior year happily intrigued with his English course. My son, who on principle refused to work for grades, was serenely content. I discovered that his comfort was related to the fact that Dr. Donald did not put grades on the kids' papers. They were to rely upon the comments. This suited my son perfectly. The course was called Semiotics. Dr. Donald had created it. As part of the course my son spent hours on hands and knees on the brick walk leading to our house observing the behavior of ants. The miracle wrought in my son stayed with me. Trevor Donald's mind is that of a philosopher whose bent is practical in that it seeks young minds while it purposefully ignores the horrors of adolescence. He appeals with a perversity and deadly intent to haul out of them what is best in them. What is best at this age, he contends, is their burgeoning intellect. Trevor digs them out of themselves, and captures them. No kid's mind is in better hands. No beginning teacher could have a more inspiring model. He can, without a qualm, seize and, in his words, "ruin" the minds of his students. That is, he can change them irrevocably, without a twinge. But he holds what he calls his "baby teachers" to a different challenge. They may copy, but not too close by. It is as if his fear is that his new teachers will follow without internalizing, without creating, without making things their own.

Trevor's mentoring becomes something with three sides. He supports by discussing material and techniques before class; he sits in on a class and records what went on; he evaluates what he saw and gives advice about "how to do it better." In September, Trevor said that we might each order one new book for each course. Since I was teaching one course—Craft of Writing— that meant that I could select one book. After reading the course description, I realized that I wanted to have the students create some subject matter that interested them. In a way that would trick them into multiple rewrites, I would have them transform the material from short story form to poetry to drama and back to short story form. This unit would constitute a mini- preparation for the semester that would follow. We would then do full units on the short story, poetry, drama, and, finally, a long piece in any form they chose. For a college essay the next year, one student chose to identify the cycle of poems on his friends that he wrote in this class as the most significant academic experience of his high school career. So the class was not without its successes, though I did not not know it at the time.

Trevor asked as well that in these fall writing courses that we include reading. I decided to use a short story by Joyce, "The Encounter," in the mini-unit; poetry by Dylan Thomas, James Wright, and Elizabeth Bishop; *Waiting for Godot* by Beckett, and *The Metamorphosis* by Kafka. For a "new book" I requested John Irving's *The Cider House Rules*. I had read it the summer before at the suggestion of a friend who had remarked on the equi- table presentation it made on abortion. I had read it not thinking that I would use it in a course in November. Now, however, that the opportunity was here to include the work of a working author, I jumped at the chance to introduce the kids to *The Cider House Rules*.

By November, the classes were already beginning to feel like cans of un- ruly worms. Those who would show their stripes had shown them. The stu- dents who thought they were smarter than me and who had no use for beginning teachers, had already made themselves known. Those who thought I favored them demonstrated their relative comfort. Young people with learn- ing disabilities had taught me to encourage their splendid verbal production and to work with their difficulties in writing. Amidst the chaos and order, I handed them a 600-page novel.

According to my instructions, the students were to read ahead, to push through the book ahead of me. It was a technique I had learned from Trevor. For several days I heard from both sections of Craft of Writing that *The Cider House Rules* was disgusting. One girl in particular, an athlete, a somber girl who felt she could not write, accosted me directly. "Mrs. Larsen," she said one day. "This is a truly disgusting book." She paused. "In fact," she went on, "this is the most disgusting book I have ever read." I think I simply did not want to hear it. Somewhere I must have reasoned that I had read it in the summer and had not found it offensive, so projecting my own proclivities onto her, I opined that she must be overreacting. That night I went home to read chapter three in anticipation of tomorrow's classes. The words flew off the page: "The naked woman lay with her long legs spread-eagled on a rug—a wildly confused Persian or Oriental (Homer Wells didn't know the difference)—and the pony, facing the wrong way, straddled her . . . ." It was only a postcard, but to me that did not matter.

How could I have given that to 16-year-olds? I could not see how I could get beyond the maw that had now opened up before me. It was easy to imagine irate parents beating down the doors of the school. Whatever deficits of character for which I maligned myself in fits of pique had finally come out. The game was over. I had been impulsive and irresponsible in my choice. In despair, I realized that my career was over before it had begun.

I dragged my pink book bag and myself into Trevor's office the next morning, threw myself into the orange chair against the wall by the door and said, "I have done something terrible."

Trevor looked up, on alert. "What's up?" he said, peering at me over the frames of his metal-rimmed glasses. His pipe, already lit, smoldered away in the ashtray.

"I gave the kids this terrible book to read," I said. I cannot even now recall how I conveyed its contents to him. "They came complaining to me and I didn't listen."

Eyes lit, he looked down at me and said, "Now, you've done it, Larsen."

Well, I had done it. There were 500 pages to go and though I had skimmed them last night, I was terrified that I had missed some equally salacious segments. I have always felt that when I make one mistake I should stop, and not continue to compound an error. Using this principle, I came up with a solution.

"Okay," I said. "I could take the book back." The humiliation of having injudiciously spent money from the department weighed as heavily for me at that moment as the fact that I had ruined some perfectly innocent 16-year-old souls. I had spent time in the night thinking about issues of censorship, about what responsibilities teachers ought to take in selecting materials for their students to read. The idea of taking the book back was the first clue that I had that the crater that had opened before me was beginning to fill with some sort of rough terrain. The possibility began to grow inside me that I might in some mysterious way make it across.

At this Trevor began to smile. "Ah," he said, warming to his subject. He raised his eyebrows and clasped his hands together as he placed his elbows on the desk. The crazed blue stone of his gold ring flashed into view. "Shall you have them unread it,?" he asked.

At this I burst out laughing. It was the most ludicrous of my absurd solutions and his reply was vintage Trevor. He went on to offer a solution to the dilemma. He told me to take the problem to the kids, to tell them how I felt about the chapter, how I felt about having given it to them, to ask their advice about continuing or discontinuing the reading.

I did that with both classes. It was a moment with adolescents that I had not anticipated. They were somber, judicious, and practical. We decided that they should continue with the reading but that if they came upon a section that offended them and they wanted to skip that section, that they might do that without feeling that they were not giving John Irving his due. I was impressed with the maturity of their response. For a moment I felt in spite of other disruptions in the classes that I could trust them.

Moments like that when Trevor bailed me out of some particular stupidity in which I had enmeshed myself made me feel warm and cared for. When Trevor had to come into my classroom to observe—which he had to do three times each year—I was terrified. My journal tells me that Trevor's first visit came on a Tuesday in October. I remember it as if it were yesterday.

Most teachers find evaluations quite uncomfortable. Twenty-year veterans will whisper to you that they still get nervous when the chief walks in. Trevor says, "You will get used to it." When Trevor sits in on a class, he is looking first for the teacher's bonding with the text. Next, he is looking for the teacher's bonding with the students. Finally, he is looking for the students' bonding with each other. He walks in and deliberately puts himself in the position of a student in that class. If the bonds are in place, nothing breaks the dream for him. He can go through an entire class without being reminded for a minute that he is there to evaluate. If, on the other hand, there are disjunctures, he looks up to see what is not working. The things that are not working are the subject in the evaluation conference. It is 11:35 A.M. The students straggle in. Trevor has not yet arrived. I used today's lesson plan, not knowing which mistakes would surface in Trevor's evaluation. My mind is blank with terror. A master teacher whose technique leaves me in awe is about to walk into my class. In my primitive soul I gave him permission to demonstrate to me all the mastery in his repertoire, but never in a million years did I say it was all right for him to come to see my paltry attempts at teaching. He once said, "The pain comes from what you did not do." I want to agree, to say, "Yes. You're right. What I did not do was to keep you out of my classroom." What he says, of course, is far more agonizing for me. I must do things. The question is *what* things?

I wanted to say that I wore something appropriate for the occasion—like black crepe. I wore instead a pleated blue skirt and what for me is obligatory, a black turtleneck jersey. The black jersey I wear as a symbol, of my aspirations as a writer, a link to my imagined hippie past. What the students see is a woman with light brown hair that is graying, who stands at the podium tapping her fingernails on its wooden top and fiddling with the yellow pencil that she always has in her hand.

A crash of thunder. Are the kids in their places? Trevor had appeared at the door. In case you wondered, my heart has stopped. A pit has appeared before me and it is as clear to me as anything throughout this entire year that I will not get beyond this moment in my life. Trevor smiles at me from the door jamb. "Hi", he says. "Mind if I bring my portable computer in to take notes?" Mind? I think. Mind? No, why should I? Just because I am about to execute this flying six-and-a-half triple twist into this paper cup of water and ruin my career as millions watch amazed and appalled. Why should I mind if you have the audacity to record it all on your handy-dandy laptop computer?

"No, I don't mind," I say. "C'mon in." Ever gracious in the face of annihilation. When I first contemplated writing about this scene, it occurred to me that it could be compared to an execution where the executioner asks the condemned man if he minded if the executioner were to use a machine gun rather than the rifle. He comes into the classroom with peaceful intent, to see what his "baby teacher" needs in the way of a little guidance. But I cannot receive him yet into my classroom without considering the option of throwing up first.

Trevor settled into a desk at the back corner of the room. The students were arranged in the places they usually chose around the circle. The intense athlete scholars sat in the right-hand corner while the self-contained girls sat at the left. Near them sat various characters: the girl with the long nails painted red who wore a baseball cap during baseball season; the boy with the spiky black hair who would go on to write poems about his friends; the two friends who wrote their first "encounter" pieces in their mini-unit—unbeknownst to each other—about the reconciliation of their relationship which occurred in our class; and the boy whose mom left me a note saying, "David tells me I don't have to worry about his English this year. He says you're a good teacher." At the end of his senior year the next year David would come by to thank me for making him read *The Cider House Rules*.

I heard the sound of the computer almost immediately. At least I would not have to worry that Trevor would be looking at me. I could concentrate on the class. I had prepared a poetic term I thought he would like: "cruciate retrogradation." It gives off the idea of something in a cross shape that is somehow receding. It is the term, hard to find even in books of poetic terms, that is used to describe the pattern of repeating words at the ends of the lines of a sestina. I was pleased that I had found it to surprise Trevor and the class. It is a hard concept as I see it now. The first year I had no sense that getting that sort of concept across takes careful preparation.

Fifty minutes then seemed like an eternity. I planned to start with a small poem, then move to two poems by Elizabeth Bishop, her famous poem, "The Fish," and my favorite, "Sestina," which I would of course cap off with the startling revelation of the term "cruciate retrogradation." I had three stacks of poems on the desk. I divided the first stack, half in each hand, which I then handed to the students sitting closest to me. Once the poem had been passed around we began. It was simply called "Poem" and began in the first person. "Tracy," I asked a blond, curly-haired angel in front of me, "Would you please read the poem?" The poem described itself as if it were an apple, with juice which would drip down your chin. "Now," I addressed the class, "what do you think it is?"

Silence. How can I afford silence, I thought, when there is all this work to do? I was right, of course, to be concerned, but what was wrong was not the silence, but "all this work to do." But something else was wrong as well. First, I had not prepared them for the poem at all. To hand out a poem with no preliminary remarks seems to me now almost irresponsible. Without a clue as to the angle from which I would be examining this poem, they were made to feel uncomfortable and awkward. Surprise sometimes energizes, but in general I think I avoid it when I have a choice. Second, and what I think is of far greater concern, is that I did not like the poem. I gave the kids something I thought was silly and not worth spending time on just because I wanted to have some kind of beginning to the class to prepare them for the poems I really cared about, which were the ones by Elizabeth Bishop. Many things were wrong in just the first minute of the class.

"I think," said Jessica, rubbing her head, "that this poem is about a pickle. In fact," she went on, "I am sure of it." Jessica is a tall, athletic girl who is my fiction teacher's daughter. Her mind created characters such as Jake, the affable bum, who loved silver, lived in his plaid wool shirts, and frequented bars to talk to innocent strangers. Jessica was lovely to work with, but "a pickle?"

"No, no," I said again. I felt stumped and arbitrary. "Someone else give it a shot." Trevor tapped away at his computer. "It's a poem," I said, not waiting for an answer, not taking the time to go carefully over a poem I did not care about. Dividing the second stack, I handed out "The Fish." It was the first time they had seen the work of this poet and the first time they had seen this poem. And I told them nothing about this poet. Under the circumstances they did quite a respectable job.

"The Fish" is a single stanza of 76 short, unrhymed lines. I decided that because there are no stanza breaks that the poet intended the form of the poem to represent the intact fish. The poet has caught a fish, which I imagine she holds dripping over the boat. The poem contains her observations of his shiny eye, his scales, which hang off like old wallpaper, and above all, the hooks and lines, which depend from his lips as if they are medals on the chest of some ancient warrior. That the stanza was unbroken told me that the poet at the end of the poem would drop the fish back into the water. In the class before in which I had practiced this "lesson plan," I had asked the kids why the poet had left the poem as a single stanza. When they did not guess "correctly," I took my copy of the poem, held it above my desk, above my head, opened my fingers and the poem floated indecorously to the ground. I then explained what I thought. I did not dare to do that with Trevor in the room. The irony of that statement amuses me now as I realize both that I never completed the lesson plan with the first group, though I did by golly with the one Trevor observed—my reaction that first year was to press harder to "get it all in" under the 50-minute deadline—and second, that I did much more appalling things in that class than simply drop a piece of paper to the ground by way of demonstration.

Trevor stopped typing and looked up at me. Ah, yes, press on, I thought. I asked a student to read the poem. Kevin read it carefully. When he had finished, I asked the class what had happened. They told me that the fisher-man had let the fish go. "Good," I said. "Why did the fisherman let him go?" I asked, having no idea of whether they would be equipped to dig out an answer to that one.

"He let him go because he was an old fish,"said one.

"How did he know?" I inquired.

"Because his skin was peeling off," was the reply.

"Is that all?," I asked, looking at others in the room.

"No, that's not all," said Aaron, who always sat with his back to the right corner of the room as if to guard the mouth of a cave from the bald attacks of a would-be intruder. "He let him go out of respect."

"Wonderful," I said. "Now, what does respect have to do with it?" I felt rather happy that we were putting some stuff together here.

"Well," said Aaron. His curly brown hair intensified his wound-spring look. "The fish has been through all these battles and he has won."

"Yes," I said.

"And the fisherman," he continues, "who has won this battle by getting the fish into the boat feels that rather than execute the defeated fish that the fish has earned his life. He feels he has earned the right to fight again and so he throws him back." I sigh with satisfaction, hoping that Trevor feels the same type of compassion for the fish he has on his hook, hoping that he will throw it back and let it fight again. In my rapid reverie I forgot to check to see that others in the class have understood. I dance over the top of the class like a fairy sprite in my ignorance deciding that because one kid has understood that they all have understood. At this moment I do not even realize that I have an obligation to see that Jessica understood as well as Aaron did. I think that because one student was able to make sense of the poem that I have suc-ceeded. I divide the final stack and hand each section to the nearest student.

Here is the poem I loved when I heard it taught to a senior advanced placement class when I was a student teacher. I still remember the heart-stopping moment when as I followed the discussion of the poem I suddenly realized that not only were the line endings of each stanza the same five words, but that there was some sort of pattern in which the words recurred. I had hoped to re-create that moment for these students.

Well, indeed. I had ten minutes to go. Could I wait for them to discover the endings and the pattern? No. I would have to "jam it." That meant I would have to tell them exactly what I wanted them to know. We read Bishop's "Sestina." I pointed out the repeated endings and then I turned to the board. I am tempted to say that the moral of this story is never, never turn your back on your evaluator, but I think that would miss the point. On the board I wrote the words, "Cruciate retrogradation." As I completed the final "n," I heard Trevor begin to laugh. In the euphoria that can come at the end of an ordeal, I felt joy and relief. At last, Trevor was enjoying himself. I went on to explain to the class that this was merely the term given to the pattern of repeating end words in a sestina. On the wave of Trevor's laughter, I dismissed the class. The kids filed out as Trevor put his computer back in its case and sidled toward the door. The sides of his jacket showed smudges of chalk. I loved the chalk on his jacket. Like the fish's hooks and lines, chalk was a badge of honor.

Trevor, still laughing, said, "That was fine." He paused. He went on, "I'll print out what I have written so that we can both have a copy, and meet you in my office in ten minutes."

"Fine," I said, pleased with myself both that it was over and that I thought it had ended so well. At that moment I truly believed that I had made out like a bandit.

As the post-trauma haze faded, I began to realize in horror, that Trevor was not laughing with me but at me. His expectation that I would take the experience like a good sport was not rewarded with cooperation on my part. I pity evaluators when I realize that they go into classrooms and observe the work of their perfectly heretofore sane colleagues and they are critical as they invariably are, that their heretofore sane colleagues turn into swine before their Ulysses. Trevor ten minutes before had left me laughing as I straightened up my classroom. He turned up in his office ten minutes later to find a depressed morbid sullen molten lump of humanity barely breathing. Attila the Hun would have found his enemies more alive at the end of his barbarism than Trevor found me when he returned from his printing the transcript of my class. When Trevor evaluates, he puts himself in the place of the students. He says to himself, "Do I understand this? Am I interested in what is going on? Do I care what this teacher is telling me? Do I feel comfortable in this class? Do I feel happy with these classmates? Do I feel cared for by this teacher?" He holds up before you the mirror so that you can see, no holds barred, what he saw.

Now in his office he says to me, "How do you think it went?"

I am truly chastened. In later postevaluation sessions I will ponder whether I should be defensive, a dubious posture at best, in order not to suggest weakness. Now, I say it was awful and mean it. Trevor slowly at first and then without holds gives me the bad news. "Why didn't you hand out all the poems at once?" he asks.

"I never thought of it."

"You were pushing them so fast; they wanted to please you and they were going as hard as they could," he said, pausing to let that sink in. "You have to be careful," he said at last, "because they will do anything to please you."

My reaction was nothing but guilt, and then shame, that I had not thought enough about the kids to think of their reactions. Finally, Trevor turned, as he always does, to what can be done about it. "Teach to the kid who talked about the pickle. If she gets it, the others will get it, too." I nodded. I assumed that he meant "teach to the kid whose thinking is still concrete," that is, a kid whose thinking is still at an earlier operational mode. One of the things that had floored me about teaching was that while I would present the kids with a story or poem that required a certain amount of abstraction to understand and I would expect them to begin at the concrete level and we would work up; the kids would immediately announce the abstract meaning and I would figuratively stand at the desk with my mouth open wondering where I would go from there. In such a case, Jessica's concrete reaction would be helpful. Indeed, those who could already put the abstract pieces into the puzzle could help her to arrive at the abstract level with them. I have learned that some concrete thinkers can arrive at more complex concepts faster than the abstract thinker. Trevor thinks that it takes five years to make a teacher; I only hope that is it not an underestimate.

I found myself jarred by that wrap-up session. On the one hand, it takes courage to put yourself in the position of demonstrating to others that you do something new particularly badly. It seems to be an experience of youth, like skinning your knees. My pride wore the scar last summer when I fell and skinned my knees; my pride also wore the scar that attempts to bind up the wounding it takes in the evaluation process. I found myself comparing myself with my peers, asking myself if Marla would ever have tripped so badly in class. But this is useless, for whoever learns without making his own mistakes?

Evaluation involves three visits from the department chair and one from another administrator. By the end of the first semester that form of torture is behind you. I guess what you realize through the medium of the evaluation is that the diagnosis is worse than you thought and the prognosis is grimmer. As long as you remain in that state of innocence "unevaulated," you can maintain the fantasy that you are really, in fact, probably, pretty good at this stuff. Part of what had to fall away in that first evaluation session was that very fantasy, that my secret hope was that I was pretty good at this stuff was just that, a fantasy, that the reality was that in fact things were pretty grim. Maybe an evaluator needs to say to a first-time evaluatee that he knows he will find, that he always finds in the first evaluation, a dashing of hopes and a release of fears. But, how can you say this to a person? For now, I just need to be the evaluatee.

Both sections of Craft of Writing came to a close at the end of January. I felt out of control once again, both from the point of view that I could not deny that things had not gone well, even though I wanted to, and with two new sections of a remedial reading course before me and a humanities course for juniors, all of which required curricula that would for me be produced for the first time; I felt as if I were throwing myself off a cliff. As I hear teachers now lamenting the amount of reading they must do in the summer for two new courses they have never taught before, I smile in sympathy, glad for the moment I will be returning to the courses I have already taught.

Once again Trevor came to my rescue. But memory now reminds me that it was a reluctant Trevor who came to my rescue. I decided that I could not bear the multiple uncertainties that came with untried books, untried methods, and untested numbers of assignments. It was too frightening to have to deal with all those variables at once. Trevor was teaching a section in humanities as well. I decided to ask him if, so that I could know what it felt like to teach a course in which the assignments had been tried and the novels had been tested, I could use his syllabus to teach humanities that semester. I thought it made sense; nothing ever made me change my mind.

My request left Trevor horrified and unbelieving. His question was why would I want to do that? Put off, I though about it for a few more days. It had seemed to me that if I had a tested grid against which to work, that I could concentrate on the teaching without worrying, for instance, that a passage such as the one in *The Cider House Rules* would disrupt what I already knew was going to be a challenge beyond my grasp. It made sense to me. I pursued my quest and Trevor gave in. Not only did he give in, but he spent hours with me talking about each work before we taught it. When I see him take other new teachers under his wing, talking to them for long hours; when I see him arrange seminars so that several of us can discuss approaches to particular works, I also think that Trevor is doing what he ought to be doing. That is, he is passing on in the best way he can what he has learned about teaching in the past 30 years, to those who need the knowledge.

The Humanities course rolled itself out in the majestic way that Trevor had planned it. I read until I was bleary-eyed, trying to prepare all the works I had never read before. While my husband was away on a trip, I spent February vacation on the blue couch in my living room reading *Rasselas, Siddhartha,* and *All Quiet on the Western Front.* I asked two parents to talk about art, one parent to translate Calvino's *Invisible Cities* from Italian into English, just for us, and, when we read *All Quiet on the Western Front,* one parent to talk about his experience in Vietnam. The one contribution that I could make to humanities was the addition of art history to the study of literature. Trevor even asked me to prepare a set of art slides for his class, and I felt proud that I had something to offer him in return for all that he had given me. Often people say, "Tell us something good about the first year of teaching." I think it would be that, that eventually you begin to be able to give back in return for all that has been given to you.

Other moments of happiness come from working with the students. In that class were three kids who would be accepted early to Harvard, one was the brilliant best friend of a natural philosopher who had been in Craft of Writing first semester, one student who corrected my pronunciation of Telemachus, who translated a poem by Hugo for us, and turned out after a tremulous start to be a great lacrosse goalie. Where does one end in talking about the kids in the class? In your class they are just adolescents. As the years go on, they grow larger than life, their lives overlap yours, they become and remain part of your life. To write about them is to begin to write about family. Teachers collect kids like a dock collects barnacles. First of all, you end up caring for the kids who truly need you. It is not that they do not get all they need from their parents, or that they are needier than the rest. It is that they need what you have to offer. And is is with those kids that you make a special bond. I think there are a couple of kids from each class, even sometimes more than a couple, who really need what you have to offer. Those kids are willing to, as Trevor says so eloquently, "lay down their shields." They let you get close to them so that you can teach them what they need to know.

The curious question about teaching is: Who is teachable now, at this moment? And then, how do you go about reaching them? I think back now on conversations that I had with Trevor when I was a parent and not a teacher. I remember asking him how he reached the kids and if he reached all of them.

The answer I recall his giving was that he does manage to reach all kids, that if the kid would not allow himself to be caught in class, Trevor would find him in the halls, after class, in the afternoon. Trevor would tease him, joke with him, and weave his way into that kid's heart. I have seen Trevor in class and I think he sort of romances his students. They come away with the sneaking impression that he likes them. I think that is Trevor's magic. What kid could resist that kind of attention from the guy who stands up there in front of his class, that guy with chalk on his coat, with his wire-rimmed glasses, whose fingers splay out and turn as he talks about the novel that he holds in his left hand, who puts the book face down on the desk before he turns to the board to draw a diagram. He charms and engages them. He pulls out of them their best selves. I heard him say once to an informal group of teachers that he did not like children. They reacted with disbelief and proclaimed their own love of children. They, and I, said to each other, "Oh, that's Trevor teaching again, saying what we don't expect him to say so that we will have to think about his meaning."

I asked Trevor about it later. He said that that was what he really meant. He really does not like children. He likes adults. He does not find their adolescent antics charming. What he does find that he likes is inside. He finds their intelligence, that which will stay once they become adults, pulls that out of them, in spite of their adolescent nonsense, and nurtures that. Trevor holds onto the wheat and ignores the chaff. They will indeed leave his classroom never to be the same again.

Trevor engages the students in and out of the classroom. In the poetry lesson he observed, I was able to engage the material I was teaching, but I was linked to only a few of the kids and I could not link the kids to each other. I needed to work on those linkages. Out of class, I was more successful in engaging the students. At one point Trevor worried that I did not like the performance element of teaching. It took me some moments to realize that I would enjoy that part of it as soon as I got better at it. Success breeds you know what.

The variety of students in this large public high school seems to surprise people. In the remedial reading course I had kids whose sights were set on going to work right after high school no matter what their abilities. The magic moment came when I taught them that school meant being so absorbed in the work that they forgot about the time. It meant seeing success for one student who was much older and a ward of the state as helping her to complete this year at the high school so that she could go on to another place where she could complete her high school equivalency exams. In humanities, where the students were upper-level college-bound juniors, it meant learning how to deal with combative high-level boys who challenged a teacher's authority, knowledge, and teaching ability at every turn. Those kids pushed and challenged me. I found myself in the driver's seat, when they failed to understand that the Duke of Ferrara in Robert Browning's dramatic monologue, "My Last Duchess," has killed his former wife for smiling on all with equal favor and is now negotiating for a new wife; I set for the kill as Trevor does and practiced pushing to the extreme their untenable idea that this duke was a darling man who was mourning the death of his adorable wife. Trevor also taught me to take the opposite position on an issue in order to force them to defend the position that is a better one. By defending it, they convince themselves. This takes courage to do; I practice it when I am with a group of kids I trust.

The kids who are easy to relate to are generally those whose needs are clear. I asked one student in the remedial class if someone had once told her she was not bright, because she acted as if she did not expect anything from herself. Tears began to well up in her eyes as she chewed down on a stick of gum and crumbled the silver wrapper in her hand. She nodded and said, "She told my brother he wasn't bright either." I told her that I did not care whether she ever acted on the following information or not, but I wanted her to have heard it once that that was not true. She was plenty bright and I thought she ought to get to work. You may ask if that is part of a teacher's job. I guess my answer would be that until a kid feels supported she cannot get down to work. You cannot tell a kid something that is not true; but you need not feel afraid to tell a kid something nice when it is true.

The humanities class was a profile of talents, even if it took a while to discover them. While Sam had the most analytical mind I have ever run across and he and Nora, insisted on reading the 1000 page translation of *Les Misérables* while the rest of us limped along with a shortened version, Robert, the intuitive star quarterback of the football team, asked to be in my section because I made it comfortable for him to talk in class. Steven, a rotund extrovert, needing to be told that I liked him, was appointed to attend School Committee; while Harvey, who could talk well in class but whose writing was well below average, turned out to be severely dyslexic. Philip, the tall wild-haired artist, a tenth-grader in the midst of juniors, engaged with me in shouting matches until I told him that I knew what I was doing wrong, that I wanted him to concentrate on his own mess, and he did. Cyrus, also 15, told me I was flat-out wrong when I was encouraging intuitive thinking rather than linear thinking, figured out the ingenious numbering system of Calvino's *Invisible Cities* and came round to give me the benefit of the doubt. Ira was something of a jewel set in a class of super-scholars. With his dark ringlets, tortoise-shell glasses, and intense manner, Ira would make some brilliant statement and then retreat to the safety of his desk where he would complete only one of the two essays on the weekly quiz. Finally, I called Ira up after class and leaned on him. "Ira," I said, "in the first place it is very hard form to be a junior and not to complete your work. Sophomores who are flailing about getting their lives in order do it all the time, but juniors may not. I do not care how well or how poorly you do your work, but when you are asked to take a quiz on two books, you will write on both questions."

Ira was very patient. He had an itchy way of shifting his weight back and forth. He shrugged his shoulders and said, "My parents tell me that all the time." I waited. Sometimes I drag out the old saw that says that this time next year you are going to be real unhappy when you do not get into college. It helped Philip; I sensed it was not going to help Ira. So I left it in my bag of tricks. "The thing is," Ira began, "that it's about to be sailing season." Ira's excuse usually related to sailing. It was either too early for sailing season and he was too nervous and had nowhere to put his energy, or it was during sailing season and he could think of nothing but sails when the wind blew the curtains of the classroom into the room. Once when he sprained his wrist, he was depressed because he could not go sailing. "I am, you see," he intoned, "an intellectual." He paused. I think: "Oh Lord, an intense adolescent, bright, and ambivalent." "But I am also a jock," he continues. I smiled. And where, Ira, is the key? What knob do I twist to get all your pieces in place so that you can go on with your work?

I said, "Ira, there is another thing, too. I don't care what you do. I am not going to give you anything lower than a B for this course." Somehow when put between the parameters that "juniors do all their work" and "I will give you a B no matter how hard you fight," Ira got his act together. It happened to be the right box for him. He went on to discover that he loved to write poetry; a year later, he was fighting me about how to put his free-form poetry into form. I will win, I know I will; but in the meantime Ira has put his life together without losing his integrity.

The girls of the class were sleepers, except for Nora, whose quiet insistence on an education without shortened novels made a significant impact on the business conducted in the class. Cathy and Tara and Louise said almost nothing. When I asked a male teacher in whose writing class they had been the semester before, he told me that they had been quite vocal in his class.

Either the shift to reading had turned off the spigot or I was missing some crucial information in establishing relationships with those three. Mary, a dark-haired sophomore, had an on-off relationship with me until I finally realized that I knew her mother. When I understood what she was saying to me about her mother, once I realized that I knew who her mother was, I could finally establish my expectations for her work and Mary was able to settle down and get serious. When it came time the next spring to identify courses for her senior year, Mary told her teacher she wanted a course just like mine. She said that it was not really class that did it, but it was talking with me after class that made her realize what English was all about. Her teacher told me about it later when she realized that I was writing about that year of teaching. It seemed important to both of us that a student's life would be changed, even if the incident that changed her life took place in conference and not in the classroom.

When Jill walked into the classroom that first day she caught my eye immediately. She had long, straight blonde hair that she would throw back behind her as she sat at her desk at the opposite side of the room. Her manner was open and warm. I remember wondering how long it would take to forget how absolutely stunning she was, and how long it would be before I would no longer be captivated by her unadolescent warmth and considerateness. I did eventually see that Jill had a small bumpy turned-up nose, and, more important, I did find that Jill in taking on every cause at the school from drug counseling to theater, and out of school, from her share of the dinner-making and dishes in the apartment which she shared with her mom to babysitting every weekend for her tiny half-sisters who lived with their father and her stepmother an hour away by train, had no time to call her own. When I would say, "Jill, you must set time aside for yourself and for your studying," Jill would smile at me, sometimes even give me a hug, and say, "I wish I could but," when we had been talking about her weekends, "those little girls are so important to me. I have to be with them on the weekends. You should see how big the little one is getting. I can't believe she's about to go to nursery school."

With a comment like that, Jill could have been the little girls' mother, rather than their adoring big half-sister. The most formative year in Jill's life seems to have been when she was five and she and her mother and father, before their divorce the next year, lived in a commune in Chicago. When Jill wrote her essay for college, she wrote about a photograph that she has of that extended "family." She and her mother and her father keep in touch with friends from that communal life. When one of the men died recently, they were all affected by that death.

Jill got into the Boston University two-year college and into U. Mass/Amherst. We talked about the advantages of each. She chose U. Mass where she is two hours away from her families. She has a better chance of breaking away a little at least for four years to get an education.

Jill and Ira have in common that they put the needs of other people ahead of their own. They have both subjugated their needs into the needs of their parents. In the complicated world of children growing up and separating from their families, school plays a perhaps unwitting, perhaps witting, role. We provide them with the means by which they can gain competence and independence; they then decide how much and by what method they will negotiate their passage into adulthood. It is not an unimportant role.

It is not right to leave a discussion of a first year of teaching without mentioning the other teachers who make up a big part of that experience and that world. Since I had been a parent in the school and since I had been instrumental in creating an extensive parent-teacher organization for the school, my expectations were that I would not be welcomed by the staff. When I mentioned my concern to the former headmaster and to Trevor, they said I had nothing to worry about. In large measure, they were absolutely right. Teachers have so much to do that they cannot be bothered by who has come on board to lend a hand. They need the hand and they reach out for it. Though I heard a lot about teacher dissatisfaction when I was "on the outside," I found that on the inside teachers care about their subjects, they care about being better teachers every year and they care about each other.

There was not a single teacher in the English department who did not in some fashion or other reach out to me that first year. It did not matter that I was older than many and certainly older than most first-year teachers. It did not matter that as one teacher told me later she was surprised to find someone spending her first year in this department where there is so much choice in choosing curricula. Her sense was that most beginning teachers go first to departments where there is more structure and then come here. To her, teaching at the high school was like skiing the expert trails; this school had a black diamond on it. I certainly negotiated much of that first year by the seat of my pants, but I am still here, and in spite of bandages and bruises, I have learned a lot.

Two teachers in particular amused and supported me through that first year. One, who had taught my younger son, caught my heart when she announced the first day of school that she had not slept the night before. I looked at her through bleary eyes and asked her to explain her statement. She said in that lilting way that she has that she never sleeps the night before school starts. I stared at her in amazement. I had not slept, but I assumed it was a result of terror. "Why," I asked, "do you never sleep?"

She answered, "I think I am so excited to find out who I will have in my class." Think of that. A teacher who has been teaching for 30 years has the freshness and honesty to admit being excited on the first day of school every year. I once admitted to Trevor that each year in my mind in August, I lay out my knee socks, my matching sweater, the pale yellow shirt and green pleated tunic of my uniform, and I wait for school to begin. He smiled and said, "You are a teacher." I guess that is how you know. My year has always begun in September. I guess it always will.

One teacher—Robin—stood for me as the emblem of the nurturer, the listener, the one who was always there. I would walk down the hall, terrified, and I would see Robin at the door of her room. She would flash her hand at me as she ushered the last straggler into her classroom. With a bemused look she would reach down for the doorknob to close the door and begin her class. I always wondered if I would ever be that cool. Usually in the second block of the day Robin would poke her head over the wall of my carrel and say, "Coffee?" I would grab my purse and accompany her down the hall to the faculty cafeteria, running to keep up with her long strides. "How did it go today?" she asked as we sprinted to the coffee line.

"Something today made me cry." That line came from the journal I kept through the first year. I feel like Ulysses, who cried as he told his listeners about the home he missed on Ithaca. I cried, usually later, sometimes when things did not go well in class, sometimes when Trevor hurt my feelings, sometimes even when things went especially well, but most of the time the serious sad cry would come from a time when a student would hurt my feelings, and I did not think I could fix whatever the complaint was. It was a cry of total frustration and despair.

"Tell me about it," Robin said. And I would blather on, about the kid, about Trevor, about how to teach some particular thing. Robin would listen and give me advice to "try it this way" or "try it that way." Robin made me feel that my struggles were okay, that I would live through it, when I was quite sure I would not. I do not know how first-year teachers live without a Robin.

Toward the end of the year Trevor gave me some advice that was so important. I went into his office one afternoon to talk about a novel that I was going to teach. We argued and argued. The more we argued, the more I began to realize just what I was arguing. I always tried to get into the point of view of the author writing the novel. I thought once you had figured out the author's position on the novel, that the reader's work was over. Whenever a student would offer a suggestion, I would make sure that he examined his idea from the point of view of the author. To some extent this method is so ingrained in me that I fear I may never rid myself of it. Perhaps I do not need to. In any case, Trevor listened to my maddening persuasion and finally said, "You may want to find where the author is sitting; I want to know where I am sitting." It was a moment of truth for me. Trevor does not care what the author thinks. He does not care what theme the author cared to propound. He does not care what the author meant.

Trevor cares about what the novel means to him. And he wants the kids to care about what the novel means to them. If you use my method, the novel repairs to a discreet distance; it sits on the hill and looks over at you. If you use Trevor's, you become part of the novel. You are in it. You make it part of your experience. As some of my kids in Humanities the second year said, "Experience can be acquired, not just by going to sea yourself; experience can be acquired by reading about someone else's experience at sea." Who is to say one is valuable and one is not?

Trevor believes further that the teacher having become part of the experience of the novel is the embodiment of the novel for the students. They struggle with the experienced teacher, which is the same as saying they struggle with the novel and they come away with the experience of the novel under their skin. Using the method of finding where the author sits, kids only come away with the novels in their heads, in their intellectual understandings. Using the method of engaging with the novel themselves, they come away with the novels in their guts. This concept is so subtle and so complicated that even as I write it, even though I taught the second year using this concept, it still slips away from me.

One day, toward the end of the school year I stopped in to talk to Trevor. I was on my way home for the weekend, allowing euphoria to drown out my sense of shame that the year had not been a triumph. I was relieved that I could soon put behind me the mistakes of the year; I was geared up to repress all the mess. In my experience of joy, I was surprised to find a morose Trevor in his office. His curly gray hair gave him a sense of well-being. Only the faraway gaze in his eyes gave him away. "What's the matter?" I asked, not knowing whether or not to intrude on his melancholy.

He turned his desk chair to the light coming from the window that overlooked the brick courtyard of the school and said, "I just hate the dying." Trevor had told me this many times in earlier years. I had taken it lightly, as some sort of intellectual belief that, as he had said, "Kids' brains rot over the summer." I had assumed that it was on principle that Trevor felt kids should "keep their shoulders to the wheel." On the contrary, as I looked at him now, pipe out, jacket off, I knew that he was serious. He had talked in earlier times about his sense that each fall the kids create for him the teacher part of himself. They know all his ties; they know all his suits. When summer comes, he has to put away that part of himself. He goes home to be just husband, just father, just friend. He misses that part of himself. He mourns for it every spring. He mourns the loss of the minds of the kids. That is what he mentions when he completes his statement about "the dying." He hates the sense that after he has opened their minds and set them on a track that he must let them go to the summer and they will shut down again.

I say mild things about fields needing to lie fallow; Trevor says that fields never need to lie fallow. "But, Trevor," I protest, "what about the rebirth in the fall?"

"Yeah, I know," he says, disconsolate. "But I just hate the dying." And I realize in that moment that though I must now go home and put behind me the things that never seemed right, the students whose needs I could not meet, the lesson plans that never came off, and though my overwhelming emotion now is relief, I hope that the day will come when I can say as well, "I just hate the dying."

EPILOGUE

Though Jane's husband and her mentor are still speaking to her after enduring 12 months of rewrites, she has thought it best to seek refuge in a more formal writing group. Betty, Eugenia, and Mary bravely assumed the responsibility for seeing her through the final draft. Scott Walker, author of another essay in this book, and Jane, who works at the same urban-suburban high school, will team-teach a freshman class in the fall in their attempt to discover whether or not two teachers in their tenure year will go down the tubes together, or some equally attractive permutation. They are hoping they will not.

QUESTIONS FOR DISCUSSION

8.1. Larsen writes that what is good about the first year of teaching is "That eventually you begin to be able to give back in return all that has been given to you." What does she mean by this statement?

8.2. The relationship that exists between Larsen and Trevor Donald, her mentor and department head, turns out to be a supportive, maturing one.
   (a) In what specific ways does Trevor Donald help Larsen to be a better teacher?
   (b) What potential disadvantages might there be for a first-year teacher's mentor to be the administrator who is responsible for officially evaluating her teaching performance in the classroom as well?

8.3. During one of their meetings, Trevor Donald tells Larsen that, "The pain comes from what you did not do."
   (a) What does he mean by this remark?
   (b) In the poetry lesson that Larsen teaches, and Trevor Donald observes, she does a number of things that she later observes as "mistakes." What are some of the specific errors that Larsen makes in the teaching of this class, that in retrospect, cause her "pain"?

8.4. What, for Larsen, seem to be the greatest "rewards" she gets from teaching?

Chapter
9

The Vulnerable Tutor

Paula Maki

The Faulkner School sits up in the hills in a quiet residential area of Washington State. It is surrounded by greenery and overlooks a large playing field owned by the parks and recreation department. The classrooms are large and airy, laid out side by side, so that each classroom opens directly outdoors. My first impression of the place was very positive. The school's openness and warmth as well as its hills and greenery reminded me of the school I had gone to in Hawaii. I immediately had the feeling that I would like working here.

It was April, and I was in my final semester of a master's program in Boston: job-hunting time. After having lived in Boston for several years while in college and graduate school, I decided that it was a good time to look into moving to the west coast, which I had been considering off and on for the previous year or two. If I moved to Washington, I would be closer to my family in Hawaii, and I had friends and relatives in the state. I sent out résumés, and scheduled interviews for my spring break.

My interviews were at private schools and clinics that specialized in working with children with learning disabilities. I had a master's degree in reading, and would soon be completing an MAT in secondary English. I had also completed a nine-month training course in teaching reading to children with learning disabilities. My goal was to work as reading specialist in a tutorial situation. I enjoyed working one-on-one with students, and being able to address their specific needs, and I liked working with learning-disabled students, who were often very bright, but who needed to learn through methods different from those used in most "regular" classrooms. Having done classroom teaching for two summers, and been frustrated by the amount of time and energy I had spent on discipline, I did not want to teach a whole class. In a tutorial situation, discipline is not usually a problem, and a tutor can directly address the child's specific needs.

I found the Faulkner School by chance. During my trip, I had called medical centers in Washington to inquire whether they had reading clinics at which I could apply for a position. Most did not, but more than one center suggested that I call the Faulkner School, a private school that specialized in teaching students with learning disabilities. It had a good reputation and was quite well known in the area, so I quickly called the school and was able to schedule an interview with Mary Wedman, the head of Faulkner's tutorial department.

Mary was a woman in her 50s, warm and personable, and with a no-nonsense quality about her that I liked. The interview went well. Mary was pleased with my credentials and made it clear that she wanted me to tutor at Faulkner. She encouraged me to take Faulkner's summer training program, so that I could learn the teaching methods that the school used. After the training course, I would be part of Faulkner's tutoring staff. Students would be referred to me, and I would be paid on an hourly basis through the school. I could be as busy as I wanted to be, after the initial slow month or two, since September and October tended to be slow in terms of requests for tutors. Although I was nervous about not being on a salary, the job sounded like it was just what I had been looking for.

I spent the morning at Faulkner, sitting in on different classes. The school had about 300 students, and offered classes for students from first grade through high school. Each class had a maximum of 14 students. The classes were structured and orderly, since the teachers believed that learning-disabled students usually benefit from structure and predictability. But far from being straitlaced and stodgy, the teachers were energetic and creative, with lots of hands-on activities for the children. The students were responsive and interested, and did not seem bothered by having an observer in the room.

I was impressed by what I saw. Faulkner is an expensive school, and therefore had many students from affluent backgrounds, but the school also has a firm practice of giving scholarships based on need, which I was glad to know. The staff was a dedicated one that worked long days on less pay than they would get at a public school. The atmosphere was a friendly, cozy one, as all the teachers seemed to know each other well. On a gut level, Faulkner felt "right" for me, more so than any of the other schools and clinics I had visited. I also liked the area it was in. Faulkner was located less than an hour from a city, and was in the next town over from where my cousins, to whom I am quite close, lived. When I returned to Mary's office, we chatted for a bit, and were astonished to discover that Mary's son-in-law had been my high school classmate. The imaginative side of me said that it all came together too well to be coincidence, that this was where I was supposed to be. To my disappointment, Mary told me that she was to retire from Faulkner the very next day. However, she would make sure that her successor knew about me.

Two days after I finished my last final exam in June, I moved to Washington, and the day after that, began the training program at Faulkner. It was a disorienting time, as I moved into an apartment, purchased my first car, tried to learn my way around, and spent eight hours a day in an intensive summer program. It was all rather overwhelming, but I enjoyed the program, which was well organized and thorough.

The summer school director, who was also the asssistant principal of the school, was a woman named Joan, whom I guessed to be in her late 30s. She was friendly and charming, and had an effectively diplomatic way of handling problems that arose. Toward the end of the summer program, Joan asked whether I would be interested in teaching my own class during the school year. Though I was pleased to be asked, I told her that I was not very good at handlng a whole class, and that I preferred tutoring. She then asked whether I might like to work as an aide with small groups within a class. Since the aide's position would not require me to prepare lessons, I could still tutor after school, she said. She was not sure whether such a position would open up, but said that she would let me know if one did.

Early September was a slow time for tutoring, as both Mary and Joan had warned. Parents usually waited until their children were showing definite signs of struggle with their school work before requesting a tutor. My first student was a sixth-grader named Chris. He had been a student at Faulkner for two years and had done very well—well enough to return to a regular school in a regular classroom. His mother wanted him to have some additional support with his schoolwork while he made the transition back to his old school. I was nervous about meeting Chris and his mother. I chose carefully what I would wear, so that I would look like a professional, and wrote a careful lesson plan. To my surprise, Chris and his mother appeared nervous about meeting me. Chris's mother spoke to me with deference, saying that she would leave it up to me as to what I thought Chris needed to work on. Chris, a good-natured boy with a cherubic face, was polite and tried hard at all tasks. Two weeks after I began working with Chris, his mother asked if I would also work with Chris's six-year-old sister, who also had learning disabilities. I felt happy and relieved to be asked—Chris' mother must have felt confidence in me to ask me to work with both children. I relaxed more after that.

Chris and Jenny were the ideal students to begin with. Both were bright and fun to be with, and they tried hard in everything they did. Their parents were supportive of their children's efforts, and of my work with them. I tutored Chris and Jenny in their home, and their mother always made sure there was a quiet, comfortable place for us to work. I enjoyed working with them, and was impatient for more students.

I was worried about the lack of referrals, particularly from a financial point of view. My parents had put me through many years of school, and though they offered to help, I wanted to be able to support myself. There was also a matter of pride. Unlike most of my friends, who had gone into medicine, business, and computer programming, I had chosen a field that was comparatively low in both pay and prestige. I felt a bit like the "black sheep" of the group, and I wanted to prove to myself that I had chosen the right career.

In mid-September, three weeks into the school year, Joan called to ask whether I would still be interested in working as an aide. She explained that I would "wear many hats" in the job; my job would involve working with small groups, or with individual children who needed the extra help. The job would include work in classrooms at a variety of levels, which would allow me to observe and learn to teach students of different ages. I would also supervise a recess period—"Really, you'll just be a body out there, " Joan said offhandedly. The recess consisted of only five to seven junior high students who did not need much supervision. Although the pay was low ($6 per hour), I would have dental and medical benefits, and Joan would try to schedule tutees for me at the school for the time right before or after school, to make the job worth my while. I looked forward to observing and helping the Faulkner teachers, by whom I had been impressed, and I saw the job as a way to have a steady base income, to be supplemented by my tutoring. I accepted the position.

Almost immediately it became apparent that the job would not be the idyllic situation that had been described to me. In the classes where I was to help, the children eyed me suspiciously and some resented my presence. One teacher clearly did not know what to do with me, though Joan had said that the teacher desperately needed me to work with two of her slower students. The high school math teacher I was to help asked whether I would be willing to work with a small group of students in math, and I found myself with my own separate class. I was also asked to teach math to a small group of fourth-graders who were not able to keep up with their class. With both the high school math class and the fourth-grade group, I was responsible for planning the classes, finding appropriate materials, and grading papers. For both periods, I was still paid the $6 per hour aide's rate.

The junior high recess was the worst part of the job; in fact, it was one of the most unpleasant experiences I've ever had. The 5 to 7 students whom Joan had described turned out to number 12 to 15. These students were the ones who had either been kicked out of the school's sports program, or had chosen not to participate in it; therefore, I was in charge of students many of whom had already been "troublemakers" at the school. From the first day, the students tested me. They kicked balls into trees or onto the school roof, fought with each other, climbed up the hill where they were not supposed to go, and pulled branches off the shrubbery to throw at each other. To make matters worse, students from the sports program would wander over to add to the melee. When I sent a boy to the office for kicking the sports equipment all over the schoolyard, his girlfriend and her friends began to taunt me openly, calling me names and being rude. I felt angry, frustrated and hurt. I also felt like a fool for being out there, for having such a degrading job. At the same time, I felt the whole recess fiasco was my fault. I still thought highly of Joan, and she had said that the recess would be so easy. If I couldn't handle such an "easy" recess, I must be ineffectual.

At the end of the week, I did go to Joan's office, and admitted that I was struggling with the recess period. Joan listened sympathetically and said to bench offenders, or to send them to the office. She also proposed that I organize some kind of game, like four-square. Needless to say, these students would have none of four-square, but after I sent a couple of students to the office, we settled into a quiet antagonism.

Not all of the students were difficult. I gradually began to know some of the boys who were not part of the rowdy core group. There was Alden, a stocky dark-haired boy who steadily practiced shooting baskets for most of the recess, and Jake, who spoke to me about his unhappiness concerning being dyslexic and having had to leave his old school. There was also Evan, a small, thin, frail-looking redheaded boy who was jeered by some of the other students. In an attempt to be accepted by the others, he brought to school a large supply of pens, which he handed out to the students. They took his pens, then said he was weird. He too spoke of his unhappiness about having had to leave his old school and friends.

Evan did not stay long at Faulkner. Several weeks later, I heard that he had transferred to a school for students who had both learning and emotional problems. It saddened me. He had been unhappy about being taken from his regular school to go to Faulkner; now he was another step removed from his old friends and environment.

It was not unusual for children to come and go during the course of the school year. While most students at the school stayed for two or three years, there were latecomers who joined the school in mid-year, when it was evident that they needed more specialized teaching than their schools were providing. There were also those children, like Evan, who left Faulkner, some because they had more complex difficulties than Faulkner was equipped to handle, or particularly in the high school, there were students who did not want to be there, and chose to leave.

My high school math class was made up of seven boys, ranging in age from 14 to 16. They were all taller than I, but they eyed me curiously and shyly, though without hostility. I tried to act as though I knew what I was doing, but in fact, I had never taught high school math before, and had no training at all in teaching math. I had been given a textbook and workbook to work from, but I soon saw that I would have to find much additional material. Learning-disabled students need much reinforcement and practice of skills, and most textbooks do not have enough practice problems. I spent much time looking through other books and photocopying pages from them. Because the students forgot easily, we did a lot of backtracking. When we got to working with fractions, I saw that most of them had forgotten what they had learned about fractions in previous years and we had to go back to the beginning.

After the initial week of being quiet and polite, the boys relaxed and became their boisterous and friendly selves. There were many days when I wished they would go back to being quiet and polite. Rob, a six-footer at age 15, with curly blond hair and a genial round face, was the leader of the group. He was outgoing, dressed with a distinctive style, and had added status of having a girlfriend at a nearby public school. Because most of the students in the school were boys, most of my students did not yet date. Rob, being a head taller than I, would sometimes jokingly get on his knees to look me in the eye. Rob accepted me as a teacher early on, and seeing that, the others followed suit.

While the feeling within the class was generally very positive, I had some feelings of trepidation regarding two of my students, Josh and Richard. Josh was known to have an explosive temper, and had recently had a shouting match with the assistant director of the school because Josh felt she was on his case too much for being late for school. He was already on probation for fighting with other students. Richard's behavior was erratic, sometimes seeming quietly angry at everyone, while at other times totally spaced out. I wondered whether drugs were involved in Richard's case. I was careful not to push these two students too far, and tried to use humor to cajole them into doing work when they did not want to. I wanted them to know that I expected them to complete their assignmens, but I was also afraid of any explosions.

It was hard to know where to draw the line of expectations, particularly in light of their learning disabilities. All of them had experienced failure in other schools, and I did not want to lower their self-esteem further; nor did I want them to feel they were doing work that was beneath them. My lessons were based on trial and error. Some lessons that I expected to go well were totally confusing to the students, while they breezed through work that I considered to be more difficult. The students learned slowly and forgot easily, so I learned to review constantly. I was not able to plan lessons more than one or two days in advance, because we rarely covered in class what I expected we would. I began giving quizzes every Friday so that I would have a tangible, numerical way to measure progress, and to see what needed to be covered in the following week. The quizzes also allowed the students to see how they were doing, and I found that the students liked the regularity of the Friday quizzes.

The number of fourth-grade students in my other math group varied from day to day, depending on whom the teacher thought needed the extra help, but the core group that was with me most of the year consisted of four students: John, a sweet, bright, and very learning-disabled boy; Sarah, a tiny blonde with solemn blue eyes behind her blue-framed glasses; Adam, a sensitive observer of people and one of the few black children in the school; and Bobby, a mischievous towhead. Other children were sometimes added to the group, but these four were my regulars.

The children's regular teacher sometimes made suggestions about what I should be working on with the students, and offered to show me material I could use with them. However, because both our schedules were full, and did not coincide, most of the time it was easier to just find my own material. Because the students were at such different levels (John could barely subtract, while Bobby was learning long division), I made individual folders for each child, and had them working at their own levels. This took quite a bit of time, particularly until I knew where each child was in terms of their math knowledge, but it seemed to work well. However, the children were very aware of who was working ahead of whom, and sometimes tried to race each other.

In mid-October, another aide, Maggie, was hired. When Maggie arrived, I was released from my junior high recess duty (which was given to an unsuspecting Maggie), and I helped with the lower school recess instead, to my great relief. Maggie and I got to be friends quickly, since we both used the same small room as our home base. We shared the lower school recess duty, and often ate our bag lunches together while correcting papers and planning lessons. It was nice to have someone who was in the same position to whom I could talk and sometimes complain. Maggie soon dreaded the junior high recess as much as I had, and I began to think that the difficulties I had had with the recess were not solely due to my own shortcomings. Maggie was also teaching for two periods a day, and we both were taking a good deal of work home with us.

Maggie had had previous experience working as an aide at another school, and she realized that we were being taken advantage of. I had suspected as much, but thought maybe it was all part of being an aide. When we gathered up our nerve, we went into Joan's office and told her that we were doing preparation at home for two groups a day, and we needed some preparation time. Joan listened understandingly, and said that she was very glad that we had come. She said she hadn't been aware of how much we were actually doing, and that Faulkner tended to push its employees until they said, "Enough!" We were each given a daily 45-minute period of prep time, and for one hour a day we would be paid $10 rather than our regular $6. Joan explained that Faulkner could not affort to pay us $10 an hour for both hours that we were teaching. The next day Joan left a bouquet of flowers in our room, thanking us for the work we were doing. While Maggie saw it as a sign of how sweet and sincere Joan was, I secretly regarded it as a calculated move on her part. While I still liked Joan, I had noted in my journal that she seemed to "hedge a lot" when it came to discussing duties and pay.

By this time, I was getting to know the children in the classes I helped in, and rather than resenting my presence, they began asking for my help and wanted to chat. I was familiar with the routine in the various classrooms and felt more comfortable in the job. However, I was finding that I was always tired, and often irritable. On weekends I usually got together with friends or relatives, but I was always aware that there were lesson plans to write or papers to correct when I got home. I was glad that I had chosen to live alone rather than to find a roommate—on most days, I would get home and collapse on the bed and not want to move.

My days at Faulkner had been strictly scheduled by Joan. School started at 9, and I worked for the first 50 minutes with a 10-year-old boy who could not keep up in reading or spelling with his classmates. I then had my 45 minutes of prep time. Then I went to a junior high classroom for half an hour, walking around the classroom helping individual students who needed it. Next I had an hour in a fourth-grade classroom where I supervised half the students while the teacher took the other half for a reading lesson. The next half-hour was spent on the playground, supervising the lower school recess, followed by a 15-minute break. My fourth-grade math group then came for a 40-minute lesson, after which I had a 35-minute lunch break. Then I had my high school math class. After school I tutored. Although none of the duties were particularly difficult, I found it tiring to switch gears so constantly and quickly. Though my main focus was still tutoring, I found that by the end of the day, I did not have much energy left to tutor.

In October, I began working with two more tutees. Albert was a man in his early 20s. He was the first adult student I had ever worked with, and it was refreshing to teach someone who was so motivated, and who really wanted to be tutored. My other new student was a seven-year-old named Jessica. Jessica was another first for me—my first difficult tutee. She was a sturdy first-grader, with curly brown hair and wide eyes. She lived with her parents and little sister in a mansion in a posh residential area. I rarely saw Jessica's parents. Jessica was usually alone with the maid, whom she terrorized, when I arrived. She did not want to read or spell; often she would lie on the floor and refuse to get up, or would run out the door. When I asked her to do something, she would snap, "This is my house." I noticed that on the rare days that one of Jessica's parents was at home, she was cooperative and pleasant. After a few unproductive weeks with Jessica, I discussed her behavior with her mother and asked whether we could reschedule the tutoring for a time when a parent was at home. Her mother replied that it was not convenient to change her schedule. I felt that I was getting enough aggravation during my day at school, so I suggested that Jessica's mother find another tutor.

Toward the end of October, Josh was becoming more and more rowdy in the math class, talking loudly and turning in very little homework. While he was still pleasant and polite with me, and would work diligently if I stood next to his desk, he would continue socializing as soon as my back was turned. I moved his seat away from those of his friends, which helped temporarily, but the general noise level was bothering me, as some of the other students were becoming distracted by Josh. I noticed that the class was much more studious and effective on days that Josh was absent. I called Josh's mother about the homework situation, and she was very supportive. For a few days afterward, Josh turned assignments in, before reverting back to his old ways. I had to laugh when one day, when Josh was rowdier than usual, he asked meekly, "Are you going to tell my mother?"

I worried that I was not being authoritative enough with Josh, but I was rather pleased when I was able to stop a fight from happening between Rob and Josh. Josh had taken Rob's sunglasses before class and refused to give them back to him. After a few verbal insults, they both got up and were ready to exchange blows. Josh had already gotten into trouble at Faulkner for fighting, so I knew that he would indeed fight, if it came to that. There was not any time for me to stop and think of what I should do, so I stepped between Josh and Rob. Feeling that Rob would probably not be the one to swing first, I addressed myself to Josh, telling him that I did not want him to get into trouble or to be suspended again. While I talked, Josh kept looking from me to Rob, and back to me again. Finally, after a few more insults had been exchanged, both went back to their seats. It was not an important incident, but it gave me some confidence in my ability to cope.

My fourth-grade math group also had its difficult days. Micah, a boy who joined the group for several weeks, had been diagnosed as hyperactive. On some days, he was unable to concentrate or to accomplish any work at all. He made faces at the other children and acted silly to make them laugh, and distracted the others until they became irritated with him. His teacher suggested that I send him to the office when things got bad, but after a couple of periods spent in the office, his behavior didn't improve. I began pulling his desk outside the door when he couldn't function in the room. Coincidentally, at about the same time, Micah began taking medication to control his hyperactivity. Micah's ability to learn and focus improved dramatically with the medication, but Micah himself attributed his improvement to having had to work outside. Thereafter, whenever one of the other children misbehaved, Micah would tell me to put him or her outside. "It made *me* good, " he would say proudly. Micah improved so much that he soon caught up to the rest of his class and rejoined them for the math period.

While I generally enjoyed my fourth-graders, there were days when I thought I would scream if I had to teach long division for another day. However, the children were forgiving. If I was grumpy, they did not hold a grudge. If we had a bad day together, the next day it was forgotten and we began anew. I stopped regarding a bad day as the end of the world; it was only one bad day.

Financially I was struggling. In November, I still had only four tutees. Joan had not followed through in scheduling students for me to tutor right before or right after school, as she had originally said. I put a classified ad in three different local papers, advertising tutoring services. I got three or four responses; only one materialized into an actual client. I was now double-checking my paychecks from Faulkner carefully. Once they had made a mistake on how much they should deduct for taxes, and on two occasions they forgot to pay me for tutoring.

It became increasingly hard to go to work in the mornings. I wondered whether I had gone into the wrong field. I just wanted to tutor, but I did not have enough students to make a living at it. I had taken the job as an aide for a base income that would allow me to pursue tutoring, but the job was taking up so much time and energy that I was too tired to tutor. After Thanksgiving, Maggie gave her notice that she would work only until Christmas vacation. She was frustrated with the job, and unhappy with the junior high recess. I wondered if I would last much longer.

As Christmas drew near, however, I was caught up in the children's excitement, and things were generally more enjoyable. I helped children make Christmas decorations and gifts for their parents. One class had a feast of "stone soup," following the children's story about the beggar who convinces different villagers to contribute vegetables and other ingredients to his soup made with a stone, and he ends up with a delicious stew. The children were excited about the project, each bringing an ingredient and helping to chop it up. The teacher decorated a long table in the classroom, complete with tablecloth and flowers, and we had a wonderful sit-down meal. Even the children who claimed to hate vegetables had two or three helpings. The director of the school set up an elaborate smorgasbord in the teacher's room for all the teachers and aides. I was touched when I received Christmas presents from the children.

However, over the vacation, I again mulled over my career direction. I considered changing fields, and began looking into business or law schools, fields that had never interested me. If I was going to be unhappy in my work anyway, I may as well get a good salary for it, I figured. I began scheduling interviews at other schools, and also at publishing companies, the only kinds of jobs I seemed to be qualified for with my background. I also began taking an evening class in accounting, preparing myself for a change in career.

In January, a new aide was hired to replace Maggie. Anne was in her mid-50s and was returning to teaching after having been in business for many years. I was disturbed, but not altogether surprised, when Anne told me that she was being paid $10 an hour for two hours daily—the amount Joan had told Maggie and me that Faulkner could not afford to pay.

In late January came the last straw. Alex, a new administrator, was put in charge of the aides. Soon after beginning his job, Alex called me into the office to discuss my schedule. He said he had noticed that I had been given too much preparation time and that I would need to be assigned to work in yet another class. He explained that the PE teacher did not have time to work with the first-graders and that it would be very helpful if I could take over with the first-graders. The whole idea seemed ludicrous to me, and stunned, I said that I had no backgrond in teaching PE and that I wouldn't know what to do with PE. I told him that if the issue was my having too much prep time, I would be willing to help in another classroom. It became clear, however, that the PE class was Alex's objective, and he politely implied that if I did not take the class, I should not be paid as a full-timer and could lose my benefits since I was not working the full amount of hours per day. The whole thing was absurd. My days were fully scheduled as it was, and I went from one class to another except for the time Joan had given me for preparation. That prep time was rarely enough, and I usually took work home with me, which aides were not supposed to have to do since we were not paid for it. Joan, who was the one who had assigned me the disputed prep time, sat in the room the whole time at the next desk, and said nothing.

I was shocked; the situation felt like a nightmare. I felt defeated and manipulated. It was clear that neither Alex nor Joan had any respect for me as a teacher or as a person, and after thinking things over, I wanted nothing more to do with them or with my job. A couple days later, bypassing both Alex and Joan, I went to talk to Charlotte, the director of the school, whom I respected and liked. I had rehearsed to myself what I would say to explain the situation as I saw it, and that I wanted to resign. Much to my embarrassment, after I had gotten to the part about resigning, I broke down in Charlotte's office. Charlotte kindly joked and spoke of other things until I collected myself, then told me that they needed me to stay, particularly to continue with my high school math class. In the end, I agreed to work for just two hours a day, to teach my two math groups.

My finances were in shambles, but I was much happier after that. I no longer had the frustration and boredom of recess duty and helping in various classrooms, and I had more energy for my math groups and my tutees (who now numbered six). And I was no longer under the supervision of Joan and Alex. I began to enjoy what I was doing, but my parents had to help me financially, and I knew that after the school year ended, I would need to have a job that could pay the bills.

My high school math class had shrunk in size. Rob had chosen to return to his old public school, and Josh had been asked to leave Faulkner. Richard had dropped out of school completely—he did not want to bother any more. A new student joined the class, bringing the total to five. Although I missed the three who had left, it was nice having the small group. The more quiet boys became more voluble in the absence of Rob and Josh, and their sense of humor came to the fore. By February, it seemed that the students had come to terms with being learning-disabled, and were able to joke about it. "Oh Steve," one student would say to another when he was irritated, "You're *so* dyslexic!" When I gave them an assignment that dealt with completing se-quences, and one sequence involved letters written backward and upside down, one student did a double-take and laughed, "Is that letter backward, or is it my dyslexia?" At the high school talent show, a group of students per-formed a series of pantomimes, each preceded by a title printed on a card that a student would carry across the stage. When the card carrier crossed the stage a little too quickly, a member of the audience yelled, "Hey! Slow down!" The card carrier retorted, "Well, read faster," to which the first student, with-out missing a beat, said, "We can't—that's why we're here!"

The students were generally supportive of each other, and did not make fun of each other's difficulties. When Wes finally memorized his multiplica-tion tables, the other students applauded. I found them to be more sensitive and generally more kind to each other than were nondisabled teenagers.

Through trial and error, I found some tactics that seemed to work with my math groups. Because the fourth-graders came to me right after lunch and were therefore not much in the mood to study, let alone to do math, I usually had six problems on the board when they walked into the small tutoring room that we used. The problems usually included one addition problem, one or two subtraction, one multiplication, division for those who had gotten that far, and perhaps a problem involving fractions, decimals, or measurement, de-pending on what we had been working on. Having the daily variety of prob-lems helped to keep fresh previously learned skills. After Bobby totally forgot how to do two-digit multiplication because we had been so busy with long division, I realized how essential the review was. It was also helpful because the children would walk into the room, take their seats, and on their own, begin to copy the problems onto their papers. They settled down quickly, rather than their previous habit of coming in, talking, and laughing while I tried in vain to shush them, and it got their minds in gear for math.

I was learning that though the children liked to goof off, they became irritable when the classroom was too noisy. It was John who suggested that I put a list of the students who were working well up on the board. Almost every day I would write names on a "super-citizens" list, and as soon as the children saw me pick up the chalk, they would bend studiously over their work. I rewarded the super-citizens with stickers at the end of the period.

The stickers served a dual purpose. Not only did they reward good effort, they were also something special for the children to show the rest of their classmates. The students in my group were the "slower" ones who weren't able to keep up with their classmates, and they were well aware of that fact. The stickers were something extra that gave them some status in the eyes of the other children. At times, some of the other children tried to talk their teacher into letting them join our group, much to the delight of my students. Surprisingly, although I used the "super-citizens" list and stickers throughout the school year, the children did not tire of them, and were rather put out on the days that their names did not appear on the list. On a couple of occasions that I forgot to replenish my supply of stickers, Sarah arrived the next day with stickers from home so that I would have some to give out.

The children's regular teacher used a lot of manipulatives when teaching math, and she encouraged me to do the same. She was very generous in lending me her materials and in giving me ideas on how to use them. However, though I did try to use manipulatives off and on, I never was able to feel comfortable with them, and I usually ended confusing both the students and myself. From time to time, primarily out of nagging feelings that I should be using them, I would pull the manipulatives out and try to teach with them. But primarily I ended up just using math books and workbooks, along with different activities, such as having the students draw pictures that illustrated certain fractions, or having them measure the perimeter of various objects in the room. We usually ended the period with five or ten minutes of math games, such as "Around the World" or "Subtraction Bingo," which the children loved.

With my high school group too I did a lot of review, along with work from various math books and workbooks. With this group, I also felt guilty about not using more manipulatives, and so initially I did some teaching with them. However, I just did not know enough about using manipulatives effectively, and soon gave up. When the group seemed to be losing their motivation to do good work in math, I had them pair up or work in teams on a math puzzle or worksheet. The first group to finish the work accurately won. The boys themselves helped to decide who should team up with whom. They tried to balance the teams so that a quicker student would work with a slower one. In this class, some peer teaching went on spontaneously and effectively. The students seemed to try harder when it was one of their classmates showing them how to solve a problem, and the peer teachers were patient and clear in their explanations.

In the spring, I had some trouble with one of the high school students, Jake. Jake was a rather short, stocky, 15-year-old with curly black hair. He had a quick wit, and he reminded me a little of Bruce Willis. Because of his sense of humor, and the fact that he was not at all mean, it was difficult for me to be consistent with him in terms of discipline. Jake had gradually come to the conclusion that he no longer wanted to be at Faulkner. He had been envious when Rob left to return to his public high school, and since then, his cooperation had deteriorated. Before class started, he would fill his mouth with water at the water fountain, then come into class and squirt the water onto one of the other students, which would start a water fight and mean that half the period would be gone before the students were settled down and in gear to work. His classwork and homework were often not completed. He was having problems in his other classes as well, and was often the topic of teachers' meetings. His parents were concerned, and there was much communication between Jake's parents and teachers. Detention was assigned for disruptive behavior or incomplete assignments, but this practice became worthless when Jake would blithely run up five detentions in a single week. I sometimes sent him out of the room when he was disruptive, which he disliked because he hated being away from his friends, but it did not serve to improve his habits or attitude. In the end, it was up to Jake to improve or not. I was told that there were many family discussions at home during which Jake and his parents and even grandparents talked together about Jake's future and motivations, and over a period of eight or nine weeks, Jake seemed more willing to try. In his case, I did not feel the school could do much besides give Jake time and support.

Working with the students every day, I could not see their progress, and I found myself wondering if the children were learning at all. However, in April, Sarah's mother told me that although math had always been a sore point for Sarah, she was now very confident in that area. Sarah told me that math had become her favorite subject. In end of the year tests, Sarah and Adam showed significant progress in their math scores. Adam had gone from pre-first-grade math to a fourth-grade level. John and Bobby had made a little progress, but were still significantly below their age group. In my high school class, all the boys except for Jake showed good progress in their math scores. It was a relief for me to see evidence of their improvement, since I had often felt that it was a case of the blind teaching the blind.

In the meantime, I had continued my job search. I had enjoyed my accounting class, though it was for me like learning a foreign language since I was not familiar with any of the business terms. I was interested in training programs in business, and when I saw an ad in the paper for applicants for a computer training program, I applied right away. In May I was called for an interview, and I was excited and nervous about what I saw as my chance to get into another field.

The bank headquarters were new and impressive. The employees sat at orderly desks looking very professional in beautifully coordinated outfits that clearly were not intended for chasing screaming children around a playground. To my surprise, however, as the day of interviewing progressed, I felt less and less sure that I wanted the job. I really didn't care how much money the bank was making. I wondered if I would be able to deal with the office politics, since the bank employees themselves admitted that politics did play a large role in whether or not someone would move up the ladder at the bank. By the end of the day, rather than being impressed by the expensive and stylish outfits I saw everyone wearing, I wondered what the point was of looking so nice if all one did all day was to sit behind a computer terminal. I knew I could never care about the bank nearly as much as I cared about Sarah, Josh, or even Jake. The bank interview was a significant turning point for me because it confirmed my decision to teach. I felt that, now knowing what I was getting into, I was choosing to be a teacher.

Soon afterward, I was offered a tutoring position at an organization that I liked very much. At Faulkner, Charlotte was pleased with my teaching and the gains my students had made, and asked me to return for the following year. I decided to work part-time for both organizations, though I was apprehensive about returning to Faulkner. I know that had it not been for Charlotte, who was open and supportive in her dealings with me, as is her style, I would not want to return.

The past year was truly a mixed bag of experiences for me. Part of the problems I had with school administrators stemmed from the fact that I worked for a small private school that, I learned later, had not had full-time aides before. Aides are at the bottom of the totem pole as it is, and there was no consistent policy for classroom aides at Faulkner. I felt that Joan and Alex, while being outwardly friendly toward me, never doubted that I was dispensible and easily replaceable. They had no reason to respect or accommodate my wishes, since they could easily find someone else to do the job. It was also a difficult year because I chose to work out of the mainstream, where there is no union protection. Not only was I in a private school that deals with special education, but I was not a regular classroom teacher. My job was made up as the year went along. My first year of teaching was a rude introduction to the real world. Thankfully, this year looks to be much better.

EPILOGUE

Paula Maki is now working as a full-time tutor with dyslexic students. She tutors both for the Faulkner School and independently, and loves the work. She has abandoned any and all plans for business school, and feels that teaching was the right field, after all. However, she would not like to relive that first year for anything.

QUESTIONS FOR DISCUSSION

9.1 Maki openly admits, "I have never taught high school math before, and had no training at all in teaching math . . . my lessons were based on trial and error."

(a) What might be the advantages of learning to teach by trial and error?

(b) What are the obvious disadvantages?

(c) In what ways, if any, might it be possible to minimize the first-year teachers' "trial and error" approach to instruction?

9.2 Maki expresses a number of fears about teaching during her first year.

(a) What are some of these fears and in what ways does she learn to cope with and conquer them?

9.3 Teachers often use threats or "punishments" as ways of controlling student misbehavior. Maki, however, discovers a positive way of controlling her students.

(a) What is the method she uses and why do you think her students respond to it?

9.4 It is partly out of innocence and partly out of ignorance (as a fledgling uninitiated teacher), that Maki accepts the $6 per hour wage, although she holds a master's degree, and her daily schedule and responsibilities are very similar to those of a full-time teacher. Many private schools cannot afford to pay teachers salaries worthy of their talents and dedication; yet, in this instance, it is obvious—as Maki suspects that she is being taken advantage of.

(a) Why is it especially unethical and shameful for a school administrator to take advantage of a young professional's naïveté and good will? What kind of message is the administrator giving to the teacher?

(b) Could such a practice occur in a public shool? Why?

Chapter
10

In the Proximity of Foolishness

Scott Walker

After a year of teaching I am convinced that there must be a clown in the heart of anyone who starts off on this journey, regardless of how seriously he or she takes the profession. It may not be the clown that interviews for the first job, or stands in front of classes during the first few weeks. He may be silent on the first parents' night, and appear to be entirely absent the night before first-quarter grades are due, but pretty soon he has to come forward and make himself known.

Don't get me wrong, a teacher's job *is* serious business, and I started off with a heavy dose of that attitude. How could I avoid it? In 1986 when I prepared to teach for the first time there was enough in the air to sober up anyone. From presidential commissions and corporate reports on down to conversations with parents in my Boston neighborhood, I was surrounded by the awareness that there was a lot at stake in our classrooms. The schools were at risk. There was a national and a local call being sounded and I rallied to it.

In this frame of mind I remember venturing to my assigned classroom for the first time on an August morning several weeks before school opened. The building was empty and each step echoed as I walked down the freshly waxed corridors. I found room 263 and sat there for a while, first at a few of the students' desks and then behind the teacher's desk at the front of the class. As the minutes passed and I looked out at the vacant chairs I began to see hands raised in the third row. Over by the windows a couple of kids whispered furtively. I began to feel the close gaze of eyes in the front seats, and caught a head lowering in the back. The still room was alive with bright and threatening prospects.

Prompted by these imaginings I went to the front blackboard and wrote out Jesus' words, "Come unto me all ye that labor and are heavy laden, and I will give you rest. Take my yoke upon you, and learn from me for my yoke is easy and my burden is light." Even though one of my assignments was to teach a law class in a public high school, the division of church and state was irrelevant to me at that moment. Some custodian would find the boards needed cleaning and erase them before September. Like an explorer staking his claim on the beachhead of a new world, I wanted to leave a token of my hope that the space would be a place where students and I would quest for truth and find compassion. Yes, I felt this was serious business, a mission in fact. But I had little idea that entering this work would be a bit of a clowning matter as well.

A clown is gladly a fool in order to connect with the hearts of others. He personifies human sincerity hampered by the ridiculous potential we all have for awkwardness and miscalculation. Something about that combination of un-abashed sincerity and awkwardness hits close to home, and people laugh and are put at ease. My first year of teaching was hardly aimed at making students laugh. Nor did it put them all at ease. But given who I was, a teacher much stronger in my dreams and in my care than in the wisdom and confidence of experience, I walked in the proximity of foolishness and learned to make the most of it.

I was 29 years old when I started teaching. As a history major in college I never seriously considered becoming a teacher. The thought was confining. The traditional classroom was a place to be launched from, I thought, not a final destination.

Graduation landed me instead in Boston's inner city, combining part-time odd jobs with work in a church-related organization coordinating a summer internship program for college students. These were mostly students from middle-class, suburban backgrounds like my own, who were unfamiliar with the society of the city but who felt compelled to learn and to serve. My job was to find summer work opportunities for them and to design seminars that served to orient them to the culture and needs of the city. Because I was so young and new to that environment myself, it was a job that involved constant exploration.

Over four years of doing this with concerned and impressionable students, I came to the realization that despite my college prejudices, I loved doing the work of a teacher. There was something immensely stimulating to me about mixing things together into learning experiences that could help someone grow. Two years later I was on the other side of a master's degree in teaching and headed into my first school position as a social studies teacher. I was a rookie with some sense of perspective about himself, but a rookie nonetheless.

If being a new teacher is a challenge in itself, to be one at Jordanstown High School, where I started, involved some unusual hurdles that I did not expect. Jordanstown had a reputation, but it was far from the grim reputation that I had come to associate with the challenge of public education. As a teacher in training, my reading and limited experience had left me anticipat-ing the first year to be something of a *To Sir with Love* experience: hardened apathy and spitballs from kids, and fossilized conservativism from older teachers and administrators. The need for reform was being publicized everywhere, and my imagination followed the cue.

Jordanstown High did not fit this image. The challenge it presented was of a different nature. I got this impression immediately upon receiving my first correspondence from the school. The stationery heading read "The High School," as if it was obvious what high school that meant. I had heard of "The Game." Only Yale and Harvard were presumptuous enough to call their traditional football contest by such a title. Was this local high school assuming such a singularly classic identity, I wondered.

As I learned more about the school in subsequent weeks, it was obvious that Jordanstown High did have a tradition. Originally an affluent bedroom town adjacent to Boston, Jordanstown had a longstanding commitment to excellence in its public schools. The town had remained faithful to this commitment through recent decades of demographic change that brought new racial and ethnic groups into the schools. The result was a rare school system that prided itself on both its resources and its social diversity. At the official orientation for new teachers we were given pins to wear with the picture of a lighthouse on them, signifying the educational prominence of the system. For a first-year teacher it was a school bright with promise, but overshadowed with the pressure of high expectations.

I ran into these expectations on my very first day. I had come in early to finish setting up my classroom. While I was cautiously experimenting with different seating arrangements, as only a novice would, a student walked into the room. This being my very first contact with actual student life at the school, I eagerly looked up and smiled.

"Hey, where's Mr. Bergowitz?" the girl asked, looking bewildered.

"Mr. Bergowitz isn't teaching at Jordanstown any longer. I'm Mr. Walker. I'll be in this room this year."

The girl seemed stunned. "Where'd Mr. Bergowitz go?"

"I'm not sure, but I think he's working for a state senator now."

"But I signed up for his class this semester! My friends told me I had to take him."

"Yea, I hear he was a good teacher," I paused, "but you can still take the course."

"Awh, he's great. My brother said he was the best teacher he ever had. So who's teaching American Rights and Responsibilities now?"

It took some effort to get the answer out. "Well, I'm teaching one section, and Ms. Howe is teaching another."

"Oh," The girl paused for a moment. "Do you teach like Mr. Bergowitz?"

I didn't really know how to respond to that. I laughed and told her that I wasn't sure, since I didn't know him. I didn't dare share my real thoughts. The truth was that I wasn't sure how *I* taught, let alone how Mr. Bergowitz did. The student left and I returned to arranging desks, wondering how Mr. Bergowitz had arranged them.

The ghost of Bergowitz haunted me two or three more times that week, climaxing in a conversation I had with one of the school administrators. Upon introducing myself to the man, he shook my hand and replied, "Oh, you must be the new Mr. Bergowitz." I asked him what he meant by that and he explained, "You're interested in teaching about the Third World, aren't you?" I nodded. "Well, social studies teachers at this school are known for their specialties and that was Mr. Bergowitz's specialty. I know that the social studies department was hiring with that need in mind. Besides, Bergowitz had a beard as well!"

As I thought about the role I had unwittingly inherited from some veteran expert, I felt the privileges of youth being suddenly snatched from me even before I had begun! Yes, I knew a thing or two about history and political science, but I really was a beginner in the classroom teaching business. The only specialties I could claim in that setting were unproven dreams and raw, relatively naïve energy.

The high expectations were not always so directly stated. In fact many of my colleagues were more than sympathetic with the trials of the first year, and they made it clear to me that they would help whenever I needed it. But for someone who needed to get used to launching out on my own, the assistance was sometimes a problem as well as a help. This was the case with Celia Woodson, a fellow history teacher whom I met during the first week.

Celia Woodson had taught at Jordanstown High for 15 years and had been at other schools before that. When she first greeted me in the department office, her outward eccentricities were immediately disarming to me. She had a slightly disheveled appearance and a peculiar twitch that caused her to blink incessantly. As the year passed I became convinced that this twitch was probably a necessity, a kind of metabolic circuit breaker that helped her manage the intellectual energy that was continually pulsing through her. As we talked and she learned that I was teaching two sections of the freshman Law course, she invited me to make use of curriculum material that she had developed for the course when she had taught it, and then left me with some of her lessons.

I didn't look at them until later that evening. When I did, their impact was so great that I slept fitfully, dreaming that with every toss and turn I was turning over yet another page of the Woodson curriculum with no end in sight! What I saw before me as I read her lessons was the stuff of my loftiest aspirations, the kind of material that I could only imagine and hope would be the culminating work of my career as a teacher. It was marvelously engaging, inviting kids to enter into various decision-making roles that contribute to the functioning of the American legal system, while requiring them to develop important thinking and writing skills along the way. I was certainly left inspired, but I was also left feeling a bit naked, and wondering whether I should scrap the design I had come up with for my entire first unit.

It was too late for that, of course, and the encounter with the competency of Ms. Woodson and others during those first weeks finally served only to reinforce the fact that I had no choice. I needed to wear fully the limits of my knowledge and experience, and to see the constant presence of refinement around me with the grateful eyes of an apprentice. More importantly I needed to tap my youthfulness for the valuable connections it could lead to with kids. If I was feeling vulnerable and uncertain, how did I think most of them were feeling in the height of their adolescence, one among 2000 others in this high school? The thought led me to try out something different in my American Rights and Responsibilities class that first week. I wasn't the only one concerned about expectations, and that connection could be useful.

This was a sophomore class and typical of all my classes during the first days. The room was hushed when I walked in. I went to my desk in front of the room and kept the silence as I unpacked my bag and took out a stack of course guidelines to be handed out to the students. With the most business-like voice that I could manage I read through the class list and then took up the course guideline sheets and walked around to the front of my desk before the class.

"Good morning. My name is Mr. Walker and this course is American Rights and Responsibilities. I'm glad that you have decided to take this course and I expect that you will learn a great deal from it. It is important though, before we begin, to make clear what I expect of you in this class." At that I handed out the course expectation sheets and waited to see what would happen. Interspersed among some true and respectable rules of mine I had planted a couple of bombs. Here is one of them:

> While lively discussion is expected, open disagreement with the content, method, or purpose of my instruction will only make learning more difficult. If you choose to disagree with something said or done in class, I will consider your opinion only if expressed to me in a private note.

As I expected, two things happened. First, the students were clearly pained. Eyes grew wide. A number of them sat up much straighter in their seats. There was some coughing, and here and there students shot distressed glances at their neighbors to see if others were reading what they were reading. But, even after inviting their comments and questions, the majority of them said nothing. Only one or two raised questions about the fairness of the rules. After a minute or two of responding to these in poker-faced seriousness, I paused and then stepped out of role to ask, "Do most of you guys really think these rules are fair?"

The ice was broken and after exhaling a chorus of relieved exclamations, the kids talked openly about why silence had reigned. They had a lot to say about the pressure to make a good first impression on me and their peers despite the fact that they were aware that important rights of theirs were possibly being violated. In a course designed to emphasize the fact that legal rights don't become actual until citizens know and are willing to claim them; it was a good opening discussion. For a first-year teacher beginning to struggle with his own burden of unreasonable expectations in comparison to his colleagues, it was also an experience of holding secret communion with my students to the benefit of us both. I understood their feelings and by encouraging them to be boldly honest, I was encouraging myself.

Youthful empathy for my wards had its liabilities as well as its benefits. It could prove costly in terms of the advantages that some students presumed they could take as a consequence of my understanding ways. An incident with a girl named Lydia, a bright and hard-working history student of mine, serves as an example. Midway into the school year on the day of an important full-period test, Lydia showed up with only 15 minutes left in the class asking if she could take the test the following day. Her excuse: "I had to take a chemistry test."

"During your history class?" I asked incredulously.

"Well, I didn't finish during my regular chemistry period, and the teacher said that we had to finish it sometime today since he was figuring grades for the marking period tonight," she said, eying me with the most pained expression.

"Lydia, you had a test to take in *this* class today as well, You knew that. Why didn't you wait to finish your chemistry test during a free period or after school?"

"Mr. Walker, I couldn't. I didn't have a free period, and I have to go to work after school. Won't you let me take the test tomorrow?" she pleaded.

I could hardly believe the audacity of her request, and what was more exasperating, she didn't seem to understand how I could refuse her. In her own frustration she finally explained the rationale for her behavior, "You see, Mr. Walker, not all teachers are like you. Mr. Owens is really mean. He won't make exceptions, no matter what your circumstances are! And I'm not on his good side. I thought you would understand."

What upset me the most was that Lydia had not even attempted to tell her Chemistry teacher about her circumstances for fear of further damaging her position in his eyes, and yet she had little difficulty counting on my "understanding" and sacrifice to allow for this lack of honesty on her part. It took a long tearful meeting the next day to explain to her how much I didn't understand her behavior, and why she would have to be penalized on her test. It was a valuable discussion that eventually led to the heart of the matter; the pressure Lydia felt to be perfect, and the possibility of learning from failure. It took such experiences to demonstrate to students that being understanding did not mean being easy on them, but rather being willing to listen to them and deal with them considerately, something that I expected from them as well.

When it came to grading essays, my empathy and inexperience combined to create another problem: It slowed the process to a snail's pace. From my desk at home every student essay whispered up to me one of two compelling messages. First, there was, "I am something precious. I am the personal thoughts of another individual entrusted to you. Listen carefully." And there was also, "No matter how illogical or illiterate I am, I am quite possibly the best effort this young mind has ever produced. Warning! Warning! Someone's self-image may be on the line here."

Prompted in this way, I pored over each paper, not only explaining what was lacking in logic and literacy but also trying to make as many encouraging comments as possible. Did the mini-treatises I produced at the end of these papers make a positive difference to my students? The opposite seemed more the case. It took me such a long time to correct papers that by the time I handed them back my comments were almost anachronistic. Eagerly anticipating my students' attention to what I had written, on the day papers were returned I was often confronted instead with the question, "When did we write this paper?" I soon learned to curb my appetite for commentary but not without some struggle with my conscience.

Whether it was planning lessons, dealing with parents, or commenting on papers, often what I felt inspired or compelled to do proved to be impracticable. Through trial and error I gradually learned, but even so, I had an amazing capacity during those first months to rebound from a miscalculation only to venture into another unrealistic experiment.

The problem was partly managerial in nature. Three courses to prepare each night and four to five classes to teach a day meant always having to proceed with something that was less than fully thought out. There was always room for the unforeseeable. It was also a fact that I was only just beginning to gather a working knowledge of the capacities and interests of my students. My initial ideas about what was of interest to them and what they could manage were sometimes on the mark, but sometimes woefully misguided. When I was off the mark, the disparity between my total investment in what I was doing and the students' lack thereof, was painful. In terms of self-confidence, a few too many experiences of this disparity without an interlude of either successes or of vacation days was dangerous.

It was my interest in John Woolman, the eighteenth-century American Quaker, that propelled me into my first experience of this danger. I had spent part of my summer reading Woolman's *Journal*, a remarkable account of one man's anguish and struggle over the moral shortsightedness of his generation. On the issues of the white man's relationship with Native Americans and with Africans who were enslaved, Woolman's profound social conscience and his commitment to win over his errant countrymen through spiritual force alone was deeply inspiring to me. I wanted my honors section of United States History to be exposed to this unusual eighteenth-century personality whose insights seemed so timelessly relevant.

The opportunity presented itself during a unit on the Native American "problem" in the colonial and Revolutionary periods. The unit had not come together as well as I had hoped, and I looked to the Woolman reading to help capture and focus the attention of the students in the final days of our study. It was worth a try.

On the day the reading assignment was due Daniel walked into the class looking angry. That was a bad sign. Daniel was a weathervane. His reactions to me in class, or to my assignments, often served as early warning signals of the disposition of the majority of his classmates. He wore his heart on his sleeve, and his discontented look or exclamation could make me shudder. When it came to classroom decorum Daniel was tactlessly unreserved. In principle I respected his open honesty. I could interpret it as a sign of his active concern. But in the heat of the moment, especially at the beginning of class, I dreaded the criticism of this oracle of doom.

Typically, Daniel had a comment to make that day before I had a chance to open discussion.

"Why did you give us this reading?"

Had it come from a place of intellectual curiosity, this perfectly reasonable question could have served as a springboard into discussion. But the level of exasperation in Daniel's voice made it clear that his was no eager intellectual query. He didn't wait for an answer.

"Did you really expect us to understand what he was talking about? His vocabulary was straight out of the Middle Ages!" It was as if a floodgate opened as others took up the chorus of complaint. The discussion went nowhere. Many of the students had not completed the reading, and others, alienated by his language, had only read it perfunctorily. I made the most of their disinterest by probing its sources, but it did not salvage my discouraged hopes, nor my frustration over the hours I had apparently wasted selecting excerpts and preparing study questions especially designed to make Woolman's thoughts accessible. At the end of the day I was in no frame of mind to return to the drawing board to resuscitate what now appeared to be a dying unit.

My frustration was heightened by the fact that in the economy of my first-year schedule, at that time I could not easily afford to prolong the attention I had been giving to this one course. Lesson-planning was like juggling. Just as only one or two balls can be held at any given time, and the others must be left in the air until it is their turn to be propelled once again, so it was with my attention to the three courses I taught. But what do you do when the renewed propulsion you give to one course seems to flop and gravity is pulling the others down at the same time? Because I could not bear the responsibility for another day of disillusionment in a history class full of bright students, I ended up with my hands more than full that night.

Into the early morning I worked, this time pursuing an idea for wrapping up the history unit with an imaginary high-level government planning meeting in which students would play historical figures with contrasting views about Indian policy. Combining the interpretation of primary sources with a little dramatic debate had the ring of a winner, at least to me, tired and desperate as I was.

Armed with instructions, biographical sketches, and primary source excerpts, I walked into class the next day weary but excited. The excitement was *not* contagious.

"You expect this to be done in two days?" was the first remark. Daniel had yet to speak but his eyebrows were knit with consternation over the possibility of unfairness. It was as if nothing had changed from the disposition of the class the day before, and they hadn't even finished reading the assignment! There was no sign of the enthusiasm that I had expected.

Angry at their narrowness of concern, but wanting to shield my defensiveness I threw open my hands, "Hey, you're here to learn aren't you? Enjoy it! I'm giving you guys the chance to step back in time and use your imaginations. This meeting could have taken place and these people could have changed the course of American history. Get into it! You'll have today's class and tonight to prepare. That's plenty of time. Now finish reading the assignment."

I felt defeated just having to say that much. As they read on, I carried on my own inner conversation: "I thought this was meant to be a fun assignment, Scott. If it's such a grabber, what are you doing putting on a hard sales pitch? What's wrong with these kids? Where's their love of learning?"

It was their problem, not mine, I thought, and I was beginning to reconcile myself to playing more the taskmaster for this exercise than I had expected when I noticed Lynn's hand raised in the front row.

Lynn was one of my brightest students. She was an extremely quiet and diligent Japanese girl whose family had moved to Jordanstown that year in order to enroll her sister and her in the public schools. They hoped the move would improve her chances of acceptance at a competitive college. Lynn did not speak often in class, and when she did she always spoke with the utmost courtesy and respectfulness.

"Mr. Walker, do you expect us to know what our character really thought from this single quotation, or will you be giving us more information?" she asked looking up at me sweetly.

Lynn did not usually need to have assignments clarified. I looked down at my copy of the assignment materials, which suddenly seemed much more humble than I had thought. I looked back at her, "That's all you have to work with. Do the best you can based on what's there." Lynn seemed puzzled, but managed with effort to hold a smile for her teacher.

It was a smile that stung. Even Lynn was having trouble. The spectre of another assignment gone sour loomed before me. It was now not so evidently their problem as much as mine. I moved through more questions and got the class down to work, but the look of dull resignation on some of the students' faces was deeply depressing to me.

By the end of the day I was exhausted. I had left the planning for my other two courses relatively unattended the night before, since they had not gone well that day, and the thought of going home to breath a new life into them for the days ahead seemed ridiculous. Where was the breath to come from? A tug-of-war was mounting in my heart between the wounded teacher who had had enough and was demanding rest, and a fearfully conscientious one who saw that more had to be done no matter what.

As I prepared to leave, the battle broke wide open in a flush of angry resentment. Straightening my room I felt like hurling the desks across the floor, and I could barely resist the urge to shout out. I held it in until halfway home and then, feeling that the road was ultimately only taking me back to a waiting desk, I pulled over into an empty restaurant parking lot and let loose.

As water rose to my eyes I shouted, "What do you want?" in part at God, in part at myself, and in part at the whole institution of Jordanstown High School. I wanted to blame, but I wasn't sure where blame ultimately lay. One thing was certain, I was tired of what was becoming a day-in day-out experience of hand-to-mouth teaching. The disparity between what I sensed could be done if I had more time and experience, and what *was* being done was becoming intolerable. I stood mocked by the educational ideals and dreams that I so much wanted to realize. I got out of my car and started walking.

I was also getting tired of being *just* a teacher. Like cruel mirages, my weekends had begun to vanish into the desert of my teaching obligations. Yes, I had been warned by my older colleagues not to allow this to happen. "You've got to keep a balanced life outside the school," they had sternly counseled. Just how to do this eluded me though. Weekends tempted me with time to "finally " catch up with this or that course preparation or correcting. But when I succumbed to this temptation and devoted extra weekend time to schoolwork, I never came away from it with the degree of organization and control that I hoped would result. Regardless of the sacrifice, that degree of control seemed always just beyond my grasp.

And the sacrifice was real. There were plenty of other things I wanted to do, not the least of which was spend time with a woman whom I was considering marrying. Romance and first-year teaching are a volatile combination. I had been cautioned against this by a sage in graduate school. His was practical advice, but in the arena of the heart, practicality was one of my lesser guides and I did not heed his words.

Instead, my fiancee-to-be and I tried to make the most of the time we had. This meant drinking deeply of the blissful freedom of Friday evenings and parts of Saturday, then creating little oases throughout the rest of the week to keep in touch; a brief rendezvous for dinner here, a late afternoon walk there. When school pressure was high though, it was difficult to manage even this. At such times we sometimes consoled ourselves by grading homework assignments together, but that was a poor substitute for a social life. As I walked alone that day anticipating another abbreviated weekend, I wondered whether it was all worth it.

I kept walking around the block, oblivious to my surroundings and to the increasing chill of the late afternoon. By my third lap I began to know what needed to be done. I was isolated. I needed to ask for help. I had not practiced this simple solution enough. Something about the high expectations that I felt at Jordanstown High had inhibited me from being fully honest about my sense of inexperience and ignorance. Instead of continually asking for lesson ideas and other helpful tips, I had been postponing the request until I could gain a greater sense (and appearance) of having things under my belt. Sure I asked from time to time, but after each request I felt hesitant to ask again too soon lest I be a nuisance. Instead I wanted to be known as someone who could earn his own keep, and who carried his share of the load.

It was an easy trap to fall into. Months earlier, on opening day of the new teachers' orientation in September, we had been welcomed by one of the top administrators of the school system with a paradoxical statement that had set the trap for me. With a broad smile and in an enthusiastic tone he had said, "You are entering a rich and lively educational family here in Jordanstown, and I can promise you that you will find among us ready support and assistance when you look for it." It would have been fine if he had ended there, but he went on, "But, do make sure your needs are voiced. We have hired you with great confidence in your abilities, and aren't assuming that you will need any help unless you make it known." To my ears it was a double message,

"Please feel free to ask for help, but if you do we'll know that you aren't quite up to what we've hired you to be." I knew this made no sense, and yet under the vulnerable circumstances of my first months of teaching these words haunted me, and had sometimes silenced me when I should have spoken.

Now, months later, as I returned to my car, I knew that I could not afford the isolation. My own energy and vision were nearly sapped, and it was entirely unnecessary. I drove home determined to swallow my pride and reach out for more help.

The opportunity to do just this presented itself that Sunday night. My sophomore Law classes were preparing for the final exercise in a unit on the rights of the accused. The finale was scheduled for that Tuesday when the students would act as attorneys in simulating parts of the famous 1920s murder trial of Sacco and Vanzetti. To bring greater realism to the simulation I had told the kids that I would try to find someone in the legal profession to judge the activity. It was Sunday night, and with 25 students eagerly anticipating a guest expert for Tuesday's simulation, I had no one lined up.

The easiest solution was to judge the event myself. My threshold for enduring student disappointment had not fully recovered from my experiences the week before, but if it had to be, it had to be. There was another option though, and I reluctantly knew it. One of my students had mentioned that his father was a criminal lawyer. I could call him and see if he was free and interested.

It was a perfectly reasonable idea, but the more I thought about it the less I felt like calling. First, I was not at all sure what this man would see on Tuesday if he came. My sophomore classes were not exactly exhibition material. Class sessions could get boisterous. As I imagined the possibility of this respectable attorney *and* parent presiding over something that resembled more a circus than a trial I froze before the phone. Furthermore, I was considering calling him less than two days before the event, a sure giveaway that my act was not all together. I pondered the dilemma for a few more seconds, knew I needed to turn over a new leaf, and picked up the phone.

Mr. Franklin was more than happy to come that Tuesday, and when he did there was nothing spectacular about what he saw. As usual a few kids started off with stage fright and read their roles with deadpan deliberateness—eyes glued to their prepared scripts. Then there was Tom, one of the student attorneys, who felt it was such an honor to be acting in front of a real lawyer that he couldn't stop saying, "I object your Honor, that's irrelevant!," regardless of what the opposing attorney asked or said. He exhibited not a trace of the understanding of the rules of evidence that he had had the day before, and that I had labored to teach him for three straight days! Other students had similar lapses of memory.

Yet even with these humbling problems, Mr. Franklin was so invigorated by the chance to share his knowledge, especially with his son sitting in the class, that the students' troubles only served to enhance his enjoyment. His explanations were so informative and engaging that I soon relaxed and lost all sense of concern for how the class appeared. We were all learning and the students were loving it. To my surprise, at the end of the period Mr. Franklin thanked me two or three times for asking him to come. "What a significant job you have. This is where people can really be changed," were his parting words.

The whole experience testified to the value of keeping an open classroom and an open life during that year regardless of the risks. The Law class probably could have been better prepared, but in the economy of my first year I had done all that I could for this one lesson. That day it took Mr. Franklin to do the rest, and he did so by taking advantage of students' confusion, the very evidence of my weakness. I don't think the final result could have been much improved, no matter what I might have done, and it certainly could have been much less if I had been unwilling to risk looking foolish.

The circumstances of first-year teaching were a continual invitation to such risks, and behind every invitation was the dual prospect of connecting more personally and vitally with my students and also being exposed in my inexperience or ignorance. Like a swimmer in a heavy surf, the trick was in learning to ride these circumstances of vulnerability toward beneficial ends rather than wasting time struggling to avoid them. Like a clown capitalizing on the potential of his very vulnerability, I learned to use what I sometimes would have preferred to hide in order to teach well.

Strangely enough, on the very afternoon of Mr. Franklin's visit to my Law class I ran into Mr. Bergowitz, whose classroom and classes I had inherited. When he asked me how I was doing, and I mentioned my excitement over the attorney's visit, I had to laugh at the irony contained in his response, "Gosh, bring a parent lawyer to that class! I never would have dared in my first year." Without the vision of a clown, I wouldn't have either.

EPILOGUE

Scott Walker continues to teach at the high school where he started. He "wisely" married at the end of the first year of teaching, and now has a son to keep his teaching experiences rooted in reality. Since his first-year's experience, besides getting more sleep, he especially enjoyed collaborating with other teachers in creating and developing curriculum. He hopes to continue to teach, but is still in the pursuit of the holy grail of balance between the demands of the profession and the other priorities of life.

QUESTIONS FOR DISCUSSION

10.1 Walker titles his essay, "In the Proximity of Foolishness."
  (a) What does this title mean?
  (b) How does it relate to this beginning teacher's experiences?

10.2 Jordanstown High School differs from Scott's stereotypical view of a high school.
  (a) In what unique ways did it challenge him?

10.3 Recall the incident of Lydia, the girl who arrived late for the test.
  (a) What does Walker's solution tell you about him?
  (b) What would you have done?

10.4 Finally Walker asked for help.
   (a) What made him take that step?
   (b) What kept him from asking for help earlier?

10.5 A lawyer-parent who came to Walker's class said, "What a significant job you have. This is where people can really be changed."
   (a) What did he mean and do you agree?
   (b) If you agree, in what ways could Walker change his students?

10.6 Toward the very end of his account, Scott speaks of risks he needed to take as a teacher.
   (a) What were these risks and how do they relate to his thoughts about being a clown?

Chapter
11

Bright Lights

Mary Vesprini

It wasn't until this summer, the summer after my first year of teaching, in a place very far from my high school, that I was able to make any sense about what went on in my classroom. The adage that claims one must be a student to be a true teacher (perhaps it isn't an adage but something of my own fabrication) seems to smack of cliché, yet in my case, becoming a student again, inadvertently triggered the series of reflections in this essay.

For the moment my particular area of "expertise" need not be discussed. As a first-year teacher I'm sure my experiences have much in common with those of any first-year teacher. It was explained to me by my department head that as the newest member of the team, I'd be starting with the lower level students, the beginners. In a sense, we probably deserved each other. "They're not bright lights," my department head informed me, "but they're a good bunch of kids." I have since pondered, during those rare moments between frustration and exhaustion, what makes a bright light. The benefits of an upper-middle-class education so formed me that my superiors, mainly my department head and principal, referred to me as "bright," "dynamic," and "energetic." Such qualities tend to excuse a multitude of professional blunders. Never before had I found myself in a job situation where so many wanted me to succeed. Nonetheless by November, the terms "rookie" and "fresh out of school" began to grate on my nerves. It soon came clear to me that certain colleagues were anticipating the death of my idealism and enthusiasm, which seemed to annoy them slightly.

I did take the extra time to earn a master's degree. Unlike many who claim that a university education does not prepare you for the first year of teaching, I felt that the more I could learn, the better. I found the exposure I had while working on my master's to be extremely relevant and helpful. It soon became clear that my colleagues did not share this view and quite often dismissed the slightest mention of the "theoretical" as intellectual rubbish. They, the "seasoned" educators who had been purged by the fires of exasperation, knew better. I wager that a mixture of professional insecurity and an acceptance of monotony made it difficult for such individuals to accept change. They thought that their experience as educators had provided them with sufficient insight and expertise. However, some of the teachers I came in contact with were dedicated and excited about their profession.

It would be presumptuous and unfair of me to accuse such people of incompetence. They had been teaching longer than I and certainly knew something. However, in this perfectly acceptable suburban school system, so many members of the staff seemed reluctant to change, as if any new information or approach would expose some hidden inadequacy. After countless hours in the teachers' lounge, I realized that the exaggerated bitterness toward the school system and its small time politics, which occupied most of the conversation, was a defense against an unfair but widespread opinion that accused the public school teacher of being an unfit professional. Although this classification is now being challenged, many teachers are still easily threatened. Some of my colleagues had allowed themselves to become mediocre professionals because they eventually began to accept the accusations of public opinion. As the "newest and brightest star" I soon found myself fighting feelings of alienation. I was surrounded by decent people but the environment was still unstimulating. Too much time in the teacher room could and did lead to depression, so I took my lunch and my theories elsewhere, the last refuge being my department head's office.

My department was considered one of the more conscientious groups about the place. We were often accused of working too hard and our annual fair, "a festival of food and fun" was hailed by all as the most exciting cultural event of the year. I remember our first meeting concerning the fair. I naively suggested that we try to involve the students in more culturally oriented activities. An older member of the department decided that I was getting too carried away and abruptly told me that I could stay after school if I chose, however I was incorrect to assume that others shared my interest. The group went back to planning how many main courses could be furnished by the sophomore class. After the shock of being publicly attacked passed, I silently resolved to cool my zeal.

My colleague's remark hurt and angered me but I tried not to let it spoil the amiable rapport we all shared. I didn't have much in common with these ladies. They had all been teaching for at least five years, if not ten or fifteen. Most of them were married with families; I was single. Although my inexperience demanded that I focus most of my attention on my career, my lifestyle allowed me to do so. The other members of my department had to reconcile the two very demanding occupations. These women were for the most part dedicated and committed to their jobs. To combat the perpetual state of frenzy that can so easily undermine the working mother, they had mastered the system. In the time it took me to make one photocopy, they could correct a stack of papers. Years of managing dinner at 5:30 had taught these ladies a multitude of shortcuts. Yet mastering a system and mastering one's profession are not necessarily the same thing.

Our lunchroom conversations covered a range of topics. Sometimes we talked about particular students; for some reason, the superlative was a big issue: "Who was the smartest, Who used the worst language." The subversive policies of the guidance department was another favorite subject. The latest news in culinary arts and home furnishings, along with various theories about the peculiarities of men were never overlooked. Usually by lunch time, the state of exhaustion in which I found myself, welcomed this kind of small talk. After four hours of teaching, I can say without shame that talking about various theories of learning quickly lost its appeal. Unlike the business world, where the lines between personal and professional business are more clearly defined, lunch time provided these ladies with an opportunity to ask me very direct questions about my personal life. While I knew their interest was sincere, I still found it to be somewhat of an intrusion. Nonetheless, my need to feel accepted was so great, that I responded by overconfiding. As our conversations got more intense, it became obvious that we had very different perspectives on life. The fact that I actually enjoyed being single did not shock them, but whenever I implied that this could be a permanent life style they seemed immensely bothered. This was somewhat ironic, considering that our department head, a woman with an extraordinary capacity for administrative duties, in addition to being probably one of the best teachers I've come across, had for whatever reasons chosen to remain single. It suddenly occurred to me that although I clearly lacked the experience of these women, my lifestyle and the possibilities it held for me threatened them. For my part, the feeling that I did not really fit in made me reconsider whether or not I was right for the job.

Even when we were all at our worst, I did enjoy and like my students. This and the constant fear of losing my job kept me after school at the computer center well after the school day had ended. As the days became shorter, I began to appreciate the need to leave the premises with everyone else. By the end of September, I was on a first-name basis with all the custodians. On Halloween I experienced my first major crisis. On returning to my car, I discovered that someone had removed the stereo. I knew that this act of aggression was not directed at me personally, yet it was extremely demoralizing. That same evening, I resolved to leave the building at a more reasonable hour and beg my parents for a home computer for Christmas.

Time, or more precisely the lack of time, was probably the most frustrating aspect of my first-year experience. A variety of administrative tasks ate into my much-needed preparation periods. I didn't mind the study halls, attendance-taking could be mastered, and hall duty did not present any true danger, however the lunchroom responsibilities proved to be particularly offensive. I often wondered how students could take seriously any teacher who had to push a trash barrel. I was aware of such duties before I entered the profession. After all, any form of employment has its unappealing aspects.

However the push to make me, in the words of my principal, "a real part of the high school environment," often interfered with my plans to become a decent teacher. I was supposed to be teaching language, French in particular. Language teachers will try anything from verbal tap dancing to sponsoring a French bakery. This was the area where I felt I should direct my energy. Yet as a first-year teacher, was required to establish loyalties. Before I was hired, the principal more or less told me that I would be expected to be a class adviser. This is the sort of activity that tenured teachers don't have to deal with. I am not against school spirit, I was perfectly willing to chaperone dances, buy raffle tickets, and even sell candy to support the football team. It is important for teachers to be involved with their students, yet as a new teacher I found this responsibility to be very demanding on my schedule. There were days when I felt overwhelmed and I wondered why administration couldn't leave first-year teachers in peace.

What I have discussed up until this point has been peripheral. The colleagues, the administration, these are all normal frustrations that one learns to deal with. To dwell on the inadequacies of the system can only be self-defeating. Part of learning to survive within the public school system involves developing a set of strategies that allow one to cope with inefficiency. My real concern throughout the year was the kind of relationship I had with my students, the "dim" lights. These children ranging from the ages of 14 to 16, were my severest critics. I felt, and still do, that my first obligation is to them and not the administration.

I had five classes, two of them French I. One consisted of 21 mischievous and noisy freshmen who had had a smathering of French at the junior high level. My other French I class was a group of 10 or 12 youngsters, a mixed bag in rank and ability, that had ended up in my class because guidance most likely did not know what to do with them. My second-year students consisted of two honors groups, somewhat brighter lights, and a standard group (last year's standard French I class that had been promoted).

I accepted the fact that I was going to make mistakes. I knew my students would try and take advantage of my inexperience. The first few weeks were fine. My students were so enthusiastic that the neighboring teachers had to put paneling against the doors to drown out the rousing choruses of "Quel jour sommes nous?" Unfortunately I established a rather severe, according to my students, routine of homework and quizzes. I thought that this would give me the appearance of an experienced teacher. I soon became caught in a web of inflexibility. By mid-October the anticipated slump settled on my classes like a dark cloud. My students were in a slump and I was afraid to change my initial policies for fear of appearing incompetent. My first quizzes were abysmal because they were too hard. One of the best pieces of advice I received in college was from a professor who told me to always test what you teach. I took this sage piece of advice too far and assumed that my students were going to go home and learn everything I taught.

Like all newcomers my ego was frail. I wanted my students to take me seriously. Some of the bolder ones would try to undermine my confidence by asking me right out how long I had been teaching. Many of my students assumed that a pleasant demeanor could be easily manipulated, and constantly tried to change the subject during the course of our lessons. I resisted these attempts by cracking down even harder. I became unpleasant at times and continued to drill my students on grammar and vocabulary. I would sometimes stare down at those weary faces and conclude that I was carrying out acts of torture.

My task as a teacher of French became increasingly difficult as new obstacles arose. Lack of student motivation is probably the most discouraging problem for teachers. It certainly frustrated me. I spent hours trying to think of innovative ways to approach language instruction. I was full of enthusiasm, yet my methods confused and intimidated many of the students, who were used to being unresponsive in school. As I jumped around, writing on the blackboard I knew some of them must have been thinking, "Who is this nut?"

Nonetheless, I tried my best to be a one-woman show and eventually got some response. Even the most timid began to tell me the time and date in French. The more boisterous students were into making noise. This is the trap that an inexperienced language teacher can fall into. An animated language class can degenerate into complete pandemonium if the teacher has a discipline problem. I would often try to stimulate "verbal responses" through games and role-playing. With some of my older students this was quite successful because they wouldn't act up. However most of my students were freshmen. I have come to the conclusion that no species on earth is more charged than your average ninth-grade students. During those first few months of teaching, noise took on a new dimension for me. I had tried everything from role-playing "Le Supermarket Star" to a technique called Total Physical Response (TPR) to encourage students to respond physically to the teacher's verbal cue. These activities invited bad conduct.

What kept them in line was the spirit of competition. If you give two kids a piece of chalk and a verb to conjugate they'll fight it out to the death. I suppose I should have let them play more games, yet I was far too concerned about appearing soft. Besides, I wasn't very good at game-playing. A parochial school child from way back, I fundamentally believed that learning was work. I still do believe this, however the hindsight of my first year has taught me to appreciate the notion of integrating fun and work. I would either go out of my way to entertain my students, which was exhausting for any prolonged period of time, or crack down on them with an excessive set of worksheets and assignments when they refused to participate. The noisier students interpreted such action as punitive and their reaction was one of resentment and resistance. It was unbearable to teach on such occasions. All my energy and dynamism turned to anger and I would yell, knowing that I was doing the wrong thing, yet unable to deal with frustration and rejection.

On those initial days when my students were openly hostile and critical, I assumed that I ruined the year. My students were much more resilient than I suspected. They could be rude and uncooperative one day and then the next day come to class and behave quite well. It occurred to me that perhaps I wasn't entirely at fault. I never quite understood why professors of methodology often brought up the problem of the physical surroundings. I naïvely assumed that a really good teacher could make the students forget uncomfortable surroundings. Although I had days when my approach was off, I also realized that the time of day, the temperature of the classroom, as well as the noise level around us, were factors that couldn't be underestimated. For instance, Friday afternoon was not the time to introduce a new concept. Likewise, I began to dread teaching last period on Tuesday, when my high-spirited honors students turned into a bunch of noisy brats. It was some consolation to know that I was not solely responsible for what at the time appeared to be subversive behavior. Still, even on my better days, I wondered if I was really getting through to them. I had no pretensions about making a radical difference in their lives. I just wanted them to like French enough so that if they were ever stranded in some distant French-speaking province they would not starve. It became apparent that this was no small task.

With the exception of a handful of honors students I had a hard time collecting homework assignments on a regular basis, despite my threats that homework counted for 25 percent of their grade. I found myself thinking thoughts that showed my age. "When I was in school," I reasoned, "I did my homework." I did not misbehave and was genuinely interested in learning. During those bouts of frustration I had to tell myself that I most likely ended up in education because I was a good student. Moreover, I also came from an environment where discipline problems did not exist. The nuns, for better or worse, seemed to keep everyone in line. As I became closer to these students, I realized that the majority of them lacked motivation because their energies were elsewhere. They were interested in their own culture. This was no shock to me. Youth always has its own culture, its own idols.

It was still disturbing to see how these kids had become so entrapped in a culture that capitalized on the sensational and the extraordinary. So many of them seemed to exhibit a growing sense of inadequacy. They actually believed that they just couldn't measure up to what the media dictated. Because I was younger than the other teachers, my students put me in their camp, and were eager to learn about my personal life. They were intrigued by the fact that I had spent so much time in another country, yet they also realized that such an experience indicated that we were from different social classes.

With the exception of my honors students, the majority of my students came from working-class homes. Through the course of the year, it became clear that these students viewed any difference or deviation from the norm as strange behavior. They were so acculturated in their working-class background that it was difficult for them to appreciate the value of a foreign language or culture. Many of them believed the popular misconception that the French are a pretentious and affected lot, who dislike Americans.

It was not a coincidence that the students in the honors group had a greater appreciation for things French. Most of them came from homes where the importance of academics was stressed, whether they liked it or not. Their parents were the ones that actually came to Open House. So much of the tracking that goes on in the classroom is a matter of class structure rather than ability. I really can't judge whether or not my honors students were significantly brighter than my standard group. I have a difficult time with the whole concept of "brighter" and "smarter." The students who were into school for school's sake were the ones with the high test grades. They knew how to study, they knew what to study, and they knew that their remote future (getting into college) depended on their success in high school. They could also see the purpose of learning a foreign language—even if it was just for the sake of reading a fancy menu. Some of them I'm sure will even go off to spend a year or two in a foreign country. Such things are determined by upbringing rather than intelligence.

It became increasingly evident as I observed my classes and monitored my study halls that for many students school was a holding ground. About 60 percent of my high school's graduates went on to college. This is not an exceptional figure either way. I wondered about the other 40 percent. Some of the lower-level students had three 45-minute study periods out of an eight-period day that included a 30 minute lunch break. These students did not have enough homework to fill their free periods and for the most part sat and stared or talked for an hour-and-a-half every day. It was no wonder that they were bored and restless. The school couldn't really give them much to do so they were kept in study hall until they were old enough to join the workforce.

It is not my intention to discredit my middle-class honors students; on the contrary, their consistent positive response was one of my few real support systems. My low-level students, on the other hand, suffered from a collective inferiority complex. Some had emotional problems or conflicts at home that prevented them from concentrating on the external world. Others had problems with reading and writing, making it nearly impossible for them to master the troublesome system of French spelling, a nuisance even for natives. I felt like a hypocrite. I told these kids that the most important thing for me was that they try to speak, which they did. However, they knew as well as I did that ultimately they would be graded on their test scores. Whether or not these children learned any French or not seemed secondary to their ability to test well. I often wondered whether or not these students should be taking a foreign language. However, as my department head pointed out, the security of my position rested on the enrollment. I was advised to pass as many students as I could. The plight of those who were truly failing was left to my so-called "discretion." I then learned an unspoken truth about grading. For all the fuss made about homework and test scores, grading is still a somewhat subjective enterprise. What I came to label as the "fudge factor" breathed new life into my falling class averages. No teacher can actually ignore test grades and averages; however, like statistics, they can be manipulated.

Just as I was forced to evaluate my students through grading, I was observed by my department head and principal 12 times over the course of the year. "That's it," I would say to myself before each observation, "this time, they'll see right through me." For the most part the observations went well. Surprisingly, my students transformed themselves for me. Even the most

rambunctious calmed right down. Not only did they behave, they participated. During my first observation I was so nervous I misspelled a word that
was left on the blackboard. As I proceeded to bump into the wastebasket and
drop my chalk, I noticed one of my students trying to get my attention without alerting my department head. This frantic freshman was trying to show
me with his book that I had spelled "disque," the French word for record,
"disc." "They like you," my department head explained, "otherwise they
wouldn't have tried so hard." Of course what my department head didn't
know was that after each observation I was forced to reward their good behavior with a night off from homework. So my students liked me and I liked
them. I had my favorites, I suppose any teacher does, but I liked all of them.
I'm sure some of them doubted it when I let my frustrations get the best
of me.

I was having a very good first year, yet I felt something was fundamentally
wrong. My observations went well. But when a friend suggested that I let my
students fill out an evaluation form, I got scared. My superiors wanted me to
be a success; they couldn't be entirely objective. My students were a captive
audience; I wasn't ready for their criticism, however constructive. I tried to
convince myself that the only reason they found French difficult was that they
just didn't study enough. I doubled up on homework assignments and threatened lack of attention with surprise quizzes.

I knew a purely grammatical approach was not the best way to go about
teaching a language but as the year progressed my energy and creative forces
were ebbing away. The slump had taken hold. I did have somewhat of a revelation while preparing for our foreign language fair. Many of my students
wanted to do projects dealing with things French. I offered to give them suggestions. It suddenly dawned on me as I talked about a variety of topics from
Louis XIV's fetish for hummingbird tongues to Gauguin's retreat to Tahiti,
that my classes were silent; they were interested. I got the same response
when my beginning French class decided they wanted to sponsor a French
bakery. When I started to talk about French culture and the fact that French
people eat snails, I got a response. True, a lot of what I was telling them
confirmed their suspicions that French people are weird because they eat
weird things, but at least they were listening. One of my fundamental mistakes was that I was trying to teach a language without teaching about the
culture that spoke the language. I was so obsessed with trying to teach in the
target language I overlooked the fact that France was not a real place for some
of these kids. They did not trust the words. The fact that *j'ai faim* was a perfectly normal way for a French speaker to express hunger was incomprehensible. In desperation, one of them exclaimed suddenly, "Why can't they just
say 'I'm hungry,' like Americans?" The bakery was a success. My least-
motivated group had one of the best projects of the fair. When given something that they could do, these students became positive and interested. It
changed the way we would relate to one another for the rest of the year. As I
came to realize the need these kids had for positive reinforcement my quizzes
became easier. I finally learned something of value: So much of good teaching

depends on the teacher's ability to respond to different needs. It is impossible to anticipate the needs of every single student but I was so concerned with finding the best method to teach language that I was not really taking a look at what I had in front of me.

In May, I finally decided to give out that evaluation form. I devised a series of questions that would not allow my students to attack me personally. I asked them how they would teach a language. Although some of the suggestions were promptly disregarded (French parties every week, no homework), others were quite helpful. As I had expected, they wanted to play more games. There was also a general consensus that more emphasis be put on cultural affairs. They also expressed a desire to see "real" French people. I was apparently a "fake" French person. Of course, the school budget prevented me from importing live specimens, but I could always rent French films. Even subtitled films could be instructional for beginners.

"For a beginner," I had forgotten what it had been like to be a beginner. This was probably why I had such a hard time relating to my students. Intellectually I knew that learning a new language was difficult, but I understood everything I was saying, even if they couldn't. I thought I explained things clearly; I tried to speak slowly. Of course I knew that many people, especially teenagers, feel embarrassed when they attempt to speak a foreign language. It has something to do with taking on another identity. We all take language for granted. After all, it's the thing that differentiates babies from small pets. Losing one's ability to communicate is not only frustrating, it tends to make one feel extremely foolish. I had forgotten all this. I had been speaking French for too long. I had forgotten all about the day my first French teacher, Sister Norma, threw up her hands in despair at my horrible pronunciation. Everything came back this summer when I arrived in Salamanca, Spain, two days after I finished my first year teaching.

When I was hired, my department head told me that I should, for job security, learn Spanish. I had no idea she expected me to do it this summer. I had taken two semesters of Spanish nearly ten years ago. Upon my arrival I knew my French would help to an extent, but it did not help me to speak or understand. "With your language ability," my department head exclaimed before my departure, "you'll pick it up in no time." I tend to think that my facility with language stems from an inability to keep quiet for a prolonged period of time. Trying to convey a variety of ideas with a limited linguistic inventory amused me. Yet even for someone who likes language learning, without any syntactic base, a month in a foreign country does not lead to mastery. My initial days in Spain were filled with frustration. I couldn't talk. No one could understand me. Resorting to baby talk did not bother me, until I started class at the university. We were a diverse language group, and my courses were entirely in Spanish. Our teacher focused on grammar and tried very hard to get us all talking. I never felt uncomfortable when speaking to my Spanish landlady, but my inhibitions got the best of me in class. For the first time in my language-learning career, I was actually afraid of making a mistake. I was experiencing the very same frustrations that my students must have felt. My teacher was well prepared and very organized, but she was teaching her native language and did not fully realize that many of us just did not understand.

Relying on my language background, I passed my test. My tuition would be reimbursed by the school system even though I did not come back speaking fluent Spanish. I would have been better off taking an intensive course at home, but what I learned about language learning was well worth the trip. I recommend that anybody who becomes too comfortable with what it is they're teaching go out and learn something entirely new. What illuminates a bright light and not a dim light? This is still a very important question, yet it does not concern me half as much as that, bright or dim, they all need consideration. When I am absolutely sure that I've exhausted every approach to learning I can come up with, then I might understand what catches a bright light.

EPILOGUE

Mary Vesprini is alive and well and teaching in Wilmington. Her second-year students have decided to open a bagel shop in Paris, having been convinced by Mary that the product is nowhere to be found in that city. Mary, on the other hand, plans to continue to teach, to travel, and to hone her language skills.

QUESTIONS FOR DISCUSSION

11.1 According to Vesprini, the term "bright lights" describes both her and all of her students.
   (a) How?
   (b) What does Vesprini think of the term "bright lights" and its accuracy in describing students and in predicting their futures?

11.2 Vesprini felt she did not "fit in" in her school environment.
   (a) In what ways?
   (b) To what degree was her discomfort caused by others' expectations of her?
   (c) What were some of those implied expectations?

11.3 Throughout much of her first year, Vesprini describes her teaching methods by recounting her various successes and struggles with students.
   (a) What was her predominant teaching style?
   (b) Based on her account, what was her philosophy of education?

11.4 At the end of her first year of teaching, Vesprini relearns first-hand how one feels as a student.
   (a) What is that experience?
   (b) What insight does it provide Vesprini about her students?

Chapter
12

Fighting the Good Fight

Stacy Dwyer

The photographer and I chatted idly as we waited for my seventh-period students to file into the classroom. And file in they did, dressed to the hilt in all kinds of outlandish costumes, each representative of a character from a book they had read that year. Huck Finn chewed nonchalantly on a piece of straw while listening to the Great Brain explain his origins. Karana, looking remarkably well after her isolation on the Island of the Blue Dolphins for 18 years, elicited applause from her peers. And, five or six Billys, complete with coon hounds and baking soda cans, making them look as though they had just stepped out of *Where the Red Fern Grows,* roamed about my desk. No one seemed shy about having his or her picture taken. And for one brief, but wonderful day, I shut out all the horrors and hurts of the past school year. How I had managed to emerge from my first year as a public school teacher still standing and breathing on my own was beyond my own comprehension. But here I was, surrounded by the students I had grown to love. I could reflect on the negatives later; today was a day for positive thinking.

Today was a day we had all looked forward to for several reasons. First, the end of school was just a day away. Even the sturdiest of teachers and students breathlessly await the final bell. The atmosphere was one of celebration and their final class with me had all the trappings of a gala event. I called the local newspaper, for I believed that what my junior high students had accomplished over the school year deserved coverage. They had completed a year of reading, and in my eyes, they were "hooked on books." These students, many of whom had wandered aimlessly about the classroom and local libraries in September, had read anywhere from 10 to 20 books. Now, in full costume and surrounded by giant paper ice cream cones depicting the titles and authors of completed books, they surrounded the photographer, eager to answer his questions. They also eagerly glanced my way for I was the keeper of the real ice cream. It was quite a feast and a well-deserved finale to a difficult year for my students, and me.

I begin my story of this past teaching year in a rather unusual place—the end. The significance of that day brings to light what I must have been feeling all along. I called the newspaper because I had always known that what was transpiring in my junior high English classroom was quite important. Here were kids of all academic levels who were devouring book after book when there had been little or no appetite for reading before. Watching them read and recommend books to one another gave me a real sense of accomplishment. My colleagues were equally enthusiastic, as were parents and members of the school committee who voted to allot me funds for more reading projects. But through it all, the administration remained negative. It had been a year-long battle, sometimes silent and cold, other times verbal and heated, between principal, vice-principal, and teacher. In the end, I called the newspaper to help my students celebrate what they had achieved despite my anger and frustration. We ate ice cream from 8:00 AM to 2:00 PM—and that is what I have chosen to remember first. The rest will follow.

I had never harbored any thoughts that teaching in Brockton was going to be easy. Here was a city that bore close resemblance to my hometown, Buffalo. Both were home to a diversified population of working-class families. But, Brockton had the reputation of being a tough town and I wasn't quite sure what I would encounter when I headed out of Boston for that first interview. Kids were kids as far as I was concerned and I was just eager to start teaching. Hence began my introduction to public schools, their students, their teachers, and their administrators.

I had just completed a full year of graduate studies at Boston University when a friend informed me that Brockton was in search of junior high English teachers. I had known for several months that I was ready to be on the other side of the desk. I was even looking forward to those telltale chalk marks on all my best clothes. Besides, one gets tired of lectures and workshops on teaching when the desire to teach is foremost in her thoughts. In literary terms, this magnetic attraction to teaching could be likened to the call of the wild, a call to get away from all the talk about teaching and to do the real thing! Whatever it was, I heard and responded.

Looking back on those initial job interviews in Brockton, I should have been alert enough to sense ensuing problems with the administration. Oh, but we are so eager and carefree when the summer sun shines upon us. I wanted to teach; they wanted a teacher. So I cast aside my negative feelings for this principal who had drilled me with scenario after scenario of discipline problems, a kind of "What would you do if . . ." interview, and accepted the position at Bennett Junior High. As he so blatantly stated, I was being hired on the high recommendations of the English department head. In his opinion, I was a lowly "new teacher," a title he was to bestow upon me throughout the year. Here, in the public school forum, he was sure I would discover what teaching was all about. He did not hesitate to add that I probably would not survive. I challenged this man from the start and fortunately I had a wonderful department head who stood by me all the way, as well as supportive and concerned colleagues. If it had been otherwise, who knows how true his prediction of failure might have been.

What teacher, however seasoned, is not a bit nervous on opening day? There is excitement in the air as well as a sense of wonder, intermingled with a wave of dread. The first pitch is about to be thrown and you have box seats. While I am not a true baseball fan, I do know a bad pitch when I see one. The one thrown from the mound that day brought moans from the crowd. Here was yet another indication that it was to be a year of frustration for both new and returning teachers.

Addressing an assembly of freshly scrubbed students dressed in the newest of fashions, the principal opened by reading a recent news article on the soaring dropout rate. With his voice rising and falling with the passion of the moment, he warned the students before him that they too could and would amount to nothing if they didn't pull their weight this year. He then itemized negative things a 12- to 14-year-old was capable of doing—and foolishly dared them to do it. Teachers and students shifted uncomfortably in their seats. Babyish seventh-graders grew wide-eyed while the superior eighth-graders smiled knowingly.

And so, there was no welcome back, no positive reinforcement. Only a principal and a vice-principal who had never heard of or had long forgotten the theory of teacher expectations. Like archenemies, they had challenged the students before them, and there would be many who would respond throughout the year with the negative behaviors that had been highlighted for them. And with that, I was instructed to march my students off to their new homeroom. Welcome, teachers and students, to Bennett Junior High.

There were, indeed, many indications of the perilous times ahead, but my eagerness to teach acted as a blinder. At a department meeting, I had chosen to ignore or interrupt my colleagues' desire to give me a brief synopsis of my students' past histories. Special attention had been given to my homeroom list. Something told me that I was better off, and so were my students, if I greeted them without any preconceived notions.

So, while the other teachers threw sympathetic glances my way, I tried desperately to appear confident as I called out each student's name, giving him or her what I hoped would be the perfect seat. Little did I know how permanently some of those names were to be etched in my mind; Floyd, Robert, Stephanie, Carlos, Darnay, Michael. As those first few days ticked by, the reality became all too clear—here was a homeroom beyond all homerooms, one the other teachers shook their heads at and clicked their tongues over, murmuring "What an awful first experience," "Be firm dear, don't give them an inch," and "Better you than me." By the luck of the alphabet, I had been blessed with the sweetest of girls, thoughtful, polite, honor students who were trapped in a den of wild animals. They had suffered through seventh grade with the same homeroom companions and they were now bracing themselves for yet another year of mayhem. Even before September drew to a close, several of these girls quietly began to keep track of how many days remained until they were free from the cruel hand fate had dealt them. Like me, they and a scattering of quiet boys were tough. We survived together. But that isn't to say that we weren't shell-shocked. There was never a dull moment in Homeroom 221.

There will always be one particular student whose name shall remain etched upon my mind throughout what I hope will be a long teaching career. Over the course of several months, this name became a catchall for every bad thing that could happen to both new and experienced teachers. When colleagues inquired about my day, I had only to utter this student's name and warm nods of understanding would follow. In time, even teachers who were fortunate enough not to teach this student began to utter his name in reference to their own misfortunes. The name was Floyd and the student who bore it was many a teacher's nightmare.

From the beginning Floyd and I were never close. His reign of terror in my classroom opened my somewhat disbelieving eyes to the total incompetence of our vice-principal, the designated disciplinarian. Floyd was a student who demanded discipline and firm boundaries from the start, but because of this administrator's decision to pamper rather than scold, he was allowed to run free as he had been in seventh grade, bullying other students, robbing them of their lunch money as well as any feeling of security. He talked back to teachers without any fear of reprisal from a higher source. His behavior toward his female classmates was beyond disturbing. Floyd was a student crying out for help, but such help was unavailable in a school where the administration failed to support the teachers. I knew early on that Floyd was headed for a big fall, and I worried that he planned to take me down with him.

I had decided from the onset to be firm yet soft-spoken with this student. At 15, Floyd's large imposing frame, bedecked with gold jewelry (complete with brass knuckles until someone confiscated them), was rather intimidating. Bennett Junior High schooled students of numerous ethnic and racial backgrounds. Floyd was just one of the many black students I taught that year. I never grew to associate his temperament or his behavior with the color of his skin. I had several problem students, black and white. Floyd was just the meanest. He looked mean, he acted mean. His favorite vocabulary word was "fuck" and he loved to begin each homeroom period by spitting on the books of a particular Haitian girl. He would then lead several other boys in a lively, vulgar discussion of this girl's anatomy, her mother's anatomy and what he would like to do to them. Along those same lines, Floyd was also fond of leaving condoms in the hallway outside my door. He seemed intent on shocking me, but I was more repulsed than shocked.

I sought guidance from an understanding colleague two doors down. Her sympathetic advice was to avoid yelling; she had found that it only served to make Floyd more rebellious. There were times when Floyd and I would have rather pleasant exchanges and I could subdue him with flattery or genuine concern about his fatigue or sulkiness. But, these moments were few. Needless to say, I began each morning hoping that this would be a good day for

Floyd and, in turn, for me as well. He wielded that much power. There were days that began and ended rather serenely, when I found myself able to concentrate on my other students and the lessons I had planned. But on others, I was not as fortunate.

Floyd was always ready to explode. His presence was immediately felt by teachers and students alike. His deskmate, a pretty, vivacious, and patient girl, would sigh with relief when it became apparent that Floyd was absent. But, despite a few occasional outbursts that the vice-principal had rendered "harmless," things remained relatively calm until the third week of school. As usual, I was instructing Floyd to be silent during the morning announcements. But, as usual, Floyd ignored me, voicing the challenge that no one set rules for Floyd. He had been made to stay after school for such behavior before and I was now forced to inform him that the time for just such another extended stay was upon him once again. Waiting for the explosion they had come to expect, the other students glanced in tennis tournament fashion from offender to defender. Who would get the point?

Much to my surprise, Floyd gave no reply and even went as far as reporting to homeroom for the final afternoon bell. Unusual, in that he was notorious for being AWOL come 1:50 PM. But, that was as far as his good behavior went, for when the dismissal bell rang, it was painfully apparent that the events of Floyd's day had erased all memory of the morning's incident. As he approached the door to exit with the other students, I spoke gently. "Don't forget you owe me time after school today. Go back to your seat."

With those words barely out of my mouth, a flash of anger streaked across Floyd's face. Walking toward me, he shouted and slammed the desktops. He would not stay! Who was going to make him? My steady voice was now on the verge of betraying my quivering insides. My head was pounding as I told him to return to his seat, take out his homework and the time would pass quickly. But the gods were not with me that afternoon. Floyd had no intention of staying; rather, his one intention seemed to involve testing my limits. Just how far could he push me? On impulse, I decided to make what I thought would be a strategic move. I stood in the doorway. Stupid move. Forgetting my less-than-intimidating physical presence, I was now faced with an approaching cyclone. If one is to learn anything from my story, let it be this: If a student threatens you with bodily harm, get out of the way. Don't waste time wondering if he means it!

Fortunately, I have lived to tell the rest of the story. I saw the clenched fist approaching and, with little time to spare, I ordered a curious onlooker to get the vice-principal—quickly. Help would be there soon. I was sure of that. I was angry and scared, but if I just stood tall and kept talking. . . . But now the fist was closer and it demanded that I move. I demanded that he sit down, but Floyd's feelings were expressed by tossing books and obscenities. Approaching footsteps. Thank God. My face would remain intact.

But any image I held of the three of us, teacher, disciplinarian, and student reaching some solution to this problem was soon obliterated when the same student I had just sent on this mission of mercy returned with the words, "Mr. Landry says he's busy with the bus students." Needless to say, some very unprofessional thoughts raced through my mind at that moment. Floyd had heard the response to my plea for support and it made him smile. Eyes still fixed on Floyd, I told the student to get a neighboring teacher. As I prayed, my calm, slow-talking male colleague appeared in our connecting doorway. Together, we compelled Floyd to sit down and this angel of mercy stood sentry while I went in search of the "busy" vice-principal. He was too busy to help a teacher in need?

Remain calm. Be professional. Explain the situation. Be firm about having him return to the classroom with you. I carried on this conversation with myself as I strode boldly down the corridor. Those were my new-teacher-in-deference-to-a-senior-administrator thoughts. My irate-woman thought process is not quite as printable. Deep breaths and the brisk pace at which I walked were helping me to resolve the two. But such a resolution was shattered when I gazed out the front door of the building and saw this man wrestling good-naturedly with several students. He was busy? I stormed through those swinging doors with the ferocity of a hungry predator closing in on its prey.

"Mr. Landry, I would like to speak with you please." (Not bad for a mind struggling against saying something altogether less gracious.) Smiling, he left the students and asked what he might do for me. I inquired as to whether or not one of my students had asked him to come immediately to my room a few moments earlier. Obviously my tone caught his attention. He answered in the affirmative and suddenly Mr. Happy-Go-Lucky became Mr. I'm-in-Charge-Here. Here was a very busy man. Without mincing words, I informed him that I thought reports of an angry student threatening to punch a teacher should have been enough to bring him running to my room regardless of what he was doing. I now expected him to make the trip and contend with the situation. Score one for a professional statement.

I then quickly turned on my heel and began walking toward whatever lurked ahead. Hearing the heavy footsteps of the vice-principal behind me, I held high hopes that this incident would be brought to a proper close. In my mind, displays of violent force and destructive behavior by a student demand strict discipline. This was coming from someone who smiled all the time and spent countless hours worrying about each and every kid. Here was a disciplinarian with a commanding voice walking behind me. He was a tall man with a muscular build. The veteran teachers at Bennett had initially been impressed by his stature and seemingly stern approach to discipline. They had bid adieu to a burned-out vice-principal in June and were looking forward to a new face and, a new no-nonsense approach to discipline. I momentarily forgot about any previous encounters I may have had with Mr. Landry and felt confident that his booming voice and intimidating presence would silence Floyd. Now that he had arrived to offer support and lay down the law (and I was willing to forget his absenteeism once justice had been served), I would explain the situation and turn Floyd over to him.

Silly me for harboring such thoughts. In the heat of the moment I had forgotten that I was dealing with a vice-principal who believed in the buddy-buddy approach. His goal was first to be a friend to all students. Teachers were obviously excluded from this wave of understanding and friendship, or at least I was. I stared in total disbelief as I watched this man place his arm around Floyd's shoulders and then inquire what the problem was. Streetwise Floyd was smart enough to know the game and play it well. He proceeded to spin tales of a sick mother waiting for him at home, appointments he had to keep, and a not-too-bright teacher who didn't know that she couldn't keep him after school without 24 hours notice. As Mr. Landry listened to this tale of woe with closed eyes and a head bobbing in sympathy, my sentry, Mr. Giordano, quietly exited the room, gesturing for me to remain calm in the face of adversity. From the first week of school, he had sensed that this man was a nice guy in the wrong job. He would never discipline the students, only the teachers.

If I had thought I was going to be offered the chance to recount my views on what had transpired that afternoon, I was being naïve once again. Escorting Floyd from the room, Mr. Landry only stopped long enough to ask if I was sure Floyd actually meant to strike me. Funny, I hadn't really thought to stand there and debate that issue. The clenched fist had somehow impeded my thought process. I stared at him in total disbelief for now it seemed perfectly clear that without proof of his intention to strike me, Floyd was off the hook.

Floyd was allowed to go home shortly after that. I was not privy to the conversation that ensued between him and his buddy, our vice-principal, but once he was dismissed, Mr. Landry asked me if I was aware that Floyd's mother was on welfare. Was that to be Floyd's excuse throughout the year? If so, hundreds of other students in our school would also be given free license to intimidate and bully their classmates and teachers. With that one question, Mr. Landry thought he had wrapped up the situation and left. The month of October didn't look too promising.

Floyd, with the help of the very person I had requested to come and help me, had been sent home with a pat on the back and a laugh and a smile to soothe his nerves. I, on the other hand, had been left sitting in my classroom, chastised for disturbing a busy professional for no apparent reason. Doubt engulfed me. Maybe I didn't know how to discipline my students. Maybe I was weak and had no place in this system. I won't cry, I told myself, because that's what the administrators would like to see me do. Slowly, I began to pack my things to go home. Tomorrow just had to be better—maybe Floyd would be sick. I did have some great plans for my classes. . . .

I walked by Mr. Giordano's room. He waved goodbye and smiled in my direction. But nice as that was, it suddenly wasn't enough. A student known for violent behavior threatens a teacher and the teacher is reprimanded? My footsteps fell harder as I approached another colleague's door. Noticing my anger and then tears, she beckoned to talk. When the story had been told, she confessed to expecting to hear as much. She had been wary of this buddy-buddy approach and now her worst fears had become reality. Here was the new vice-principal they had anxiously awaited that summer, one who barked orders at his teachers, siding with the worst of students while incident after incident was reported. Clearly he intended to do nothing with repeat offenders such as Floyd.

Together, we walked to our cars. By saying very little, she convinced me that new as I was at this public school game, I was not alone in my confusion and frustration. It was imperative that I keep up the good fight. This was Floyd's third year of battle at a two-year school and he had already succeeded in reducing to tears a majority of the faculty, herself included. My emotions thus changed from depression and self-doubt to anger.

This anger was directed not at a student who was obviously surviving under a tremendous burden of insurmountable problems, but at a 50-year-old vice-principal who continued to cut me down with insinuations of incompetence. He was the incompetent one, as incident after incident would reveal. And, as a result, the students were taking control of the school, well aware that their teachers received no support from their superiors. Sure, they would be the vice-principal's buddy, often calling him by his last name minus the respectful title of "Mr." They would walk boldly out of the afternoon detention sessions to tell him, their buddy, how they had been wrongly accused. How could we as teachers blame the kids? They were smart enough to know a pushover when they saw one. I hated to see all my colleagues suffer, but took some comfort in knowing that I wasn't alone.

I confess to glaring quite frequently in my bathroom mirror; taking pains to transfigure my usually smiling countenance into a look that can stop a troublemaker dead in his tracks. Friends and relatives often express disbelief in my ability to be gruff. Ask my students about that, especially Carlos, who stopped that last day of school to say, "You were sure different than I thought. I was sure you'd be a pushover." So, those glares had worked on all but Floyd, but I tried to put him out of my mind from 8:00 AM to 1:50 PM. It was then that I really labored, pushing books, diagraming sentences (yes, some of us still do that), checking vocabulary, reading creative writing assignments—all the while roving in and out, up and down the classroom. I know that at times my students wished I would just sit down, but I wouldn't. Something told me that I had to keep them going, and to do so, I had to be aware of where they were. There was so much to teach and learn on both ends. And, since the school year had just begun, I was still fresh on my feet.

Meeting my students for the first time had both worried and excited me. Who are they as individuals? What can I possibly offer them? What will they leave with come June? Who will shine? Who will turn sour? I couldn't help but wonder who would appreciate my sense of humor and who would moan in dismay. Please, dear God, I begged, don't ever let me give way to cutting sarcasm.

Here was a new experience for me. Classes, levels, and students would continually move throughout my day as an English teacher. While there was something of a movie quality in faces passing, I also saw disadvantages. The quick pace of the day would make it difficult for me to get to really know all 100 of my students. It was painfully obvious to me that there were bound to be those who remained hushed in the background, who would come and go without me ever really knowing them or what their lives were all about. I knew that in those first few weeks, some students would shine as memorable.

There would be those who captured my attention through academics. Even the worst of discipline problems would force me to take a closer look. But what about the average quiet kids? The thought then that some kids were going to slip by me was depressing. I wanted to be there for everyone. I vowed to try my best.

Looking back on the first six weeks of school, I can see that I was overwhelmed by the "publicness" of my new position. I was constantly being evaluated and I was constantly questioning whether I could say or teach this or that. With what I felt were a million eyes looking my way, I moved methodically through the designated curriculum. While a voice within urged me to open my eyes and use the creativity I knew I possessed, I felt stonewalled. This was a public school with an entire English department and curriculum chairperson to whom I was accountable. I was only one of six English teachers and low person on the totem pole at that.

My "reading is great" sensibilities had immediately zoomed in on the fact that the vast majority of my students saw reading as a heavy task rather than a delightful pleasure. My brain whirled as an introduction to Aesop's fables brought cries of "Yeah, I saw that on Bugs Bunny! Why read it?" I pushed aside what I know to be true—that these kids needed to get reading—rebuked by the mounds of teaching materials and curriculum charts that lay before me. I trudged from colleague to colleague, posing that age-old question, "How do you balance grammar, vocabulary, spelling, writing, and literature into five 45-minute periods each week?" Each had his or her own answer, stressing that which he or she saw as most important.

For one, grammar was the end-all, complete with intricate diagrams. "If we don't teach it to them here, they'll never get it," one colleague explained. "They can't be bothered to teach parts of speech in high school. It interferes with literature and the writing process." But, were we really supposed to be saving literature for the high school?

Another colleague was big on the writing process. His kids were writing but not reading. I was sure there should be a connection.

I stayed away from the one who sang the praises of worksheets. "Keeps them busy," she would remark as she ran off bundle after bundle. It seems that once she handed them out, she spent the better part of class time visiting other rooms. True, her students never moved, but I had the awful feeling their brains were turning to sludge.

My department head sympathized with my plight. She also wanted her students to think for themselves, not spend the year going from one textbook exercise to another. Under her supervision, her students read a tremendous amount of literature, analyzing and critiquing all the way. The work they produced was remarkable, but they were also a class of advanced eighth-graders with a tremendous vocabulary and a sound understanding of English grammar. I, in turn, pondered the fate of my standard-level seventh-graders who seemed to be in limbo in all areas, as well as my seventh-grade honors students, who, while very bright, still needed a strong foundation. Then there were my eighth-grade basic students who arrived sleepy-eyed and terribly bored every morning. How could I possible cover everything and still be vivacious and interesting. I wanted to be challenging but fair, and I wanted everyone to love coming to class. Naïve? No. Just optimistic.

So, in the opening round, grammar, vocabulary, and spelling stood front and center. Funny, though, how junior high grammar texts devote four to six weeks to parts of speech while in reality, those four to six weeks are required just to wake your students up to the fact that they have heard of nouns and verbs before and English isn't a foreign language for the majority of them. I droned on, boring the bright ones and frustrating the already frustrated. I would occasionally interject some creative writing or literature assignment as a "treat," but not for very long. After all, we were only on verbs. I secretly wondered when we would ever get to those intricate diagrams.

My role as a public school teacher seemed to terrify me. I was unsure when I should have been confident. In the midst of adhering rigidly to the assigned curriculum, I had somehow forgotten about my opening day activities with my students. Back then, I had made inquiries about what books, if any, they had read and the day had been filled with my promises to get them excited about reading and writing. I wanted to do just that, but I felt as though I needed a full day with each class, not 45 minutes often cut short by ridiculous announcements about the boys' baseball uniforms and a vice-principal who thought he was covering the territory by breezing in and out of my classroom. He would slap a few kids on the back and then pretend to read what they were writing. I often thought that my attempts to teach amid such distractions would be a good story line for Woody Allen. I would even go one step further at times and find myself wondering if perhaps I was trapped in one of his zanier films. I could see myself in "Radio Days."

As we plodded along, and the boredom and frustration continued to grow in my standard classes, so did the discipline problems. Such an outcome was inevitable but I hadn't seen it coming. Two boys in particular just seemed to slip away from me and I remain disappointed in my inability to have somehow caught them before it was too late.

Scott was the typical wiseguy, smart enough to know that his constant disruptions ate up valuable class time. Unable to do the work, he chose to create turmoil instead. Attempts to keep him after school to discuss the problem proved futile. He was always the first to cry, "You have to give me 24 hours notice. I'm a bus student." (I always resented this policy. Why didn't the students have to give me 24 hours notice when they were about to wreak havoc in my classroom?) So, I had to let Scott go and he would arrive beaming the next day, minus the 24 hours, with another excuse in his hand. He had more dental appointments that year than I have had in a lifetime—and I spent five years visiting an orthodontist.

One of the few times I did manage to keep Scott after school for extra tutoring proved quite memorable. Standing alone, away from the cronies he loved to entertain with bad behavior, he was an immature adolescent with little self-esteem. He was clearly frightened of the work assigned to him. He wouldn't read out loud because he was so unsure of many pronunciations. His horrendous handwriting helped to disguise numerous spelling errors. Scott revealed at this meeting that his one great love was scuba diving, but while I tried desperately to tune into that, I never quite reached him. His frequent absences and a two-week "vacation" in Florida despite protests from his teachers helped to ensure his downfall. Scott made me mad, at him and at myself. It gave me no pleasure whatsoever to have to fail him for the year.

If Scott angered me, Doug made me sick at heart. Carrot-colored hair, freckles, and a keen mind hid Richie, a boy secretly enrolled in my class. In those early weeks Doug was eager and interested, but perhaps just a wee bit shy, something I attributed to the seventh-grade jitters. He was a little fish in a big pond. Yet, as October approached and then slowly dissolved into November, Doug's shyness gave way to isolation. Often the target of cruel adolescent ridicule because of his hair color and disheveled appearance (dress to be cool in seventh grade), he slowly slipped into his own little world. I, too, was excluded.

Here was a boy who had shown such promise only a few weeks earlier now lost and befuddled in the far corner of my room. My attempts to reach him in class were unsuccessful; directing attention to him only brought bursts of laughter from those around him. They were so with it; they had friends and Doug didn't. There were obviously problems outside of the classroom that my role as teacher could not obliterate. I quickly dissolved my stern "do your work" approach and tried to spend some time with this troubled boy before and after class. There were times when he would talk to me and others when he barely seemed to note my existence.

Scott and Doug were two other totally different problems, or that is the way it appeared on the surface. Scott was loud and disruptive; Doug was quiet and withdrawn. Neither did well academically, one hindered by achievement, the other impeded by outside forces. Scott had all the material things as well as some good buddies to pal around with after school. Doug appeared to be the victim of poverty, neglect, and loneliness. Much to the amusement and disgust of his classmates, he began to wear the same outfit each day, grime-bespeckled jeans and a faded flannel shirt. With his hair now dirty and tangled and a week's worth of soil etched into his hands, Doug no longer bore any resemblance to the all-American Richie Cunningham. Phone calls home left me frustrated. I only managed to inform a weary voice of what she said she already knew. What was a mother to do, she wondered. I wondered what a teacher was supposed to do. Numerous complaints to the guidance office seemed to echo about those four walls and then drop dead. Promises were made; they would talk to Doug. I was never really sure that they ever did.

Meanwhile, I continued to muddle my way through the curriculum and struggled to hold my floundering standard classes, of which Scott and Doug were members, together. Doug came to class but no longer felt the need to bring books, pen, or paper. Maybe he thought I had nothing to say to him—and maybe I didn't at that point in his life. Grammar and all those other lessons I was trying to juggle didn't seem important at that stage; Doug's mental health did.

While I groped about for answers, other teachers began to express their concern. Some just labeled Doug lazy, others wondered what could be done for him. And the guidance office offered no answers. Too late, they revealed to me that Doug was a victim of attendance boundaries. Although he had attended a grammar school for six years with one group of students, he was compelled by his address to attend our junior high while his friends traveled collectively to another. So here he was, in a school that even I found intimidating at times, a young, frightened seventh-grader surrounded by a sea of unfamiliar faces who taunted rather than comforted him. While I had been wondering what to teach and how to teach it, Doug had slipped away from me and I would never quite catch him. It was an awful lesson, but there it was; our students have no time to spare during our personal moments of struggle and doubt.

It is now painfully obvious to me that any confidence I had in myself as a creative and knowledgeable teacher was pushed behind a dark cloud. Discipline problems in my standard classes, ranging from Scott and Doug, to Jim, who arrived with a terrific hangover every morning, to Jeff, who was too smart to be there, to Anna, who kept running away from home, to Allison, who barely looked at me, kept me on the run. Homework was assigned but barely trickled in, leaving me to wonder if I had been foolish to ignore the advice of the other teachers. From day one, I had been told by several to watch my students' eyes. Those of my honors students would surely be bright, reflecting the eagerness and intelligence not to be found in the dull, vacant stares of my standard classes. The joke went further to explain that I would be lucky to have a basic student who even made an attempt to open his or her eyes so I might get a chance to categorize them. Sadly enough, there now seemed to be some truth to that disturbing bit of junior high folklore.

This realization disgusted me, as did the notion that these same teachers appeared right on target again when they suggested the following homework schedule: none for basics because I would never see the books, let alone the assignment again; twice a week for standards since more would only cause me frustration and anger; and four times a week for honor and advanced students because they alone could and would do it. But, tempted as I was to follow these guideline and make my life easier, I just couldn't go along with this concept of the prepackaged student. To do so went against everything I believed in. I truly expected something from these kids, regardless of their level. All I was asking was that they do their best and at this point, I was sure they weren't doing it.

Teaching junior high English is a tremendous task. I wanted my students to write, but then I needed to read all 100 papers. Take too long to do so, and their interest and momentum was lost. The concept of peer evaluation (students reading students' papers) always sounded great during the workshops, but was disastrous in the lower-level classes. Each paper inevitably came back with a brightly colored A+ scrawled across it. When questioned, the peer evaluator could be counted on to shrug his or her shoulders and say, "I thought it was great!" But then, how could I expect them to check for that which they hadn't even mastered yet themselves?

Journals started out strong but subsequently fizzled when I again found myself unable to respond to their entries quickly enough. The kids were eager to write, though there were exceptions, and I was eager to read, but the stacks and bundles I carted home each night left me tired and discouraged.

Reading the essays of my honor students was another story. They were a delight to peruse each evening. I devoured every word they wrote. The kids were certainly growing as masters of the written word, many with just a snitch of help from me. But, pick up an assignment done by one of my standard kids, and the night stretched into morning. No paragraphs, no sense of structure, and total confusion on my part. There I sat with a folder bursting with 42 often-unintelligible papers and an alarm clock ready to shatter any hopes of sleep at 5:30 AM. I was overwhelmed to say the least by the task before me, and jealous of, if not angry with, the teachers who shot through those swinging doors like clockwork each day at 2:25 PM clutching only their car keys. I, too, had a life apart from the classroom, or so I was thought. The burdens of life as an English teacher had left me little free time. I was sure my husband-to-be would veto an apartment overflowing with adolescent literature, stacks of journals, and mounds of spelling and vocabulary worksheets. I had to get my act together and there didn't seem to be a moment to spare.

Fortunately, a light beaconed. How could I have missed the answer I needed lying dormant in my desk drawer all along. It was there that I had stored my students' written responses to those opening-day inquiries about their reading habits. As I glanced over them absentmindedly one afternoon, it suddenly dawned on me that I had known what to teach and how to teach it all along; I had just allowed other pressures to knock my sensibilities about. I had been like Dorothy in the *The Wizard of Oz*, asking everyone how to get home when the power had been with her since day one. What about reading for pleasure, for growth, for writing, grammar, and vocabulary skills? Somewhere along the way, I had lost sight of my wish to get books into the curriculum and off the library shelves. While my attention had been diverted to the daily struggle of keeping the kids and myself going at a steady pace, the boredom and frustration on their faces indicated a failure on my part. They seemed to stare at me, curious as to which direction I would take next. It was then that I put aside any mental pictures of Scott sitting with his arms crossed or Allison staring at the floor, and boldly wrote across my plan book in big block letters: INTRODUCE BOOKS. That was all I wrote, but those two words meant the difference between a year of total defeat and a year of partial victory.

I worked feverishly throughout the weekend, going through stacks of index cards I had kept for the past three years. These bore the names of books for adolescents, books I had read and had perhaps already recommended to some students. As Sunday evening approached, I grew anxious. Here I was, book lists ready for distribution and instructions meticulously set out for all classes, but I was plagued with feelings of self-doubt. Would they bite the bait I had prepared? Would I be cutting short that which I was required to teach as outlined in the curriculum guide for what I wanted and needed to teach? Would my professional relationship with the ever-watchful administration continue to deteriorate based upon this transgression from what the older, and more respected teachers were doing? I knew I was probably setting myself up for some major conflicts, but I threw caution to the wind.

I went to bed that night virtually challenging the new day to dawn. It's funny how one, as a teacher, can face conflict after conflict each day, often wrestling with feelings of fear and self-doubt, and then push it all aside, in the promise of the next day. I have heard it said that in matters of love, the heart is a pretty resilient muscle. So, too, must be the inner workings of the being we call "teacher."

And so, despite the reality that I still had to begin and end each day with Floyd and his homeroom cronies, my actual teaching gained new momentum and freshness with the introduction of books and the concept of reading for pleasure. Many irritating discipline problems became more manageable or disappeared altogether once classes commenced with a five-minute silent reading period. My standard students had always arrived immediately after lunch, injected with a chaotic vitality one could only obtain from a hastily eaten lunch of grape soda, potato chips, and sugar-packed pastries. Now, while they still scattered noisily to their seats, they soon settled in for a good read. Reading deadlines were set for all students, and those who failed to complete their books by the designated date soon saw the necessity of utilizing these precious five minutes each day. For some, reading in school meant more time to watch television at home. For others, it was a good way to keep a great story going. Either way, I was pleased because I now had tangible evidence of my nonreaders reading. They kept reading and I acted as a role model, reading my own book as they read theirs.

We were not reading just to fill up the day. No, from such prolific reading stemmed a vast array of writing and literature lessons. A great deal of attention was still given to grammar, spelling, and vocabulary skills. Reading pulled everything together; by reading more, the kids were able to see the language at work. The majority of them seemed to be improving academically. Still, I had this nagging feeling that curriculum mismanagement would be the charge leveled against me by my superiors. While my department head was just as enthused about the reading program as I was, we both waited for the principal to respond negatively during an ensuing evaluation. But, I pushed that worry aside. What else could I do in the face of such enthusiasm on the part of my students? Was I to say to them, "Read at home, but not here. Reading for pleasure is not a priority at school?" Perhaps I could have told them to read at home, but since so many of them were obviously not in the habit of doing that, I felt compelled to get them going in that direction. I had to go with what I believed: Get them reading and all else will follow.

I was to spend the remainder of the school year caught up in this dilemma. The administration eyed me carefully; they couldn't deny that my students were reading rather than sleeping during study periods, but they did blame me for what they saw as not planning my lessons effectively. Spot evaluations often "caught" students and teacher engaged in three to four different activities; silent reading, book talks, grammar lessons, and writing assignments. For the one evaluating, this translated into absentmindedness on the part of the teacher. Such a barrage of activities, often coupled with chatter, could only mean that I had failed to plan anything and was once again filling up the time with random assignments. On the contrary, such activity required a tremendous amount of planning and organization. But, a mistake one morning set me up for harsh criticism and the threat of a poor formal evaluation.

That morning I was rushing about the apartment in an attempt to gather materials scattered about the evening before: essays, folders, posters, and my plan book. It was not until I was 40 minutes into my journey to school that I realized I had left the plan book at home. It was Monday, the day when all plans must be turned into the department head. Upset as I was, I was not about to turn back. Someone would just have to understand.

The department head did understand; the principal did not. This was the day he had chosen to evaluate me, a Monday morning of all things. Fortunately, my plans for the day were etched in my mind and I carried them out with what I viewed as great success. But, here I was, being cited for a lack of planning. The class had been busy. Here were five eighth-grade basic students reading and working together, their enthusiasm clearly evident, and the principal's parting comment? "Just as I expected. No plans." With that, he walked out of the room, leaving me to wonder what education in that school was all about. I had set myself up for this criticism. I had even predicted it. I had no written plans in sight to back up my activities. That was what he needed to see, not the actual activities of my students. I thought back once again to yet another piece of teacher advice that had proven true: "Keep the floor tidy. He looks for messy papers littering the floor. He likes well-lined rows. (Too late. Early on I had paired off desks, enabling students to work together on writing assignments.) And, this was gospel, always have your lesson plans ready to show him." One colleague even confessed to repeating the same plans week after week. It was only a matter of having the proper squares filled in the plan book.

Yet I had committed the ultimate sin. I had taught a class without the benefit of a plan book. I would admit to such a crime but I was not willing to be labeled incompetent because of it. As my Irish temper flared, so too did my need to voice a complaint. These day-to-day incidents of "me versus them" had left me worn out, weepy, and frustrated. I was having success with my classes, but absolutely no success with my administrators. Were they incapable of saying something positive about the work I was doing? I was angry and at that instance I, the raw teacher, became feisty. It was obvious that my lack of tenure made me fair game for sharp, unconstructive criticism from those above me. I swore I would stand up to them and challenge their accusations. No longer would I cry quietly or scream at the empty air as I drove home each afternoon. I would now voice my complaints in any way I could. And, I reminded myself, I would never, ever give them the satisfaction of leaving my plan book at home again.

Visions of a long-ago toy commercial complete with catchy jingle came to mind. I could see before me cute, round, wooden people called "Weebles."

True to their form, "weebles wobble, but they don't fall down." Funny, I suppose an English teacher should mark a major turning point with a more classical, poetic reference, but the image of those toys being rocked about by reckless children and always popping back up did it for me. I would wobble, but I would not fall down.

My first vocal protest, beyond the usual conversations I had had with my colleagues, was made to my department head, an intelligent professional who also seemed to be at odds with this administration. She had, on an earlier occasion, recounted the tale of her first meeting with Mr. Landry. It was late August and all the department heads were meeting to discuss fall scheduling problems. They were all eager to meet the person who would replace the previous vice-principal. They were obviously hoping for the best. Her own personal enthusiasm vanished when he greeted her with a twinkle in his eye and a proclamation of "Sweetheart, I sure hope you baked something for this crowd of hungry men." She was the only woman in the group and immediately made it clear that she regarded his comments as highly unprofessional.

As she listened to my story unfold, it was quite obvious that she too was angry at the way my earlier complaints had been dismissed by Mr. Landry. She was even more disturbed by my recent encounter with the principal and agreed that my evaluation should not reflect this one-time absence of my plan book. Taking the time to listen to and then discuss the problems I was having, she offered some important suggestions and some much needed encouragement. I was doing a remarkable job; I was a good teacher. I had no discipline problems that she could see when observing me teach, only a few notorious incorrigibles who were quite pleased with the buddy-buddy system extolled by the vice-principal. This, she reminded me, was an administration that detested students parked outside its office. Both the principal and the vice-principal seemingly wanted no part in the discipline process and therefore resented any teacher who made repeated demands for their assistance. She herself would love to shut the classroom door and exclude those day-to-day problems that kept creeping in and taking us away from all we really wanted to do—teach our students. But we both knew that these problems were, unfortunately, part of the reality of teaching.

With that realization, she vowed to be my advocate when needed. There were many times after that initial cry for help that she did just that. It was comforting to know that I had someone in a position superior to mine willing to do battle for me with those who were above us both. She did, beginning with the complaint that my evaluation should not insinuate that I had not thoroughly planned my class. She reminded a startled principal that he was the one who had once bemoaned the fact that the students never seemed to read. Wasn't I getting them to do just that? She emphasized that this was a major accomplishment on my part. Parents and other teachers thought so. He was forced to admit to such and, with that, I had achieved my first small but important victory. I was ready to fight the good fight.

There were many instances of conflict between the administration and me from Thanksgiving on, but somewhere along the way, I learned to evaluate each predicament better. At times, it was a matter of my being right and they (usually the vice-principal) being ridiculously wrong. And, at other times I made some unfortunate mistakes and learned some good lessons. Whatever the particular case, I could not afford to develop ulcers and destroy years of orthodontia by grinding my teeth at night. Teaching my students was most important and I tried to keep that belief foremost in my thoughts. Thus, when conflicts inevitably arose that I felt seriously impeded the learning process of the majority, I no longer meekly asked the administration for assistance; I demanded it. True, I often blinked incomprehensibly at the new aggressive me, but I stood my ground. It was this new me, steady and confident, that finally demanded that something be done about Floyd.

With the onset of what was to be a long winter, Floyd grew more incorrigible than ever. He was now in the habit of arriving after the first bell. He would slam his locker to announce his late arrival and would proceed to wreak all kinds of havoc for the remaining moments of the period. He continued to spit on the Haitian girl's books because he "didn't like her face." Other mornings he mimicked the announcements in a loud and boisterous voice, throwing in a few obscenities here and there for flavor.

Any action I took against him seemed futile; keeping him after school left me physically ill since he spent the entire period slamming things with his fists and badgering me incessantly. Floyd had succeeded in creating quite a rift in the homeroom. There were those who stepped back cautiously, afraid to cross his path. Others cheered him on, eager to see just how much he could get away with. So far, he had gotten away with quite a lot. I felt like I was in a prizefight of some sort, and the referees were taking bribes.

Floyd obviously had many problems. Neglected and abused as a child, his adolescent years were incredibly turbulent. It did not take a psychiatrist to tell me that this kid was looking for attention the only way he knew how. But try as I might, I alone, in the role of homeroom teacher, could not make up for all the past injustices he had suffered. There were others, too, who, like Floyd, needed more than I could, not would, give, This was a difficult realization for one who wished to be all things to her students. Floyd needed outside help, but when I tried to explain this to the vice-principal, I was again brushed aside. In his opinion, I was making too much of Floyd's outbursts; all he needed was some "motherly" attention. The suggestion was made that I try soothing him with my feminine ways.

As I stood listening to this lecture on discipline, the blood rushed to my face. Thoughts of Floyd responding to my feminine ways—whatever those may be—raced through my mind. He was a young adult, not a little boy, who had time and time again demonstrated a total lack of respect for members of my sex. I was not about to endanger myself any more. Since Mr. Landry had reaffirmed that he had no intention of interceding in this matter, I was compelled to make some important decisions.

I had come to dread Wednesday, because it meant homeroom period, complete with Floyd, lengthened from 10 to 45 minutes. It was a special period designed to involve students in extracurricular activities they might not otherwise enjoy due to strict busing schedules. But, true to the reality of education, it excluded the "bad" kids, leaving them with their homeroom teachers. For almost 12 successive Wednesdays, my life had been hell. I had learned to tolerate Floyd for 10-minute intervals, but 45 minutes left me weary and, at times, physically ill. As I walked to my homeroom that particular morning, I made my decision: Floyd had to go.

Beckoning him to join me in the hallway, I instructed him to gather whatever materials he would need for 45 minutes of work. He fought me all the way, swearing and hurling insults, but I left him on the vice-principal's bench. There he sat and there he remained as I told the vice-principal that he would no longer be admitted to homeroom as he could not abide by the few rules I had set down. Without waiting for a reply, I returned to a relatively quiet class. Only a curious few ventured to ask what had become of Floyd. The majority seemed to know instinctively; it was as though they had been waiting for me to do it for some time.

For one full week I escorted Floyd down from his locker to the office bench. And each morning I reminded the vice-principal that Floyd would only be allowed to return after the three of us had met to discuss his behavior. I waited for him to schedule the meeting; I could handle having Floyd out of homeroom for any length of time.

Things were unusually subdued until a beaming Floyd appeared in the doorway one morning and, in sarcastic tones, relayed the message that he could return now. He had promised the vice-principal that he would be on his best behavior!

I confess to some very unprofessional thoughts, and there they were, plaguing me again. Asking a colleague to keep an eye on the class, Floyd and I began the journey to the office again. My steps were angry; his seemed to be laughing at me. Was I losing my mind?

When the school secretary saw me, she knew the problem immediately. She herself could not believe that Floyd had been given permission to return. Since both administrators were out of the office, she promised to deliver my message; Floyd could not return to my homeroom until a previously discussed meeting had been held.

The principal was at my door in ten minutes. Who was I to say who could and could not be admitted to my classroom? (This was a position he used against me several times: Ignore the behavior of the student in question, and yell at the teacher instead.) Much to his surprise, I interrupted him by handing him a letter I had just completed, detailing the entire situation. As I relayed the facts, his anger toward me gradually subsided and was eventually redirected at the vice-principal. Victory! He himself would hold the meeting that very afternoon and Floyd would not return to class until after we had all met.

Fortunately, my fears were without merit. I was allowed to state my case. Floyd must abide by the few simple rules his classmates seemed to follow with little incident. He had to be on time; he could not speak during announcements; he would stay away from property that did not belong to him.

To my delight and surprise, the principal further emphasized that if Floyd did not follow these guidelines, he would be transferred to another junior high, one, it appeared, that he was to have been attending all along. Disbelief took hold. But there it was on paper—one infraction and he was out.

Naturally, several teachers encouraged me to send Floyd to the office if he even blinked when spoken to, but I would not. He did make an attempt to behave and I was always the first to compliment him. But, while he may have been behaving for me, he was venting his pent-up anger in other ways. Swearing at teachers, instigating cafeteria fights, responding rudely to a polite request to pick up a piece of paper; all infractions were duly recorded in the citizenship books kept in the office. Floyd was warming the office bench once again, but something strange was happening. The vice-principal, fully aware of the stipulations set down by the principal, was shielding Floyd. When Floyd did appear at the office with a note from an angry teacher in his hand, he was briefly spoken to and then sent on errands. Anything to get him out of the office. I kept quiet about this, figuring that my intervention would only create a bigger rift between Mr. Landry and myself. I knew something had to give, and soon.

Chaos erupted the week before Christmas vacation. Floyd made the mistake of swearing at the wrong person. Here was a teacher who had learned to take his students directly to the principal as soon as they pushed him over the edge. He had quickly learned in those first few weeks of school that the vice-principal would do little, if anything, in the way of discipline and that the principal would be sure to become irate if the behavior problems started drifting into his office. Floyd was expelled that day and, despite his efforts to plead his case with his buddy, Mr. Landry, he was not allowed to return to school.

Floyd had caused many problems from September until that noteworthy day in late December. Why then was he given free reign to do just as he pleased? Why were his teachers chastised for sending him, time and time again, to the office? Why was this disturbed young man not helped sooner? It is this final question that bothers me the most. Floyd's expulsion and subsequent enrollment in another school, though a relief for me, only caused distress for another undeserving teacher. How was Floyd helped by this action? Perhaps I could have done more for him but I have to admit that it is probably not true. I needed assistance and support, and the school disciplinarian was unwilling to give it. The only feedback I received—up until the meeting with the principal—was criticism. I was weak. I complained too much. I was incapable of disciplining a boy. Not true. What, in fact, was true was that I was ineffective when handling Floyd alone.

Looking back on the year, I feel I have highlighted the bad and forgotten the good. It seems that my dealings with Floyd and the vice-principal left me wary of everything I did. This was the wobbling motion I have attested to, but it was January, I was still standing. I emerged from a restful Christmas vacation angry that I had been forced to expend so much energy against what I and my colleagues viewed as total incompetence on the part of the new vice-principal. Those who had been teaching at the school for many years were particularly disturbed. The school seemed to be failing around them. As an individual in a position bureaucratically superior ours, we expected him to know and do more. I know I expected more, and at this halfway mark in the school year, I was beyond disappointment; I was disgusted.

We, the teachers, had the insiders' view of the whole dreadful situation. We were the ones who overheard our students discussing how so-and-so had just escaped punishment via a sob story he had told in the vice-principal's office, or how such-and-such a teacher was reprimanded by this same individual in front of her entire class. I was deeply distressed to hear several of my students admit that they should have been suspended for a recent prank, but were not, because one of their friends contradicted their teacher's story to Mr. Landry. These kids had savvy; they knew a push-over when they saw one.

Conversations in the faculty lunchroom were dismal. Try as we might to cheer one another, we were all just too tired and too angry. One discouraged teacher after another voiced his or her own personal tales of woe. One woman had her grade book destroyed by a very well aimed cup of coffee. With a room full of witnesses, the decision came back that the boy "needed mothering, not discipline."

Another teacher had tried to offer suggestions on how to improve assembly behavior, and was cut down with the proclamation that this school was like a ship, he was the captain and he gave the orders; we, naturally, were to follow them.

The women seemed to suffer more, for we bore the brunt of sexist remarks. A student was joked with, rather than reprimanded for lying to me. "After all," the student was told, I was "such a pretty young lady." No mention was made of my role as teacher and adult. Later, I made quite sure that the student had no doubts about my role. Despite the vice-principal's suggestion that a simple apology would be enough, the student spent detention with me, and was later heard to remark that he had not been able to get away with anything at that time.

My refusal to permit a nasty-tempered youth to remain in an overcrowded study hall was labeled as "female hysterics," even though the male teacher I shared study hall duty with had issued the same order.

For the most part, the men ignored the situation, voicing their complaints at times, but often just laughing off what they christened "the good ole boy" image of the vice-principal. They could afford to do this because by virtue of their maleness, their complaints to him were somehow seen as more valid. They offered us their sympathy and many did speak out on our behalf, but there seemed to be no overcoming the fact that we were dealing with a person in a superior position who was highly favored in the proper political circles. So, we kept teaching, continuing to have our very good and very bad days, all the while hoping that someone, somewhere, would listen and act on our complaints.

I have often wondered if teachers in Florida and California dread the months of February and March as much as their northeastern colleagues do.

Oh, what a dismal time. Cold rain, heavy snow, those dark, dark days. It is certainly hard to find anyone with a bubbly personality roaming the hallways. A peek into several classrooms revealed teachers, myself included, putting aside curriculum-bound lessons in favor of anything to charge the atmosphere.

Although I had suffered crisis after crisis at the main office, my classes certainly kept up my spirits. My first period honors class was an absolute joy. I loved to watch them file in, ready and able for whatever the day would bring. True, there was Josh to contend with, a boy who had earlier tried to persuade me that he was deaf, but subsequent hearing tests proved otherwise. I guess I was too much for him, because after failing the first term, he quickly switched into a higher academic gear. I was inspired by the work of the entire class—writings, discussions, test grades, everything.

Another seventh-grade honors class, proved to be more of a struggle, due most likely to their class time at the end of the day rather than their actual ability. They were quite a mixed group, ranging from hoodlum to future prom queen. This class was beset with grape gum chewers, a habit and an odor I detest. Much to their dismay, I had a very keen sense of smell, especially where grape was concerned, and as they hated to spit out a "fresh wad," many stopped chewing. This was a difficult class; so many brains, so much potential, but so many problems. Many's the time I spent in the guidance office with parents, ready to complain about low grades or poor behavior only to be silenced by the reality of the hard lives many of these kids lived.

My eighth-grade basic students were slugging it out, the three who remained anyway. I had lost one student to a special needs classroom and another two to their parents' lackadaisical attitude toward attendance and schooling in general. Anna, Ramon, and Peter were my star pupils. Peter struggled with everything he did, but he never threw in the towel. I never once heard him say that he couldn't do something, even though his poor reading skills kept him fighting at every turn. His passion for baseball led him to read books he never dreamed he could read before. He devoured them while I searched the library for more. I let him move at his own pace and we were both pleasantly surprised by the outcome.

Anna was quite a smart student, but her difficulty with English as a second language kept her at a basic level. There she worked diligently and was frequently rewarded with her favorite grade, an A+, even though I had been instructed not to give the basic students such high grades.

Ramon was also inhibited by problems with the English language but he too continued to try his best. That was all I was looking for. All three students would beam with pride when I passed out the usually dreaded mid-term progress reports. They had learned in November that such slips could also relay good news about their outstanding efforts and amazing progress. These three pupils were my stars for several reasons; one was that they appeared every day in a class plagued by a high absentee rate.

I continued to have my ups and downs with my seventh-grade standard students. Signs of improvement would suddenly flash brightly only to fade later due to illness or other problems. Adam, a rather large, sluggish student was out of school for six weeks following major surgery, only to return with the explanation that he wouldn't be allowed to stay after school for extra tutoring. Brian, my comic book hero, had agreed to set down his six binder collection of *Amazing Comics* to read *Tom Sawyer*. But Christmas vacation steered him off course, as was the case with many in the class, and it looked as though I would have to begin anew.

Now, with the sleepy month of February upon us, I turned to what always perked me up, regardless of season—ice cream. My students had long known of my passion for ice cream. I had earlier confessed to a one-cone-per-day-habit. Feeling that each class needed some tangible evidence of their success in reading, I began all my classes one snowy day with Shel Silverstein's poem "Eighteen Flavors." The tale of an 18-scoop cone tumbling to the floor left even the coolest of kids giggling. From there, they began to fashion their own giant scoops from construction paper, decorating each with the titles and authors of the books they had read. Most importantly, these scoops, then displayed on giant cones around the room, bore their names. Instant classroom decorations, instant positive reinforcement, instant friendly competition between other students and classes, instant success! As many of the students later pointed out, our room looks much more inviting than many of the other stark, gloomy classrooms that made up the school. This was a startling realization for me. The simple act of decorating a classroom seemed to make a difference to the kids.

Come spring, we had giant paper ice cream cones tumbling out the door and down the otherwise bleak hallway. And, no one ever did deface them in any way; instead, they seemed to spark conversations about who had read what. This was what I had been looking for all along, a feeling of pride on the part of my students. Oh, and the administrators' comments? They just hoped I wasn't using transparent tape on the painted walls. Peels the paint, you know!

Thus, February and March went by faster than usual. A week's vacation and several snow days that can only be likened to gifts from God helped to ease the doldrums. But, the days would not pass without heartache. A tragedy occurred, knocking both my students and myself down with a force we barely knew was possible.

Brian was a wonderful sort of boy, a shining star in my seventh-period honors class. Handsome and freckle-dotted, he would begin to wave to me frantically as soon as he rounded the corner and began the long walk to my classroom. He was the boy who withstood snorts of laughter from his classmates to inform me that his name had been erroneously omitted from my detention list. "I cannot tell a lie, Ms. Dwyer. I didn't do my homework either." He wasn't being a goody-two-shoes. Deep down the other kids knew that; he was just being Brian, honest and lovable. His death in late March deeply affected us all. It also, unfortunately, set the stage for another administrative blunder. Perhaps they had never had to deal with the death of a student, but their handling of the situation made a real tragedy somehow worse.

Living outside of the area, I was not privy to the daily newsworthy events until briefed on them by my colleagues the following morning. That Monday seemed filled with promise, as I bustled about my classroom in those first few moments. A voice in the doorway startled me. I turned to face the principal and wondered why he wanted to know if Brian was scheduled to be in my class that day. Thinking that Brian may have somehow managed to get himself into trouble late Friday afternoon, I began to extol his many virtues. I just felt that way about Brian.

It was worse than I feared. Suddenly, my cheerful song of praise was interrupted with the words I had never planned on hearing in my career. "He was killed over the weekend." A newspaper clipping, complete with haunting picture, was flashed before me. That was all. Having given the necessary information, the principal was gone. At that moment, my grief for Brian, his family, for the kids, and for myself took hold and shook me violently. Despite the bell ringing and the masses flocking toward me, I fled to the faculty room. There I cried, remembering my own grief upon the news of my father's death several years earlier. How would these kids who, until now, had only associated death with the old and infirm, handle the death of a classmate and a friend? I knew I had to pull myself together for their sake.

Since my homeroom was comprised of eighth-graders, the morning's brief announcement and moment of silence had little effect. Not so in the seventh-grade homerooms. Eerie cries of anguish could be heard above us. Many, it seems, had been with Brian Friday afternoon and had seen or heard the car that struck him as he darted across the busy street on his bicycle. But up until this moment, the only report had been that Brian had been seriously injured and had been flown to a Boston hospital. Now, the word "dead" stunned them, as it had me. What made it worse was that the voice on the intercom continued with the habitual, if not hypocritical statement, "Let's have a good and productive day."

The seventh-graders filed into my room with the first bell, many of them sobbing and swollen-eyed. Most had known Brian since kindergarten. How could I possibly speak to them? What could I say to ease their pain? I prayed for guidance and what followed was an admission of my own sadness. Without once considering that I was a Catholic in a public school, I spoke to them about my own views on death and how I was just now coming to terms with the death of my own father. Together, we talked about our feelings and what Brian had meant to each of us. Some students were silent, others more vocal. These kids were hurting.

By third period, the guidance office was inundated with pleas from various teachers for assistance. Many felt inadequate to meet the needs of their grieving students. Was there to be nothing more than that brief morning announcement? Requests were being made for special in-school counseling sessions but those were rebuffed by the main office. The response was that the kids would get over this. Certainly they would; but it seemed painfully obvious that anything we could do as their teachers to help them should be done.

Finally, the new guidance counselor took control. Appearing in my doorway, he requested that I bring my seventh-graders to the library. Once there, he, several other teachers, and I joined forces with a visiting social worker and listened to and spoke with the kids. The principal was angry that classes had been disrupted, but he attended this gathering.

The meeting was sad, but helpful. Students cried openly at the mention of Brian's name. Witnesses recounted the accident and expressed anger at the innocent driver who had struck Brian. We all knew it was important and necessary to the grieving process for emotions to surface, so we just let the kids talk. Slowly, the conversation turned to happier memories of Brian and a reaffirmation of the impact he had had on the lives of those present. Both students and teachers took turns remembering a silly thing Brian had once done. Tears and laughter intermingled.

As our hour drew to a close, powerful feelings of grief gave way to a discussion of how we, as a community, could best remember Brian. From then until June, the students worked feverishly to collect money for a worthwhile tribute to their friend and classmate.

Brian's funeral took place on one of those cold, rainy March days that seem to ridicule the possibility of spring. Only two teachers were given permission to attend the service, and they had to fight to do so. The administrators made it clear that they saw no need for any further interruptions in the school schedule. They themselves had failed even to attend Brian's wake. We who remained behind that morning taught sparsely attended classes; most of the seventh grade was absent. I stayed in my classroom and talked to what students I had about Brian. Most of their inquiries were directed at what I would do with his ice cream scoops. His name seemed to stare out at us from around the room. Later, we agreed as a class to leave them hanging. Brian had loved talking about those books.

Time served to heal many wounds. During the ensuing weeks, my students wrote letters to Brian's parents and brothers, sharing with them stories they recalled about the friend who had been their son and sibling. The kids wrote these letters voluntarily at my suggestion. I had explained to them that I knew what they were going through. Their eyes grew wide as I talked about my father's death and how my family had been comforted by the many cards and letters we had received following those first shock-filled days. At that moment, I think I was suddenly more human to them, cracking voice and all. Teachers have fathers? They know what it is like to hurt? To miss someone? The letters they wrote were simply beautiful, a real expression of love and friendship. As the thank you note from the family later stated, their happy memories of Brian meant a great deal to his family. As young as they were, the kids took real solace in this fact.

It is true that children do seem to bounce back from life's painful moments more quickly than one might expect. Many of my students were examples of this phenomenon. But the loss of their friend deserved more attention that those in charge wanted to give. Brian's death drove home my own need to be more educated on issues of childhood grief and how I, as a teacher, could help ease the pain of my students should such another tragedy occur. I felt the principal and vice-principal were wrong in not realizing the effect that their brief announcement, coupled with their refusal to bring in outside help, would have on the students. The question of whether we as educators were here merely to teach academics to the students rose to the surface. Were we never to stray from the designated schedule to address those devastating issues that were part of our students' lives, issues such as sexuality, drugs, and death? In this case, many of us were unprepared to discuss death with our students and we failed them somehow. Other such tragedies will occur; other students will die during the course of our careers. I wanted to be able to help those left behind as much as I could. It was this realization that led me to allow a student, without a single word of reproach, to etch the following into the side of a desk; "Brian sat here. He was the best."

When spring finally did arrive, and there were times when I wondered if it ever would, the days seemed to fly by with incredible speed. Spring brought with it feelings of self-doubt. I wondered if I would ever be able to wrap up what I was supposed to teach over the course of the remaining weeks. As checklist after checklist appeared in my mailbox, I began to alter my agenda. I would forego friendly letters, but business letters were a must! The grammar textbooks glared at me menacingly, taunting me with the fact that so much of their scintillating material was mystery to my students. And what about the novels we had just started reading together as a class? The kids were quite capable of completing them on their own, but there was one obstacle: The books couldn't leave the school. Thus, a great deal of class time would need to be utilized . . . and the glare of those grammar books seemed unrelenting.

There was still another obstacle to finishing the academic year; despite my dedication to my profession, I felt absolutely no guilt. Even teachers were allowed a brief respite to get married. If my fiancé were devoted enough to still want to marry me after my trials and upsets of the past year, I was not about to disappoint him. The kids would just have to struggle on without me!

I have yet to meet a student who is not overjoyed to learn that his or her teacher is about to be one of the missing in action. Mine were no exception. I left an explanation of why I was to be absent for ten days until the last moment. Better first to assign them the work they thought they would miss come the day of the substitute and free study periods. When I finally did tell them, the honeymoon jokes I had half-expected were few. Instead, I was greeted with applause, handshakes, and even a few hugs. The crowd was clearly with me on this one.

My return to school found me even more rushed to squeeze a million important lessons into four weeks. Why is it that just when you are rushing full-steam ahead, you are forced to a grinding halt by an endless amount of paperwork. Report cards were due, for some unfathomable reason, two weeks before the last day of school. Now there was a real teaching trick. I had to keep the kids working diligently even though most of what they did would have little or no bearing on those all-important grades. While I must confess to enjoying those final two weeks of grading, I felt guilty deceiving the kids. But, as any teacher of adolescents can verify, crowd control was a must at that point. Let them know that they could no longer help nor hinder their grades and cries of "party time" would erupt. While it made me uncomfortable to lie knowingly, I couldn't tell my students the truth when belittled with the question, "Does this count?" Here was a true lesson in how to subdue the unraveling masses. I kept them moving and thinking.

When the first of June hit, I was forced to accept the inevitable. I couldn't cover everything. Let the powerful shoot me if they must, but even business letters would have to be forsaken. At that point, I felt that a final synopsis of all the literature we had read, discussed, and written about was crucial. I had been gearing my students toward a final book report, and I had decided the report would be oral, coupled with an art project.

The mention of "oral report" always seems to hit a nerve with the junior high group. Tediously written papers and whimsical ice cream cones had been one thing, but get up in front of the class? Moans and groans issued forth from all. Cries of "slave driver" and "student abuse" failed to soften me though. They just couldn't believe that I would make them work so hard when two glorious months of freedom loomed so close at hand. But, work they did (most of them anyway), and the final fruits of their labors were gratifying for both sides.

The ten days devoted to oral presentations kept everyone in the "get into reading" mode I had long ago sought to create. My students and I seemed to work as one, eagerly asking questions about the books being discussed and recommended. All attempted to soothe the frazzled nerves of the speakers. We were really enjoying ourselves. Yet, in the midst of it all, Mr. Landry's attempt to interrupt this oneness one morning set the stage for what was to be the biggest battle yet between us. How long ago it seemed when I timidly first introduced myself to him and became dubbed "the new teacher." Now, as the war raged on, I felt confident that I had earned my stripes. I cast aside any feelings of self-doubt to confront this individual head on. There would be no wobbling on my part.

This final debacle transpired in my first-period honors class. The oral presentations had commenced the day before and there was a tense but excited atmosphere permeating the class. The order of the presentations had been predetermined and posted a week ago. Now, the five students awaiting their turns and, as I reminded them, an absolute sense of relief when it was all over and done, flipped through their index cards anxiously and made last-minute adjustments to their art projects.

The first student called was a very pretty, shy girl named Kelly. With hands shaking and papers rattling, she stood facing the class. My heart went out to her at that moment; I knew all too well how difficult it was to remain composed when you feel the room is spinning about you. Kelly and I had a special understanding. She had spent many hours throughout the year talking to me about problems she was having. Her once plummeting grades had been showing signs of steady improvement. Looking at her from my comfortable perch on the windowsill bookcases, I smiled as if to say, "You'll be terrific!"

Kelly never stopped looking at me during her entire presentation. When her nerves caused her to stumble, I provided her with the necessary word to guide her in the right direction. The other students were wonderful, smiling or signaling to her that all was well. So intent were we on helping Kelly that no one heard Mr. Landry enter the room. When it became apparent that the class was not going to halt its activities, he cut across the room and beckoned to me. From where I sat, I could see he held pink grade-change forms in his hand. Was this to be the third discussion we would have about the changes I had requested? No! I refused to take my eyes off Kelly. Both she and the other students sensed that her oral report was to continue. I knew that if I interrupted her so close to the end, her nerves would never allow her to continue.

At that moment, two events were happening simultaneously. Kelly was engaged in a description of her book's main character and Mr. Landry was standing within five inches of me. There was no rush on those cards; there was a need to stick with this student. As he cleared his throat to interrupt my discussion with Kelly, I raised my hand and whispered, "I'll be with you in just a minute." But, rather than offer his support to Kelly, Mr. Landry stormed from the room. I was angry but I refused to show it. The kids sensed I was probably in big trouble. By controlling my anger, I forced them to re-turn their attention to their classmate. Kelly finished her report with a burst of applause. The warmth of that class at that moment somehow made me for-get that there would most likely be a showdown of sorts later.

The period immediately following that class was the dreaded study hall. Anywhere from 80 to 150 students were seated in alarmingly close proximity to one another in a cafeteria filled with long tables. My year-long stint as a study hall monitor had been a lesson in crowd control, but such experiences deserve their own book. Suffice it to say that I never found these periods to be conducive to quiet moments of inner reflection. But, in between hushing loud students and repositioning a few of the more obnoxious, I did have time to review my earlier stand. It was quite simple actually—my students came first. Kelly had been my top priority. Her somewhat tremulous condition had commanded and deserved my full attention. If the situation arose again, I was positive my role would stay the same. My hand would still go up to halt the interruption; my eyes would still remain fixed on my student; the conversa-tion between teacher and student would still go on.

As I moved toward the final moments of the study hall, I began to wonder if I had perhaps misinterpreted the vice-principal's actions. Surely, as a former teacher, he knew how imperative it was to never interrupt a student during an oral report. Naturally, he would realize that the student always came first. . . .

These sweet thoughts meandered through my head, as I made my merry way to the next class. All was right with the world, and summer vacation was just around the corner. Unfortunately so was Mr. Landry.

The words that were exchanged at that moment will remain etched in my mind forever. As I moved to ask him if now was a convenient time to discuss those grade changes, he turned on me with a voice I had grown to hate, first low pitched and then booming for effect. His message was clear: When he wanted to speak to me, I was to speak to him. There were to be no ifs, ands, or buts about it. He was irate that I had not interrupted Kelly to discuss the changes. I just couldn't believe what I was hearing, nor could the students who were passing by in the corridor on their way to class. All instinctively turned to see who was in trouble now. I was mortified.

Deciding he had made his point, Mr. Landry turned to leave. I was too angry to allow that to happen. With teeth clenched, I gave an unexpected response to his command. I would never interrupt a student giving an oral report for anything less than a life-threatening situation. Had he any idea of how difficult it was for that particular student to stand before the class and give that report? Hadn't he been able to sense her nervousness when he had first entered the room? Or was it just a matter of not caring? Kelly's self-esteem was much more important to me than any discussion of grade changes could have ever been at that point. With that, I walked away from him.

I have no idea how I succeeded in teaching my remaining four classes that day. Both my mind and body suffered the ill effects of those last few moments. While my outward appearance had been one of self-assuredness and determination, I could not deny that I had been duly stunned by my own anger. I spoke to no one about that fiery exchange. I chose to remain silent during lunch despite the concerned inquiries of my colleagues. I just knew that a further rehashing of the events would only serve to upset me further. I waited throughout the day for an irate principal to appear in my doorway. He never did. But while I had escaped his reprimand, I did suffer another kind of anguish. The whole horrid scene, complete with student onlookers, replayed itself time and time again in my head. I wondered if I had allowed this person to get the better of me. The bigger question that troubled me though was how this man, who was supposed to be in a position of authority, could be so unprofessional.

I tossed and turned for two restless nights pondering these questions. In school, I avoided the office entirely. Finally, I turned to my department head and, at my request, she agreed to accompany me to a meeting with the principal. It was at that meeting that I lodged a formal complaint against the vice-principal, complete with documentation of the incidents I have written of here. The presence of my department head added the necessary validity to my charges of unprofessionalism, incompetence and, at times, sexual harassment. She fortified my complaints with her own as well as those made by others in the department. I mentioned my hesitancy to return to a school where "new teachers" received constant criticism rather than support from their administrators. I put myself out on a limb to voice this complaint, but I had made up my mind to let the principal know how angry I was about the treatment I had received throughout the year.

Greater attention than I had expected was paid to my complaints. The principal spent close to an hour discussing the situation with us. Since school was closing, I expected to see little, if any, changes in those final days. I had requested the meeting to clear the slate; I wanted to make sure that my side of the story had been told.

It was at the conclusion of this meeting that I made my decision to phone the local newspaper with word of my students' successful year of reading. I wanted to end the year on a positive note, not the sour one my last encounter with the vice-principal might have led to. The school news editor readily agreed to send a photographer who would cover the story of a day of celebration complete with costumed, giggling students and a teacher doling out ice cream. The party was a smash hit, a wonderful way to send us all into summer. Fellow teachers stopped by to join in the festivities. The principal and vice-principal, though notified, never made it.

The last day of school came and went in a flurry of paperwork, assemblies, and hurried exchanges of good wishes. As I loaded boxes into the car and answered the inquiries of whether I would be there come September with a shrug, I knew I had some important decisions to make over the next several weeks. Would I come back?

Although I had signed my contract for another year, résumés and letters had already been sent to school systems closer to home. I wondered where I would stand if a choice became necessary between one of those schools and the one to which I had just devoted a year of my life. I had enjoyed the camaraderie of my fellow faculty members. They had always been ready to offer me their support and friendship. In truth, I had a special place in my heart for each one of the kids. The only obstacles blocking my decision to return were the administrators themselves, namely a vice-principal whom I considered unprofessional and incompetent. His position as my superior could only continue to adversely affect my role as teacher. The question was how much I would allow him to determine the path my profession would take.

For some reason, I drove away from Bennett Junior High that afternoon knowing that I would probably return in September, fresh and eager to give it another try. But, I thought, such important decisions should not be made hastily on a muggy day in June. The summer, after all, was just beginning. I definitely needed an ice cream cone.

EPILOGUE

Perhaps it was the enormous amount of ice cream she consumed that summer, or maybe she was suffering from some form of newlywed-induced psychosis, but Stacy did return to Bennett Junior High that fall. Forever the victim of eternal optimism, she just knew that Mr. Landry must have learned from his mistakes of the previous year. After all, hadn't she?

Oh, that poor deluded woman! Not only did Mr. Landry remain his boorish self, but he added a tangerine sport coat to his already stylish wardrobe. Stacy did take consolation in the fact that he continued to go bald while she held on to her naturally curly hair.

And so, with another year of combat duty under her belt, she has moved on, at her husband's insistence, to the greener pastures of western Massachusetts. The teaching continues, and our heroine rejoices in the fact that she is now free from the damage one tangerine sport coat, coupled with black pants and white shoes, can do to one's psyche.

QUESTIONS FOR DISCUSSION

12.1. Dwyer's year was filled with conflict and pain.
  (a) What does "fighting the good fight" mean to Dwyer?
  (b) What role does her anger play in her teaching?

12.2. The attitudes and actions of Mr. Landry, the vice-principal, are unprofessional and directly contrary to the true goals to which an educational leader should aspire to.
  (a) In what ways ?
  (b) What negative moral and social values does Mr. Landry unwittingly communicate to students and teachers?

12.3. Dwyer demonstrates qualities of imagination and flexibility in teaching the required skills in the seventh-grade curriculum.
  (a) How?
  (b) What is it that she teaches her students that is of inestimable value? Why?

12.4. Many first-year teachers spend weeks and months floundering and adrift before they find the content that strikes a responsive chord or until they come upon a method of instruction that deeply involves their students.
  (a) What was the approach that was most effective for Dwyer?
  (b) What are the educational principles behind her success?

Chapter
13

Conclusion: Rules for Riding the Roller Coaster

Kevin Ryan

A dozen stories. Twelve accounts of what it is like to go from being a civilian to being a teacher. Each of the over 2.5 million teachers currently employed have gone down the same road, seen the days of August dwindle, drawing them closer to the great adventure. They have all had the big moment when they go through the door of *their* first classroom . . . or have been sitting there in the quiet classroom as the first wave of curious students enters, anxious to get a glimpse of the new teacher. This is an old story in American education, but still it always seems to surprise the beginner.

There is so much happening during the first year of teaching that even the most intellectually agile beginner has trouble sorting it all out. For most, it is "data overload." Twenty-five years ago, teacher-writer Bel Kaufman began her classic novel, *Up the Down Staircase* about a first-year teacher in an urban high school with the following passage:

> Hi, teach!
> Looka *her!* She's a teacher?
> Who she?
> Is this 304? Are you Mr. Barringer?

> No. I'm Miss Barrett.

> I'm supposed to have Mr. Barringer.

> I'm Miss Barrett.

> You the teacher? You so young.
> Hey she's cute! Hey, teach, can I be in your class?

> Please don't block the doorway. Please come in.

Good afternoon, Miss Barnet.

Miss Barrett, My name is on the blackboard. Good morning.

O, no! A *dame* for homeroom?
You want I should slug him, teach?
Is this homeroom period?

Yes. Sit down, please.

I don't belong here.
We gonna have you all term? Are you a regular or a sub?
There's not enough chairs!

Take any seat at all.

Hey, where do we seat?
Is this room 2309?
Someone swiped the pass. Can I have a pass?
What's your name?

My name is on the board.

I can't read your writing.
I gotta go to the nurse. I'm dying.
Don't believe him, teach. He ain't dying!
Can I sharpen my pencil in the office?
Why don't you leave the teacher alone, you bums?
Can we sit on the radiator? That's what we did last term.
Hi, teach! You the homeroom?
Pipe down, you morons! Don't you see the teacher is trying to say something?

Please sit down. I'd like to—

Hey, the bell just rung!
How come Mrs. Singer's not here? She was in this room last term.
When do we go home?
The first day of school, he wants to go home already!

That bell is your signal to come to order. Will you please—

Data overload. "The system cannot compute!" Confronted with so much going on in one place at one time produces stress, particularly since the new teacher must appear to be in control of the situation. ("My cover is blown! They took one look at me and knew right away that I'm not a teacher. Just someone pretending to be a teacher! What should I do?")

Meanwhile there is very little time to sort out this flood of data and reflect on it because more data keeps pouring in. ("Why is that boy in the back sneering at me? Or is he smiling? And why did that girl jump up and leave the room in tears? Why would anyone want to sit on a radiator? Why, when I asked them if they had any questions on what we were going to do this year, why was the only question they asked me, "Are you married?"!)

But still the beginner has to act, has to do something! It is situations like this . . . situations not uncommon in other demanding lines of work (think of the combat soldier or the emergency ward physician or the Parisian traffic officer) in which rules come in handy. And it is against this background of fast-moving and fluid events that I offer the following advice.

Be prepared.   Yes, that's the motto of the Boy Scouts. But it can serve beginning teachers well, too. Much that happens in classrooms can be anticipated and provided for. By definition, the new teachers are assigned to a room or rooms that are new and strange to them. These are *your* workplaces. Take command of them. Your classroom is your arena, your stage. Every stage has weaknesses and strengths. Organize it to suit your goals. Shape it to fit the drama you want played out.

There is a problem of course, if you are a "traveller," and have to move from classroom to classroom. This is common for new teachers in high schools. If such is your situation, negotiate some space in each room for yourself: a file cabinet drawer, a desk drawer, a bulletin board for your students' papers.

Get to know how your room works. This is particularly important for travellers, who are continually forced to set up camp and then pull stakes for the next campground. With 27 pairs of expectant eyes on you, it is difficult to remember which of the seven keys you were given opens the closet, or where the much needed textbooks lie in wait. Not to know how to open the windows, turn the lights off and on, get into the closet, the file cabinet, or glassed-in bookcases makes you appear ineffective and possibly incompetent. If books are not available at the beginning of school, students ought to be told when they can expect them and what they can accomplish without them. So, too, with supplies, such as chalk and paper. Think of all the things you are going to need for instruction (this list is very long for the elementary school teachers) and take your shopping list to the school office. If you are not sure what you are going to need, ask some teachers.

Before the students arrive, it is important for you to become familiar with your teaching space and to have your tools ready.

Get them engaged right from the start.   First impressions count, especially in education. Ernest Boyer, the president of the Carnegie Foundation, talks movingly of his first day in first grade. The very first thing his teacher, Miss Rice, did was announce to the class, "Today you are going to learn how to read." Then with great enthusiasm, Miss Rice wrote on the board, "I go to school." The class spent much of the day tracing out the words, reciting them, even singing them. Boyer describes his excitement—running home and into his house with his paper and announcing to his parents, "I can read!" As they looked on incredulously, young Ernest took out a crumbled piece of paper with the words, "I go to school" and read them to his parents. Thus began his romance with education. The moral of this story is: Start off with a bang. Tell them all the wonderful things they will know at the end of the year. Let them know that they are going to be better people—smarter, stronger, more capable—as a result of your working together. Let them know that you have high expectations for them, but that the goals are achievable. Most students come to school in September with worries and anxieties and sorrow that summer is over, but, also, with a deep hope:

> This year is going to be different. This year I'm going to get a teacher who likes me. Not just says she likes me, but holds her lips funny when she says it. One that really likes me. This year I'm going to catch up with the other kids and be one of the smart ones.

Teach them something they don't know yet, but make sure *they learn it!* Or give them an activity that will surely involve them. ("Write down as many suggestions as you can about how this classroom can be improved and made to look better.") Giving them an activity that will keep them actively involved will also allow you the time to do some of the chores the front office wants you to do on the first day. The critical thing, however, is for the students— whether kindergartners or seniors—to leave your classroom with a sense "that something significant and interesting is going to happen to me this year. I've got a teacher!"

Make sure that there is real learning going on in your classroom.   Classes that have a direction, one that is understood by the students, are ones in which learning usually takes place. In "learning classrooms," students know what the task is; the task is understood to be reasonable; and the task is doable. These are classes that have a clear *learning vector.* Classes lacking a learning vector or direction are ones in which students are confused by or about what they are supposed to do. Or, they know what they are supposed to do and find it "too easy" (repeating something they already know) or "too difficult" (they don't have the skills or direction to complete the task). As a result the students become anxious or discouraged and they slip off-task. Aside from the issue of students learning, there are other problems. The old axiom, "An idle mind is the Devil's workshop," is certainly true when it comes to the classroom. The student who is bored by the classroom activities or who is overchallenged by them and cannot perform will find something else to do. Often that "something else" is spelled t-r-o-u-b-l-e.

Children need to feel a sense of accomplishment. Often they are learning new things, but they are unaware of it. Good teachers continually provide students with feedback on their progress and frequently remind them of what they have learned so far. They instill in them a sense that they are making progress, that things are moving ahead in their classroom.

Another method is to make sure the students have learned something new each day. (It is terribly unsettling to a parent to ask one's child at dinner, "Well, what did you learn in school today?" only to have him continue to play miniature golf with his peas and say, "Nothing again today, Dad.") Clearly focusing on one learning objective—and letting the students know they have learned something new keeps the teacher and the class on track. Many classroom discipline problems come about because students feel they are not making progress.

Discipline! Discipline! Discipline!   Research shows that a lack of discipline is one of the primary problems in American schools. For the last 20 years, lack of discipline has been identified in public opinion polls over and over as the number one problem plaguing American schools. Beginning teachers are among the most vulnerable to this problem. First-year teachers report that maintaining discipline is their most serious problem. In one recent survey, 83 percent of novice teachers reported problems of discipline. Why this is so is both easy *and* difficult to understand. Sheer inexperience is one answer. (This may startle some who, having gone through student teaching, believe they were able to discipline a class. Unseen, however, was the real teacher's authority, and authority that was present even if she or he were not in the classroom.)

A second reason is that not a great deal of attention is given to discipline in teacher education. The reason for this, too, is a little difficult to explain. Perhaps professors of education are convinced that maintaining discipline is too situational, too dependent on the particular grade level and subject being taught and the sociological makeup of the school and even more particularly by the personal characteristics of the teacher in training. Trying to teach discipline skills and strategies that will be useful in many different situations is a daunting challenge.

A third reason is that discipline or classroom control is something of a "negative topic," implying as it does that students must be controlled, suppressed, and threatened—and possibly even punished. It is much more satisfying to ignore this side of classroom life and to stress the positive.

A fourth is the sheer difficulty of managing all the humanity present in a classroom. Someone once described trying to manage a class as "trying to keep 35 corks under water at the same time." But for whatever reason, discipline or classroom control is ignored or downplayed. And, it remains a major problem for most beginning teachers.

Discipline 1: Establish order.   First, bring order to your classroom. A class is a small society. In fact, it is a small, quite crowded society. To get anything accomplished—indeed, to keep things safe—order is demanded. Order is the sine qua non of education. Children need to know what they can and cannot do, what the rules of the game are. To pretend there are no rules or that everyone can "do his own thing" is the fast lane to chaos. Order does not mean rigid authoritarianism and absolute control. It means that there is a structure in the classroom that is understood by the students and that enables everyone to exist comfortably and work toward goals. But this order does not just emerge.

Research has shown that effective teachers differ from ineffective teachers in how they treat the classroom rules and procedures during the first weeks of school. Effective teachers either have a set of classroom rules and procedures that they share with the students, or they work with the class to develop its own rules (thus giving the students a sense of ownership). However, they do not just pass out the rules or have a brief discussion about them and then move on to teaching content. Effective teachers spend a substantial amount of time in the first few weeks of school ensuring that the students understand the rules and are complying with them. For instance, if there is a rule that homework is to be turned in at the very beginning of the period, the teacher enforces the rule, and gets students into the habit of submitting homework in the proscribed manner. Or, if there is a rule that in classroom discussion students must raise their hands and be called on before they can speak, the teacher works at what one educational writer calls "grooving" the students to that rule. Ineffective teachers often are casual about their classroom rules and procedures, either because they are too anxious to "start teaching" or slightly embarrassed "by all this attention to rules." Thus ineffective teachers usually spend huge amounts of time throughout the school year dealing with the large and small breakdowns of order in their classes.

Discipline 2: Confront, but never in anger. *"Things fall apart; the center does not hold."* Literary critics usually assert that this line from William Butler Yeats's poem "The Second Coming" is the poet's prophetic vision of the collapse of Western Civilization. It is clear to anyone who has ever taught school that Yeats, in fact, was talking about life in the classroom! It is the rare, rare classroom, indeed, that does not "fall apart" sometime during the school year. Even hardened veterans have those days when the students revolt or act revolting. Even on the most tightly run ship there is always the planned outbreak of coughing or the two students who take on a clear suicide mission, in a brave attempt to steal Mrs. Sledgehammer's grade book.

Most of us like to think of schools and classrooms as society's gifts to children, places of warmth and kindness, dedicated to teaching children skills and information, and to weaving our young into the rich fabric of our culture's best stories and ideas. Kids, however, rarely see it that way. Many have a more *penal* view of the school. It is a place they are compelled by law to attend. Daily they have to get out of their warm beds and trudge off to forced labor camps. They see teachers' gentle invitation to taste intellectual riches as a brutal force-feeding of noxious leftovers. Suffice it to say, that school life is a great trial for many students, a cross that is lowered on their frail shoulders at 8:45 in the morning and is lifted temporarily by the 3:00 dismissal bell. Young bodies that cry out for physical activity and young minds that feel they are in a vise of subject matter yearn to be free. From this slightly jaded perspective, it is little wonder that even in the best of classes disorder breaks out.

Things happen: To break the boredom, the class decides to bend down and tie shoes at 2:12 exactly; coming into class after lunch, two girls erupt into a screaming fight; a boy talks back, using vulgar language; having asked the class nine times to stop talking, there continues to be a loud buzzing in the room; you have been building up to an important assignment and they inexplicably refuse to do it. Direct and indirect challenges like these are part of school life. They must be dealt with.

Instruction cannot take place amid disorder. Basic to the teacher's job is the need to maintain order. Therefore, the teacher must act. Prior to their first year of teaching, relatively few beginning teachers have had much experience being in charge of a group of people. Not many have ever been in the position where they had to look another human being squarely in the eye and say, "Don't do that!" However, in many situations that is exactly what the teacher must do.

Disorder must be confronted. In clear, firm terms the teacher must let the individual or the group know what should happen next. "Now that you have tied your shoes, everyone get up on your feet, take a great big stretch, and then let's get back to those problem sets." "William, do not say another word. Take up all of your things and stand out in the hall until I come out."

Confronting inappropriate behavior—behavior that deviates from the reasonable standards that have been set—does not mean the teacher has to be angry or even indicate displeasure. It means going to the source of the disorder—the class as a whole, an individual student—and firmly clarifying what they/he/she should be doing. "Firmly" is the trick word here. The effective teacher needs to be able to switch communication gears, so the students can tell, "Oh, oh! Listen up here, Teacher's using that voice again (or has that look in her eyes)!" Often the change is subtle, but students become very adept at picking up these small barometric changes in the classroom climate. On the other hand, new teachers frequently lack this ability to change gradually. They tend to have two communication gears: the first is all sweetness and light ("Now children, I do wish you would channel your boundless energy into something a little more constructive than hanging my best students out the window by their heels") and the second gear, blood-red rage ("I have had it with you mutants. I didn't go to college for four years in order to take this kind of abuse from you ingrates!").

Anger is very dangerous in a classroom. A teacher blows up at one student, and several are convinced he blew up at them. The charged emotions released by a teacher's anger frees the pent-up fury in another student and he loses control. It is too strong, too uncontrollable, and often provokes unanticipated reactions in students.

To say, however, that anger is inappropriate is not to say that teachers, even effective teachers, do not get angry with a student or a class occasionally. What is important, though, is not to speak or act in anger. When anger comes, smart teachers follow the wise advice and count to ten. If that does not work, they continue on to 30. Once the teacher is back in control, she can more rationally and carefully respond to the situation.

While it may not always seem so to the insecure first-year teacher, students are, in fact, at a disadvantage in a classroom. Therefore, when you confront a student with his misbehavior or poor performance, it is important not to do it publicly. While a few students thrive on attention—any attention—most students live in fear of being humiliated in front of the class. What seems to the beginning teacher to be a mild rebuke of playful sarcasm can be a crippling mortification to the student on the receiving end.

Another problem related to confronting students is verbal escalation, whereby the student responds to the teacher's merely cutting remark with her own attempt at a small insult. The teacher is not going to let it go by, so he one-ups the student, who, in turn, outdoes him. Meantime, tempers are rising and words follow words higher and higher on the temperature scale. And, before anyone is aware of it, things are said that everyone regrets.

While confrontation is often necessary, it needs to be done thoughtfully and carefully. It should be a measured response that indicates what behavior is inappropriate and what behavior should replace it. Confront the behavior. ("This is the third day in a row you have come in after the bell. I want you seated at your desk before the bell rings from now on.") Don't assault the personality. ("That's strike two, you lazy fat-head. Once more and I'll be meeting your fat-head parents!")

Discipline 3: *Quickly learn their names.* As is probably quite evident by this point, new teachers have a great deal to learn and they have to know it early. One of the most important things to learn is to connect names to those strange faces that are staring up at you. There is an entirely different psychological environment created when a new teacher coolly says, "Robert, put away that comic book and get to work on your assignment, please," than when she stumbles,

> Hey, you there in the back with the plaid shirt. . . . No, not you. You with the bright plaid shirt. . . . and the brown hair. . . . okay, okay . . . with the black hair. . . . No, not you . . . you have a striped shirt. . . . Anyway, you . . . yes, you! Put away that . . . ??? Didn't I see a comic book on your desk before? Well, okay. I hope it is clear to the rest of you that I don't want to see any comic books in this classroom Now, everyone! Back to work!

When teachers don't know the names of students, it is an invitation to "fun and games." Students feel free and unattached to the usual classroom accountability system. It is not unlike the freedom some people feel to yell things out in a darkened movie theater. Many experienced teachers suggest that the key to starting a class off well in September is to get to know the students' names as quickly as possible. Therefore, becoming familiar with grade or class rosters *before* the students arrive enables you to match names to faces quickly. Another method is to have the students wear a name card, or place cards with their names on them on the fronts of their desks.

Also, make up a seating chart as soon as possible. Then, tell the students you want them to remain in those same seats at least for the first weeks. Explain the roll-taking procedures and carry them out carefully during those initial weeks. If you have established a seating chart, then students can say their names, and save you and them the embarrassment of mangling the pronunciation of their names.

Another reason to learn students' names as quickly as possible is that everyone's favorite word is his or her own name. (Another reason not to mispronounce it.) Once students get over the shock of you learning their names so quickly, they feel pleased that you know who they are. On the other hand, it is particularly helpful to know the names of those students who may be tempted to test you ("All the other teachers let us snort coke and perform satanic rituals in class. Why won't you?" Or, "Can I be excused? I feel a bloody nose coming on. Honest!")

And, too, it is a good idea to let them know who you are. Like Miss Barrett, putting your name on the board and helping them with pronunciation is a good start.

Discipline or classroom management or control is one of those qualities prospective teachers often don't know they have until they start teaching. Also, like teaching itself, it is not one thing, as in, "She's a good teacher," or, "He's a poor teacher." Being a "good disciplinarian" is not one quality, but rather a bundle of skills and strategies. Although maintaining a positive and work-oriented classroom seems to come more easily to some beginners than others, these skills and strategies can be learned.

Like many other tricks of the teaching trade, there are discipline skills that one can acquire. One of these is the famed "withering look." I once had a teacher who had a look that I swear left burn marks on my clothes, and a coach whose cold stare killed four errant referees in one basketball season. (Or, so it was reported in the boys' locker room.) These teachers were, in effect, great actors. And, it would not be surprising to learn they had practiced those withering looks for hours in front of a mirror.

We all have had a teacher who we were convinced "had eyes in the back of her head." This is another acquired discipline skill: Watching all the students at the same time. Or, better still, make your students think you can watch all of them at the same time. It is only the most daring student who will misbehave if he thinks he is being observed. This sense of the teacher being aware of what is going on can be accomplished by developing the habit of continually scanning the room, checking to see who is on task and who is off. Often, just noticing one is being noticed is enough to get students back on track.

There are many, many more skills and strategies—ranging from point systems for good behavior to demerits for offenses. The new teacher, though, is a romantic at his own peril. While being an effective disciplinarian would not be a concern in an ideal world with ideal children, nevertheless in the real world of schools, the teacher must maintain order. William Lauroesch, my mentor and first department chairman, told me on the day he was hired, "Remember, you have to *keep school* before you can *teach school.*"

Many young people are uncomfortable with the idea of being an authority figure and with the concept of "being in charge." However, being an authority figure, like other aspects of teaching, simply comes with the territory. But where the territory is strange and frightening, you need a guide, which leads us to the next rule.

Get help.   One of the big surprises of teaching for many beginners is how isolated they are. Isolated in a sea of students. They are thrown in with just their own resources, only to discover all too often that their resources are considerably fewer than they expected. And, the people who have the resources—fellow teachers, curriculum specialists, and administrators—are often hard to find. While the isolation that many first-year teachers experience is unfortunate, it is usually a solvable problem. There is help available and it is up to the beginner to seek it out.

Perhaps the most important thing to do is find a mentor. Mentoring is a fairly new concept in education. It comes from the name of the character in Homer's *The Odyssey* who was left behind by Ulysses to watch over his son Telemachus. Mentor carefully guarded over Telemachus and helped him reach adulthood relatively unscathed. Usually, a mentor is an older, experienced teacher, someone who is settled in the school and is not preoccupied with his or her own teaching problems. The mentor plays many roles—from being a shoulder to cry on to explaining the school's real power structure.

Margaret O'Bryan taught in a school district that had a regular mentor program, in which skilled teachers were given extra responsibilities and extra rewards for helping beginners. For Margaret, having a mentor was a key element in helping her weave herself into the faculty and solve some vexing teaching problems. Other teachers, like Jane Larsen, found a mentor in their department chair. For Jane, this relationship with her mentor is perhaps the most significant part of her first year. Other teachers drift into a relationship with their mentors. They see a sympathetic face in the faculty lounge or someone almost literally takes them under their wing.

The choosing of a mentor (when you have a choice) should be done with some care. In the same way one would not choose the most eager native or the one asking the lowest price to be your guide on a potentially dangerous safari, so it should be with the choice of a mentor. Many schools have teachers who have soured on the administration or who are alienated from others on the faculty and are seeking allies. They lie in wait for new faces, people they can enlist on their side of what is often an all-but-forgotten battle. Under the guise of helping, they are enlisting you in their Cause. Beware of these people!

Mentors do not necessarily have to be the most skilled teachers on the faculty, either. While it helps to have a master teacher for a mentor, as apparently was the case with Jane Larsen, there are other qualities that are more significant. One quality is time. The experienced teacher who is busy raising a young family or who is kneedeep in teacher association politics may be the natural person for you, but he or she simply lacks the time.

Experience with mentor programs and research suggest that the best selection is someone who is in their middle years and who has the time and the inclination to help. This point about "inclination" is important to remember. Mentoring is a two-way street. While the new teacher (sometimes called by the dubious phrase "the mentee," making the poor soul sound suspiciously like an after-dinner chocolate!) clearly is the major beneficiary in the relationship, nevertheless the mentor typically finds the work satisfying, as illustrated by recent comments from mentors:

I felt important again!

It was great . . . like being given a new friend.

I was flattered when the principal asked me. I didn't know anyone ever thought I was together enough to do something like this.

I felt young again!

I felt old. All of a sudden someone was asking me for help.

The point is that many teachers find the experience deeply satisfying in that it fills a need at a time when teaching may have become somewhat predictable for them.

Besides a mentor, there are other sources of help and advice. Many school districts have curriculum specialists, or instructional specialists are there to support teachers. Often they have the time, training, and resources that are simply not available to regular classroom teachers. In some schools the principal—or another member of the staff—is very good at supporting new teachers. It is best, though, to check with more experienced teachers to find where the best sources of materials, advice and help are. Do not let problems, like discipline or the lack of an evaluation system, drift. Go out and find the help you need.

Don't look for love. Settle for respect.   There is an old line that goes something like, "Show me a person who says they don't want to be loved and I'll show you someone who will lie about other things, too." We all seek to be loved. Children, adults; the Beautiful People and the Not-So-Beautiful People; students and, yes, teachers. It is a natural drive to seek those signs of approval and affection that indicate to us that "We're okay. We're safe. We're loved."

This desire for tangible signs of being warmly regarded becomes particularly acute for people when they are in a new situation, when their normal support systems are absent. Being uprooted from one's familiar environment and thrust into a strange, new milieu is upsetting. If we add to this a situation in which the individual is required to perform a complex task in front of and for the benefit of an audience of knowledgeable critics . . . well, we are describing the world of the first-year teacher.

In his essay, The Discipline Game, Michael Knoll describes with great courage and candor his quest for approval and how his every attempt to be accepted made life more difficult. He wanted to be liked. And not being exactly sure what he was supposed to do, he began looking to his students for clues and indications that he was on track. Students, like trapped animals, can smell the new teacher's desire for approval, for signs of love. Some students use the new teacher's vulnerability and uncertainty to wheedle favors or better grades. Some use it to lower the new teacher's work expectations. ("None of the other teachers give homework on weekends! How come we get it?" Or, "All the other teachers [Read: all the real teachers who know what they are doing, Rookie!] let us keep taking the test until we learn the stuff! How come you don't?")

Without the confidence that comes with years of experience, it is difficult to tell a child she is not working up to capacity or to turn back a group of assignments that you judge to be below standard ("Whose standards? Mine? What do I know? Just a few months ago, I was in school having my assignments turned back!") Without the self-assurance that comes with the years, it is difficult to insist that students keep working on math facts or memorizing irregular verb forms or mastering the use of the comma. Without the aplomb that comes with "time in the trenches," it is difficult to hear that young woman who has come to your desk and announced for the second time this week, "I gotta go and I gotta go now!" and then to look her squarely in the eye and say "Melodie, either go back to your seat or take your books and report to the principal's office."

The teacher is, de facto, an authority figure. Indeed, he needs this authority to do much of the work of the teacher: To get people to do tasks they would rather not do and to keep them on task when they would rather be wool-gathering or "chatting it up" with their friends. Many new teachers shy away from using their authority in the hope that students will do what they are supposed to do out of affection for them. They rarely do. Indeed, students often deeply resent teachers they regard as weak and vulnerable and ineffective. They want their teachers to be strong, to be confident, and to be in charge—all of which is, of course, a great deal easier to write than to put into practice.

There is, however, useful information from the inspirational writer, Scott Peck. Several years ago, Peck, then an unknown writer, published *The Road Less Traveled*, which subsequently became a bestseller. As happens to successful authors, Peck began receiving invitations to address large audiences of people. He quickly discovered that his success as a writer did not carry over to public speaking. He reports that he was a bomb, a terrible keynote speaker at several important conventions. Peck decided to become a student of public speaking and took every opportunity he could to observe skillful platform performers. He noticed that most started with a joke or a good story. They kept eye contact with the audience. They varied their voices. And so on. He, then, systematically tried to adopt those skills. He reports that his motto became "Fake it until you make it." And, apparently he transformed himself into an accomplished public speaker.

While this method may not be for everyone and may strike some as unauthentic, acting like a teacher until you feel like a teacher does have merit.

As we come to the end of our tour of the Roller Coaster Year, I am uneasy. Have I made the career of teaching about as attractive as trying to enforce Robert's Rules of Order in the middle of revolution? Has the reader decided to consider more sedate careers, such as stunt work or demolitions expert on a SWAT team? Clearly, the picture of a career in teaching is not balanced. In fact, this volume does not present an even-handed portrait of the first years of teaching. The 12 contributors set out in good faith to tell the unadorned truth about their initial years, but undoubtedly the conflicts and failures and lapses crowded out the smiles from appreciative students, the moments of camaraderie with other teachers, and that special compliment for a fine first year from the praise-stingy principal. Unquestionably, this final chapter has presented a distorted picture of problems and threats to one's authority—if not one's sense of self-worth. This was done purposefully.

That famous educational philosopher, Woody Allen, titled his autobiography, *Guilty, But with an Explanation.* I plead guilty to the charge of distortion and overkill. My explanation is that over a 30-year career in education I have witnessed legions of new teachers march into school in September with high hopes and with rose-colored glasses, only to be blindsided by the dear little beasties they came to serve. Discouraged, some slink off in June. Worse yet, some come to think the students really are beasties and they stay on to even the score. It is hoped that being forewarned is to be forearmed, forearmed against unrealistic expectations and unanticipated disappointments.

Finally, it is important for the first-year teacher to know that this, too, shall pass. The first year is an unnatural one. It is a year of intense and sometimes painful learning. And, while it is a year with its own acute satisfactions and, for most, a year that ends with a profound sense of having accomplished a great deal, those pleasures are only the beginning.

The Roller Coaster Year is one of a kind. In the hurly-burly of this unusual year, beginning teachers often lose sight of some of the ideals and intuitions that attracted them to teaching. This same thing happens to doctors and social workers and other people-serving professionals, but it is unfortunate when a teacher loses sight of the sheer nobility, the sacredness of the calling. Teaching is work that, aside from its vacations and daily victories, offers a deeper satisfaction: the luxury of always knowing that no one does more important work than a teacher.

Index